Challenging Macho Values

Challenging Macho Values
Practical Ways of Working with Adolescent Boys

Jonathan Salisbury
David Jackson

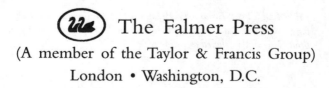 The Falmer Press

(A member of the Taylor & Francis Group)
London • Washington, D.C.

UK   The Falmer Press, 1 Gunpowder Square, London, EC4A 3DE
USA The Falmer Press, Taylor & Francis Inc., 1900 Frost Road, Suite 101,
       Bristol, PA 19007

First published in 1996

**A catalogue record for this book is available from the
British Library**

**Library of Congress Cataloging-in-Publication Data are
available on request**

ISBN 0 7507 0483 7 cased
ISBN 0 7507 0484 5 paper

Jacket design by Caroline Archer

Typeset in 10/12 pt Bembo by
Graphicraft Typesetters Ltd., Hong Kong

*Printed in Great Britain by Biddles Ltd., Guildford and King's Lynn on
paper which has a specified pH value on final paper manufacture of not less
than 7.5 and is therefore 'acid free'.*

Contents

Acknowledgments   vi

Acting Hard — *A poem by David Jackson*   viii

Preface by Jeff Hearn   ix

1 Introduction: Why Should Schools Take Working with
   Adolescent Boys Seriously?   1

2 The Secondary School as a Gendered Institution   18

3 Boys' Sexualities   40

4 Sexual Harassment   86

5 Violence and Bullying   104

6 Media Education, Boys and Masculinities   139

7 Language as a Weapon   166

8 The Ideal Manly Body   189

9 School Sport and the Making of Boys and Men   204

10 Boys' Well-being: Learning to Take Care of Themselves and
   Others   216

11 How Boys Become Real Lads: Life Stories about the Making
   of Boys   232

12 Playing War   250

13 Fathers and Sons   274

Bibliography   292

Index   298

Acknowledgments

The authors and publishers would like to thank the following for permission to reproduce materials used in this publication:

'Smalltown Boy': Words and Music by Jimmy Somerville, Larry Steinbachek and Steve Bronski © 1994. Reproduced by permission of Jess-E Musique Ltd/ EMI Virgin Music Ltd, London, WC2H OEA.

'Smalltown Boy': Words and Music by Jimmy Somerville, Larry Steinbachek and Steve Bronski © 1994. Reproduced by permission of Bucks Music Ltd, London, W8 7SX.

'Smalltown Boy': Words and Music by Jimmy Somerville, Larry Steinbachek and Steve Bronski © 1994. Reproduced by permission of Larry Steinbachek.

Living and Learning (Cambridge) Ltd for permission to use material from *Taught Not Caught*, H. Dixon and G. Mullinar (eds) and *Greater Expectations*, H. Slavin (ed.).

The Guardian for permission to use the article 'Bare Faced Cheek'.

SMASH (Sheffield Men Against Sexual Harassment) for permission to use their Sexual Harassment questionnaire and 'The Lads' cartoon.

Richard Yerrall for permission to use material from his privately published *Anti-Sexist Practice with Boys and Young Men* (1989).

Rykneld Support Service, Derby for permission to reproduce material associated with whole school policy on bullying.

National Council of Voluntary Organisations for permission to use material from *Boys Will be . . .* , Neil Davidson, Bedford Square Press (1990).

Prentice Hall, Englewood Cliffs, New Jersey for permission to use 'Being a Boy' by Julius Lester from Men and Masculinity, Pleck and Sawyer (eds).

Neti Neti Theatre Company for permission to use material in the bullying section.

Mike Davis of Hackney Downs School for permission to use material from their 'Skills for Living' course.

David Pickersgill for his preparatory work in the sexual harassment section.

Val Lindley, Head of Lower School and Dance Teacher at Redhill Comprehensive School, Arnold, Nottingham for her contribution to boys and dance.

Derbyshire County Council for permission to use material from their HIV/AIDs pack.

Max Biddulph for advice and assistance in the Boys' Sexualities section.

Bob Vincent and Mike Wilkinson for his reading of the text, advice and encouragement.

Acting Hard

He wants to be the giant King of Hard
smirking beneath his back-to-front
baseball cap. Proud of his blood-grazed knuckles
he tries to push his fist through another
locked door. Sprawls insolently across
three seats on the bus home. Knows
that he was born to own space.
He threatens to jump out of this poem
to head-butt YOU.

But this giant King of Hard
is afraid to take off his bomber jacket
before the hissing showers. He knows
they would rip his towel away, sneer
at his hairless dick. He sees their jeering
faces in his Dad's shaving mirror — the place
where he practises looking mean.

This King of Hard has jelly feet.
He tries to put his shoulders on again
and the upturned cap that hides his eyes.
But it's too late; the iron lung is cracking.
These are real, human tears that are scalding
his cheeks. Now nothing can stop
the dark, wet stain from seeping right through
his 'Red Devils' football strip.

David Jackson

Preface

There are good reasons, albeit different ones for women, for men, for girls and for boys themselves, why boys and young men should be challenged and changed. Many girls and women, whether they are sisters, students, friends, mothers or partners, would like to reduce the power of boys and young men, to increase their safety from them, and where appropriate to improve their relationships with them. Perhaps surprisingly, the reasons why it might also be in boys' own interests for boys and young men to change are rather similar — equalizing power, increasing safety, improving relationships. For example, it is well documented that young men are particularly at risk of violence from other young men. From the point of view of men, challenging and changing boys and young men, whether we are brothers, friends, fathers, or whatever, is also a matter of concern. In addition, many men carry with them sadness from their boyhood that they would like to shift in themselves and see shifted in others. For some people, all these issues are complicated by the ambiguous authority that comes from being a teacher teaching boys and young men — and of having to face the question 'What on earth do I do with these boys?'

So how did we get here? How has it come about that the need to challenge and change boys and young men is being increasingly recognized?

Like many stories of this kind, this is a long one. Boys and young men have often been seen as a breed apart, as naturally quite different to girls and young women. In the late nineteenth and early twentieth century there was a clear emphasis on the separation and segregation of boys and girls. And although it is easy to overstate the operation of such 'dual spheres', there was certainly a strong pursuit of 'natural' separation, so that boys could be and could become boys. That was the way things were in schools, in religious and paramilitary youth organizations, and even in many workplaces.

This 'natural' regime with its own firm distinctions has remained with us since. Indeed my own schooling in the fifties and early sixties was strictly based on the idea of boys becoming the way they should be, through sport, study and segregation from girls — a strange and inconsistent mixture of nature and instruction. However, by the sixties there were movements towards mixed schooling and mixed youthwork. Interestingly, this mixing was accompanied by the creation of 'youth', 'youth culture' and the 'youth problem', in which the naming of boys and young men was liable to be lost. Despite the fact that 'youth culture' and the 'youth problem' usually stressed what boys and young men did, they usually remained unnamed. 'Youth' was a word without sex or gender even though it generally meant male youth. This second regime also continues — so that talk of 'youth', 'youth problems' and even 'youth crime' often fails to really address boys and young men. Accordingly, male youth can be all too visible yet rendered invisible.

Both of these regimes — the supposedly 'natural' and the supposedly 'neutral' — have been challenged by feminist and pro-feminist interventions. They have reminded us that the experiences of girls and boys are different, gendered and pervaded by power. In this context, there has been a return to girlswork and then boyswork. Similarly, *Challenging Macho Values* challenges both of these regimes and the approaches to boys and young men that are associated with them. Boys and young men are named as such, but not so as to suggest that they are fixed and unchangeable.

Challenging Macho Values is designed for teachers, youth workers and all who work with boys and young men. It combines commentaries on the key issues and lots and lots of practical suggestions for doing boyswork. Most of these exercises can be put into practice with a minimum of resources and equipment — they rely above all on the experiences of the boys themselves. The topics covered include sexuality, harassment, violence, bullying, media images, language, the body, sport and much more.

Challenging Macho Values is equally useful for working with boys and young men who are stereotypically sexist and aggressive, and those who behave in other ways; those who use violence and those who don't; those who are more or less successful; those who are black or white, heterosexual or gay. The boyswork that is described draws on a general awareness of sexism and anti-sexism and a specific awareness of power, safety and relationships. Boys and young men are no longer just the way they are. Read on.

Jeff Hearn
University of Manchester

Chapter 1

Introduction: Why Should Schools Take Working with Adolescent Boys Seriously?

The Theory

One of the authors can remember a particularly striking lesson in a working-class comprehensive school in Sheffield. He was sitting at the back of the classroom, observing a mixed class of twenty-one students, with eight boys and thirteen girls. The memorable aspect of the lesson came from the wild antics of two boys sitting at a front desk. They spent most of the lesson singing or humming, putting their feet up on the desk, fighting, pinching each other's books, calling out, having a laugh. The lesson was interrupted, time after time, by the two boys demanding attention from the teacher. It was like having two over-grown cuckoos in the classroom, with yawning wide beaks crying out for immediate satisfaction.

The two 13-year-old boys clearly expected to take up the centre of the stage in that classroom. They gave the impression that they knew how to get their own way in everything they did. They didn't seem to know that other students, with separate needs and wants, existed in that classroom. Out of twenty-one students, these two boys controlled almost all of the events of that lesson, and effectively blocked any serious learning from taking place.

After the lesson I had a word with the teacher about the two boys. I could remember from my own teaching days his defensive, guarded response which probably came out of an anxiety about his threatened control as a teacher. What slightly surprised me was his resigned acceptance of their behaviour. Nowhere did he seriously question the actions of the two boys. What he seemed to be implying, between the lines, was the taken-for-granted assumption that 'boys will be boys'. He seemed to be saying, indirectly, that this was the natural and normal way for boys to behave and that was why he was turning a blind eye to what was going on, right under his nose.

Many other teachers share this grudging acceptance of boys' behaviour at school. Admittedly, there are other complex factors at work here, influencing teachers' perceptions. There is the influence of daily school routines normalizing the aggressive disruption and, also, an individual weariness at the huge burden of having to take a stand against every incident encountered in the course of an average school day. But, at its heart there is some kind of biological determinism shaping many teachers' perceptions of the problem of boys. The unchallenged assumption is that boys act in the way that the two Sheffield boys did because the causes are in their genes, and therefore there is nothing the teacher can do about that.

Out on the street, and in different communities up and down the country, the story is the same. There is a real problem with boys, especially between 10–16, and nobody seems to know what to do with them. With the demise of the traditional model of the male breadwinner, in regular work, bringing home a 'family wage', the old incentives to become a respectable, working man — status, pride, security — are collapsing. What many boys are left with is a lawless, aggressive culture of masculinity. In this culture, boys often prove themselves men through criminal rather than work activities.

So today, in the 1990s, boys are trying to turn themselves into men through smashing things up, hanging around in a menacing way, being hard, not listening to adult voices, joy-riding, looking for a fight all the time, burgling, breaking into places, and burning community buildings down, often schools. The unofficial syllabus of the streets is about learning how to be a 'real man' for many of these boys. So what are we to do about this destructive, masculinity training? Some women are protesting but, often, their voices aren't being heard. Some men, often in positions of authority — police, judges, teachers — are either looking the other way or indirectly condoning the boys' behaviour. One municipal manager, reported by Beatrix Campbell (1993) in *Goliath: Britain's Dangerous Places*, said that 'When women make complaints they're told by the police that "lads will be lads" '.

These 'Boys will be boys' assumptions need to be vigorously challenged now, in school and in community education projects, at a time when boys' and men's aggressive and dominating behaviours are being increasingly exposed. If we accept that boys act aggressively because it's in their chromosome structure (see Mahony, 1985) or hormones then the possibility of personal and social change in men and boys is wiped out. As a result, the struggle to change girl/boy, woman/man power relations becomes a waste of effort. So it's urgently necessary to go on reminding ourselves that traditional, manly characteristics, like being strong, powerful and controlling, aren't innate qualities that all men and boys are born with. But, alternatively, are mainly social constructions forged out of culture, ideology and history. Alternative, educational choice and change is made possible because of these social and historical processes. From this perspective, conventional manliness stops being fixed, natural and eternal but, instead, temporary, artificial and something all teachers, parents and students can change through their own active efforts.

Why Should Schools Decide to Work with Boys as a Matter of Importance

So why should already over-worked teachers concern themselves with working with boys? Why should teachers put energy into mainstream, curricular work that interrogates and changes some of those traditional, masculine values and behaviours exhibited by those two Sheffield boys? The first answer to this question is to explicitly appreciate how much teacher time, energies and school resources already go into picking up the pieces after boys' routine, daily acts of vandalism, classroom disruption, bullying and harassment of girls and boys. The overwhelming majority of school students involved in short-term and permanent exclusions from school are boys.[1] The majority of school truants are boys. The majority of school cases involving sexual invasion of students' bodies are perpetrated by boys. Less spectacularly, boys' attention-seeking strategies take up an enormous amount of classroom time.

At the moment, too many schools just passively react to boys' disruption. A policy of containment or just getting by seems to be the order of the day. Why can't that valuable time, energy and resources, now being spent on short-term clearing up the mess after the event, be more profitably channelled into more preventative, pro-active, whole school programmes that deliberately challenge conventional, masculine values, behaviours and relationships?

Feminist work on gender and education has already shown the way forward. This work has drawn attention to boys' power and control within mixed, secondary classrooms. Boys' monopolizing of linguistic, social, psychological and physical space in mixed secondary classrooms has been made increasingly visible in the work of Mahony (1985), Spender and Sarah (1980), Stanworth (1983) and others. But the case for change is even more wide-ranging than that. Perhaps we can best indicate the scope and range of those arguments through the use of a list of central points:

1. Schools are places where boys' bullying, sexual harassment, physical and psychological abuse are seriously damaging to girls' emotional and physical lives, and to the lives of marginalized boys (gay, disabled, asthmatic, effeminate/heterosexual boys, some black boys, etc).

2. Boys' domination of physical and psychological space in mixed, secondary schools often prevents girls from fully participating in and making use of school resources in developing their own lives and careers.

3. Boys' identification with macho values and relations, where school learning is seen as unmanly, often leads to a significant academic underachievement in some groups of boys (particularly working class and some black groups). Conformity to peer pressure also works against boys' academic success as the two recent research reports (Homerton College, Cambridge and at Thirsk School in North Yorkshire) on boys' academic behaviour indicate. The researchers comment: 'For many boys, their emerging masculinity placed them in direct conflict with the ethos and aspiration of the school.'

4. Restricted notions of heterosexual manliness often prevents boys from taking emotional and sexual responsibility for their lives and the lives of others — at a particularly dangerous time of AIDS and sexually transmitted diseases. Fear of unmanliness often leads to a contempt for condom use and other safer-sex, risk-reduction behaviours.

5. The school playing field, the playground, the changing room and the gym are some of the most important institutional sites where boys masculinize their bodies (often with very damaging results) in attempts to physically embody force and superiority.
6. Traditional models of manliness are not only destructive to other people, but are self-destructive. Pursuing these traditional models traps many boys into severely limited subject, curricular and work choices as well as damaging the range of their emotional lives and social relationships.

The continuing struggle for greater gender equality in schools is entering a new phase. Initially gender work in schools was seen mainly in terms of empowering girls. While that is vitally important to extend and continue, it is also urgently necessary to stress the connections between the formation of femininity and masculinity in gender work in schools.

The Historical Foundations of Gender and Education Work

Gender and education work that focuses on the social construction of boys, men and masculinities has its historical roots in the re-emergence of feminism in the late 1960s in Britain. Working with boys is a direct response to those challenges and it needs to acknowledge its debt to those criticisms, campaigns and transformations in which so many women took part.

But that history has not only been transformative, it has also produced a historically specific approach to gender work in schools that might not be appropriate for gender work with boys.[2] To understand this difference in emphasis and approach, we need to quickly trace the historical development of gender work in schools.

Our present model of gender and education work grew out of the radical, feminist initiatives of the early 1970s that later became formalized in two pieces of legislation, the Sex Discrimination Act and the Equal Pay Act of 1975. Although the results of these acts were slow to effect practice in schools, gradually the influence of the new legislation started to seep in and began to support women's efforts to reduce the power imbalance in schools. Many active women teachers wanted to give girls the positively assertive skills, the confidence and the qualifications to stick up for themselves in a 'man's world' (Whyld, 1990). Backed by the Equal Opportunities Commission, set up to monitor the Sex Discrimination Act, some women teachers started to examine and change the system of gender inequalities in their schools. Subject and career choices for girls were challenged; boys' domination of the classroom, corridors and playground were drawn attention to; exam results were analysed; text books and reading schemes were revised and class registers were 'de-sexed' (Weiner, 1985).

By the 1980s a 'number of schools had devised their own equal opportunities policies, posts of responsibility had been created at school level, national projects were under way' (like the Schools Council for Sex Differentiation project, and Girls into Science and Technology).

By this time the dominant version of gender work in schools had developed into the primary aim of empowering girls and women teachers through an equal opportunities approach. This 'equality of access, for both girls and boys, to existing educational benefits' approach proved to be deeply contradictory. On the one hand it failed to recognize the unequal starting points and power inequalities between girls–boys, women–men in an equal access approach, while on the other hand, many women teachers used it to struggle for a more radical, anti-sexist approach that concentrated on the development of a girl-centred education.

Despite courageous initiatives like the 'Skills for Living' course at Hackney Downs school[3] and the ILEA conference 'Equal Opportunities — What's in it for Boys?',[4] many boys and men in schools were left confused, hostile and very defensive by these developments. Equal opportunity work on gender in schools felt at that time, to many men and boys, like just doing something on girls' and women's issues. After years of expecting centre of the stage attention, they now often felt rejected, or left out in the cold. Predictably, they reacted to gender work in schools with open hostility, indifference or suspicion. Many male teachers became obstructive to whole school approaches to gender work, or became skilled in using the empty rhetoric of equal opportunity, without ever personally applying the insights to their own lives. At the classroom level, many boys turned away from a didactic approach that made them feel rubbished or inadequate. As one boy student commented, 'Gender work is against boys — everyone's trying to tell me I'm wrong' (Askew and Ross, 1988).

On a more positive note, more promising gender and education initiatives that focused on the social construction of boys, men and masculinities were developing more vigorously in other statutory and non-statutory agencies. Innovatory approaches to working with boys were pioneered through youthwork initiatives like 'Working with Boys', Trefor Lloyd (1985), and Neil Davidson's (1990) work on sex education for boys and the sexism awareness training approach for male youth workers held at Plow Hatch Hall, June 1983. Other collective efforts were also influential, like the work of Sheffield Men against Sexual Harassment in the SMASH pack (originally published in 1984, revised in 1987). There was a new, cutting edge to the valuable work of this voluntary group. They represented a fresh, practical approach to issues like sexual harassment in schools, rape, the sexual abuse of children and pornography and male sexuality. Later, 'The Him Book', compiled by Chris Meade (1987), followed up this work by introducing a range of concrete ideas 'for men looking at masculinity and sexism'. What came through in this new work was a different, energizing emphasis on men and boys looking at masculinities (including their own) and taking personal responsibility for emotional, sexual and material problems related to sexism. They weren't trying to work through an inappropriate, equal opportunities, educational model but were taking up a clear anti-sexist focus that critically highlighted the problems associated with the social construction of men and masculinities.

The prevailing tendency for men concerned about sexism was assuming that they should (a) see themselves as feminists, and (b) focus politically on women and 'women's issues' was effectively challenged by Jeff Hearn (1987) and seen by him as 'misguided'. He saw that 'men cannot be feminists. Men can clearly be interested in and instructed by feminism', but 'political participation by men in the women's movement will be likely to interfere with and reduce its autonomy . . . it still leaves men's main problem as ourselves, not women.'

This criticism helped to change approaches to working with boys. As a result, a new kind of more balanced interaction between men and women working in this area can be envisaged. What this might mean is a more carefully coordinated mixture of separate gender work initiatives (with women teachers mainly working with girls and male teachers mainly working with boys) linking up, occasionally, in whole group work on common gender problems.

It's high time then we questioned the adequacy of a conventional, equal opportunities approach to working with boys in school. As Connell (1989) argues, 'A compensatory logic will not work for the privileged sex.' Because of their inherited power and privilege, most boys need a more clearly defined anti-sexist way of working that encourages them to investigate traditional, masculine entitlement. And later, to work with them in such a way that boys feel they have alternative choices to conventional, bully-boy culture in schools.

The Limitations of Using Sex Role Theory in Approaching Gender Work with Boys

Part of the problem of using an equal opportunities approach to working with boys, is that it's theoretically informed by a severely limited sex role theory. From this perspective, boys are seen as fixed, passive victims of gender socialization. Schools are also seen as places where boys learn to fit into a pre-existing gender role or script that trains them up in aggressiveness or competitiveness. Boys don't seem to have any ideas of their own but unquestioningly conform to certain masculine norms. Even the pioneering book *Boys Don't Cry* by Carole Ross and Sue Askew (1988) — which is particularly strong on the school as a patriarchal institution — works within the confines of an over-deterministic sex role theory:

> We take it as given that much of the behaviour described as 'masculine'
> is learned (as opposed to being innate) and reinforced by stereotyped
> ideas about what it means to be male in this society. (p. 5)

All this talk of 'internalizing dominant stereotypes' doesn't give any critical purchase on questions of boys' resistance, the variety of masculine forms, historical changes and the contradictions in the lives of most boys and men.[5] It doesn't analyse boys and masculinities in such a way that allows them to accept active responsibility for their own changes.

The restrictions of the sex role approach is also apparent in the classroom practices that are often linked to this theoretical perspective. These practices overemphasize 'Spot-and-breakdown-the-gender-stereotype'. This approach can be useful but too often it presents a static, conformist version of the varied and complex ways men and boys wriggle and squirm, sometimes protesting, sometimes giving in to dominant pressure, in the living processes of constructing and reconstructing masculinities. Viewing boys as passive 'victims of gender socialization', where boys just slot into a sexist role or script, doesn't do justice to the complicated dynamic of boys' struggles and resistances in the processes of becoming masculine.

Rethinking Boys, Men and Masculinities

The alternative priorities of a new curriculum design and a changed approach to teaching and learning in the field of working with boys is tied into a radical rethinking of boys, men and masculinities. This rethinking has been provoked by the recent explosion of interest in the 'crisis of masculinity' and the related expansion of a critical men's studies literature, especially over the last five years.[6]

The key themes of this rethinking are best summarized, point by point:

1. There is no such thing as masculinity — only masculinities. Lumping all men and boys together, as in phrases like, 'All men are . . .', doesn't do justice to the many varied forms of masculinity. Masculinity is never unified or homogeneous.

2. Masculine identities are always full of cracks and fissures, as they shift across history and different cultures. They are complex and contradictory, often revealing inconsistencies between their emotional attachments and how they rationally present themselves. They are never harmoniously integrated or rationally coherent.

3. Masculine identity is always fragmentary and multi-faceted. Every single man or boy is made up of multiple masculine identities struggling for dominance. Within each man and boy there is a conflict going on between the fiction of a fixed, 'real me', masculine self and more fluid, alternative selves.

4. There is an internal pecking order between these varied forms of masculinity. There is always an internal, men against men, boys against boys, conflict going on between the different interests of ruling 'top dog' masculinities and more marginalized and put down masculinities, like gay, disabled, asthmatic, effeminate/heterosexual boys, and some black boys.

The old equal opportunities approach to gender work with boys worked within the simplified polarity of female virtue and male vice. Boys were often lumped together in a very frozen 'either/or' kind of a way, and any sense of internal divisions and contradictory struggles was obliterated. What these fresh ways of looking at boys, men and masculinities have allowed us to do is to open up a new way of theorizing gender work with boys that can lead to changed and more effective classroom practices. Instead of seeing men and boys as representing an undifferentiated, monolithic system of power that is static and unchanging, the new literature has drawn attention to the transformative implications of *variety, difference and plurality* both between men and men and within individual boys and men. It has also stressed the positive results of the *contradictoriness* and *fragmentariness* of boys' masculine identities. Finally, it has pointed out that *gender relations are historical* and always in a state of constant flux, depending on the prevailing, governing models of masculinity that are in the ascendancy, at a particular time in society.

Because there isn't a mechanical one-to-one correspondence between the prevailing system of male power and *all* boys and men, it allows us to see how *some* men and boys in schools can actively work against conventional, patriarchal power. Although most boys benefit from the institutional privileges of being a boy in a school system that is organized in the interests of male power, there are many fissures and cracks in boys' relationships to that system that come out of this new emphasis on variety and contradictoriness. The tensions between the ruling models and images of manliness and the real conditions of boys' lives always gives rise to doubts, mismatches and confusions even within the lives of the group cocks at school. These mismatches create the possibility of an opposi- tional space within which new work with boys can begin.

There are two main areas of positive contradictoriness that work with boys can creatively harness. The first, outer kind of struggle, is a product of the intensity of opposition that many marginalized boys experience towards the ruling cocks of their classroom, staffrooms, playgrounds and corridors. *Outlaws in the Classroom* (City of Leicester Teachers' Association, 1987) makes it clear what it feels like to be a gay student in the school system, having to put up with phrases like, 'Here come the three benders!' or 'Backs to the wall, here come the girls.' These other voices from excluded and ridiculed masculinities bear dramatic testimony to the potential power of protest and opposition, simmering just below the surface and just waiting to be supported and brought out into the open.

> You have to be careful about what you let out about yourself . . . You've got to be careful not to let the other kids think you're soft. (Askew and Ross, 1988)

> Anyone who might be a bit slow, or dim, or weak, or ugly, or poorly dressed is liable to be called a poof or queer . . . (Trenchard and Warren, 1987)

The other, more inner area of positive contradiction comes out of the conflict between multiple identities within boys' lives. Just below the swaggering, boast- ful public face are often suppressed, alternative identities demanding to be heard. At unexpected moments, in the awkward breaks in heroic performances, you can often hear these other identities struggling to get out, like in Gary's recog- nition in 'Boys against sexism':

> I'm not always trying to be hard, get into fights, stuff like that. Some- times I like to be sort of different, sensitive, in a sense, right? (Channer and Channer, 1992)

The range and variety of these hidden boys' identities need to be more explicitly acknowledged in public. Underneath boys' brave mouthing you can hear other choked voices straining to come through:

> Not all boys try to act macho and tough. I mean, I try not to go around looking like a macho man, girls think it's daft.

> Some of the time I like to hang around with girls more than boys because they talk more sense about life and everything.

> I could see how often people just started fights and then pulled knives out and I didn't want to get involved in that. (Channer and Channer, 1992)

Some boys are learning to turn their backs on violence, to talk about their feelings, to be non-competitive and to value close relationships over trying to get their own way in everything that they do. Some of them are being nudged into a different kind of awareness about themselves as boys through their relationships with girls. Admittedly, many boys are still clinging onto more traditional values about being masters of their households — 'You can get someone to do your washing and cooking' — but there are signs that some boys are beginning to look around themselves and are turning a questioning eye on themselves.

In some recent work on boys' behaviour, Sue Lees, Diane Reay and Angela Phillips have all drawn attention to the fact that traditional, gender stereotypes of boys are far too monolithic and simplistic. Indeed, there is a lot more going on in boys' lives than the literal surface impression would suggest. There is always insecurity, fear and self-doubt co-existing with boys' boasting and swaggering. Any movement towards challenging traditional, macho culture needs to start from this new emphasis on variety and flux.

The feasibility of making different choices amongst competing identities shows the real potential for change here. As teachers who work with boys we can learn how to make friends with these buried voices, bring them to the surface, make them more visible. In Gary's case, for example, we can positively reinforce Gary's wish to be 'sort of different'.

But a word of warning is necessary here. The peer group pressure to become accepted as one of the lads can block some boys' motivations to oppose macho values. These pressures work on boys' fears of being isolated, mocked, made to feel the odd one out. Therefore to support marginalized boys in making visible their sense of difference, there is a great need for the classroom to be organized in a way that provides safety, trust and reassurance for boys to feel confident enough to voice their dissatisfaction with conventional models of being a boy. Given a coordinated 'working with boys' effort across a substantial number of staff, and a belief in carefully chosen pair work, and appropriate small group methods, useful progress can be made. A social climate in schools, however small and fragile it is, that supports boys to look at their fears and insecurities about doing this kind of work is absolutely necessary if this kind of work is to develop.

The Different Levels of Change Needed in Schools

Secondary schools aren't just mirrors that reflect the macho values of the social world outside, although they are partly influenced by them. Like other important institutional sites (like the family, the workplace, sexual relationships) that form masculine, gendered identities, school is a place where masculinities are actively made, negotiated, regulated and renegotiated.

It's this daily, dynamic giving and refusing of consent to the prevailing, governing models of masculinity that ensures that schools can be places of change and intervention. Schools aren't rigidly over-determined by structural factors outside the grip of staff and students. Instead, they are involved in a daily struggle for power between the shaping forces that control their lives and their active efforts to remake those forces.

This constant, dynamic renegotiation takes place in three main areas of school life. If whole-school approaches to working with boys are to be effective, then links between these three areas or levels need to be firmly established. These three different levels are the institutional, the hidden curriculum and the classroom levels:

The Institutional Level

Secondary schools are often heavily gendered institutions with male-dominated cultures. These cultures are frequently made up of paternalistic, leadership styles, competitive hierarchies, an over-emphasis on success, individualism, performance and getting ahead.

White, middle-class, heterosexual men mainly hold power in our schools and they sometimes block change from taking place because they are power- and gender-blind about their own taken for granted positions and social relationships. Staff development inservice work is urgently needed here to develop more self critical, gender-aware perspectives on some of the following organizational structures:

- Styles of leadership/management
- Discipline/authority
- Pastoral organization
- Streaming/setting/mixed ability
- Hierarchies in school
- School culture and ethos
- Teaching styles, relations with students, school values

(For more practical details, see our chapter on the secondary school as a gendered institution (Chapter 2). Also see the excellent suggestions for working with male staff in *Boys Don't Cry* by Askew and Ross 1988, Open University Press.)

The Hidden Curriculum Level

The unofficial curriculum — under the desk knowledge acted out along the corridor, behind the bike sheds, in the toilets, and all that is muttered and whispered in classrooms behind cupped hands — is often more important in the making of boys and masculinities than the explicit courses teachers provide. That's why a conventional, equal opportunities school policy that only focuses on the explicit curriculum is missing out on the really powerful, gendering forces in schools.

What is often being brushed under the carpet about boy's behaviour in schools, are the ritual insults, jeering, sexist jokes and name-calling made against girls and put-down boys; the touching up and sexual harassment of girls[7], sexist graffiti, the sexual teasing; the bullying and psychological intimidation of girls and marginalized boys, like having your hair pulled, being laughed at, pinched, pointed at as well as punched, kicked, slapped and thumped; boys' constant invasion of physical and psychological space and boys' informal masculinizing of their bodies to express force, power-over and domination.

We've attempted here to directly address those absences in the official curriculum. In our organization of the book we've tried to explicitly acknowledge what's usually left out. So in our selection of chapters we've included at least half of them that focus on the unspoken problems of boys in the hidden curriculum. These chapters are the ones on Male Sexuality, Sexual Harassment, Violence and Bullying, the Ideal Manly Body, Language as a Weapon and some of the School Sport chapter.

The damage and intimidation done to so many children's lives as a result of macho, schoolboy culture is so urgently pressing that gender work on the hidden curriculum shouldn't just be side-lined to the outer spaces of pastoral and tutorial time or personal and social education, although some valuable work can be done there. A freshly designed, anti-sexist programme for boys, working alongside a positive action programme for girls and women teachers, deserves to be taken very seriously indeed. Practically, that means a gendered awareness of boys and masculinities informing the quality and direction of the mainstream curriculum and school organization. For example, that awareness would have to affect biology courses on the subject of violence in people and creatures, critically examining male violence as an innately aggressive instinct or a socially constructed action to gain and maintain power and control over women and some men. English and language development courses might investigate boys' use of language as a defensive weapon, as well as studying gendered patterns of language interaction in mixed groups in classrooms and staffrooms. A whole-school programme that wanted to challenge gender-divided career choices for both male and female students would have to run consciousness raising courses for boys investigating the narrowing of their choice of primarily scientific and technical subjects and 'masculine', educational routes (see Arnot, 1984). Physical education and sport might want to try out some of the detailed 'positive alternatives' suggested in the chapter on 'School Sport and the Making of Boys and Men' (Chapter 9).

The Official Curriculum Level

The formal, academic curriculum in schools is often blind to the personal and social forces that are currently shaping students' lives every minute of the day. Traditional, masculine language and social behaviour in boys (like bullying, jeering, teasing and touching up) is, along with race, nationalism, sexual orientation and social class etc, one of those largely ignored forces in schools. There is often an uncomfortable silence surrounding the latest outbreak of boys' bullying, petty vandalism, graffiti in the toilet or show of rebellious defiance to classroom authority.

What we want to argue for is the urgent necessity of breaking that silence, at all the different levels of struggle indicated here. This destructive and self-destructive, 'real lad', schoolboy culture needs to be reflected on, investigated, challenged and changed by both teachers and students (especially males) through their official and unofficial work and relationships. In doing this we want to question an academic version of the curriculum that divorces itself from students' critical understandings of the everyday circumstance and conditions that they find themselves within. The selection of archaic 'contents' that favour the interests of white, middle-class, male students contributes to the muzzling of this alternative, curricular agenda. Clearly, for an awareness of boys and masculinities to influence the making of an alternative, educational agenda, it has to be a part of a wider approach to curricular design. Therefore, we want to argue for a working with boys approach to be an integral part of a wider, socially critical approach to the curriculum.

The priorities of a socially critical curriculum (that emphasized a critical unmasking of masculine privilege along with linked and overlapping work on race, ethnicities, gender relations, sexualities, class and green issues) are the skills of analysis, of concepts and ideas and principles, rather than of specific and outdated 'contents'. What seems most 'natural' and 'obvious' in boy students' personal and social worlds, like learning to mend cars and motorbikes rather than learning to bake cakes, would be opened up to an emotional and critical unpicking.

In this kind of critical curriculum, investigative work that focused on the gendered process of becoming boys and young men would be a positive starting point. Then, branching out from that would be work that challenged and changed privileged, masculine expectations about 'getting their own way in everything' like those two boys in the Sheffield comprehensive school. Boys learn best when they can start from their own personal histories, feelings, curiosities and actions. Some kind of personal validation is needed before they can take seriously any other perspectives on that experience.

But this approach wouldn't just stay there. Through a gradual process of learning, confidence building and dialogue, students are encouraged to extend their critical grip on what they thought was most 'natural' and 'normal' for boys to say and do. Then at a later stage, through the meeting of alternative perspectives on their own personal experiences, students can learn to strip off the over-familiar layers to their habitual ways of viewing their personal and social worlds, and a more rigorous, critical interrogation of conventional, masculine behaviours can begin.

Teaching Methods: Harnessing Boys' Spontaneous Interests in Gender Work

There is no lack of interest in questions of sexuality, gender and sexual politics among boys and young men . . . For many it is a matter of absorbing concern. (Connell, 1989)

Boys aren't just brainwashed by macho values. They don't just swallow the dominant models of manliness in a docile, passive manner. Instead, they have a much more wry, contradictory approach — half-mocking, half-accepting — both contesting and buying into these models. The majority of boys aren't the super-cool, swaggering, hard cases they sometimes would like to think they were in their fantasy world. Actually, they are much more fearful and self-questioning, trying to sort out the myths and lies that surround the puzzling world of sexuality, manhood and the difficult world of social relationships.

Teachers who are trying to develop work with boys have to learn to tune into that fearful self-questioning, and not accept the manly blusterings at face value. In contexts of safety, boys will often allow their spontaneous concerns about questions that concern them to rise to the surface — Should men and boys cook, clean, do the ironing? Do men and boys need big penises to be 'proper men'? How does AIDS affect me now? Am I a 'poof' if I like to dance? Do I have to impress girls to be able to go out with them? Only if teachers can get alongside those awkward puzzlings, can they persuade boys to engage themselves in gender work on boys.

Developing effective work in this area depends on teachers being able to negotiate with boys' real, questioning concerns about their own identities as boys and young men. Instead of viewing boys as blank pages, teachers need to value and respect what boys already know about these issues. Teachers need to go on reminding themselves that not all male students are taken in by macho values and images. A recent Strathclyde University research project on alcohol advertising revealed that 'many teenagers have a highly sophisticated understanding of the "messages" behind the "ads"'.[8] After watching a series of beer ads, one of the 16-year-old boys said that he thought they showed that beer 'is for the macho type of man who can get all the girls'. So instead of patronizing young male students and treating them as cultural dopes, we need to devise classroom approaches and teaching methods that positively harness these tacit, 'sophisticated understandings' and 'absorbing concerns' in learning about boys, men and masculinities.

Effective ways of working with boys must start by rejecting the old equal opportunities approaches to gender issues that, very often, only generate shame, guilt and hostility in boys. Teachers need to reject that teaching style that preached at boys, from the front of the class, about what they were doing wrong. Or told them what a 'right-on' boy should be thinking about these issues. This approach not only put boys' backs up so that they switched off from what was going on, but, in learning terms, it was totally ineffectual because it didn't start by validating and then extending those 'absorbing concerns'. Such a prescriptive/didactic approach is ineffective because it drastically under-values boys' potential for getting engaged in and developing critical understandings of these questions of gender and sexual politics. As a result, boys often feel rubbished and then react aggressively or defensively. Any teaching method that stands a chance of working has to negotiate with boys' best versions of themselves — their self-doubts, their puzzled contradictoriness, their spontaneous questions and their active sense of being able to change themselves and others.

Conclusion — So Why Should We Take Working with Adolescent Boys Seriously?

As we have already seen, there is a pressing urgency about doing something about the problem of boys. In school, at home and on the street, many boys are violent, damaging to others and to themselves and systematically under-achieving, academically. We can't go on turning a blind eye to what's going on in boys' lives or excuse them by saying, 'Boys will be boys'. We need a fresh approach to gender work in school that doesn't just focus on girls or operate within a conventional equal opportunities approach (as commented on earlier). It needs to recognize that 'a "compensatory logic" will not work for the privileged sex'. This new approach must avoid getting stuck in the sex-role socialization trap. Instead it needs to face up to the complex and contradictory relations between femininity and masculinity that lie at the heart of the making of gender identities today.

Instead of seeing boys and men as exercising a monolithic, unchanging system of patriarchal power so that girls are always going to be positioned as victims, we need to view secondary schools and youth centres as important arenas of power, where masculine and feminine identities are actively made, on a daily basis, through the dynamic processes of negotiation, refusal and struggle. That means that there are real, social constraints and power imbalances but that gender regimes are more shifting and contradictory than we supposed back in the late 1970s. And perhaps there are more opportunities for changing gender inequalities.

At the present moment, enormous amounts of time, energies and resources are being wasted on a merely *reactive* approach to boys' disruptions and violence. On a regular, daily basis, teachers, ESWs, educational psychologists , behavioural support services, mental health teams, the police and probation and social workers are spending a great deal of time picking up the broken pieces after boys' routine acts of vandalism, arson, violence, intimidation, stealing, display and disruption. So perhaps it's the right moment for secondary schools and youth centres to be more pro-active in designing courses, programmes and teaching approaches that begin to challenge the dominant culture of aggressive, heterosexual manliness that thrives in many areas today. And in these new approaches to gender work men and women need to go on learning how to work together in these projects. But the changes that we are talking about aren't just programmes to be taught. We are also referring to the ability of male members of staff to create bridges between these educational approaches and their personal lives and to recognize that whether they like it or not they are giving out powerful messages about how to be a boy and a man in that institution. Boys need an alternative vision of being male. That alternative vision cannot be achieved unless male members of staff take this challenge on themselves in their own lives.

Practical Uses of the Book

Although the two male authors are white, middle class and heterosexual we have both been personally and politically involved in men's groups and social action groups. We are pro-feminist and gay affirmative and committed to changing harmful male-making in our own lives and in the lives of growing boys.

In the book we are aiming for a balance between theory and classroom-based practice. As a result most of the chapters are made up of four elements:

- A thematic introduction to each chapter called The Theory.
- Classroom Strategies — practical suggestions for classroom use.
- The Session — a short, honest account of actual, classroom experience. It describes how a group of secondary school boys got on with the classroom strategies and asks the question 'How much learning went on?'. Such sessions could work equally well in youth group settings outside the school curriculum.
- Selected further reading to advise and inform those seeking to take issues further.

We don't imagine that readers will read the book from cover to cover. We envisage a more dynamic negotiation with different parts of the book when the need arises. We see the need to dip into the theory for a time to reflect on what's going on in the lives of boys in the home, the classroom, the youth centre and the streets. It will help to make sense of the sometimes confusing, whirling atmosphere which can be present when boys are gathered together. It will provide time for reflection and insight into how to effectively proceed.

Through 'The Session' sections we offer the ways in which another facilitator worked with both the young men and some of the materials. We want to encourage the trying out of classroom strategies, but would encourage their remodelling in the light of specific local needs. We have made the Classroom Strategies a series of non-prescriptive suggestions. They are a framework of options which define a method of approach more precisely for both participant and facilitator. The user is welcome to take on the materials as they are or to discard and work out different routes to suit individual and group needs.

What we recommend is a group of no more than 15 boys. In schools this can be half a class group, with girls involved in issues of personal development, assertiveness and equal opportunity/gender work in a separate place. Such an approach involves the cooperation of staff or links with support services to make the sessions possible. In other youth settings we would recommend that groups be closed at a fixed number. We recommend assessing the mood of the group and that facilitators do what they feel comfortable with. It is worth asking questions before groups start, to work out what the young men are bringing to the group from their own resources and backgrounds. We need to continually create bridges between young mens' own developing interests/curiosities/questions and the resources in the book. For facilitators everything needs to be flexibly tailored to suit the context and circumstances they find themselves within. In whatever setting it is important to begin gently with trust games and exercises. This allows boys who can be very anxious in these situations to become more comfortable with each other and with their surroundings. Stressing the confidentiality of the sessions and continually reminding them of this is a very powerful aid to group cohesion.

We advocate a mixture of individual work, pair work and sharing in small groups. Whole groups even of 15 can be very difficult in the early stages. It is important to constantly break activities down so that there is more emphasis on small intimate sharing. This is part of the whole development process for young men. This is the way in which they can become differently masculine. In some senses the activity being worked on becomes irrelevant as the building up of trust between young men takes place.

Since schools are such important places in the making of masculinities we also want to generate a new kind of staffroom discussion about education for boys. We would like to use inservice training days to help create a climate where what goes on in staffrooms isn't frustrated moans about boys but becomes a shared, more purposeful talk about what can be done for them.

We envisage a new kind of climate of cooperation — of making alliances not only between teachers in schools but also between schools, probation services, social work departments, the youth service and community health teams. In this way groups of people engaged in this work can act as a support for each other when things get tough but also as a source of motivation and new direction. For example, at a Nottinghamshire comprehensive school a boys' masculinity group has emerged out of negotiations between the local probation service, the Youth and Community service and the school facilitators: all the services involved will be working with young men on issues of violence and aggression.

Selected Further Reading on Boys, Masculinities and Schooling

MAC AN GHAILL, M. (1994) *The Making of Men: Masculinities, Sexualities and Schooling*, Milton Keynes, Open University Press.

ARNOT, M. (1984) 'How shall we educate our sons?' in DEEM, R. (ed.) 'Co-education Reconsidered', Milton Keynes, Open University Press.

ASKEW, S. and ROSS, C. (1988) *Boys Don't Cry: Boys and Sexism in Education*, Milton Keynes, Open University Press.

CONNELL, R.W. (1989) 'Cool guys, swots and wimps: The interplay of masculinity and education', *Oxford Review of Education*, **15**(3), pp. 291–303.

SKEGGS, B. (1991) 'Challenging masculinity and using sexuality', *British Journal of Sociology of Education*, **12**(1), pp. 127–40.

Notes

1 Evidence from a Derby Comprehensive School. Between 8 September–23 October 1992 there were 114 referrals made to Room 20, a school 'sin bin'. Out of the referrals, 105 were boys and 9 were girls.

2 This whole introduction is indebted to CONNELL, R.W. (1989) 'Cool guys, swots and wimps: the interplay of masculinity and education', *Oxford Review of Education*, Vol 15, No 3.

3 See the description of the course in ASKEW, S. and ROSS, C. (1988) *Boys Don't Cry*, Milton Keynes, Open University Press.

4 'What's in it for boys?' — this pack can now be bought from Whyld Publishing Co-op, Moorland House, Caistor, Lincolnshire LN7 6SF.

5 This part of the argument on sex role theory is deeply indebted to CONNELL, R.W. (1985) 'Towards a new sociology of masculinity', *Theory and Society*, Vol 14, No 5.

6 Books like BROD, H. (1987) *The Making of Masculinities*, London, Allen and Unwin; KAUFMAN, M. (1987) *Beyond Patriarchy: Essays by Men on Pleasure, Power and Change*, Milton Keynes, Oxford University Press; KIMMEL, M. (1987) *Changing Men*, Sage; CONNELL, R.W. (1987) *Gender and Power*, Cambridge, Polity Press.

7 See JONES, C. (1985) 'Sexual tyranny: male violence in a mixed secondary school', in WEINER, G. *Just a Bunch of Girls*, Milton Keynes, Open University Press; MAHONY, P. 'Sexual violence and mixed schools', in JONES, C. and MAHONY, P. (eds) *Learning our Lines*, London, The Women's Press; and, MAHONY, P. (1985) 'A can of worms: the sexual harassment of girls by boys', in MAHONY, P. (1985) *Schools for the Boys?*, London, Hutchinson.

8 From a 'Guardian' article.

Chapter 2

The Secondary School as a Gendered Institution

The Theory

Male power works quietly and secretly as an institutional reality in secondary schools, as well as showing itself via more overt examples of male domination. Its power is in its secrecy and taken-for-grantedness. The majority of headteachers in secondary schools in England and Wales are male and men also dominate numerically and proportionally the senior management teams (SMTs) which form the policy-making bodies of those schools. A particular example, typical of many, is provided by the comprehensive school in Derby where one of the authors has worked. On the surface the head seems kindly and approachable but dig a little deeper at the point where his authority is challenged and the full weight of a system of male authority and strong leadership becomes rapidly apparent. This process is repeated throughout all the varying levels of school organization.

Such a system provides the framework for the conduct of staff–student relationships. Teaching is seen to be about control and authoritarian certainty. It is also the visible face of material male power in the establishment. The characteristics of effective teaching become talking from the front and controlling any child's responses. It is also about a system of duties, patrolling corridors and the constant checking of students' presence. The atmosphere of control will be underpinned by the need to impose a strong, hard, authoritarian disciplinary system. Students don't accept it. They get their own back in disruptive ways. They are active agents in the process of kicking against authority. They squirm and wriggle against imposed limits by showing boredom, indifference, insolence and rudeness. Such behaviour provokes so many male teachers in so many schools to experience a sense of shame around loss of control. Losing face or control means not measuring up to the manly ideal and fear and drives men to buy into the security provided by strong leadership and patriarchal values.

It is at times like this that male power also gets reproduced through ideology, culture and fantasy. There is a fear of internal chaos if personal power is challenged or within the institution if leadership is weak. This leads to the eager espousing of patriarchal values around certainty and control as something natural which must be affirmed in schools. It seems so natural that it stops any realization that alternatives exist, and promotes fantasies to help sustain the masculine feelings of power and control within.

Male staff at a Derby secondary school would joke with each other from time to time about employing a 'Basher'. Such a fantasy of control would arise when the pressure of ever increasing marking and peripheral paperwork coincided with a larger than usual number of classroom confrontations with difficult students. We would all contribute money from our salaries; a PE store would be converted into the 'Basher's' room. There the 'Basher' would wait within carpeted and mattressed walls to deal with the deviant, antisocial pupil to be sent to him. One visit would be enough to solve the problem for staff and school.

Of course, this was a male fantasy shared by male staff but it serves to show how the dominant culture works through fantasy and it has such a tight grip on us because it works through our unconscious desires. All the men taking part bought into the fantasy at some level. In the face of a downwardly spiralling disciplinary system, our collective imagery, taken from the popular culture of what it is like to be a 'real' man reasserting control, takes over from the inside. Our heads were colonized with images from popular culture of what 'real' men would do in this situation and thus violence or threats of violence through the image of the big, faceless male 'Basher' gave us back the power and security of a 'males-on-top' identity which was seen to be slipping away.

At one level, the 'Basher' is a light-hearted relief from stress; at another, what lies behind the masculine creation of the 'Basher' is the fear and anxiety around the world of patriarchal values slipping away. The 'Basher' story is a reaffirmation of those values, a desire by male staff in the secondary school system to work in an atmosphere of certainty and being on top, cushioned by the elaborate web of male power. It is an illustration of the way male power exists in schools in an institutional or material sense but is also present through a cultural, ideological and fantasy framework. They are like complementary forces at work, existing both simultaneously but with lives of their own as they affirm the structures of male power as a response to the uncomfortable fear of uncertainty.

Institutional Practices

The reality of these patriarchal values lies in a solid material power base but also in cultural and ideological power. Their driving force can be seen and felt within schools as an interplay between the reality of a system of male power and a sense of anxiety around losing that power. So male staff in schools use their power in a variety of ways to protect their position within the pyramidal hierarchy, within the classroom and also to often unconsciously breathe life into the patriarchal values system without which their sense of order and stability would crumble.

The more vicious side to fear and anxiety is the male need to exercise power over women. Male power has a strongly taken-for-granted heterosexual stance which establishes itself through homophobia and misogyny. Thus the atmosphere of male conversations is filled with attacks and justifications around women and gay men and their perceived threat to expressions of 'real manhood'. Boys are more open and use phrases like 'I'm not gay!' or 'You Woman!' to control each other's behaviour. Male staff display the same behaviours within the framework of homophobic jokes and put downs of women staff which highlight their perceived incompetence in male terms. It is only by stepping back from a whole series of incidents in schools that it is possible to notice with clarity what is happening. The taken-for-granted naturalness of the processes and behaviours makes the participants blind to the subtle, and not so subtle, ways of power affirmation.

What is it about the male senior teacher that is so controlling that women staff feel that they have to play up to him, make jokes and humour him? Inside they cringe at how this ingratiating behaviour makes them feel — but they feel powerless around any alternative. If they don't respond openly and willingly to his sexually charged physical presence then they will be punished. By this is meant that there would be 'awkwardness' and veiled hostility around issues individual women staff felt to be important or that move cover slips for taking the lessons of absent colleagues would be coming their way. Thus the senior teacher succeeds in giving clear messages about power and control. He further demonstrates his anxieties around loss of power by drawing other men into his fears. He takes other men on one side to share his misogynistic comments, his remarks about women's effectiveness in the school and about how much better things were with more hard-line (male) tactics in a former school regime. To disagree with his philosophy is to court the same sort of vindictiveness which was felt by the woman head of PE. What makes the senior teacher so important is that his influence is layered on top of the school's official rhetoric around equality issues, openness of access to sources of power and a philosophy which cares for all.

It would be easy to just declare this example as a case of sexual harassment and try to have it dealt with appropriately. The dilemma lies in the fact that the senior teacher's behaviour arises from the taken-for-granted organization of male power which is ever present in the cultural ethos of the school. It is there alternately proclaiming its power in a myriad of subtle ways and also in anxiety, policing the boundaries of any erosion of that power.

The wall of male power, built and maintained by the senior teacher, seeks to define the naturalness of patriarchal values against marginalized others who in some ways are seen to threaten the male power structure. So it is that certain staff can be dubbed as ineffective, irrational, hysterical and not as able. They are being subordinated as feminine as staff are graded along the hard–soft continuum. Their contribution to the life of the school can be written off or marginalized. Such marginalized others may include women, black people, people with disabilities, gay people and other males who do not conform to the real male value system. In the main, people from such groups cannot achieve the same degree of power and success because of the way the system oppresses them.

They find themselves silenced by the dominant voices in a variety of ways. Just as the senior teacher demonstrated his power by draping his arm round the shoulders of the head of physical education, so he was demonstrating the way the institutional organization and dominant culture squats on people with its tentacles around them. In this way, the head of PE tolerated the senior teacher's oppressive behaviour to make life easier for herself in the short term. Other women teachers are silenced or make similar compromises for fear of being ignored as ineffectual or ridiculed as strident and hysterical. Gay teachers are silenced because the dominant culture makes it unsafe to openly acknowledge their sexuality. Male staff whose persona and style are different from that espoused by the male power system find themselves and their work undermined and attacked.

Boys recognize this power all around them. They sense that schools are influenced by patriarchal expectations of a 'boys first' approach with its pressure to compete and succeed. They notice the atmosphere of competition and success being actively shaped in the school hierarchy and feel that same pressure on themselves. Such attitudes, together with men's continuing commitment to at least some of the dominant images of masculinity, means that men's interests get put before those of women. The work of caring and nurturing inevitably gets down-graded in such an atmosphere of masculine power and authority. Thus it is that the male deputy head, responsible for school timetabling arrangements, is able to place a 'soft' subject like personal and social education at the most potentially difficult times in the school day, either just before lunchtime at the end of a long morning, or as the last lesson of all in the day. 'Hard' subjects like maths, English or science receive a far greater proportion of allocations at times when student attention spans are likely to be at their best.

Whether boys wholeheartedly buy into a 'compete and succeed' atmosphere or not, the quality of the capitalist masculinist discourse touches them at some level. Avoiding showing sensitivity and hiding emotions is essential if boys are not to be thought of as weak. Boys recognize the toughening process which is at work as they skilfully avoid the pitfalls of ridicule. Success for one of the boys was avoiding the nightmare of being seen as different. As a result, boys learn to devalue the possession of openness and sensitivity with each other because it is at odds with the examples around them of what a successful working and social life really means. One of the authors asked a student what was important for him in the term 'ambitious'. His answer encapsulated the 'boys have to get on' notion. He had noticed it all around him: 'You've got to get on or you end up poor, with no home and no money.' This was likely to happen if he spent time 'behaving like women do'. For him 'getting on' implied having money for a wife and family and being recognized as competent and efficient within the chosen sphere of work.

Schools are agents in the construction of masculinity. It is not the explicit school curricula which exerts the most powerful influence on the ways boys develop. Although this external force shapes boys, they are also simultaneously shaping themselves as they interact with each other. They turn themselves into masculine subjects and adopt as masculine the restrictive, unhealthy, holding it altogether aspects of manly values. Of far greater importance is the need to look at different ways schools are organized and how these institutional practices reproduce dominant patriarchal and capitalist values. Many of the examples of the subtle workings of these institutional practices on the minds of boys within the school system are derived from one of the author's experiences at an inner-city comprehensive school in the East Midlands.

Discipline and Authority

Many male teachers maintain their authority over pupils by a 'hard-line' rule of fear. They control by threats and a loud voice to reduce students to frightened silence. From such an aggressive disciplinary style boys learn that 'this is how you get what you want'. Male teachers are also very competitive around their ability to establish firm discipline. There is ridicule of 'soft' members of staff behind their backs. Defining others as less strong in a disciplinary sense also serves to foster the competitive nature of their own sense of power and respect within the school.

Some adolescent boys identify with the 'tough male' approach and are less willing to respond to the self-disciplinary approach of other teachers. Unable to set their own boundaries, they push hard at the teacher targets they label 'soft'. In so doing they achieve a kind of notoriety and fame which gives them kudos in the eyes of their peers. Other boys seeking status and prestige within the school structure push hard against the hard-line conformity to make statements about themselves. One such boy is Ian Davies. Ian is white and working class with a family background which includes drug addiction and fundamentalist religious fervour. He resists all attempts to make him work or abide by the social mores of the school. He scorns encouragement, regarding academic work as a waste of time. He intimidates weaker boys to get his own way and his sense of bravado in bucking authority is widely admired by those among his peers who have a sneaking admiration for what he gets away with. Ian provides a good example of a boy who, in rebelling against middle-class authority, chooses to exhibit the aggressively macho behaviours which often co-exist with class rebellion.

Other boys who find it difficult to be so rebellious in the face of staff within the school, use bullying as a way of establishing self. Just as male staff threaten and intimidate to get their own way, so too does David Lomax (aged 14) who uses his size and strength to bully and intimidate and also to attract 'friends' around him.

The traditional male staff response to the problems posed by Ian Davies, David Lomax and others like them. is to assert hard-line disciplinary authority. Indeed the voices of dominant male values police the edges of the disciplinary system to maintain their power. The voices are critical of counselling approaches that are regarded as being soft and which will undermine the established hard-line system of pupil control. Thus the nurturing, soft, feminine approach of the women deputy head and the male school counsellor is the subject of mocking comment. Their work has a different quality from the critics' favoured approach of displaying hard, masculine discipline and again is the subject of ridiculing comment. The object of such criticism is to set up a climate of opinion which portrays their work as ineffective. Anyone who disagrees with this can be marginalized and made to feel uncomfortable.

Another way in which male power resisted change that may have had disciplinary connotations was over the suggestion of a new teacher to the school. She suggested that staff be referred to by their first names by students. The barometer of male anxiety over lack of control swiftly led to a mobilization of forces to highlight the foolishness of such an idea.

The Pastoral System

Pastoral care in schools really means dealing with student problems. It can scarcely be otherwise since National Curriculum demands and new forms of recording students' achievements provide a greater workload for all those in daily and direct contact with students. Schools try to create systems that value all students' contributions to school life but inevitably the form tutors, heads of year, heads of house or heads of upper and lower schools are going to be drawn in by the problems presented by troublesome students. Pastoral care inevitably becomes an extension of a system steeped in the discipline and authority structure of the school. Although some students resist school rules and regulations, the system is about social control. In addition the pastoral system regulates gender identities, not just the social well-being of boys and girls.

A detailed example of the structure of the pastoral system at Etches School, an East Midlands inner-city comprehensive, is full of examples of social control. The head of lower school is Les Newton. As a classroom teacher he has an authoritarian approach and has regularly used girls to sit next to boys to regulate the boys' behaviour. As a head of lower school, he likes to keep tabs on everything himself. He is busy, hard-working and involved. His deputy was a woman who had great difficulty in knowing what her job was since Les Newton found it very difficult to delegate. Students thought Marjorie Etherington, the deputy, was Mr Newton's secretary. When it was realized that she did have a role, it was obvious that she was the caring person while Les Newton was the aggressive, hard, disciplinary person. Students between 11 and 14 were learning that men were powerful and authoritarian while women were kind, understanding, caring and powerless (like secretaries).

Les Newton's influence goes further since he regularly takes school assemblies. One particular assembly provided a fund of gender-related material. Ostensibly the content was about the value of helping each other within the school. The story was told as follows (abbreviated version).

A man was walking through the woods a long time ago and was feeling very tired and hungry. He didn't know how much further he could go on. He came to a cottage where an old woman lived. The woman was reluctant to let him in but the man pleaded with her, saying that he would make them both nail soup which was really thick and nutritious and all it needed was some water. At this the old woman let him in. The man put the nail in a pan of water and heated it over the fire. He persuaded the woman that the soup was very good but that it just needed a small carrot which the woman provided. This was repeated a number of times until the woman had provided enough vegetables for what turned out to be a rich vegetable soup which they both enjoyed. The moral of the story was about mutual help to get something which is worthwhile.

In the days that followed, one of the authors asked boys for their comments on this assembly. They recognized that it seemed natural to turn to women if men were in trouble and that the woman was in the wrong for not wanting to help. Some boys recognized that it showed that women could be easily taken in, while a few wondered whether it was right for an old woman to let an unknown man into her house for any reason.

On another occasion, some Year 7 boys were waiting to go into the hall for a dance lesson. They were showing themselves to be keen and eager to get in and start. Les Newton passed them and commented on their enthusiasm by giving a limp wrist, 'camp' gesture. In view of the prevalent homophobic atmosphere around the school, what should boys be thinking about themselves in relation to dance in the eyes of the head of lower school? What a clear message is contained in this signal to boys since, according to the behaviour of the head of lower school, dance has no place in boys' lives if they are considered to be real boys. What an opportunity has been missed here to extol the virtues of men becoming more connected with their bodies and feelings through dance as a physical exercise.

One more example is important since Les Newton likes boys to be like 'real boys'. He is openly scornful of boys who cry and one of his favourite sayings is around wimps who are 'too fond of their mothers'. The young adolescent who desires approval is going to be very careful not to be upset and to take his chastisement without showing his feelings.

Les Newton has a new deputy. He is a karate black belt with much success in competitive karate. He exudes male power, literally inflating into his power as he constantly uses his own name to boom his displeasure. As a black man, originally from Mozambique, he is like other black men who use macho power and dominant models of manliness as a compensation for economic powerlessness and racial discrimination. While patrolling corridors he carries a Mr T (*The 'A' Team*) mug. He shares Les Newton's views that boys should be able to take their punishment and behave with manly dignity. Boys admire his strength and his power. He is also very kind, particularly with girls where he exudes a patronizing warm friendliness. He taps girls on the head as if they were dolls and encourages them to be good. In a non-uniform school he is openly critical of girls' dress, bewailing the fact that he would much prefer girls to wear dresses, particularly in the summer.

Out of a pastoral care system, which is reactive to individual problems, there still emerge powerful messages for all students about the way boys and girls should behave to ensure the praise and respect of the two men who run the pastoral system. Boys know they are to show strength of character and that too much sensitivity is a bad thing, while girls are to be good, pretty, caring and supportive of men's enterprises.

The Academic Masculinist Curriculum

What gets taught in schools fulfils the wishes of the government via the National Curriculum documents. The selected knowledge can at one level be seen as something which is abstract, neutral and value free, but at another level as a selective form of 'academic' knowledge drawn from university disciplines. Thus the important, serious knowledge that schools transmit is what counts as serious to the ruling groups within society. The university connection guarantees that what is taught is invested with a sense of reliability and has status as significant knowledge. The ruling groups have legitimized, validated and authorized a particular type of knowledge.

School knowledge retains the academic form of a self-referring, abstract body of knowledge which strongly separates what is learned from the personal and social experiences of the learner. Knowledge is also organized hierarchically from the less difficult to the more difficult. This emphasizes the idea of there being one path through the material which is necessary to follow. The way knowledge is imparted is by means of transfer teaching, i.e., something the teacher knows is transferred to the mind of the student, i.e., a 'delivery' model. This still occurs by means of chalk and talk and teaching from the front so that impersonal science demands an impersonal teaching style with no attempts to link what is done with the emotional lives of the children. Links with students as people are superficial because of the way teachers know their subject and desire to impart subject knowledge. Knowledge control and what constitutes what needs to be known is in the hands of men. The opportunity is lost to engage in collaborative learning where the everyday knowledge of the student is validated by a process of interaction with teachers' knowledge.

At Etches School the concept of a masculine curriculum is very noticeable. National Curriculum demands have reinforced the need to teach a body of knowledge. Thus in some areas of the school the approach is impersonal, abstract, scientific and objective. This is masculinist knowledge. All the science staff are men and they teach from the front keenly and enthusiastically, telling students what they need to know and cajoling those who are resistant. The technology area shows what is really valued when the making areas in wood, plastic or metal are regarded far more favourably than the textiles or food areas. Lessons like personal and social education (PSE) and drama create a sense of panic. One supply teacher (a former long-serving regular member of staff) refused to take a PSE lesson as set because it did not fit in with his view of children listening and doing behind desks in a classroom organized in a traditional way. He wanted careful instructions which would have enabled him to teach a body of fact.

Another implication of an academic masculinist curriculum is the way some teachers concentrate their time and energy upon boys in the classroom. Boys elicit more approval and disapproval than girls. Hence figures for very high achievers show a large number of boys while, at the same time, the figures for disruption show far more boys than girls attracting teacher attention. Boys grab attention by 'acting out' behaviours that attempt to hog the show. Research by Walkerdine, Stanworth and Fuller, confirmed by one of the author's observations, shows the loudness of boys in the classroom, their sexual harassment of girls and female teachers, their demands for attention from peers, their desire to impress each other and their attitudes to girls in their class as the 'silent' or faceless bunch. Even after three years of being in the same class, some boys do not know the names of girls with whom they spend a considerable amount of time each week.

However, it should be noted that recent developments in boys' and girls' approaches to school learning has produced a more complex and contradictory picture. Now girls are out-performing boys at every educational level and there has been an improvement in many girls' self-esteem in schools.

On the other hand, there seems to have been a collapse of morale amongst many boys. A combination of low aspiration, under-achievement and a drastically reduced motivation has resulted in many boys lacking purpose and direction in school.

Although some boys still expect to be treated in a privileged way in the classroom, a great many other boys are more focused on proving their manliness in the eyes of other boys than achieving academic success. Some of the reasons for this seem to be connected to the break-down of traditional certainty in the lives of many men and boys.

With the undermining of the male breadwinner and Head of the Household roles has come the erosion of male confidence and self-respect. With unemployment, poverty and increasing separation and divorce have come a lack of motivation in working hard at school. Why should they work hard when the usual incitements for academic involvement — well paid, satisfying, secure job prospects — have all but vanished? Why should they choose working hard rather than messing about when they are surrounded by adult male role models who are often depressed, listless and lacking in energy and any sense of future vision?

National Curriculum demands have made sure that all children study maths, English, science, technology and have some continuing link with a foreign language, if not to GCSE level. Girls still display a greater affinity for arts and humanities so that the female culture still revolves around literature, art, languages, music and domestic crafts. Marginalized boys also opt into the feminine culture as a deliberate rejection of the masculine culture that throttles them. It can be both a refuge and a torment for such feminized heterosexual or gay boys in the school system. On the one hand they might have group support from others within the subject areas, but on the other they must also suffer the taunts of the 'real lads' who have sometimes forced themselves into 'hard' male subjects to keep themselves safe from similar bullying.

The National Curriculum is heavily biased in favour of male interests so that boys' interests in science and technology and the careers they give rise to, are actively fostered — but at the expense of the development of boys' emotional and artistic selves. As personal and social education in secondary schools is slowly forced off timetables, so the encouragement of boys to think about human values, wider social issues and their personal lives, is drastically reduced. In some schools such goals for boys have scarcely ever been visible at all. Thus boys concentrate upon obtaining skills for living in only one sphere of social life. They will probably leave school ill-equipped for personal independence and for taking responsibility in home and family life. They are poorly prepared for dealing with people and with their own emotions.

The more general implications of this pattern of academic masculinist curriculum is that through such subject choices and through styles of teaching, a specific ideology of the traditional nuclear family is being perpetuated. The Year 10 boy talking of ambition had learned the school's message well. He saw it entirely natural that he had to 'get on', he had to get a job and be the breadwinner of the family. He spoke of having a wife and children who would be dependent on him.

Teaching Styles and School Values

The teaching of an academic, masculinist curriculum reflects the masculine qualities and values of the school and encourages boys to notice the type of masculine behaviours and attitudes of which society approves.

When the talk is of what constitutes real work at school there is a marked understanding that work means really doing something with a viable end product. Interactive collaborative activities, which rely on social exchange, are not recognized as real activities by boys and are devalued accordingly. Boys' resistance is demonstrated by their inability to stay on task, to create diversionary agendas, or to withdraw from non-product-oriented activities altogether. Boys perceive such activities as a threat to masculinity. One of the authors has run boys' groups in schools and has seen lessons involving boys sharing feelings together, rudely and deliberately sabotaged by a whole range of anti-social activities.

It is not only boys who show resistance strategies when being seen to be in control is at stake, but also male members of staff. Etches School pursues a policy of having support staff in lessons to assist students who have learning or language development difficulties. All but one of these support staff are women. The work involves close commitment to individual students, together with a wide range of expertise in strategies that enable effective learning. In the classroom the teacher officially responsible for the lesson is in charge. Some male teachers are very uncomfortable with the presence of support teachers in the room with them. Their power and control in terms of class discipline are on display, together with the style and content of their lesson delivery. Thus the male teacher in charge demonstrates his control over the support staff. They only work as instructed. They make no general contributions to classroom order and offer no instructions to the whole class.

Such attitudes mean that ideas proffered by support staff are likely to be rejected if the powerful position of the teacher-in-charge is felt to be threatened. Thus it was that ideas from a lively member of the support staff with a strong interest in experiential learning, were viewed with great suspicion. She was keen to recommend her video expertise so that aspects of work in humanities lessons could be filmed. Her ideas brought forth the full range of male anxiety over potential for loss of control. Two members of staff rejected her ideas completely, making excuses about having to deliver the curriculum in a given period of time. Another member of staff would only agree if there was a third member of staff in the room (a male!) so that potential for disorder could be curbed.

Observation suggests that the secondary position of these largely women support teachers is noticed by the students. They are questioned as to their status as 'real' teachers and their opinions on lesson content are often checked with the classteacher. They are not seen as effective or important as the men who take the up-front position as the deliverers of knowledge.

Boys learn to expect dominant authoritarian behaviour from male teachers since it provides a role model for superior power and strength. It mirrors much of the power they see exhibited by other men in their daily lives — their fathers, brothers, uncles and grandfathers. At the same time boys need to assert their own power and to stand up to this authority, to prove that they too can become male authority figures like those who wield power over them. The clash is inevitable. Disciplinary problems are almost exclusively male. At Etches School, staff who have disciplinary problems can send offenders to Room 20 (a sort of sin-bin). At the end of the summer term in 1992, of the previous 100 referrals, 93 had been boys. In the academic year 1991–92 the school temporarily excluded 50 pupils for serious offences; 45 of these were boys.

This subtle and unofficial teaching of male power at the school is powerfully influential since, even in those areas where an alternative way could be shown, the choice is not taken. In the PSE area, one of the teachers wields his authority in a jokey fashion by literally using a big stick, a metre rule, which is used to gain attention and remind students of where the power in the room lies. This teacher's room is also decorated with posters showing Arnold Schwarznegger as 'The Terminator', and 'The Undertaker', one of the stars of WWF (World Wrestling Federation) wrestling. Both posters are in full colour and are prominently displayed. Perhaps his role in the PSE/school structure as the information technology person keeps him firmly in the male camp.

School Culture and Ethos

At Etches School it is male power and control that determines how the school functions. By this we mean that structural power, although continually contested exists through the institutions of the school that support patriarchal views. The most powerful institution is the mainly male senior management team (SMT) which pays lip service to the democratic and equal opportunities practices that are spelled out in the staff handbook and initiates regular consultations with staff in committees, forums and regular staff meetings. Behind all this lies the question, 'What happens when male power is challenged or when a sense of male anxiety over loss of control emerges?' It is then that the weight of patriarchal views escapes from the equality rhetoric and emerges into the light as a starkly oppressive bastion of male power.

The headteacher smiles, is approachable and keeps an open door to staff and pupils alike, but behind the smile lies the reality of male power when his own position and responsibility for activities in the life of the school are called into question. And so he came down particularly heavily on the whole of the technology department who had not mounted the fullest and most pupil participative display for a school open day. The attack was vicious and alarming, calling into question as it did the staff's motives for teaching in the school. One woman was asked if she was only working to pay the mortgage. It seemed that the headteacher's fear of public humiliation had brought out his powerful male authoritarian tendencies. In a less dramatic but equally disturbing fashion is his questioning of women members of staff in ways which would be unthinkable with men. For instance, a woman member of the pastoral team was asked whether she was anti-authority or just simply anti-men. Pupils notice the head because he is often present in corridors at break and at lunchtimes. When he wants to call attention to boys' behaviour he refers to boys by their surname but that is never the practice with girls.

One of the most influential members of the senior management team is the head of the upper school. She uses her femininity to get what she wants from both staff and pupils. She exudes a friendly, hectoring, bonhomie which brooks no refusal. She uses her sexuality to control boys' behaviour with over-familiar suggestions about whether they (the boys) love her or not. She seems to be re-emphasizing the divide between male and female to get her own way. Thus she fits neatly into the male atmosphere, even to the extent of being blind to the extent of alternative sexualities in the school, with constant references to people who are queer. Her deputies feel bulldozed into working in the way that she wants, leaving little room for individuality of style in dealing with students. This seems to be the very male attribute of 'my way is best'. Is it any wonder, therefore, that a stand taken against boys wearing Bulldog T-shirts, with their macho, racist overtones, by a black woman member of staff should be greeted by a rebuke from the head of upper school because she had been 'inconvenienced' by the parental complaints over the matter. Where was the school's anti-sexist and anti-racist stance here?

The masculinized nature of the school ethos comes through a hard, disciplinary approach linked with competitive, individualized self-sufficiency. Such an approach captures the essence of how you need to be to succeed. The only thing that makes sense for the many boys in the school is the patriarchal, individualist, competitive approach to them. For this reason it is easy to see why such boys reject the small group drama-style way of collaborative learning. They challenge the system in the school which seeks to control them but only in so far as they are trying to competitively succeed within the same framework.

Students who are more aware notice the blatant sexism that occurs. A member of the maths department made remarks to a girl student who was visiting classes to collect money for Red Nose Day. He suggested that she would get more money if she wore a shorter skirt. Subsequent inquiries revealed that remarks of this sort were a normal part of his repertoire. The girls resent it, the boys think it is just part of the culture of being male. He is a male teacher after all.

Male power in the school is also kept safe through the conversations and unspoken practices of the 'corner'. The 'corner' is in the staff room. It is literally a corner containing a circular table, inhabited by men in close proximity to the tea- and coffee-making facility. This is the corner where power fantasies are talked of and where the controlling misogyny is covertly shared but leaked with sufficient care to intimidate and control staff relations. It is the relationship between the 'corner' and the dominant masculine culture which pollutes the ethos. It is the corner which gives vocal expression to male anxiety and fear about what might happen to their position in the school. It is here that the misogynistic and racist jokes are shared, laughed at and overheard. It is here where the phrases like 'Everton played like a load of girls' are appreciated. It is here where the serious conversations go on around 'The Lone Ranger' and 'Bilko': both characters, of course, espouse the male chauvinist values which mirror the atmosphere of the corner. It is here where chance remarks about absence of women in the staffroom can be greeted with the jokey 'that's how we like it to be'. It is here where a deputy head who struggles with certain aspects of a humanities course he teaches can seek and receive help but against the background of veiled amusement. After all he should really know these things but it gives a chance for a bit of showing off to be done so he is indulged in his questions. It is here where the plot is hatched to encourage as many people as possible to opt for an inservice day workshop to be run by one of the 'soft' marginalized male members of staff. This is to be his punishment for being different and for letting down those who speak for the dominant voices.

The man who pulls the strings in the 'corner' is a senior teacher. He has been at the school for eighteen years and controls the cover for absent colleagues. He takes a full part in all the conversations but is also keen to leak information to support the cause of the powerful male voices. He is particularly hard on women, letting it be known that a senior woman member of staff is to go on a 'women into management' course. He claims she has been on a similar course before and he proclaims the need for 'men into management' courses. He picks on the counselling and soft approach of a woman deputy head who had been absent for nearly a year with serious back trouble. He ridicules her contribution to school life and also uses her participation on out of school inservice courses to unsettle other male members of staff who are having similar course requests turned down.

Attitudes from the 'corner' leak out around the school in various ways. From the subtle and varied ways in which male power is on display, students expect teachers to behave in particular ways. They expect male teachers to use power within the classroom and they learn from teachers how to get their own way. They experience a naturalness around male entitlement which was so graphically expressed by a Year 7 boy running to his next lesson and saying to a friend, 'Forget it man, we can just shove them out of the way'. Did the remark refer to sitting in a favoured seat? Could it be boys or girls in his way? Whatever the answer, he was acting out as one of the dominant voices in his peer group who felt he could use his physical power to get his own way.

Competition

Closely allied with the academic masculinist curriculum is the way learning is organized and tested. When assessment of learning is being tested, it is how much each student can reproduce as an individual that is important, not what groups can do with the material together. These emphases on isolated individuals measuring themselves against others links closely with patriarchal values. We would argue that this is mistaken and that cooperation is more important than competition. One of the authors has experienced the damaging effects of competitive learning. Competition brings up many kinds of unpleasant feelings, such as being pushy and arrogant around winning and sneakily resentful around failure. At Etches School, boys complain bitterly if someone copies off them and react with incredulity if there is a suggestion that such practice does not imply cheating but more a wish for help. The school also operates a merit system, which, particularly for boys, becomes a paper chase to see how many merit slips can be cajoled from harassed staff in the shortest possible time. All this fuels the competitiveness and selfishness of male entitlement. If merit collection enables boys to be reaffirmed in their boastful 'we are the greatest' way, then is it worth it?

National Curriculum and the demands of GCSE and A level exams encourage staff to foster competition because they too are part of the competitive system. How often has it been heard in staff rooms that a particular member of staff has got the best percentage of GCSE 'passes'? National and local publication of league tables of exam results foster the spirit of competitive learning as the only way to achieve success. It activates the notion of manly values around winners and losers and, just as football league tables can be devoured as evidence of success and failure, so too can schools' exam results.

In sporting terms the accolades go to those who play for school teams. Cricketing century makers and national long jumpers and sprinters have their competitive achievements blazoned over the school magazine. To those who are physically weaker, less gifted or overweight there follows the uncomfortable sensation of constantly feeling ridiculed, either by staff who patronize their efforts, call them wimps, or put them in situations where their limitations will be shown up, i.e., always coming last in warm-up sprints, or in pupil selected teams always being chosen last. The message is clear, that to not shape up properly as a boy in competition with others causes pain, resentment and anti-social behaviour in the form of truancy, disruptiveness and other attention-grabbing devices. After all, a competitive system that fails some boys academically and physically compels a compensatory assertion of masculine pride, a competition in machismo to enable male power to be demonstrated and admired. Perhaps this is why Tim Oldknow, a thirteen-year-old student, rebels against the PE regime. The male PE staff are hard and abrupt in dealing with boys, particularly those who are not drawn to PE and games as an enjoyable activity. On this particular day, it was cold, wet and windy and Tim would not take part. He simply refused and the conflict escalated. As the PE teacher felt his authority slipping away, he became more vocal, loud and scornful of Tim's attitude. From Tim's point of view, he became entrenched in his refusal. He sensed that to back down at this point would lose him status in the eyes of his peers. Eventually he told the PE staff to 'fuck off' and stormed away.

There are numerous other examples of individual boys standing up to the authority structure of the school. The incidents are so public that they become the cutting edge for the assertion of masculine pride, not only in confronting authority but also in the competitive element of being seen to be powerful and daring in front of peers. Such alternative hero status gives bounce to the manly strut around the school.

Ways Forward

Since we believe that the manliness of the school institution is fundamentally damaging to both girls and boys, we need to join forces with the anti-sexist work done by feminists. As a result of feminists placing the relationship between patriarchal power and women's subordination at the centre of their thinking, some initiatives have gathered momentum throughout the country's schools.

Many schools have adopted initiatives designed to give girls and young women the skills and knowledge to challenge the male system in the workplace. Wider subject choice has been encouraged to try to de-sex traditional views of what constitutes male and female learning. Books, films and other materials are checked for sexist content and discriminatory images. Initiatives in assertiveness training for girls have been applauded to enable a sense of female solidarity to be fostered, together with ensuring self-confidence and motivation. Of similar value are evenings set aside for girls-only activities within schools. Women's groups for staff are an invaluable source of self-help around the stresses of the teaching experience in a male dominated values system.

Etches School has initiatives in science technology to encourage girls. Laboratories have been renamed after women scientists and posters of important women scientists are displayed prominently in corridors. Humanities programmes have been tailored to take into account the past and present experiences of girls and women emphasizing the richness of women's creativity in the past and around the world. In such ways some attempts have been made to put girls and women at the centre of the educational experience rather than at the edges.

All such practice is nevertheless conducted in a male defined and structured education system. Women and girls may succeed as products of this system but does this really constitute any sort of victory at all? Although recent research suggests that some boys are failing academically, the wider system is still designed to allocate success to the male, middle-class, white, able-bodied, heterosexual majority. The only way to achieve a system which is not just girl-centred but gives girls the space, freedom, time and help to fulfil their full potential, is to replace the structural power system which feeds on the patriarchal values of competitiveness and authoritarianism.

Despite examples of good practice which many schools can cite, girls' experiences within educational institutions gives room for concern. Expectations placed on girls by boys or expectations made by male staff of their women colleagues, are still demonstrably different. This results in expectations girls and women assume for themselves are very much tailored to the inescapable feeling that they are living in a man's world.

How does all this affect boys? There is an illusion of sameness when boys are referred to and this has the effect of masking the variety and contradictions of boys' experiences in schools. We need an equal opportunities approach that recognizes the power inequalities between boys and girls. At the same time as asserting the power of girls, it needs to challenge the traditional models of a single masculinity. We need to make visible the neglected problem of boys within the institution. Do all boys feel happy with maths, science and techno-logy? Do some boys want to do child development and can't do so because of peer pressure? Pressure from the peer group is so crucially important for so many boys. The peer group regulates acceptable masculine behaviour. As more and more boys are failing academically, we would maintain that there is a link between restricted notions of masculinities and the diminishing learning possi-bilities for boys. Fear of falling foul of scorn from the peer group, fear of being ridiculed and dubbed as feminine prevents boys from acknowledging their full affective and emotional sides. Espousing rational objectivity and being 'one of the lads' will keep them safe within the peer group but at what cost? Resistance to cooperative learning and group work in personal and social education settings is widespread. Attempts to engage boys in working at understanding themselves can easily disappear in a welter of disruptive and anti-social behaviour. Gender expectations are actually failing boys academically and emotionally.

Ways forward involve a variety of practices for looking at the whole of school life. We list eight areas of the official and hidden curriculum and apply these to the experiences in one school.

Gender and Sexualities Differentiation in Whole School Areas

Schools need to look at gender-related choices for girls *and* boys that trap their emotional and educational development through too narrow a choice. It means gathering information about option choice at 14 and analysing exam entries and results, but it also means making the boys' connection with all this more explicit. It is about looking at ways of moving beyond science, maths and technology as a taken for granted route for 'real lads'. Finding different routes through subject material is important. Collaborative learning techniques will present a different emphasis from traditional, authoritarian patriarchal styles. Thus, even within a traditional 'male' subject, boys' experiences of learning can be different. It is also about creatively finding ways to support boys and girls to make choices without fear of put-downs and ridicule from peers. In personal terms, schools need to prevent a repetition of the case of Kevin Newbold, a fourteen-year-old student. Kevin has a real gift with small children and was prevented from choosing child development as an option. He was not put off by peer pressure but he did succumb to staff pressure to choose 'something more appropriate'.

Sex Bias in Reading Schemes, Text Books and Teaching Resources

One of the best ways of doing this is to allow pupils to look critically at the material they use. They are able to spot sexist stereotyping and notice omissions which render material irrelevant in their lives, e.g., boys in nurturing, caring roles rather than active and controlling roles.

Sex Bias in Specific Subjects or Departmental Areas

Each department in a school could be analysed from the point of view of staffing patterns, exam entries and results, student attitudes and option choice. Look also at the traditional models of manliness which move boys in a particularly gendered way towards certain subjects. The whole will give a sense of the prevailing atmosphere within a department. For whom is the department friendly? What attitudes need challenging?

The large technology department at Etches School exudes a catch-all, entertain-all atmosphere and works well with both sexes. It is difficult to escape the conclusion, however, that it is a male values dominated department. The textiles and food technology aspects are marginalized as less important and both women staff involved feel less valued. The main 'Making' or construction part of the department appointed a woman member of staff in 1991. She was praised by the male head of department for not allowing her feminist views to 'rock the boat'. On the other hand she was patronized by the oldest male member of the department who teaches this rich and creative subject by the time hon-oured male method of teaching from the front with boys and girls working individually at desks. She feels undermined by him as he waits for her to fail.

How can marginalized boys admit to their uncertainties around work in this department? This is the subject area where 'real lads' can be creatively inventive so those who are not attracted to 'Making' and electronics, experience the internal conflict with the male values on display. They are silenced and sub-ordinated by them. They do not speak out and just learn to fail.

The 'Hidden Curriculum' — Looking at the Implicit Assumptions and Messages that the School Encourages in its Daily Practices

At Etches School there are still examples of boys and girls lining up separately for certain members of staff. There are examples of girls being used to control boys' behaviour. Tutor group lists have recently been sex segregated, officially to make it easier to identify boys and girls in a multi-racial school! It is also important to look closely at assembly content and teacher and pupil attitudes and expectations.

Classroom Relationships

This means observing, monitoring and working with the group dynamics in the classroom. It means looking at the relationships between boys, between boys and girls, and between pupils and teachers in the classroom situation. Such observations would involve seating patterns. Who do boys sit with? Who do they avoid? Which boys are marginalized and how is that noticed? What is the physical and emotional distance between boys and girls in the class groups? Another area for work would be the conversational language of the classroom filled as it is with sexist assumptions and put-downs. One of the authors at the start of a new boys' group module at Etches School heard five different and very common put-downs used by boys of each other within the first two minutes of boys entering the room. Thus was heard, 'I'm not gay', 'You woofter', 'You woman', 'You're a tramp' and 'You're a dickhead'. Using this kind of here and now experience and beginning to find out the fears, anxieties and contradictions that lie behind such language is a way of enabling boys to begin to look more honestly at their behaviour. Similar challenges can be made around boys' har-assing behaviour around girls and women.

In relation to boys it also means noticing the collusion that occurs between male members of staff and boys. What kinds of masculine models are being communicated covertly and overtly within classroom? It is about male members of staff being encouraged to have an awareness of the social relations which go on within the learning process and the effect that less authoritarian and partriarchal teaching styles might have on the levels of confidence within the classroom. This means recognizing that the male view of the world is not the only one, and that there is an alternative to the pushy, aggressive, competitive model of being a man. The alternative puts the teacher as listener or part of a collaborative process of learning within the classroom.

In addition, it means noticing how boys and girls might experience discrimination in terms of disciplinary matters. At Etches School boys demand far more attention and they make up 90 per cent of the referrals to the school's temporary exclusion zone (Room 20), but how much of this is about staff actually treating boys and girls differently? How many male teachers become trapped in the power and control spiral and send boys to Room 20 immediately they sense their own dominance in the classroom is being challenged? How many teachers send no-one to Room 20 for fear of being seen as weak? How many male teachers have different expectations of girls' behaviour? How many women teachers find alternative, non-confrontational ways of negotiating behaviour? What could male staff learn from this?

Careers Education — Examining the Effects of the Content and Focus of Careers Advice

Are subject and work choices being approached in an anti-sexist way? Is there any preventative, positive action work with boys on how their choices are affected by gender? The careers educator is a crucial influence here; and it is disturbing to realize that the person responsible at Etches School refers continuously to women in responsible jobs as lasses or girls. He does not refer to men of similar age or experience as lads or boys. When challenged on this as an example of the way men diminish the dignity of women, both as people or in response to their workplace contribution, he suggested that 'it wasn't the words that mattered, it was the practice'. Would he ever refer to black people as 'niggers'?

Language Use in Schools — Undertaking Studies of Language Use in All Areas of School Life

What messages are given by the use of gender-specific language in classrooms, assemblies and in school information that goes out to parents? How do young women in the school respond to being referred to as girls or lasses by the careers teacher in the example above? Above all how does such usage feed the atmosphere of 'acceptable' male entitlement in the school? What message is such language giving to boys? Gender-specific language feeds the atmosphere of male entitlement, which is also perpetuated in the unofficial language usage of the daily exchanges and conversations of day-to-day affairs. Such language of superiority and power touches all boys as the corridor and classroom banter and verbal jousting testifies (see Chapter 7 'Language as a Weapon'). How does this atmosphere affect the marginalized males who feel uncomfortable with the macho messages which are at odds with their desire to be more open about their emerging roles as caring, sensitive, nurturing young men? Is it any wonder that in such an atmosphere girls and young women in the school system either adopt very low profiles or 'act out' in an anti-social fashion. Is it any wonder that women members of staff who join the school with ideas of equality and partnership and with a feminist perspective find that initiatives like the women's support group slide quickly into anonymity and oblivion.

The Changing Curriculum — Looking at Changes in the School
Curriculum Brought About by Different Patterns of Employment and the
Growth of Computer Technology

It is also important to look at subject-specific sexist content with a view to removing certain items from the curriculum. One obvious example at Etches School is the 'Witches' English project for Year 7 pupils which actively and blatantly encourages a misogynistic view of women. There is no alternative balance provided so that students can understand the view that witches were actually women who espoused ancient matriarchal traditions and wisdom, and who were hounded by male attitudes in society which led to the systematic destruction of literally millions of wise women.

One of the author's experiences of a number of different boys' groups has shown that the boys thought that much behaviour attributed to western men is natural. In one group Colin suggested that 'it was natural for men to like fighting'. Others disagreed on the naturalness of fighting but felt that it was part of the expected attributes of men in this society. There have been other debates around the naturalness of women in child-care arrangements. It would be helpful, therefore, to look at gender aware curriculum interventions like 'What does it mean to "be a man" in different cultures around the world?' An examination of the non-competitive, non-violent, masculine behaviours on Tahiti and in Malaysia could be undertaken (see Gilmore, 1991, Chapter 9).

How effectively and enthusiastically such a school survey could be undertaken depends on the attitude of the male power system within the school. Such activities provoke fear and alarm which leads to disruptive behaviour and an undermining of initiatives which threaten to strike at the heart of that sense of male entitlement within the school. Inservice training for male staff will have to be carefully structured and sensitively handled. Early work could revolve around examining the question: What do I do, as a male, which could be seen as a threat to women's and marginalized boys' experience of school life — in my language, body posture and general demeanour? Courses structured in this way may then lead to a serious examination of questions of male entitlement and looking at positive alternative ways of being for men.

Meanwhile, a really fruitful area for challenging assumptions of male power lies in the male pupil population of the school. Boys' work can focus on three areas of damage:

- the damage that male power and control does to women and girls;
- the damage that restricted and limited gender expectations do to boys through restricted models of being men, restricted interactional styles, restricted subject and work choices and restricted exam results in areas where 'head work' is seen as feminine;
- homophobic damage to marginalized boys, boys who would want to explore much more wide-ranging diverse possibilities for being working, relaxing, nurturing men.

Doing boys' work can produce benefits in so far as boys learn to be more honest with each other, to take down their shields, to stop pretending and to learn to give and receive emotional sharing with each other. The result is potential for better psychological and emotional health since there will be less need to succeed at all costs, less need to play power games, less need to strut and show off, and less need to learn to be the hero, innovator, provider in life. As boys' sensitivity to each other can grow, so their potential to be more available to girls at an emotional level becomes greater. They are better equipped to show empathy and respect for the emotional and social rights of women.

Individual benefits of working in this way need to be linked to the context of male power. Individual shifts won't be sustained shifts if we fail to look at the context of male power at work secretly and get behind the brick wall of male authority. Both the authors were involved in delivering an inservice training day to the dozen male members of a senior management team at a Nottingham College of Further Education. We had been invited by the male principal. He had identified the stultifying and damaging effect of entrenched masculinity within the life of the college. His vision was to encourage his male members of staff to look at their masculinity and the way it damaged both their own lives in the college and also the equal opportunities initiatives that the college was keen to espouse. We took on the task, despite misgivings about the enforced nature of attendance by participants. We would have the principal's support or so he said, but when the personal work around manly expectations got difficult, it was a shock to find that it was the principal who panicked and retreated from the implications of what he had set up. He twice sabotaged our efforts, giving his reluctant male staff permission to turn on us as facilitators of the day. There was to be no breaching of the brick wall of male authority that day.

As the college experience shows, it is easy to be pessimistic about institutional change in schools. However, there is a more active dynamic going on between personal and institutional power. There is a gradual chipping away so that males in power positions in schools are learning to pay lip service to equal opportunities rhetoric. They learn to be silent about their sense of male entitlement at a personal level, knowing that such views will not be well received institutionally. Sometimes the personal creeps to the surface. There is the head who speaks the equal opportunities rhetoric with conviction but after a woman deputy angrily left his room after a heated disagreement he was heard to say, 'No woman has ever walked out of *my* [his emphasis] office before.'

Two strands do give grounds for optimism around challenging male domination. One is the sense that by choosing the language of change in schools, when more explicit changes around equal opportunities practices are mooted, the grounds for objection become increasingly difficult to sustain. The other is the real sense of crisis around boys in schools as bullying, abuse and ridicule increase. More and more schools are noticing this and realizing that they need to understand what is going on. They need to challenge themselves in terms of masculine entitlement at every level in the school from senior management team downwards. It will be a difficult and painful process.

Selected Further Reading on the Secondary School as a Gendered Institution

ASKEW, S. and ROSS, C. (1984) *Anti-Sexist Work with Boys*, London, ILEA.

ASKEW, S. and ROSS, C. (1988) 'Sexism in the school structure and organisation' (Chapter 3) in *Boys Don't Cry: Boys and Sexism in Education*, Milton Keynes, Open University Press.

CONNELL, R.W. (1989) 'Cool guys, swots and wimps: The interplay of masculinity and Education', *Oxford Review of Education*, **15**(3) pp. 291–303.

Boys' Sexualities

The Theory

Learning about Sex

Boys learn about sex without really being taught about it. In school locker rooms and playgrounds, in furtive conversations in corridors, and on the way home from school, adolescent boys are struggling to learn the rules for becoming a man and at the same time are becoming aware of their emerging sexualities. In my boys' groups I have noticed the tension that exists around a desire to talk about sexual issues, together with a compulsion to shock and demonstrate knowledge to both myself and to each other. There is a teasing, tentative coyness mixed with aggressive humour as issues around sexuality are debated. The aggressive humorous approach is fulfilled by the mass of disinformation with which boys learn the sexual mores of their culture. It shows itself in the false sense of certainty that accompanies their utterances, and in the swagger and the bravado with which they embody their remarks. Seated or standing, the aggressive thrust of 'I'm going to grab her and ride her on the settee', implies that there can be no doubts about the vigorous, manly sexuality of the boy who speaks these words.

Sexual activities with girls are used as a way of confirming a gender identity as a 'real boy'. Traditional heterosexual adolescent male sexuality is defined both negatively and positively through homophobia with the vigorous assertion that 'I'm NOT gay' and misogyny with its objectification of women/girls in the expression, 'I'd like to fuck THAT'. Boys are squeezed between these two poles. The full strength of their fears and anxieties in the area of their own sexuality emerges as they struggle to reconcile the overwhelming feelings of sexual pleasure with the fears about whether they will measure up or be big enough. At the same time, boys are learning that there is something shameful about acknowledging sexual pleasure and that this is reinforced by family, friends, school, religion and media images of sexuality. Boys have that sense of denying images of sexual pleasure when in the company of family — the sense of being heavily drawn in by sexual imagery but at the same time being embarrassed and ashamed. Learning the case of shame from a father who turns sex scenes off the TV not to protect the child but to protect his own sense of acute embarrassment.

Just as the shame enables them to deny their interest to others so they learn the separation of emotion and pleasure in themselves, which emerges as a sense of emotional detachment. There is a gulf between the conversations boys have about sex, since the words they use are for public performance, separate from their confused and tangled emotional responses to what is really going on inside. All they know is that they must toe the 'real lad' line or risk the scorn and ostracism of the male peer group and the images of male sexuality which feed it.

Popular culture provides many images of what real men are like. Boys realize that to be a man in this culture they must distance themselves from anything feminine in their own character. They must also be successful and admired. They must be the providers for future families. Boys must also aspire to being confident, reliable and cool, particularly in times of crisis. Finally, manliness is about having a sense of daring, about not ducking out of fights when pride is at stake, and about risk taking in general. All these attributes can be found in men's sexual behaviour. Thus the models of being sexual as a man combine the cool, sexy, daring and sophisticated attributes. Boys notice the power and appeal of Arnold Schwarzenegger and other celluloid heroes. From their images they can construct their own sexual fantasies and sense of potency.

John Walker, a fifteen-year-old student, is very knowledgeable about sex. His viewing of *The Good Sex Guide* on television has confirmed his detailed sexual knowledge gleaned from his sister's sex manuals. He has had girlfriends for the past four years and he wants to hint at his growing sexual experience with them. It seems very important for him to demonstrate his knowledge of many aspects of sexual activity in front of other boys in the group. His imagery relies on the world of sexual activity where men do things to women. He wants us to know that he is clear about this thrusting, driving heterosexuality, where he is the dominant male giving his partner what he knows she wants. He expresses his desires which need satisfying with a sense of awful certainty. He grips the attention of the boys who waver between nods of agreement and a sense of wide-eyed admiration tinged with a feeling of 'would this all be true' (but I could make it true for me). They are captivated but with a lurking sense of doubt. It is at this point of doubt that this view of a dominant male sexuality capable only of thrusting expression needs to be challenged.

The seeds of doubt emerge because at one level boys know that the only acceptable expression of male sexuality in front of other boys is the view that grips their imagination as John Walker speaks. They aim for the image of the hard-driving stud in their minds. Around other boys it is difficult to begin to give voice to those other fluid and tangled feelings which they think also expresses their sexuality. So it is that they daren't take the risk to talk of feelings, emotions, warmth, desire and communication born of love. There is much mis-understanding and distress around as boys seek a relevant outlet for their more sensitive and caring sexual voices. Pressure to not lose face either by admitting their sensitivity or displaying ignorance is at the heart of the confusion and fear that surrounds the atmosphere in which boys struggle to come to terms with what is regarded as the 'norm' as far as sex is concerned.

Other sources of confusion exist in boys' minds since the sexual atmosphere in which boys grow up has been changing dramatically. Society's approach to sex has undergone a significant shift in the past thirty years. Single-parent families are a reality despite being the subject of a great political attack from the traditional family brigade — the New Right. More people live together without marriage with contraception more freely available and abortion legalized. In addition, there is a limited toleration of open expressions of gay and lesbian sexuality. Such celebratory processions as Gay Pride marches would have been unthinkable a generation ago, as would Parliamentary debate on the reduction of the age of consent for gay people to 16. Sex in terms of women's bodies is also powerfully present in all aspects of the media. Advertising continues to exploit female attractiveness and men's desires for women's bodies to sell products and hints of sexual availability via women's bodies pervade television, films, newspapers and popular music.

Probably the most dramatic impetus to an urgent re-think about male sexuality is the realization that HIV/Aids is now a threat to the whole population unless some significant changes to the attitude and practice of safe sex take place. Both HIV and the uncovering of large numbers of child sex abuse cases has also directly challenged conventional masculine heterosexuality. In addition, the impact of feminism, the changing role of women in society and different patterns of employment which challenge the concept of the male breadwinner, have all challenged traditional male ways of being and with it traditional patterns of male sexual behaviour.

We need a sex education that disrupts the 'taken for grantedness' of male heterosexuality. When boys talk of sexual matters they assume that the only natural kind of male sex is heterosexual. Thus the only proper male sexual activity is focused in atmosphere, imagery and reality around the harsh aggressiveness of 'screwing' and 'fucking'. There is also the assumption (inspired by the related fear of deviating from the 'normal') that this natural, top dog, heterosexuality will have power over other forms of sexual orientation so that gay, bisexual, and other vulnerable varieties are silenced and dominated.

One of the authors has worked within the framework of a deeply homophobic school culture. Scarcely a day goes by without being able to witness insults like, 'You bender, poofter, queer', etc., which serves to put down, hurt and control the recipient of the remark. To be so condemned means to be seen as less than a real boy. At the same time there is the frequently heard rejoinder of, 'I'm not gay' or many variants of the same as boys assert their attachment to dominant heterosexual masculinity. Gay men's sexuality is perceived as being unmasculine since it touches the softer, gentler side of themselves which it is difficult to show in front of other boys who are intent on demonstrating their vigorous hold on real manliness.

Thus boys throw themselves vigorously into earnest proclamations of their ruggedness as a defence against being tainted with any unmasculine and therefore homosexual traits. The fear of unmanliness provokes many boys to constantly affirm themselves as members of the male club. Various strategies serve to gain access. An interest in sporting activities of the rugged masculine kind is particularly important. Hence, there is massive energy invested in talk of football, American football and the stars of American wrestling rings. Others share enthusiasm for various types of cult popular music, while humour is used by many to ensure popularity and deflect attention from gentler natures which might be too near the surface for peer acceptability. Sexual swagger in the form of sexual boasting and bragging and largely fantasized stories of drinking activities, also serve to ensure credibility. All may be seen as avoidance strategies that prevent any talk that questions all these defences.

Working with boys around the issue of homophobia is challenging. Boys take aggressive and angry stands against homosexuality or are confused and withdrawn reflecting questions marks around their own sexual identity. The nature of the confusion shows boys as alternately fascinated and repulsed by questions of gay and bisexual life styles. They are drawn into wanting to know more while at the same time wanting to make clear their revulsion. There is so much disinformation and myth around: boys make assumptions that all gay men are drawn into penetrative anal sex and are perverts looking for boys to corrupt. When confronting the normality of dominant heterosexual masculinity there is a sense of trauma around as a world of certainty is questioned and the scary world of love, intimacy and fluid sexuality is opened up.

Using statistics about one in ten people being gay doesn't acknowledge the fact that there is no fixed sexual identity and it doesn't give regard to the variability of sexual experience at some times and moments in a person's life. Labels are not fixed and there is a swirling range of fluid sexual identities which men buy into at some time in their lives. At times of feeling vulnerable and inadequate, men and boys buy into a fixed source of identity — dominant heterosexual masculinity. Boys learn to look for safety within that source of recognition and approval — thus they take up a homophobic and any misogynistic stance which reassures them when they have a sense of losing their grip on their male identity.

In the vigorous homophobic world of the school corridor it takes special moments to capture what is really going on. Two examples illustrate the pitfalls and successes of the work. A boys' group session in July 1993 was taken over by Sean. Sean is 15 years old but is very small for his age. He is taunted and picked on by other boys. In return he is often aggressive, challenging, prone to violent outbursts and assertive of his sexual successes with girls. Although his attendance at boys' group sessions has been irregular, his interest when present has been marked and valued. He is known for his homophobic remarks so it was no surprise when at the start of a session he asserts, 'If any bum basher came round to my house I'd shoot him'. I used this remark to begin to look at the whole question of male sexuality. Other boys made comments, some helpful, some guaranteed to wind Sean up more. He wanted to know whether I was gay and began to direct homophobic comments to other boys in the room. By this time he was extremely agitated and was moving round the room issuing threats. He called me a 'fucking queer' and held a stool over my head. The threat that he would bring the stool down on my head and thus the 'fucking queer' would be punished seemed real. He was eventually persuaded to lower the stool. The whole episode which had scarcely lasted ten minutes was too challenging and too traumatic for him. The only way he could cope was to wreck it and leave. He did eventually walk out, throwing a stream of abuse in my direction. He had assured us in no uncertain terms that his rugged powerful masculinity was intact. We had threatened his sense of being a 'real lad'.

With this same group, picking out what the behaviour had been about, helped other boys to look at their responses. The boys who had taunted Sean about his boasts about sexual activity with girls were able to begin to notice what they were saying about themselves. The confessions began to emerge that they were not nearly as experienced as they made out and that they were frightened of seeming soft and inexperienced in front of their peers. The fears about being gay emerged again when Neil spoke of an all-male sleep-in at another's house when John had reached over in the night and felt his penis. John was full of denial, then said he must have been asleep but eventually was able to say, 'I'm not gay but sometimes I just wonder what it's like'. There was a silence as boys seemed to take this in. One by one they began to shyly admit their interest. Roy mentioned how it might be if you really did have a friend who was gay. I encouraged him to explore this using role play. Other times that I have used this strategy have proved very difficult but on this day Roy was able to tap into and acknowledge some of his sensitive and caring side that he seldom showed. Afterwards other boys shared how they had been encouraged by what Roy had done to share more of their feelings with those they could trust. It was no coincidence that it was this group of boys who were able to come up with a wide range of caring, sensitive sexual activities and emotions which get lost when men think of 'having sex'. Each boy chose one which stood out for him and in a rare moment of collective adolescent male intimacy they sang their words and phrases to each other.

It was as if in that moment we had reached out and grasped the notion that male sexual identities can be broadened to embrace a much wider variety of sexual and sensual pleasures. Boys need to be able to hold on to their adventurous heterosexual desire but have that desire channelled into the process of communication and contact with another person which can be an alternative source of emotional satisfaction and pleasure. Connell's work (1990) on Australian gay and bisexual men makes this clearer. He discovered that within the gay community sensuous touching and kissing was more emotionally satisfying than any other sexual practice.

As boys make their way through the minefield of sexual expectations, it seems important to try to bring boys into contact with this forgotten dimension. Such sexual intimacy as varieties of sensuous touch has only been acknowledged in boys' minds as foreplay before the goal of penetration is achieved. The gay and bisexual movement can help an appreciation of sensuous touch for its own sake — as a prelude to nothing. In this way the gay movement has much to contribute to widening the compass of male heterosexuality.

What do boys desperately need to challenge, share, explore and know in sexual terms? This central question helps us to focus on the key problem areas that affect boys as they grow up to be men.

Distancing and Detachment

In locker rooms and playgrounds, in furtive conversations in corridors or on the way home from school, boys learn to separate their emotions from sexual expression. As adolescents, boys learn the secrecy of sex, that somehow it is morally wrong and not to be talked about but infinitely exciting and pleasurable. Boys learn that there is something shameful about acknowledging sexual pleasure and that this is reinforced by family, friends, school, religion and media images of sexuality. Boys have that sense of being heavily drawn in by sexual images but at the same time being embarrassed and ashamed. Just as they learn to deny their interest to others, so they learn the separation of emotion and pleasure in themselves — which emerges as a sense of emotional detachment. There is a gulf between the words boys use in conversations about sex and their own emotional responses to what is really going on. The talk is of 'doing it', of 'performance' and of 'achieving' orgasm — in particular 'You've got to give her plenty of orgasms haven't you?' The language is of a functional job from which somehow they are separate. The penis is transformed into a tool — an instrument whereby the job can be carried out. It is as if boys learn to develop a secret sexual self that performs sexual acts and that somehow this self exists outside themselves and is only transiently and fearfully part of their whole being. Distancing prevents those painful feelings of fear and vulnerability from emerging. The dread of losing a sense of self by getting too close; the fearful fantasy of becoming a sucky little boy back in the folds of his mother's breasts with all the feelings of powerlessness is the antithesis of the feelings of power and taking control that men learn they have to display themselves to be real men.

Performance

'You've had sex haven't you Paul?', asks Sean. Paul looks shy and confused. He doesn't want to answer. He looks round for support and takes the risk to actually deny his sexual experience. The original questioner pushes on with his sense of bravado asserting that he has had sex many times. The group look at Sean half doubtful, half wanting to believe and sensing his sense of exaggeration and half admiring his sense of being experienced.

What Sean's body language is showing is that he is now a man since he has had sex. Sex is interwoven with masculine identity. Having sex expresses the pride and confirmation of being a man. In this boys' group among boys with very limited sexual experience, Sean can preen and feel sure of his male identity, at least on the surface. Beneath the boastful exterior lies the fear and anxiety which lies behind the question, 'Am I man enough to satisfy her?' It is not just the achievement of the sexual act with all its pleasure and desire but it is being caught in the process of expectation. Boys are already beginning to acquire the inflated and distorted expectations about what they ought to be doing in the sexual process. Assumptions like, 'a man should always take the lead in sex', 'men always want and are always ready for sex' and 'in sex it's performance that counts', loom large and create great anxiety about sexual contact. Boys can intellectually dismiss all of these assumptions as they talk together in a group setting but when I probe further it is obvious that there *is* an attachment to these anxieties because they *might* be important. Such anxieties get in the way of loving interactive sex. As Gordon Deakin (1988) says,

> Penis size, the maintenance of erection, duration of coitus before eja-culation, the search for simultaneous orgasms and other impersonal and pleasure destroying concerns induce anxiety and foster inappropriate goal orientation in sexual activity.

While boys are attached to the notion that sex equals erection, they will be unable to focus on the pleasure of the moment. They become attached to the notion that 'it only counts if I put it in', or 'it only counts as sex if I come inside'. Boys grow to be the men who think that they have to delay orgasm for as long as possible since that implies real sexual adequacy. Many will never have heard of Bullmoose Jackson's song *Sixty-minute Man* but they nevertheless try to live out his fantasy. They have all manner of strategies to take them away from their partners in their heads. Thoughts consciously drift to income tax, railways, football, car engines — anything to take them from the brink of orgasm. But with orgasm complete they rest with a sense of job done and pride in performance — a sense of pride in confirmed masculinity. Sex can only be satisfying if the boy hangs on to that feeling — but there is a nagging doubt about how good it really was. The only way such doubts can be eased is to be better next time, to be more in control, more sure of his power and in greater control of performance. If he is more sexually manly in this way then the doubts will go away.

Boys boast about their sexual conquests, real or imagined, to other boys. There is great peer pressure to have 'done it'. Boys can't relax and choose the right time and context for love making. With their eye on confirmed mascu-linity, achievement and performance they lose touch with their bodies. They have learned to impose their will on their bodies and of calling that feeling sexual. They haven't learned to notice the appropriate time when it feels right. Sex therefore takes place with a sense of rush in captured moments in all manner of places — in backs of cars, up against walls, in doorways, in strange bedrooms with the fear of intrusion or in company with other significantly inexperienced couplings. The experience has been fumbling, uncaring and embarrassing but the weight of virginity has been lifted and although the experience has been dis-appointing and unfulfilling this is not revealed. Mates are not told of the sense of disappointment and regret, only the sense of how good it was. What particularly comes across to other boys is the celebration of becoming a man via this sexual achievement and the realization that by repeating the experience, manhood will be perpetually confirmed.

The sexual experience has become an endurance test. Pleasure becomes almost accidental since in the partnership of sexual experience the other person is virtually absent.

Genital Focusing

One powerful source of information about boys' sexuality comes from pornography. Nearly every boy in all the groups I have been involved with has discovered about sex from pornography's distorted images. When given permission to speak of pornography it is almost as if they will not be a real man if they don't *live* a porno fantasy. In my presence the boys allude to some of the tamer images they have seen. It is enough to notice their attachment to the false idea that the women are just there for men's pleasure. Women are always seen to be gasping for it, the longer, the harder, the better. Pornography encourages masturbatory fantasies focused on parts of women. Boys speak of women with 'good accessories', meaning women with big breasts or the grossness of the imagery of the women's 'fluffy muffin' into which 'the man can hammer his nail'. Around all this is the image of 'traditional' feminine frothiness, the frills and the black pantiness against which the rock solid hardness of men is defined.

Boys talk of going out with a girl with big breasts as good for the male image — 'You've attracted someone with big tits — you lucky . . .'. Once again, the person has actually disappeared, the object of attention is only a part of her body. This is the language of objectification, the breaking down of women into the parts which can guarantee boys' pleasure. The language dehumanizes. The reality of the person is lost in obsessive references to breasts and vagina, from which they will get their fun. The talk is of doing 'it', of success and arm thrust upwards in triumph. It is the language of winning something — acquiring a trophy. What is this trophy for sexual conquest? For boys it is being able to say to themselves, 'I am a man', and if others know of your conquest, your knowing that they know is a real reward.

Boys are drawn by pornographic fantasies to consider their penises as the centre of the sexual universe. The long thrusting penis is transformed into a tool, an instrument whereby the job can be carried out. Sometimes boys talk of the penis as if it is somehow separate from themselves. It is something to be objectified and conquered. It can have names like John Thomas and Peter and it can let boys down with erections at inconvenient moments. It has a kind of behaviour of its own which each boy is somehow curiously detached from.

What boys seem to be doing in all of this — the linguistic swagger and the obsession with genitals and performance — is to keep their fears and anxieties at bay. They are covering up their vulnerability where they feel really exposed. Boys and men must be in active control.

Male sexualization emphasizes how real men are supposed to have sex. The man is supposed to be in control. Passivity is prohibited and men must constantly seek to escalate the scale of sexual activity. He assumes control of a sequence of events, 'a sequence of invasion' (Wood, 1984). The progress from 'feel 'em to fuck 'em' means that men can't be softly sensual in sex. No sooner does he arrive at a particular level of sexual intimacy than he is planning the next move. The woman is also having to consider if it is alright to progress to the next level. It is almost as if both parties are living in the future. Men who know all the answers and find it difficult to ask for help in any capacity are inevitably going to find it difficult to seek help around another's body. Sex is about negotiation and communication between two people's adventurous desires. It is about the fluidity of balancing each other's adventurous desires as the journey which *may* lead to intercourse takes place. And during this journey the negotiation may determine that intercourse is not the goal — but that at each level of mutual pleasure there will be time to pause and think and feel how soft, warm and lovely her breast might feel. Gone from this scenario is the sense of subject and object. No-one is dominant and 'the giving it to' approach has been genuinely abandoned in favour of something more mutually satisfying. Sex negotiated in such a way rids men of these fearful thoughts which follow performance pressure. Was she happy with my performance? Did I last long enough? How do I compare with others?

Masculine Entitlement

In my contact with adolescents, I have noticed how the power dynamic operates between the sexes. Girls' rights to physical space are eroded as they are brushed aside in corridors and classrooms. Girls' interests and enthusiasms are ignored, dismissed or mocked. However, gifted, talented and bright girls are, there are so many boys who make assumptions that their own maleness gives them rights which girls would be foolish to challenge. It is an assumption of privilege that boys come first.

In the sexual politics between adolescents, boys have expectations about being in control of the sexual contact. Boys have a sense that sex is a kind of natural gushing force which has an uncontrollable, addictive power in their lives. It dominates their adolescent existence and drives them to see their genital sexuality as standing for their masculine identity. Fed by the notion that their needs come first, they claim their masculine identity by demonstrating power over and control of girls. It is these demands of male sexuality which seem essential to a real boy identity.

To chase the addictive sense of power, boys learn to focus on the 'natural' masculine heterosexual behaviour, but the crucial element is that it is the power differences which are eroticized rather than eroticizing the communication and contact between two people. Boys and men feel more manly about scoring than about making themselves vulnerable enough to make contact with the other person. And so boys talk the bravado language of 'shag 'em and bag 'em', getting off on the hard 'fuck 'em and ride 'em' language. They squirm and wriggle when confronted with the sensuous sensitive fluid world of love making. They fear rejection and humiliation and thus exercise control over their partners by organizing the direction of sexual activities — 'Who does what, when to whom?' Within this context of self-protection, the sexual act often gets used by boys and men to bolster a shaky, masculine identity, rather than ways of deepening pleasurable contact with another person. All of that is just too scary.

Sex and Dangerous, Wild, Risk-taking Behaviour

Tony is 27 years old. He has an athletic body transformed by regular sessions with weights. I notice him occasionally glancing at himself in the mirror and flexing those carefully constructed muscles. He knows he is a real man. His sexual appetite is large. Women fall for his good looking manliness and charm. His brand of smooth talking and endearing promises enables him to make relationships easily. He has at least six children by at least four women, although there are rumours of other children in other areas of the country. His sexual behaviour is irresponsible. Contraception is not his responsibility and he doesn't believe in using condoms. He lives the fiction of wild, unfettered sex which confirms him as a man. It is just not manly to use condoms; sex is better without. Condoms desensitize the pleasure in the penis 'like sucking a sweet with the wrapper on'. Tony enjoys the thought of having fathered children but he bears no responsibility for any of them. He turns up occasionally, expresses luke warm interest, has sex and disappears again. Tony's gender script defined through his sense of manliness puts unprotected sex high on the list of what is expected of himself as a 'real man'. Tony is not alone. There are many Tonys who adopt a similar philosophy. No fiddling around with condoms for them, they are just an embarrassment. They choose to place their sense of being 'real men' ahead of considerations about health risks to themselves or their partners. Whatever the danger, this is a risk they will take to shore up the edifice of themselves as men.

Tony's swagger has a bravado that appeals to adolescents but if they adopt such aspects of his life they will be perpetuating the link between diseases, male sexualities and gender. Sexually transmitted diseases and AIDS can be directly related to masculine risk-taking behaviours. Michael Kimmel (1991) has even referred to AIDS as the 'most gendered disease in American history'. First, in men's 'natural' acceptance of risk behaviours (unprotected sexual intercourse and sharing needles) as being more manly than safer sex practices, men put their lives in danger. Then, in their scorn for risk-reduction behaviour (abstinence, safer sex techniques, safer drug use) they buy into a more dangerously exciting obsession with manly virility that can again destroy their lives and others. As Kimmel comments,

> . . . these types of risk-reduction behaviour are in direct contradiction to the norms of masculinity. The norms of masculinity propel men to take risks, score and focus sexual pleasure on the penis. Real men ignore precautions for AIDS risk reduction, seek many sexual partners and reject de-pleasuring the penis. Abstinence, safer sex and safer drug use compromise manhood. The behaviours required for the confirmation of masculinity and those required to reduce risk are antithetical.

For boys, safer sex means creating a climate where they can learn to talk about sex and confront the vulnerable, less confident part of themselves — not the bit that hides behind the shield of virile masculinity and avoids responsibility for their own well-being.

Fundamental changes in the laws governing education have taken place in recent years. The Education Reform Act and Section 28 of the Local Government Act seek to impose a particular moral code and to promote a particular view of heterosexuality which patently discriminates against all who exist outside 'normal' stable married heterosexual units. We would maintain that the Acts also promote not only a highly mythological view of heterosexuality but also one in which stereotyped ideas about masculinity, sexuality and femininity go unchallenged. Thus as governing bodies of schools determine how sex education should be provided, the real fear is what schools will be allowed to teach.

Growing knowledge of sexual facts fails to take into account the problem of masculinity in relation to those facts. Boys' sex education has often uncritically accepted that sex for boys and men is an uncontrollable urge or impulse, and that women and girls have to be protected from their masculine predatoriness. This implies a 'boys will be boys' approach that necessitates women being given strategies to protect themselves from uncontainable male impulses. Hence it promotes the view that women rather than men should stay off the streets to prevent rapes and sexual assaults. Such an approach relieves boys of the responsibility of ever having to change themselves or challenge male power in society.

We need to stress the problems inherent in the problem of masculinity at a domestic level. A recent large-scale survey of Middlesex University found that one in ten women had suffered violence form their partners during the past year (*The Guardian*, 1 September 1993). How many boys witness such violence or are recipients of it? How many boys come from homes where their sisters or themselves are sexually abused? How many boys come from homes where there is general deference paid to the wishes of fathers in the decision-making process? How many boys witness the emotional neglect and abuse that takes place within the framework of the traditional, nuclear family unit? How many notice the ways in which men learn to eroticize power and learn to 'get off' on fantasies of dominating women's lives.

There is also the assumption (inspired by the related fear of deviating from the 'normal') that this 'natural', top dog, heterosexuality will have power over other forms of sexual orientation so that gay, bisexual, vulnerable transsexual varieties are silenced and dominated. What the ethos of heterosexism does to young gay men and lesbians is to drive them into secrecy and self-doubt with its need to lie, with its feelings of insecurity and with its thoughts of suicide. Within the school framework there is an almost complete rejection of homosexuality in all areas of the curriculum. There is a willingness on the part of the school community to condone anti-gay and lesbian attitudes and the inability to provide any positive support to young gay children with problems at school. How can it be otherwise if the head of Year 9 at a Derby comprehensive school was heard to say 'the only thing I'm racist against is homosexuals'.

And the climate is worsening as nationally the Health Minister, Virginia Bottomley, is advocating scaling down the HIV/AIDS awareness budget with the implication that it has been exaggerated in the heterosexual community — hence it's just the 'queer' disease. Again, under pressure from the Tory family group, John Patten, the former Education Minister, has been suggesting that teaching around homosexuality needs to be looked at again.

We need to help boys to discover new models of masculinity because it can challenge the controlling behaviours associated with dominant heterosexual masculinity. Sex education should be focusing not only on the inner change made possible by greater sexual knowledge when linked with feelings, loving relationships and awareness, but also creating outer change in terms of changing oppressive behaviour away from the mode of 'natural male hunter' and male sex as conquest. Can men and boys begin to acknowledge their full body sexuality, the importance of tenderness and a real sharing of bodily pleasure? Can they do this when sexual activity appears as an anxious competitive test? Is the first question in the forefront of men's minds, 'Am I getting it right?', followed by 'How do I compare with other men?' and 'I must not disappoint — real men are hard, driving studs.'

The fear engendered in boys by such questions impels boys to control fear in themselves by controlling girls. There is a real need to confront the inter-relationship between heterosexual men's power over women and the construction of their sexualities. Can they give up power over women and gay men without being afraid that their grasp on their maleness will loosen and collapse? This dilemma and the challenge centres on deconstructing the edifice of male power and control that is equated with the traditional structure of masculine identity. This needs to be done without it seeming that the giving up of power automatically implies giving up the foundation of maleness and therefore creating the spectre of impotence with all its erosion of self-esteem.

In the explanation of sex education for boys there is a continuous link with issues of men and masculinities. Boys are born into a world of male entitlement which is so intuitively accepted as to appear entirely natural. So it is that boys grow up to expect to be served and treated deferentially by women. Boys learn quickly about the privilege of being men. The corollary of this privilege lies in the lonely isolation of many men who have no responsibility for their own emotional lives and who find it very difficult to relate to women on an equal partnership basis. Our approach enables boys to critically scrutinize their lives so that light is shed on those areas which are most denied — the inner silences and uncomfortable feelings that feed the fears and anxieties about growing up as a man. Thus we not only challenge the everyday assumptions boys make but also help them to make healthy emotional relations and contacts in the world.

Selected Further Reading on Boys' Sexualities

DAVIDSON, N. (1990) *Boys Will Be . . . ? Sex Education and Young Men*, London, Bedford Square Press.
HOLLAND, J., RAMAZANOGLU, C. and SHARPES, S. (1993) *Wimp or Gladiator: Contradictions in Acquiring Masculine Sexuality*, London, Tufnell Press.
KIMMEL, M. (Ed.) (1991) *Men Confront Pornography*, Meridian/Penguin (USA).
KIMMEL, M. and LEVINE, M. (1980) 'Men and AIDS' in KIMMEL, M. and MESSNER, M. (Eds) *Men's Lives*, New York, Macmillan.
LITEWKA, J. (1977) 'The socialised penis' in SNODGRASS, J. *For Men Against Sexism*, USA, Times Change Press.
METCALF, A. and HUMPHRIES, M. (Eds) (1985) *The Sexuality of Men*, Pluto Press.
WOOD, J. (1984) 'Groping towards sexism: Boys' sex talk' in MCROBBIE, A. and NAVA, M. *Gender and Generation*, Macmillan.

The Session

The Language of Sex

It is 2.12pm on Thursday afternoon — the last period of the day. I have arrived early since I never know what kind of mood the boys will be in. I arrange the square of tables. Part of me would prefer to have them all sit in an open circle of chairs, but it is easier to deal with the written work aspect if they sit at tables. In any case we can all see each other around the square of tables.

The bell goes and they start to come in from break. There might only be ten of them but I know that there will have been some minor crisis to prevent a prompt start. By this stage there will have been the inevitable question, 'Are we doing any writing today?' I feel quite annoyed and defensive about this question each time it is put. They never write very much at all but it is beginning to be a big issue with this group. I protest to them in my mock humorous way that they never write very much at all, that they have really only dealt with questionnaires. I share my anxieties with the group that I feel very pressured by this attitude, that I do have concerns about making them write, but that I do need to have some written record of some of their thoughts and attitudes. 'In any case,' I throw in with a sense of relief, 'I think you might enjoy your writing today. It will be very different from anything you have written in school before.' I say all this with a knowing grin. Continued muttering tells me they are not convinced.

The last person arrives. It is Wesley who has had some highly plausible problem about his football. I wait for silence but there is a seemingly inevitable atmosphere of rustle and disturbance. I am beginning to get annoyed. I try not to let it leak out. There are still some groans about writing. Some are engaged in exchanges of information, others are keeping their eyes on me. Paul suddenly tries to touch Gareth in the stomach. There is some pushing and shoving between the two of them — the banter between the two of them is about noses and what's wrong with each other's faces. More seemingly unconnected banter occurs around someone wanting to change sex. I decide reluctantly that I have to 'go authoritarian'. I shout and the room quietens. I hate doing this because most of the time I am trying to model a non-authoritarian approach to create a climate filled with mutual sharing and respect. I feel uncomfortable but sense that I can recapture the mood I want to achieve fairly quickly. Thus in an altogether calm, friendly and encouraging voice, I ask them to form into pairs or threes. I give them a sheet of paper and ask them to brainstorm all the words they can think of which have anything to do with sex. I think it is important to do this since boys grow up in an atmosphere which dubs sex as dirty or naughty and even bad, but which in adolescence is an all pervasive powerful influence. What is it about boys that impels them to use talk of sex to shock adults, to compete with other boys and to impress and oppress girls? All of this leaves out whole areas of real contact which a fuller view of sexual and sensual activities would provide. All I want them to do is to look at the words, share how they are used and begin to look at what is left out. The brainstorm will be the start of that process.

Pairings and groups of three are formed fairly easily. Sex is written in the middle of the sheet and I tell them that they have five minutes for the task. There is much excitement mixed with reticence and embarrassment about what is expected of them. 'Can we write rude words down?' I explain again that all the words they can think of will be fine. I ask them not to censor themselves by thinking of something and then not daring to write it down. Confirmed with permission they get into the task enthusiastically. I look round and notice the delight they are sharing about doing something they think is really naughty — with permission.

Once this part of the task is complete, we begin a discussion of the sort of words they have recorded. What had made the boys embarrassed to write them down? The group threw in that the words were dirty, rude, hard and aggressive. There were lots of doing words and the done-to party was invariably a woman. Kevin noticed the analogy between the word penis and its use under the alternative name of weapon. He suggested that women would not think much of that and that even if the words were 'cleaner', it would still be like 'men using women'.

I move on to give each boy a sheet with four column headings as follows:

- Words about doing something to another person.
- Harsh aggressive words.
- Medical, technical words.
- Caring words.

53

I ask that they go through their brainstorms and put each word into the different categories. Some will fit into more than one column and they are encouraged to repeat words where necessary. Some help was needed as the boys wanted to check on certain of the categories, even to the extent of asking, 'Is vagina a medical word?'

I ask them to survey their finished product with the question in their minds, 'What is largely absent from the survey of what the word sex brings up in your mind?' 'What is missing?' Jagvir flippantly says 'Give me ten minutes and I'll go and find someone and come back and tell you.' His friend Ishtiaq pauses and says, 'Was it a nice time?'

I confront these two remarks with their in-built assumption of male entitlement and boyish embarrassment about the whole task. Jagvir accepts that what he said was wrong and that it was just a joke. I ask him to think more clearly about what is missing. All the boys begin to slowly realize that words revealing care and tenderness are the ones that are largely absent. Shahzad says, 'People who think of sex don't think about caring, stroking and those things.' I ask if that is true for him and he agrees. Chris, in his earnest and serious way, adds knowingly that, 'Oh yes it's got to be about caring as well'.

The boys seem quite shocked that there are so many words about 'doing to' the other person and that most of them are also sneering put-downs of a particularly harsh kind. 'What do all these words leave out?' I ask. The boys then produce a string of words that suggest that they do have a marked idea of the gentler side of love-making. Words like enjoyable, loving, hugging, kissing, love at first sight, caring for her body, and nice atmosphere were all expressed and agreed as important. Jagvir thinks that, 'her feelings towards you are just as important as your feelings towards her'. The whole atmosphere of the room has become gentler. The boys are touched by a desire to unself-consciously share that they do think like this. I reflect this back to them and question where the harshness comes from and who creates it? The boys offer ideas ranging from friends, the media, pornographic materials. The pressure to conform to this public, peer pressure view of sex as 'having a good fuck', or 'I'm going to fuck her tonight', is very powerful. I ask what impression such statements were actually making. 'It sounds like you're not friends with her,' says Husan, or that 'you're forcing someone', says Wesley. Amazingly, they ask the question 'Where is friendship?' 'All this is just lust', says Shuiab as he waves his hand dismissively over the brainstorm sheets.

Since it was Wesley who had used the expression, 'I'm going to fuck her tonight,' I ask him if he will sculpt all the qualities that are being left out if this is all the relationship actually means. I asked Wesley to line everyone up so that we could all see what was really around in this expression he had used: an expression which was in danger of being unacknowledged and unremarkable in male company. If boys forgot that they were supposed to keep up an image dictated by the 'fuck, shag, screw syndrome', as I coined it, what would they discover? Boys took on qualities as follows: Care, Love, Patience, Attention, Friendship, Affection, Relationship, Understanding, Personality, and Interest in the Other Person. I was impressed that the boys achieved this so quickly. Some added other words that came from the brainstorms, like hugs, cuddles and caresses. Each boy repeated his quality four times as they encircled Wesley so that each knew what their qualities were and that there was a whole new dimension to the idea of making love which was very different from having sex. I asked if they could try to keep the image of this circular sculpt in their mind. Wesley expressed his discomfort at being 'I'm going to fuck her tonight'. He said that he would rather join the circle as part of the tenderer side of love-making. He came in as Hugging. I asked the boys to look at each other and repeat their qualities once more. Philip said that we could sing them all. There was some embarrassment around this, but it seemed important to try as I felt that it might be a real memory to hold onto — and remember what was behind it.

Classroom Strategies

Gender Identities and Sexualities

Rather than talk in terms of sex education, it is tempting to use the term 'sexuality' as a curriculum title. A major USA educational study has argued, 'Sexuality is a tent that encloses the biological, psychological, sociocultural and ethics of human sexual behaviour' (Burt and Meeks, 1985). Marland (1989) argues for the use of the title 'Sexuality Curriculum' enabling the young man to understand himself and the choice of behaviours which he has in his life. An important part of such a curriculum would thus be 'understanding one's own gender and that of others, one's attitude to one's own gender and that of others and of one's own growing sexuality' (Marland, 1989).

Sexuality is a lifelong process and expression of sexuality has been seen as a crucial part of the difference between men and women. Our gender identities are supposed to derive from 'natural' differences in our sexualities. In reality the extent to which men and women are different sexually is a result not of different natures or differences in sex organs, but because we receive and learn from different messages as we grow to become men or women. Since sexuality begins at birth, there are numerous powerful messages told to boys and girls by parents and family relating to acceptable gender identity and sexual expression. Parents can be so inhibited in dealing with sexuality that a cycle of sexuality as naughty or wrong gets perpetuated. How many boys have had their sensuality attacked by expressions like, 'Don't be a cissy', or 'Be a big boy and don't cry'? How many others learn to take in sexual messages like, 'Don't touch that — it's dirty', or 'Don't do that — it's not very nice is it?' Such messages are informed by a view of sexuality and manliness which is reinforced by powerful institutions in society — the media, religion, schools, politics, the legal system and the scientific world.

Since all boys grow up around the same messages, the power of the peer group for adolescent boys is enormous. It influences or distantly controls even intimate and private activities of sex. Many boys and young men, so influenced, outwardly assume that the only way of being sexual is to be heterosexual and engage in what they regard as normal sexual activity with a girl to whom they are attracted. This is underpinned by the assumption that the boy is taking control, with conquest, penetration and performance as the ultimate activity models for the real or imagined intimacy that is taking place. But what of the boys who are uncomfortable with this model but who can say nothing? In these circumstances it is so important to begin to empower boys with skills that will permit them to express their own ideas, beliefs and feelings. The relationship in which boys will feel they need to express their sexualities are many and varied. It is important to realize that sexual preferences may change during a lifetime. If at any time a boy's sexual behaviour may be incongruent with his sexual identity he needs to be empowered to follow his own convictions and yet not alienate himself from the peer group.

Many of the classroom strategies are designed to help boys share the difficult areas of their lives. Boys in all the groups I have worked with have struggled with whether it was safe to be honest with each other and share what they were really scared to let others know. It is vital to examine this fear, which sees many young men fitting into the norms of prevailing peer behaviour or face the ridicule and the taunts of those peers in the face of perceived deviant behaviour however subtly it may be expressed. The exercises that follow are designed to promote the sharing of feelings around fear, being left out and what constitutes appropriate manly behaviours. The rest of this section goes on to explore sexual information and heterosexism and HIV/AIDS.

What Frightens Me?

Aim: *To encourage boys to share their fears with other boys*

Materials: *None*

Time: *20 minutes*

What to do:

Encourage the boys to form pairs.

Each boy to take it in turns to talk about, 'What frightens me'. Take two or three minutes each, then ask each boy to share with their partner, 'What do fearful feelings actually feel like?'

and 'What do I do to myself when I am feeling frightened and can't show it? How do I pretend not to be frightened?'

Bring the group back into a whole circle to share common themes, threads and feelings.

Exclude

Aim:　　To discover the feelings associated with being an outsider and to share those feelings honestly with other boys

Materials:　None

Time:　　20 minutes

What to do:

Form groups of five or six boys.

Each group excludes one of their number in turn. Those that remain in the group form themselves into a physically tight-knit group (seated or standing) to resist their temporary outsider. It is the job of the 'outsider' to get back into the group by whatever means they choose.

Do not keep each phase of the exercise going for too long and beware of boisterous behaviour.

When all have had a turn, bring the whole group back together to share how they felt about such issues as:

- Being outside the group.
- What feelings they had about wanting to get back into the group.
- Comments on the amount of effort they were prepared to put in to get back into the group.

Try to get at the honesty of their inner process and encourage them to be truthful about their real feelings about exclusion.

(Note: this exercise can often bring up quite strong emotions. Make sure that at the end each group values each of their members.)

The Outsider

Aim:　　To encourage boys to share the feelings and fears associated with being left out.

Materials:　Plain paper
　　　　　A variety of coloured pens or crayons

Time:　　30–45 minutes

What do to:

Ask the boys to find a space in the room where they feel comfortable. They can sit quietly in chairs or lie on the floor.

Explain that you are going to tell them a story. They should listen to the story and allow the images to be created in their own minds. Tell them it is best to keep their eyes closed so that they can 'see' their images clearly.

Read/tell the story — *The Outsider* (below).

When the story is over ask the boys to quietly take a sheet of paper and crayons and to draw the image of what it means to be left out. Stress that no artistic skill is necessary and that whatever feels right as their drawing is fine. Allow about 10 minutes for this.

On completion the boys find a partner to share what their drawings mean for each of them.

Finally, gather the whole group together to share anything that has come up.

The Story:

The Outsider

First we're going to relax our whole bodies, so feel the weight of your body on the floor or on the chair. Really notice which parts of your body are in contact with the chair or the floor and which parts are not . . .

Now notice your breathing — don't try to change it, just notice how your body moves when you breathe in and out . . . and now focus on your top lip and see if you can feel that little movement of air over your top lip as your breathing changes from in to out . . .

Now when you breathe in, imagine the air you breathe in is a warm relaxing colour, any colour that is relaxing for you . . . and as you breathe in, send that warm relaxing colour flowing all down your legs, right down to your feet . . . and your legs are relaxed and heavy . . . your legs are sinking into the floor, into the chair . . . now let this warm, relaxing colour come slowly flowing up your body, relaxing each part . . . each part becomes soft . . . and heavy . . . and relaxed . . . right up into your shoulders, and let your shoulders really hang down loosely . . . and now feel that warm relaxing colour flow gently down your arms . . . in to your hands . . . and your arms are very loose . . . and relaxed . . . and heavy . . . your whole body is very deeply relaxed and heavy . . . sinking into the floor into the chair . . . and now this warm, relaxing colour is flowing gently up into your neck, softening and loosening any tension in your neck . . . opening your throat . . . and now it's flowing gently into your face . . . your face is soft and relaxed . . . your jaw is relaxed, your mouth is relaxed . . . your eyes are relaxed . . . and now this warm, relaxing colour is swirling gently about in your mind, like a mist . . .

In a minute you will see that mist clear away and you will see a picture in your mind of a boy of your age walking alone to the bus stop on a school day . . . so let the mist clear and see that picture. What exactly does he look like? What is he wearing? What is the weather like? See every detail of the picture . . . he is on his own because no-one likes him . . . he gets near the bus stop and he can see a crowd of other boys he knows. They are about the same age and going to the same school. As he gets nearer, he hears someone laugh and shout, 'Here's the tramp . . . did your mum go to Oxfam again then!' No-one speaks to him. They all talk and laugh together till the bus comes. He gets on and sits in an empty seat. No-one comes to sit with him though some boys are standing up. The other boys joke and laugh on the bus but everyone ignores him.

The bus arrives at school . . . the other boys push him out of the way as they get off. They run up the school drive chasing each other and laughing. He walks up alone. Suddenly a group of boys rush up to him from behind — they push him and punch him as he lies on the ground . . . and then run off.

He walks into his registration group. All the other class members are there. The teacher says he looks a mess. Other boys snigger and whisper 'Oxfam' and 'Tramp'. He sits down by himself. Everyone else in the class brings money for a school trip but he is not going.

He goes to games, his first lesson. He has forgotten his kit. He is the only one. The teacher tells him off . . . other boys snigger . . . when the teacher is gone, they say, 'We never want you in our team anyway, you're useless.' Whilst the others play football, he sits in the classroom on his own, writing. He can see them through the window.

The rest of the day passes in much the same way. No-one will sit with him or talk. He is teased. At break-times he is tripped up. Groups of boys rush up, grab his bag and throw it around. At last the school day is finished. Evening comes and he goes out on the street. He joins a group hanging around by the shops. Someone has a football and people begin to pick sides. No-one picks him. He asks to join a team. One boy says, 'You're just a wimp'. When he looks a bit upset, they gather round him and chant, 'Weirdo, weirdo' at him. One boy shouts, 'Only girls do that', as he looks upset. The boys surround him, jeering and chanting . . .

Now let that picture fade . . . remember your feelings and allow the picture to go . . . now come back to noticing your breath, don't try to change it, just notice it . . . (long pause) . . . and feel your body on the chair or the floor . . . and slowly open your eyes . . . and stretch . . . but stay silent with your thoughts.

The Prison of My Peers

Aims: To promote discussion of the power of peer pressure. To begin to look at the manly behaviours of being accepted and the unmanly behaviours of being an 'odd one out'.

Materials: Paper and pens

Time: 30 minutes

What to do:

In a whole group use the following questions to promote discussion.

- As a boy what fears of being left out of the main group do you have?
- Do you worry about being left out of things other boys do?
- What sort of things might cause you to be left out?
- How do I make sure I stay in the group?

At the conclusion of the discussion or when it feels appropriate, ask the boys or young men to make lists in two columns of acceptable/expected behaviours which fit each of the headings.

Normal, manly behaviours essential for being accepted

Abnormal, unmanly behaviours associated with being an 'odd one out'

The Awareness Walk

Aim: To encourage boys to share the feelings and fears associated with being left out.

Materials: Plain paper
             A variety of coloured pens or crayons

Time: 30–45 minutes

What do to:

Ask the boys to find a space in the room where they feel comfortable. They can sit quietly in chairs or lie on the floor.

Explain that you are going to tell them a story. They should listen to the story and allow the images to be created in their own minds. Tell them it is best to keep their eyes closed so that they can 'see' their images clearly.

Read/tell the story — *The Awareness Walk* (below).

When the story is over ask the boys to quietly take a sheet of paper and crayons and to draw the image of what it means to be left out. Stress that no artistic skill is necessary and that whatever feels right as their drawing is fine. Allow about 10 minutes for this.

On completion the boys find a partner to share what their drawings mean for each of them.

Finally, gather the whole group together to share anything that has come up.

The story:

The Awareness Walk

Have a picture in your mind of yourself in a crowded shopping centre . . . look around carefully at all the shops . . . and all the people . . . you are sitting on a bench. You are looking at the people passing by. Some are alone . . . others in couples . . . some are in family groups. Some rush . . . others dawdle. Some have heavy bags others none. A group of youths is hanging around outside the music shop laughing and joking . . . A group of girls are nearby. Both groups are eyeing each other up and joking loudly. What do they look like?

You turn and see a cafe behind you. Look carefully at all the different people sitting here. What do you notice about them? Some are alone, others in twos, others in a family. A couple sit close together.

Now you get up and move slowly through the shopping centre. You notice all the different people shopping and the shop assistants too. You come out of the shopping centre into a park. Look around . . . there is a game of football going on. What are the players like? It's a hot day. A couple are sitting on a park bench holding hands. Another couple are sunbathing on the grass. Two parents are having a picnic with their two children . . . couples are playing with their children in the adventure playground . . . there is a lot of laughter around . . .

Now let that picture fade . . . remember the experience of being in the park and shopping centre . . . remember the feelings and images in your mind . . . now come back to noticing your breath, don't try to change it just notice it . . . (long pause) and feel your body on the chair on the floor and slowly open your eyes . . . and stretch . . . but stay silent with your thoughts.

Sex Brainstorm

Aim: To encourage boys to look closely at the ways they think about sex. To help boys to appreciate how the crude language of sexual expression misses out vital qualities in a love-making relationship. (In view of the climate around sex education in schools, this exercise needs to be handled sensitively. Only do this if you are personally confident and your governors approve!)

Materials: Pens and paper
          Category sheet (see headings below)

Time: 45 minutes

What to do:

Ask the boys to form into threes with pens and paper accessible to them.

Each boy to brainstorm what words come to mind when they think about sex. Encourage them not to self censor.

Give the brainstorm a strict 2 minute time limit.

Give each boy a category sheet which will enable them to divide up the words and expressions in their brainstorms into the following categories.

- Words about doing things to the other person
- Harsh, aggressive words
- Medical, technical, proper terms
- Caring words

When this is completed begin a discussion about why caring words figure so little in the lists. Encourage the boys to appreciate the importance of those feelings in any intimate sexual relationship. What stopped those words and feelings being recognized? (see Boys' Sexualities — The Session).

Every Picture Tells a Story

Aim: To look at sexual stereotypes from assumptions we make about the way people dress and present themselves.

Materials: A collection of photographs or cuttings from magazines/newspapers. (These should present images of both male and female, doing activities and wearing *clothes that are 'non traditional', and likewise stereotyped images of male/ female. It is worth spending time building a collection. Try and make them as varied as possible.)*

Time: 45 minutes

What to do:

This game is based on the assumption game with which many people may be familiar.

Hand out a picture of a person to each member of the group and ask them to look at the picture and not let anyone else see it. Each member of the group takes it in turn to describe their photograph without giving away the sex of the individual. (Alternatively you could make up a group of cards with words on, and ask the group to choose 3 or 4 which they feel describes their picture.) The group then takes it in turn to say what sex, age and sexuality the person is, e.g., heterosexual, homosexual, celibate, transsexual, bisexual, etc.

Points for discussion:

How did they arrive at their assumptions?
What do they associate with words such as:

- male
- female
- straight
- gay

Why do we often use words like straight to describe a heterosexual?
Do they recognize the assumptions we make about people we meet?
Can they recall a time when making assumptions about someone caused them problems?
Is it important to know another person's sexuality?
If so why?
What do they feel about:

- men wearing 'women's clothes'?
- women wearing 'men's clothes'?
- men wearing make-up?
- women wearing make-up?

What should men/women wear?
What is acceptable/unacceptable?

(This exercise is based on Davidson, N. (1990) *Boys Will Be . . . ?*, London, Bedford Square Press.)

Attraction

Aims: To question assumptions about what makes someone 'attractive'.
          To discover whether there are different standards of attractiveness for men and
          women.
          To find out if the same qualities of attractiveness are wanted by heterosexual
          women and men.

Materials: Collect postcards and magazine cuttings showing men and women. (Pictures
               of famous people could be interspersed with 'ordinary' people. Good sources
               of material are the mail order catalogues.)

Time: 30–45 minutes

What to do:

Spread out all the pictures of women. Ask the boys to pick out one or two that
stand out for them. It is possible to share a picture. Ask what it is that makes
each boy's choices attractive.

Repeat the procedure by spreading out the pictures of men. Be aware of boys'
resistance to picking out examples of attractive men. Try to work with the
resistances on display. They could range from refusal to do the task, to 'camp'
speech and gestures. All responses are valuable and can be explored.

Questions you might ask are:

- What stops you doing the task?
- What is the feeling that encourages you to behave in this way?

When boys notice each other's embarrassment is being acknowledged the task
can be completed.

Here are some questions you might like to ask to try to define attractiveness.

- What makes a woman attractive to men?
- What makes a woman attractive to other women?
- What makes a man attractive to women?
- What makes a man attractive to other men?
- What do you admire about other men even if you are not sexually
  attracted by them?
- Do you try to mould yourself into the image of a famous man so that
  you might seem more attractive?
- What is the difference between fancying someone and liking them?
- What is the difference between fancying someone and loving them?
- What is the difference between liking someone and loving them?

(This exercise is based on Davidson, N. (1990) *Boys Will Be . . . ?*, London Bedford Square
Press, pp. 91–2.)

Identifying Assumptions

Aims: To have a look at everyday assumptions people make and look at the reasons they are made.

Materials: Copies of 'Frankie and Chris', prepared using the worksheet below

Time: 40 minutes

What to do:

Hand out copies of the story and ask boys not to discuss it. Read the story aloud.

When the story has been read, ask the boys to circle their responses to each statement. It is important they do this strictly on their own.

When this task is done read out each statement and ask boys to indicate their responses. Encourage a discussion about the assumptions behind the choice.

Repeat this process for each of the statements.

The worksheet:

Frankie and Chris

Frankie and Chris were holding hands. They often did so as they felt very close to each other. Although they were both only 16, they knew that they loved each other. 'It's not fair Chris', said Frankie, 'your parents give you such an easy time. You can go out when you like. I wish mine were like yours.' Frankie's parents were strict and expected to be obeyed. Frankie wanted to finish school and become a hairdresser but at times it seemed difficult to make that choice. Frankie really felt the parental pressure to stay at school and do better. It was only Chris's support that kept Frankie going.

For Chris things were different. Chris was going to finish school and go into engineering, work hard and do really well. With parents who thought those plans were fine and expected their children to take responsibility for their own decisions and lives, Chris felt really valued and lucky.

It was sometimes hard to understand why they felt so attracted to each other as they came from such different backgrounds.

Circle your response to each of the following statements:

Statements about the story	True	False	Don't Know
Frankie and Chris plan to become engaged.	T	F	?
Frankie is a boy.	T	F	?
Chris is a girl.	T	F	?
Frankie does well at school.	T	F	?
Frankie and Chris are in love.	T	F	?
Frankie and Chris want to live together.	T	F	?
Frankie's parents want to keep Frankie and Chris apart.	T	F	?
Engineering is for boys.	T	F	?
Hairdressing is for girls.	T	F	?
Frankie and Chris are both girls.	T	F	?
Frankie and Chris are both boys.	T	F	?

Sexuality

Aims: To encourage participants to explore their understanding of the terms bisexuality, celibacy, lesbianism and male homosexuality.

Materials: Copy the statements below onto separate sheets for Bisexuality, Male Homosexuality, Celibacy and Lesbianism

Time: 45–60 minutes

What to do:

Divide the group into four smaller groups. Give each sub-group about 15 minutes to talk over their responses to *one* of the above discussion sheets.

Ask each sub-group to do a presentation of their discussion to the whole group. This may be written, spoken or a bodies sculpt of their feelings and responses. (Sculpts are ways of showing feelings through physical bodily expression.)

Process each of these as you go along by asking the whole group to comment on each sub-group's presentation.

Some interesting ideas that it may be useful to make interventions with are:

- Kinsey (1948), an American researcher into sexuality, asserted that sexual orientation is in fact a continuum for most people. A person's position on this line may change with age and may not be fixed.
- Freud asserted everyone was bisexual.
- More gay men 'come out' than do lesbians.

- Some scientists believe there is a gene that causes homosexuality.
- Most people don't see celibacy as a viable sexual choice.

The statements:

Bisexuality

David Bowie, Bette Midler and Boy George all display prominent stage images of bisexuality. They aim to be attractive to both women and men. Successful musicals such as *Hair* and the *Rocky Horror Show* mock conventional sexuality and show the possibilities of bisexuality.

Bisexuality is the ability to love and to express that love with both women and men. Most people are socialized into a role which carries with it loving people of the opposite sex. Many reject this role or never accept it and love people of the same sex. A few fit into both groups.

Why can't people love others as people first, responding to sexuality as a part of being human?

Male Homosexuality

Kissing is accepted between heterosexual people. It is an expression of affection between homosexual people as well. If you accept gay people, you accept their behaviour too.

Men may express their homosexuality in a number of different ways, at different times and in varying degrees. As for the causes of homosexuality — why is there a need to find a cause? No-one ever asks what causes heterosexuality.

Is it moral or immoral? I don't know. Can I judge? I do know that my son's homosexual relationship is a loving, caring, faithful one. What more could I want?

More people now believe that homosexuals, lesbians and heterosexuals should have the same rights, yet a person who openly acknowledges being gay still runs the risk of alienating family, friends and colleagues. Why is it that some people find lesbians and homosexuals so threatening? Why can't the law treat them like everyone else — as individuals who fall in love and have relationships and want to live their lives free from discrimination and guilt?

Celibacy

Celibacy in the past has been viewed as a temporary and transient state, except for those who choose it as a religious discipline. Celibacy is not an alternative that many people elect voluntarily. For those who do, it must be viewed as an honourable and viable alternative for life, or for any period a person decides upon. It also does not exclude physical closeness or intimacy with other people, or a long-term domestic relationship. Celibacy can be practised in and outside of marriage.

Some people come to identify that they don't need sexual intercourse. For these people celibacy is desirable, even preferable to intercourse.

I enjoy the company of the opposite sex; I am attracted to them and they to me. Since I am not interested at the moment in a sex-based relationship I try not to make myself available.

Many sexual relationships are based on one partner exerting power over the other and on domination and oppression. To honestly try to change, these kinds of relationships may require an agreement for each person to remain celibate for an extended period until they are able to relate to each other as equals.

Lesbianism

Many lesbians have had sexual relationships with men, and some have been, and still are, married. Being a lesbian does not necessarily mean hating men — many lesbians still have close friendships with men.

Life is not always easy for lesbians. Often they have to hide their feelings and lie about their close relationships and social life. There are many situations in which it would be impossible to admit to being a lesbian so they need to think about everything they say.

There are no specific laws against lesbianism because the people who made the laws didn't believe that it existed. Women have been loving and caring for each other for centuries. Sometimes this is sexual, sometimes not.

Being a lesbian means loving other women.

People sometimes ask what makes a woman a lesbian. It's as easy to ask as what makes a woman a heterosexual.

For some women, being a lesbian isn't just a personal thing, it's also a political statement. Many lesbians believe that they are stronger as a woman by not relating sexually with men. They feel that they can be more independent individuals.

(This exercise is based on Dixin, H. and Mullinar, G. (eds) (1985) *Taught Not Caught*, pp. 91–4, Living and Learning Ltd.)

Smalltown Boy

Aim: *To highlight some of the problems faced by young lesbian, gay or bisexual people growing up in Britain.*
To look at the powerful forces of heterosexism and homophobia and the powerful affect they have on people's lives.

Materials: *Copies of the lyrics of* Smalltown Boy *(below)*
A copy of Smalltown Boy *by Jimmy Somerville in his days with Bronski Beat (useful but not essential)*

Time: *45 minutes*

What to do:

If you have a copy of *Smalltown Boy* to play to the group do so. If not, let them read through the lyrics.

Ask boys for comments. What feeling does the song bring up for them?

Ask the boys to look at the short quotations beneath the lyrics and initiate a discussion about relationships in families when one of the children is lesbian, gay or bisexual.

The following questions could help.

- How do you think they must feel if they are disowned and chucked out by their families?
- Who is likely to be the most supportive, Mum or Dad?
- Does anyone know of occasions when something like this has taken place?
- How would you feel if this happened to you?
- Does heterosexism and homophobia exist in your community?
- How would you react if a close friend confided in you that he was gay? (There is scope here for some role play around how boys may react when a friend comes out as gay.)

The worksheet:

Smalltown Boy

> You leave in the morning
> With everything you own
> In a little black case

Alone on a platform
The wind and the rain
On a sad and lonely face
Mother will never understand
Why you had to leave
For the love that you need
Will never be found at home
Pushed and kicked around
Always a lonely boy
You were the one
That they'd talk about around town
As they put you down
And as hard as they would try
They'd hurt to make you cry
But you'd never cry to them
Just to your soul
No you'd never cry to them
Just to your soul.
(Jimmy Somerville featuring Bronski Beat)

Quotations

She [his mother] said I was evil and acting against God's will and asked me to leave home. (*Male 19*)

They threw me out of the house and didn't speak to me for three to four months. (*Male 20*)

I was thrown out of home. Dad threatened me with a kitchen knife. (*Male 17*)

I was 15 when I knew I was gay. I shut myself off. I was desperately unhappy. I was 17 when I took an overdose. I didn't feel I had anyone to turn to or talk to. All I needed was maybe one caring teacher. (*Male 20*)

(Trenchard, L. and Warren, H., 1984)

Boys' Sexual Myths

Background: *Boys relate to each other in an atmosphere where a number of sexual myths serve to inhibit their capacity for shared feelings, intimacy and personal well-being. It is difficult for boys to admit their areas of sexual ignorance in front of their friends because the atmosphere engendered within the boys' club is one of being well versed in sexual matters. To admit ignorance or to be found out not knowing is to be the butt of put-downs and ridicule about a boy's sexuality and likely quality of performance. The atmosphere of jokey camaraderie to which the boys aspire is fuelled by the myths relating to sexual power and performance. All are assumed to be 'in the know' and, in so assuming, perpetuate the immutability of the myths still further.*

    The intention here is to state the myths under which boys operate and to find strategies that challenge them. It is important that this deconstruction takes place in a group atmosphere which allows for an acceptance of new learning and gives opportunities for new ways of behaving as a boy. So much of the way boys talk is about scoring, conquest and performance. Sex is used to shore up and confirm a shaky sense of masculine identity. This kind of sexual knowledge is inextricably linked to being a real boy.

Aim: *To enable boys to reconsider this bedrock of perceived masculinity so that sex can be seen as arising out of relationships, their closeness and contact.*

Materials: *'The Myths' sheets, prepared using the statements below*

Time: *30–45 minutes depending on size of group*

What to do:

Taking each myth in turn, ask the boys to put themselves on a continuum showing how much of their behaviour is informed by some belief in the truth of each statement.

Each boy speaks from the position he has found for himself and shares his reasons for being there.

A lively discussion is likely as boys agree or disagree with each other. As facilitator, by using an interview technique with each boy, it will be possible to find out where the origins of these myths lie in each boy's life.

The statements:

The Myths

1 Penis size — the bigger the penis, the better the lover, the better the man.
2 Sexual performance pressure

  • Getting it right.
  • '2 feet long, hard as steel and can go all night long.'

3 Only wimps masturbate.
4 Having sex proves I am a man.
5 It's only sex if it's focused on the genitals.
6 Heterosexuality is the only normal expression of sexuality.
7 Male entitlement — 'I have the right to sexually control and use girls.'
8 Men should take the leading role.
9 Men are always ready for sex.
10 All really good and normal sex must end in sexual intercourse.
11 Any physical contact other than a light touch is meant as an invitation to foreplay and intercourse.

Contraception

Aim: To identify all the methods of contraception known to the group.
            To enable myths and misconceptions about contraception to be cleared up.

Materials: Large sheet of paper and felt-tip pens
             A Health Education Contraceptive Kit (optional)

Time: 15 minutes

What to do:

Divide the boys into groups of three or four. Each group takes a large sheet of paper and brainstorms all the ways they have heard of that prevent pregnancies from occurring.

As a whole group, share the results of the brainstorm. Ask boys to point out methods which are ineffective or effective and for what reason.

An addition to this session could be provided by acquiring a Health Education Contraceptive Kit and showing the different types of contraceptive available.

This might also be the time to demonstrate the correct use of condoms. A fat pen or a carrot could be used to give students the opportunity to put one on correctly.

Design the Perfect Contraceptive

Aims: *To enable participants to identify the factors that need to be considered when choosing a method of contraception.*
To provide a light-hearted introduction to contraception.

Materials: *Large sheets of paper and felt-tip pens*

Time: *20–30 minutes*

What to do:

Divide the boys into groups of three or four. Explain that each group is to design the perfect contraceptive method, stressing that there are no financial, social or scientific constraints to observe. Encourage them to be really imaginative.

The group draws and writes an advert to describe their perfect method — stressing its safe sex aspects.

Share the completed work with the rest of the group.

Playing it Safe

Aim: *To raise awareness about the social and sexual activities which lead to risk of becoming HIV positive.*
To help foster positive feelings towards those who are infected.

Materials: *'Playing it Safe' cards*
'Aids and Your Life' sheet (you can make these by copying each of the 40 activities on to individual pieces of card, plus cards labelled High Risk, Low Risk, No Risk, and Not Sure)

Time: *30–60 minutes*

What to do:

Give each boy a set of the 'Playing it Safe' cards (it can also be usefully done in pairs). Each boy or pair locates the cards labelled High Risk, Low Risk, No Risk, Not Sure and places them on the table in front of them. Then going through the 40 cards suggesting various social and sexual behaviours, they place the cards under any one of the categories according to whether they think the activity is linked with contracting HIV.

73

When the task is complete, discussion can follow in the following way:

- The No Risk cards are used to stimulate a discussion about the ways in which HIV *is not* transmitted. The cards will also encourage discussion about other important matters such as living with persons who are HIV positive, confidentiality, medical treatment and testing for HIV.
- The High or Low Risk cards show ways in which HIV can always be transmitted. Such cards will promote discussion about use of condoms, dangers of injecting drugs, the importance of screening for infected blood.
- See if the boys can locate the cards depicting activities which become unsafe AFTER infection by HIV.

Conclude the session by issuing the hand-out 'Aids and Your Life' which summarizes the facts about the virus to reinforce the information which is being discussed.

Answers:

Playing it Safe

Activity	*Risk*	*Notes*
1. Sharing a toothbrush	Low	No know transmission through saliva.
2. Sharing a needle and/or syringe for injecting drugs	High	Blood from infected person can then be injected into new host.
3. Masturbation	No	No mixing of body fluids.
4. Being tattooed	No	As long as a recognized dealer does it.
5. Sleeping with someone who is HIV positive	No	Terms need to be discussed. Sleeping does not mean the same as having penetrative sex.
6. Kissing	No	No known transmission through saliva.
7. Oral sex	Low	Check they understand the term oral sex. Not wise if you have open sores in or around the mouth, on the penis or vagina. In some cases a flavoured condom could be used as extra protection.
8. Mutual masturbation	Low	Check they understand the term. No risk as long as body fluids do not mix internally.
9. Anal sex	High	Without use of a condom.
	Low	With use of a condom.

74

10.	Unprotected penetrative sex (vaginal and anal)	High	Check understanding of the term penetrative sex.
11.	Being married	?	Marriage does not mean you are immune. Discuss personal and social implications.
12.	Having sex with more than one partner	?	Protected or safer sex with many partners is lower risk than unprotected sex with one partner.
13.	Mosquito bites	No	The virus cannot live in an insect's blood system. This applies to head lice too.
14.	Living with someone who is HIV positive	No	The virus cannot be caught from everyday, casual contact.
15.	Sharing a razor	Low	Stress the general hygiene problems of sharing razors, such as skin complaints. Does the possibility of cuts make it medium rather than low risk?
16.	Going to the same school as someone who is HIV positive	No	See 14
17.	Cuddling	No	See 14
18.	Massage	No	See 14. Explain massage.
19.	Love bites	No	Explain the fact that bacterial infection and Hepatitis B can possibly be transmitted this way.
20.	Using condom without a kitemark	?	A kitemark ensures the quality of the condom. Those that don't have a kitemark can split or dissolve.
21.	Giving blood	No	All blood and blood products (including Factor 8) used in the UK are screened. Sterile needles are used for each new patient/donor.
22.	Swimming pools	No	Virus cannot live outside the body for very long. Anyway the chlorine would kill the virus.
23.	Blood transfusions	No	See 21
24.	Having sex with a prostitute	?	We are not talking about risky groups. We are talking about risky behaviours — it is this which transmits the virus.
25.	Sharing earrings	Low	Greater risk of spreading other blood and skin infections.

26.	Being born to an HIV mother	High	There is a 1 in 4 chance the baby will be born infected with the virus (figures to date).
27.	Shaking hands	No	No mixing of body fluids.
28.	Crying	No	Tears are not mixed internally.
29.	Sharing a toilet	No	Safe — the virus cannot be caught from everyday casual contact.
30.	Sharing bed linen	No	See 29
31.	Sharing cups, cutlery or towels	No	See 29
32.	Visiting the doctor, dentist or hospital	No	
33.	Having a baby	No	Becomes unsafe only if the mother is HIV positive.
34.	Donating sperm to a sperm bank	No	Becomes unsafe only if donor is HIV positive.
35.	Giving blood or donating any part of the body (transplants)	No	Becomes unsafe if donor is HIV positive.
36.	Eating in restaurants	No	
37.	Unclean needles (not sterile) that pierce the skin	High	See 2
38.	Sharing sex toys	High/ Low	Depends on type of toy and use and whether toys are washed after each separate use.
39.	Inexperienced/unqualified tattooing or ear piercing, e.g., at school	High	See 2
40.	Mixing blood in blood brother/sister relationship	High	Blood from infected person can be transferred.

Hand-out:

AIDS and Your Life

What does AIDS stand for?

Acquired
Immune
Deficiency
Syndrome

What causes AIDS?

- AIDS is carried by a tiny germ: a virus called HIV (Human Immunodeficiency Virus).
- You can get HIV by having unprotected sex with an infected person or injecting drugs with infected needles or syringes.

- The virus enters the body and infects the white blood cells.
- The virus attacks the white blood cells and destroys them.
- At this stage you will appear healthy but you can pass the virus to others.
- HIV is passed on to others in blood and semen.
- Unlike the flu or cold viruses, it is NOT passed on by coughing or sneezing or ordinary contact.

How does HIV harm you?

- HIV attacks the body's natural defences and, in most people, breaks down the body's ability to fight disease.
- The virus can allow serious illnesses to develop and take hold. Some of the most common are pneumonia, cancers and damage to the brain. When this stage is reached the person is said to have AIDS.

Is there a cure?

- The virus stays in the body for LIFE.
- There are new treatments to help prolong life but:
  — there is no known cure or vaccine
  — you will DIE.

What will stop me getting AIDS?

- The only effective way of helping people to avoid this disease is to start to talk about the behaviours which cause the spread of HIV and to show how easy it is to prevent infection.

'What Do You Know about Sex?' Questionnaire

Aims: To share the level of sexual knowledge that boys have in common.
To correct some of the myths that emerge around sexual activities.
To share some thoughts on expressions of their own sexuality.

Materials: 'The Questionnaire', prepared using the questions below

Time: 10 minutes for 'The Questionnaire'

What to do:

Ask the boys to fill in the questionnaire.

Initiate a general discussion based on the answers. Use the 'What Do You Know about Sex?' Questionnaire tutor's notes. Some of the discussion points after each question provide a useful starting point for further work.

The questions:

What Do You Know about Sex?

1. What do the following mean?

    (a) Heterosexual
    (b) Bisexual
    (c) Homosexual
    (d) Celibacy
    (e) Homophobia
    (f) Transsexual

2. Why are people heterosexual, bisexual or homosexual?

    (a) Nature
    (b) Upbringing
    (c) Choice
    (d) Nobody knows

3a. What is the first physical sign of a female becoming sexually aroused?

    (a) Vagina becomes wet
    (b) Nipples become erect
    (c) Clitoris becomes erect
    (d) Heart beats faster

3b. What is the first physical sign of a male becoming sexually aroused?

    (a) Penis becomes erect
    (b) Heart beats faster
    (c) Nipples become erect
    (d) Testes rise in scrotum

4. Which in the list below may cause someone to reach an orgasm?

    (a) Fantasies/dreams   (h) Oral sex
    (b) Clitoris stimulation   (i) Using sex aids
    (c) Penis stimulation   (j) Pain
    (d) Breast stimulation   (k) Sensual body touching
    (e) Anal stimulation   (l) Fear
    (f) Kissing   (m) Any of the above
    (g) Sexual intercourse   (n) None of the above

5a. An orgasm for women results in vaginal contractions.

    (a) Agree
    (b) Disagree
    (c) Unsure

5b. An orgasm for men results in ejaculation.

   (a) Agree
   (b) Disagree
   (c) Unsure

6. Sexual pleasure does not have to be about stimulation of the genitals.

   (a) Agree
   (b) Disagree
   (c) Unsure

7. People masturbate:

   (a) In the absence of a partner
   (b) From birth and until they die
   (c) To make their sex life better
   (d) To help them relax
   (e) To give themselves pleasure

8. People always have sexual feelings from birth to death.

   (a) Agree
   (b) Disagree
   (c) Unsure

9. What is important when you are considering sex with a new partner?

   (a) Ask them about their sexual history
   (b) Have an HIV test
   (c) Practise safer sex

Quiz tutor's notes:

What Do You Know about Sex?

1. What do the following mean:

   (a) Heterosexual: people who are sexually attracted to people of the opposite sex.
   (b) Bisexual: people who are sexually attracted to both sexes.
   (c) Homosexual: people who are sexually attracted to people of the same sex.
   (d) Celibacy: someone who is not involved in a sexual relationship.
   (e) Homophobia: an irrational fear/loathing of homosexuals and homosexuality.
   (f) Transsexual: a person who believes themselves to be the opposite sex to which they were born.

79

Discussion points

Do people remain the same sexual orientation all their lives?

Celibacy can be for a whole list of reasons, cultural, religious, medical, personal choice. Do you think it's OK to be celibate?

No form of sexual orientation is abnormal — All people are individuals and have individual needs. Do you agree?

2.   Why are people heterosexual, bisexual or homosexual?

    (a)   Nature
    (b)   Upbringing
    (c)   Choice
    (d)   Nobody knows

Answer

(d)   Nobody knows

Sexual orientation (i.e., attraction to the same, opposite, or both sexes) is among the most misunderstood aspect of human sexuality. Due to the stigma and disapproval attached to homosexuality this has confused much of the research conducted in this field. Most research has focused on looking for 'causes' of homosexuality, thereby making the assumption that heterosexuality is normal and does not need any explanation.

However, what is known, largely thanks to the work of Kinsey, is that 'homosexual and heterosexual' are not exclusive categories, i.e., there is a considerable overlap between the two in terms of attraction, fantasy and behaviour. This occurs within the population as a whole, and within individuals over time. Homosexuality is as old as humanity.

Discussion points

Does it matter what sexual orientation we have?
Are you afraid of gays/lesbians and if so why?
What assumptions do we make about people's sexuality, e.g., I bet he's gay because . . . etc?
If your best friend said he was gay how would you react — what would you do, say?
Have you ever abused someone because you don't like their sexual orientation?

3a.   What is the first physical sign of a female becoming sexually aroused?

    (a)   Vagina becomes wet
    (b)   Nipples become erect
    (c)   Clitoris becomes erect
    (d)   Heart beats faster

3b.   What is the first physical sign of a male becoming sexually aroused?

    (a)   Penis becomes erect
    (b)   Heart beats faster
    (c)   Nipples become erect
    (d)   Testes rise in scrotum

Answer

(a) Vaginal lubrication and (a) Erection of penis (Masters and Johnson) (1966)

Facts

Male erection is caused by engorgement of the penis with blood. For the female the engorgement of the walls of the vagina and surrounding tissues cause a clear fluid to seep through the vaginal wall.

For both men and women, arousal can be caused by visual, auditory and tactile stimulation or erotic thoughts. The sexual response cycle is similar for men and women.

Discussion points

Have you been embarrassed by an erection that has occurred at an awkward time, i.e., in public?

4.   Which in the list below may cause someone to reach an orgasm?

(a)	Fantasises/dreams	(h)	Oral sex
(b)	Clitoris stimulation	(i)	Using sex aids
(c)	Penis stimulation	(j)	Pain
(d)	Breast stimulation	(k)	Sensual body touching
(e)	Anal stimulation	(l)	Fear
(f)	Kissing	(m)	Any of the above
(g)	Sexual intercourse	(n)	None of the above

Answer

(m)   Any of the above

Facts

All can lead to orgasm. People have different preferences or many combinations. This obviously can vary from occasion to occasion and at different stages of one's life.

Orgasm can be triggered off by either touch or mental stimulation or a combination of the two.

The brain plays an important role by enhancing sexual pleasure (e.g., through sexual fantasy). This also explains why people with disabilities can experience sexual pleasure even when they might have no genital sensation.

Discussion points

How important is touch?
How important is 'foreplay'?
How important is fantasy to sexual excitement?
What are your views on the use of aids for sexual arousal, e.g., vibrators, pornography?

5a. An orgasm for women results in vaginal contractions.

  (a) Agree
  (b) Disagree
  (c) Unsure

Answer

(a) Agree

Facts

An orgasm is extremely difficult to describe. Research by Masters and Johnson on human sexual response led them to conclude that there is only one kind of female orgasm. This is centred around the clitoris and involves involuntary rhythmic contractions of the outer third of the vagina (this is so called the orgasmic platform). This is only the answer to the physiological aspect of orgasm.

Throughout history and in present times, attempts (often by men) have been made in order to 'categorize' women's orgasms. What is certain is that when both men and women achieve orgasm, there is a sensation which is both physical and emotional, but importantly they are unique to every individual. Orgasms can be more or less intense depending on a range of social, psychological and physical factors. As women do not have 'a cooling off period' (unlike men), for some continued stimulation may lead to another orgasm.

Discussion points

Can we really define/explain an orgasm?
What is your definition of an orgasm?
Does having an orgasm matter?
What is the difference between sexuality and sensuality?

5b. An orgasm for men results in ejaculation.

  (a) Agree
  (b) Disagree
  (c) Unsure

Answer

(b) Disagree

Facts

Ejaculation in men occurs in two stages:

(i) The 'pooling' of seminal fluid in the posterior urethra.

(ii) The expulsion of seminal fluid (caused by rhythmic contractions of the bu/bospongions and ischiocarernosus muscles) from the urethra. It is usually this 'pumping' experience which is associated with orgasm.

However it is important to be aware that ejaculation and orgasm are not necessarily synonymous. For example, many men who had prostatectaries (i.e., partial or complete removal of the prostate gland) may be left unable to ejaculate, or ejaculate in a retrograde fashion, i.e., into the bladder. However their ability to experience orgasm is intact.

What is more certain is that after orgasm the vast majority of men have a 'cooling off period' (refractory) during which they are unresponsive to further stimulation. This period varies between individuals and as men get older this period tends to lengthen.

Discussion points

What difficulties might men experience with ejaculation, e.g., premature (coming too soon)?

If orgasm for men is not necessarily ejaculation, what is it?

6. Sexual pleasure does not have to be about stimulation of the genitals.

(a) Agree
(b) Disagree
(c) Unsure

Answer

(a) Agree

Facts

The most important powerful sexual organ is our brains.

People with no genital sensations can and do experience sexual pleasure. The human body has a remarkable ability to compensate. If we let ourselves, we can eroticize other parts of our bodies instead of our groins always being 'the sexual organs'.

Sexuality is more than a physical process: our circumstances, mood and emotions all play an important role in determining our response to any potentially sexual situation.

Discussion points

What is sexuality? Is it the same as sensuality?
What is erotic?
Are men and women different in how they view sexuality/sensuality?

7. People masturbate:

    (a) In the absence of a partner
    (b) From birth and until they die
    (c) To make their sex life better
    (d) To help them relax
    (e) To give themselves pleasure

Answer

All

Facts

It seems most people masturbate throughout their lives for a range of reasons. Masturbation has been deemed to be dangerous, send you mad, blind, etc., but masturbation is normal and is done by people of all ages (men and women). Some people do not masturbate for a range of reasons — this is also perfectly normal.

Masturbation is certainly safer sex. Also you are often only out to please yourself, furthermore you don't have to look your best!

Discussion points

What do you feel about masturbation?
What do you think about partners in a relationship masturbating separately?
Who is responsible for sexual pleasure?
Should children be encouraged or stopped from masturbating?

8. People always have sexual feelings from birth to death.

    (a) Agree
    (b) Disagree
    (c) Unsure

Answer

(a) Agree

Facts

Children enjoy their bodies and masturbate when unhindered. People can, if they allow themselves, enjoy sexuality for as long as they desire. Negative attitudes from some people do not expect certain groups to have sexual feelings, i.e., children, elderly, physically and mentally ill, the terminally ill, prisoners etc.

Discussion points

What is sexuality? Is it about having sex, being a sexual human being, or is it something entirely different?
How do you think it affects people?
What do you think about everyone having sexual feelings regardless of their age or disability?

9. What is important when you are considering sex with a new partner?

    (a)   Ask them about their sexual history
    (b)   Have an HIV test
    (c)   Practise safer sex

Answer

(c)   Practise safer sex

Facts

Even if you know the sexual history of a new partner it is not reliable for a number of reasons: either of you might possibly have the virus without knowing it; they might not be honest with you; if they do tell you their sexual history you don't know that of their partners'. It only takes one partner to infect you. Remember that the antibody test can only tell you about the situation up to roughly three months before the test is conducted — this is because it can take up to three months for antibodies to be produced (in some cases even longer). Another problem is that a small number of people never produce antibodies but are nonetheless infected with the virus. For a negative result to be really meaningful, there should have been no potential opportunity for infection to occur for at least three months prior to testing.

Discussion points

What does safer sex mean?
What activities can you think of which would be included? Which wouldn't?
What other advantages of safer sex are there apart from avoiding infection?

Chapter 4

Sexual Harassment

The Theory

Unwanted Attentions

Colin is 12 years old. He is a cheerful, friendly boy with blonde hair, blue eyes and a likable disposition. He is playful and mischievous and he invades other people's space. He is enthusiastic in a demonstrative way. Hence one day he was seen going up behind girls in his class to tickle them round the waist. They reacted with annoyance. When he persisted in doing this in the face of such rebukes, I sent him to the school's sin bin (called Room 20) with a note that I felt he was sexually harassing girls. I felt it was important to take this action to highlight what I had noticed as a growing problem around the school. Girls' bodies and girls' rights to personal space were being intruded upon and infringed with increasing regularity.

Colin couldn't believe he was being sent to Room 20. The girls were bemused since they regularly experienced such behaviour, but, more importantly, since Colin has an older brother in school (Year 11) the word got to this age group too. For some days it was a real talking point. 15–16-year-old boys approached me to comment on the case. I took time and trouble to explain what I had done and asked them to tell me why it was important. In our conversations came the grudging acceptance that maybe it was a form of harassment for boys to behave in this way towards girls. Unwanted attentions can be damaging and humiliating.

Craig is a Year 10 student, a friendly nuisance to all those around him. As a teacher it is difficult to curb his inventive capacity for banter of all sorts. Samantha is a young woman of similar age. There is an attractiveness about her appearance, her face and her figure which encourages boys to lust after her. On one day she was very much the object of Craig's attention. He said something to her, his face close to hers. She reacted angrily and turned away. Immediately Craig's hand grabbed hold of her buttocks and squeezed. There was another irritatedly angry remark as she got out of the way. I called Craig over and it took him some time to understand at any level why his behaviour was unacceptable. All the classic justifications came out: 'It's only a bit of fun', 'She doesn't mind really', 'Everyone does it — it's what they expect', 'It's just a laugh'. Craig also writes letters, particularly gross letters, offering his sexual services in a variety of ways. The suggestions are sexually graphic, the language is grossly obscene, the spirit of the words comes from the world of hard pornographic literature. One girl has been the recipient of such offers. She has coped by suggesting that it didn't matter really. He was just a fool. There were tears in her eyes as she spoke.

Neil's mother comes to meet him at lunchtimes and at the end of the school day. He walks home with her. He is a quiet, shy and timid boy who was once seen holding his mother's hand. This fact has been seized on by his peer 12-year-old boys. He suffers the taunts and abuse of someone who has been caught letting masculinity down. He is discouraged by the ridicule, once sadly confiding in me his wish to be like a wrestler because then maybe he wouldn't be tripped up, poked at and abused as a 'poofter'.

At another level the senior teacher came into the staffroom. Only two or three people were present. One of them was the young head of Physical Education with whom he wanted to talk about some point of school organization. He spoke in a loud, patronizing, but friendly voice and draped his arm around her shoulders, his head getting closer to hers as he spoke. As an observer, I wondered how she felt but noticed particularly how the power was being demonstrated — loud, warm, friendly and avuncular, but the arm around her shoulder and a certain tone in the voice demonstrated the power relations that were on show. I speculated how difficult it would be for the head of PE to reject all this. In a subsequent conversation with her she revealed a fear that if she crossed him by criticizing his behaviour towards her then he would be vindictive and obstructive. It is in her best interests in the school, both personally and departmentally, to allow this over-familiarity to continue without comment.

Mushtaq and Asif are studying French. Unfortunately much of their time in French lessons is spent in harassing their woman teacher. They talk loudly enough about 'blow-jobs', make pointed remarks about their teacher's early nights in bed with her husband and they continually refer to her as bitch and slag, using their family language. The teacher has made repeated attempts to complain of her harassment. Boys have been seen by the Head of the Upper School (female) but a written account of one of her humiliations was seen as a subject of some mirth by the headteacher.

In another case at a different school, the caretaker persistently harassed a woman member of staff. His continual use of sexual innuendo, reflections on what he would like to do with her if he were her husband, and attempts to kiss her, created a climate of total insecurity and fear. The woman's work deteriorated, her health was undermined and her domestic life suffered for a period of more than two years before she fought back. The case she eventually brought was proved but ironically it was she who moved school to get the fresh start she deserved. The caretaker stayed in post.

Recent high profile media cases of sexual harassment have served to bring the phenomenon into sharper public focus. The polarization of opinion around the infamous case relating to Judge Clarence Thomas in the USA can be mirrored through less celebrated cases down to the unpublicized daily harassments experienced in schools throughout the country. On the one hand is the sense of hurt and humiliation experienced by the victims. Girls speak of boys who are 'pains' when in the company of their mates:

> They think they are being funny. They come up to you and make suggestions. They try to grab your breasts and pinch your bum. They only do it when their mates are around. They think it makes them look good.

All this is said with a mixture of annoyance and wistful resignation as if nothing can be done about it. There is also a sadness because 'on their own they're all right. They don't do any of that'.

On the other side lies a sense of incredulity that anything is wrong with the behaviours on display. The boys' comments, 'It's only a bit of fun' and 'they like it really', becomes the headteacher's laughter at the experience of one of his staff at the hands of two 15-year-old boys. There is a blindness and fearful denial around which prevents boys and men from noticing the seriousness of Zoe's tears as she struggles with being the unwanted object of Craig's sexual fantasies. There is the sense that he deserves taunting because he's not a proper boy around Mark's harassment at the hands of the 'cock' boys in his peer group.

There was a time when sexual harassment had to be endured because victims had nowhere to turn for redress. It was most noticeable in the workplace where male power blindness in institutions prevented the phenomenon from being acknowledged as a problem. The growing weight of complaints from workers meant that the challenge of tackling the issue was taken up by Trade Unions. The TUC's work in defining and highlighting the problem has been invaluable. The drawback in their work was to imply that the behaviour is exclusively adult–adult and a male–female interaction. In addition, because it isolated sexual harassment within working life, it left men free to exercise their traditional dominance in other social spheres. In other words, men only had to curb their power and control practices at work. Further, male power in working institutions and within Trade Unions means that the rhetoric which sees sexual harassment as a trade union issue which affects all workers and is not purely a personal problem can easily become empty words. For instance, what is the position of the train driver known to one of the authors who regularly finds offensive graffiti in her cab. She knows that to complain she will have to take on the male power system, not only of her employers but also of her male dominated union. For this reason, many women have failed to pursue legitimate cases of outrageous harassment, preferring instead to resign their jobs, leaving the harasser to find another victim.

While the TUC publication recognized that 'teachers and other workers involved with young people can face sexual harassment from them' (TUC, 1983), it does not specifically mention sexual harassment between students, between males or between workers in such institutions. Within a school environment we are much happier with a definition of sexual harassment which removes the 'person as a worker'. Wise and Stanley (1987) suggest 'all sexual harassment behaviours are linked by the way they represent an unwanted and unsought intrusion by men into women's feelings, thoughts, behaviours, space, time, energies and bodies'.

This definition enables us to view behaviours in schools with more understanding and disquiet. It enables us to see that what is going on in schools are daily examples of a dominant and powerful masculinity exercising its power. Moreover, this 'top dog' masculinity is learning the taken-for-grantedness of behaviours which will get translated into work-based practices. It is very important to confront the issues of sexual harassment at this root level and to challenge these manifestations of male behaviour in schools.

Although we recognize that the vast majority of cases of sexual harassment involve males harassing and intimidating females, this simple dichotomy between girls and all boys, between women and all men is too generalized to be a helpful definition. What is clear is that there are examples of many and varied masculinities in conflict with each other and what we are considering is how a hierarchical heterosexual masculinity maintains its superior position. The testing ground can be seen in its most virulent form in the corridors, classrooms and playing fields of schools throughout the country. It is there where an observer would witness the aggressive bullying, abuse and intimidation of countless girls and women but also many vulnerable 'unmanly' boys and men.

Tough guy, heterosexual masculinity keeps its position by socially constructing 'deviant' cultures which define its own supremacy. It does this by clearly marking out what behaviour is acceptable as a norm. Sometimes boundaries are not clear and the dominant voices set the tone. Definition is instant and the hesitant in the pack shift their position. They join in the abuse, they take part in the punishing behaviour so that they are not found out and similarly treated for not being a 'real boy'. Any behaviour perceived as girl-like, be it inflections in the voice, a way of walking or pleasure in activities not deemed acceptable, bring out the wrath of the pack and the acquisition of the feared epithet, 'poofter'. Hence, the difficulties experienced by Mark whose behaviour around his mother caused the 'pack' to tease, taunt, ridicule and physically attack him. Fear of being seen as girlish, unmanly or physically inadequate and being publicly teased and ridiculed keeps dominant heterosexual masculinity on top. It gathers into itself victims like Mark and encourages them to join in by finding other target boys to abuse.

Spender (1982) has reported some teachers' comments on male classrooms:

> It seems to me that the boys create an inferior or outside group and level the abuse at them which they would otherwise direct at girls. The least 'manly' boys become the target and are used as substitute girls in a way . . . The sexual hierarchy gets set up but some boys have to play the part that the girls would take in a mixed school. (p. 121)

In our opinion, such boys who are not in the tough guy, heterosexual male club, are subjected to a form of sexual harassment. Askew and Ross (1988) have reported on an extreme-form of this harassment 'in one class the boy who took on the role of girl was even known as "Janice"'. All the boys called him Janice most of the time and some teachers were heard to refer to him as Janice. This is but one more example of the power that aggressive, heterosexual 'tough' boys can (and do) yield, viciously using the more vulnerable masculinities of their victims as a target. This power can also be illustrated by the ways in which such boys dominate mixed classroom situations by their use of physical and verbal intimidation and harassment (Lees, 1986).

One of the authors constantly witnesses interactions in mixed classrooms at secondary level where boys ridicule other boys' contributions to lessons. Such boys are deemed to be 'guilty' of deviant, unmanly behaviour. Their equipment is stolen and they are the subject of personally directed abuse in the same way as girls.

Mahoney (1985, pp. 34–53) has also researched this phenomena, commenting that, 'boys who do not display sufficient evidence of masculinity, or more rarely those who actively challenge the sexist behaviour of other boys, are prime targets for what is called in their case "bullying"' (p. 52). We would suggest that this 'bullying' is a form of sexual harassment — unwanted and unsought intrusions into feelings, thoughts, behaviours, space, time, energies and bodies — directed at boys who do not conform to the accepted dominant heterosexual 'norm'.

This fear of bullying, of sexual harassment, of not being one of the boys, of being seen as different, is well illustrated in *Outlaws in the Classroom*, a booklet on gay and lesbian issues. As some of the contributors put it:

> The whole situation was made worse by going out with girls. I hated every minute of it but it's so important to be one of the lads.

> After you have established that you are gay you have the big task of covering up . . . the way I did it was to hang around with the 'gang' and go around beating up the other people we thought were 'queer'. (City of Leicester NUT Lesbian and Gay Rights Working Party, 1987)

One of the authors of this book can also remember an example of such harassment from his own school days:

> I remember the humiliating fight with a boy called Bill at primary school. I'd only just begun to wear nickel-rimmed National Health specs for reading and Bill started teasing and jabbing fun at me ['specky four-eyes']. Bill's goading went on for several weeks until I could stand it no longer. One wet break I shouted at him to 'get lost!' and he threatened to get me on the way home after school. And get me he

did. We argued and nudged each other until we got to the park. Charles Atlas would have flattened Bill with one iron fist, but I was soon knocked flat on my back with Bill's knees pinioning my shoulders and him straddled across my chest nearly suffocating me. I couldn't stand being trapped underneath Bill's weight. My nose ran and tears came, and Bill left me sobbing and picking the pine needles off my jersey. That's where my elder sister found me — beaten-up, snivelling and ashamed. (Jackson, 1990)

The school, as an institution, far from taking a stand on behalf of the victims, actually reinforces the messages about how bad it is to be seen as 'unmanly'. There are the male PE staff who castigate boys as wimps about failure to bring kit for 'trivial' reasons or an inability to play certain games with the verve, skill and commitment of the natural athletes. Boys who cry are taunted by pastoral staff for their real or imagined over-attachments to their mothers. One of the authors has been told this by the Head of Lower School at a Derby comprehensive school. It is clear where his perspective lies in the making of masculinities.

Clothing is another area where it is important to not get it wrong. Boys wearing the wrong trainers, the wrong style of underpants, or brand of tracksuit will be pilloried for their lack of conformity.

Jan Humpleby (1990), working in primary schools has commented on the reaction of boys when asked to play with 'girls toys':

[They] remained deeply within the confines of the classroom . . . several showed increased aggression and noise level, seemingly as a reassurance mechanism to indicate that they hadn't lost any manliness . . . Those playing with dolls or 'pink things' . . . hated all the exercise. All . . . stated that they would never go outside the classroom with one or ask for one themselves, for fear of mockery or humiliation.

Faced with the dominant, heterosexual pack and a similar value system resonating around the institutional structure of the school, where can boys turn? Their only choice is to guard themselves from harm by adopting pack values, by joining in the abuse of girls and unmanly boys. In so doing they are damaging the feminine and sensitive part of themselves but at least they are keeping themselves safe from ridicule and physical harm.

It is important to challenge and work with boys on their sense of entitlement and expectations around girls and women which leads boys into sexually harassing behaviours in order to demonstrate their power. It is, after all, not the boys who suffer from voyeurism, gropers, sexual assaults and sexual innuendos. Boys are not in danger of having hands pushed up their trouser legs or their bottoms grabbed and squeezed.

It is not our intention to take away the sense of excitement as boys stumble towards a sense of sexual balance with girls. It is our intention to work in such a way as to confront boys with the feelings that their behaviour engenders in their victims and to question the feelings of power which being a harassing perpetrator evokes in themselves.

This sense of power growing out of the vigorous assertion of heterosexual masculinity not only affects boy–girl relations, but also occurs between males as a way of maintaining power over weaker masculinities. This form of male–male sexual harassment is often classified as bullying:

> Neil knows he is being bullied. He is being punished by the vigorous heterosexual cocks in his peer group who are not only anxious to assert their power but also to punish him for his deviance — for letting them down. Neil's response is to be withdrawn, maintain a low profile and dream of being tough like the wrestlers he chooses to admire. Occasionally when the going gets really tough he finds the abusive part of himself and lashes back at others. It seems like a sad attempt to be one of the boys.

For the protection of Neil and others like him it seems that future investigations into sexual harassment should take a more specific focus.

Instead of considering 'all males' as an undifferentiated mass, it would be helpful if one specific version (hierarchical, heterosexual masculinity) was analysed, in order to understand more clearly how it gained and maintains such a dominant position. And also how this hold can be weakened and finally broken.

Selected Further Reading on Sexual Harassment

STANLEY, L. and WISE, S. (1987) *Georgie Porgie: Sexual Harassment in Everyday Life*, Pandora.
SHEFFIELD MEN AGAINST SEXUAL HARASSMENT (1984, revised 1987) *Sexual Harassment, Rape and Sexual Abuse of Children: An Information Pack for Men*, Sheffield, SMASH.
JACKSON, D. and PICKERSGILL, D. (1992) 'Combating sexual harassment', *Working with Men*, **1**, pp. 12–14.

The Session

Behind the Sexually Aggressive Exteriors

Chris had been on holiday and had missed the session that starts with the sex brainstorm. I always find this session important and powerful because it is the boys themselves who come to realize what is missing when they use graphic expressions like, 'Grab her and ride her on the settee'. Slowly, from out of the shared riskiness and exhilaration of being able to use graphic obscenities in lesson time, comes the realization that it's OK to share the 'soppy stuff'. They begin to look behind the blustering, sexually aggressive exteriors and show each other those feelings which value the sensitive and caring aspects of sexual relationships. It ceases to become 'soppy stuff' and becomes instead something allied with the notion of love-making as an equal partnership far removed from the 'I'm gonna fuck her tonight attitude' which had begun the session. Moreover, it had been safe to share these feelings with other boys in the group. Such connectedness and sense of sharing in such a sensitive area had never happened for these boys before.

I kept my surprise and delight to myself as it was the boys themselves who wanted to tell Chris what had happened the previous week. It was they who told him of the concern for partners, the gentleness, the trust and the importance of building relationships. Most of the boys shared with Chris how their approach to sexual activity was shifting and that it felt better and more honest. Only one boy (Danny) said that he wasn't changing but that was because he really cared for his girlfriend anyway! He was also keen to point out that the lyrics of 'I'm Gonna Sex You Up' (Color Me Badd) seemed to be only a cleaned up version of the sex brainstorms of the previous week.

We move on to the way men and boys make assumptions about what is acceptable treatment of women and girls. I introduce this now because I had been disturbed by an incident at the start of a lesson earlier in the day. The door had suddenly opened and a girl fell into the room. The girl was in Year 9 and certainly other Year 9 boys were involved. I made a general enquiry about whether anyone knew of the incident or what was going on. The boys' answers reveal that the girl is well known for teasing and poking fun at boys and that she attracts a lot of attention by doing this. Sometimes boys get their own back, although her actually falling down was probably an accident. I told them how troubled and disappointed I had felt witnessing the incident. They sit in silence. I wanted no more explanations thinking perhaps that 'Just a Bit of a Laugh' will help us all at this point in the group's development.

'Just a Bit of a Laugh' is a very useful exercise (see p. 101). It is also very popular with boys because the way I use it encourages vigorous, active, involved and chaotic debate. This session (June 1991) was to prove no exception. In my teacher role, I read out a statement or short scenario with which boys may agree or disagree. Each side of the room represents the polarity points. The boys move to one side of the room or the other. If they 'don't know' they may adopt a central position. The aim is for one side to present arguments to the other to persuade them to change their minds.

The first situation concerns men whistling at young women from a building site. All previous groups have revealed some sort of split on this one and this group was no different. The majority think that this kind of behaviour is acceptable. They are very vocal in the belief. Chris told us that it was natural and that some women liked it. The others on his 'side' agreed — affirming that lots of women were flattered by attention like this. The only dissenting voice was Danny who said that it wasn't natural and that even if it was, it wouldn't make it right. With great emphasis he demolished the argument about women actually liking it because 'if you were up there whistling you wouldn't actually know if they would like it — they don't exactly wear signs saying "Whistle — I like it".' He thought lots of women would be really uncomfortable.

In this group this did actually get people to shift their position either all the way to the unacceptable pole, or at least to a central 'don't know' position. In other groups the shift was not as marked, as boys have really struggled with this seemingly innocent expression of appreciation of women. Some boys have found it immensely difficult to actually appreciate this behaviour from a woman's point of view. This issue has obviously 'lived with' boys since the results of individual internal struggles with this form of harassing behaviour was often only noted in the evaluations at the end of the course or in follow up individual interviews six months after each course ended.

Jokes about the size of women's breasts were universally condemned. All could appreciate how uncomfortable and degrading that would be for the women concerned. I was surprised to find that there was some level of support for the acceptableness of a woman being touched-up on a crowded train. I felt it important to demonstrate this by some form of action method. The boys all became commuters hanging onto imaginary straps. They were squashed tightly together as the train rattled along. One of the boys who thought touching-up was OK was in the middle of all this. I ask Parminder what he is feeling in this crush. He says that it feels uncomfortable. I suggest that he thinks of himself as a woman in this crush. Once the predictable ribaldry at the suggestion is over, I ask him to speculate on his fears about what might happen to him. He hopes nothing will. I suggest that the 'commuters' tell him the sort of incidents which might happen. The 'commuters' oblige with various indecent suggestions. What would he feel if some of these practices were carried out? He says that he would feel angry but, at the same time, not sure what to do. What does he feel like saying? He wants to tell them to 'Stop!', 'Leave me alone!' and 'Who do you think you are?' I encourage him to use the words. He decides that women should not be touched-up on a crowded train.

The next situation was a group of young men staring at two girls in a pub. The confusion with this scene actually hinges on what the boys understand by staring. Chris says, 'Surely it's alright to look at girls.' There is a hint of despair in his voice. My keenness to act things out is once again to the fore. We create the pub scene. Two boys agree to become girls. There is much predictable silliness around this. The 'girls' get chided and ribbed. I again ask the boys to look at what they are doing here. It's important to accept these boys as girls and to treat them accordingly. After some time, order is restored. The four boys from the staring group settle in to the task. The others in the group observe, prepared to make comments later. The scene is briefly enacted. At the conclusion I ask the 'girls' what they had been feeling. They acknowledge that had they really been girls, they would have been worried about what might happen to them. They felt that the starers had been 'undressing them'. The observers commented that they could have been followed or raped. The starers were very much aware of the difference between staring and glancing. Glancing they said could be done without the girls really noticing, but staring 'made me feel powerful and important'. 'The more I did it, the more I enjoyed making them feel uncomfortable.' 'It was like making love to them with your eyes.' These remarks came from the starers and emphasized the power relations which are on display in this scenario. I ask what prompts men to behave in this way. There is a grudging acceptance that it might be around showing power. I could sense that some in the group were moving towards the position of 'What right have I got to be powerful at the expense of someone else's fear?' Maybe the move-ment was only towards Chris' point that 'It was only a game, but I can see how cruel it is'. I felt it was important to have each of the starers say how they were not like the people they had played so that they did not carry any of the bad feelings away with them. They each did this and demonstrated it by going to the side of the room which showed staring as unacceptable behaviour.

There was no debate necessary over the question of 'husbands having sex as a right'. I was impressed that some of the boys knew about the recent change in the law making marital rape a crime. They felt it was important to respect when women weren't 'in the mood'. A debate took place about things to do to encourage a wife to be in the mood, like buying things or doing nice things. Suddenly, seemingly from nowhere, Danny said, 'Look, women's bodies are their own — without the woman's consent it's rape.' That seemed to shut everyone up and highlighted that men should respect women's rights and if a woman says 'No', it is better to assume that that is exactly what she means.

A boy making a 'heavy breathing' phone call to a girl in his class as a joke provoked an interesting dilemma. Some boys thought it might go too far and you might get caught. I reflected this back to them that what they seemed to be saying was that it's OK if there's no chance of being caught. I got shouted down since what they were really saying apparently is, 'It's OK to start off making a phone call like this as long as you own up quickly. If you don't do that it might scare the living daylights out of her. She might think he's outside.' There is still some ambivalence about this but all agree that the girl should not be fearful over a period of time.

The questions relating to fathers showing porn magazines to sons and daughters revealed an interesting split. No-one in any group thought that it was acceptable for a father to show a pornographic magazine to his daughter. In this group the hostility to this was marked and it was Chris who said quite angrily that, 'it might even make her think she is expected to do this'. When this issue became fathers and sons there was some initial feeling that this was one of the ways in which you learned things and that it was OK. Indeed, earlier in the year one of the groups had voted almost exclusively that this was part of the 'way of life' and were unshakable in this belief. In this group those who found it unacceptable were saying that although they looked at porn magazines, they knew that they contained all the 'harsh, unacceptable stuff around sex'. Jagvir was also bothered about what he would think of his father who showed him these things. He looked up to his father and he didn't know if he would be able to if he showed him such material.

The last two scenarios both concerned rape. The first was a judge acquitting a man after the rape of his step-daughter because his wife was pregnant and not interested in sexual intercourse. This provoked a particularly unified and angry response. 'How did this guy become a judge?' 'This guy needs sorting out.' 'Rape is rape' was the phrase from Chris which seemed to capture the mood of complete bewilderment that a judge could be so crassly stupid. Chris' remark was very appropriate in view of the second incident which concerned a man raping a prostitute. There was some confusion here since they were all aware of their very recently confirmed view that rape is rape. 'Perhaps prostitutes expect to be raped' said Parminder. 'No they don't, they expect to be paid — if they're not paid and forced to do it then it must be rape.' 'A woman is a woman and none of them go out to get raped.' Such arguments seem to confirm that they were right to think that rape was rape and should be universally condemnned.

A brief discussion followed on why women became prostitutes which became a wider discussion on why boys and men sexually harass women. The boys were very good at coming up with a range of 'having fun', 'to impress', 'jealousy', 'desperate for love'. There was some appreciation that men actually harassed women to show they were superior and more powerful than women.

In conclusion, as time was running out, I asked how the boys in the room stopped themselves from being unkind to women. Some were honest enough to admit they they had hassled girls in the past in what they regarded as minor ways, but said that now they would 'think about the consequences more'. Because of what they had been doing on this morning, it seemed that the boys would not feel good in themselves about the effects their behaviour might have. I was glad no-one was silly enough to say that they would never harass again, but pleased that all said they would think first about what the consequences of their actions might be.

Classroom Strategies

Sexual Harassment

Boys make assumptions about male privileges and entitlement. Some of them believe they have the right to invade girls' space and bodies by grabbing, pinching, groping, whistling and making sexual innuendoes. The object of this classroom strategies section is to encourage boys to notice how this behaviour operates to put down and humiliate. We are offering boys the opportunity to be in situations which encourage them to feel what it is like to be on the receiving end of such behaviours. The activities begin the process of challenging these taken for granted assumptions.

Thinking about Power and Oppression

Aim: *To get in touch with feelings we have all had of feeling powerless or humiliated or unfairly treated and to make connections with the way sexism affects women.*

Materials: *None*

Time: *30–45 minutes*

What to do:

Ask the group to think of a time when they have felt humiliated, unfairly treated or made fun of and yet felt unable to do anything about it. Get them to describe what it was like. If you feel confident in using active methods then individual scenes could be shown by means of role play.

By whatever means feelings of powerlessness are highlighted, allow the feelings to be discussed in the group and suggest that this is how women often feel in the face of sexism and discrimination.

If used carefully this is a good way of getting boys to make the connection between various forms of oppression. All of them will have personal stories of some form of this as children in relation to adults. Young black men, those of minority religions or young gay men and young disabled men will have an even more extensive experience of this.

The Lads!

Aims: *To raise issues about young men's attitudes towards women.*

Materials: *Copies of the 'The Lads!' cartoon (from the SMASH (Sheffield Men Against Sexual Harassment) pack)*

Time: *30 minutes*

What to do:

The cartoon contrasts the view of two young men. One (Mick) has opinions which undermine, oppress and harass women, while the other young man is very critical of this attitude and says so.

The following questions could act as stimuli for discussion:

- In what ways does Mick show that he does not think much of women/ girls?

- What do *you* think of his attitude to women?
- What do you think of the attitude of the blond-haired young man? How far do you agree with what he is saying?

Where Men Are Men and Women Are Women . . .

Aim: To provoke thought and discussion about gender roles and about the relationships between men and women.

Materials: Set of Statement cards, prepared using the statements below

Time: 30–45 minutes

What to do:

Get the group to divide into three areas of the room according to whether they 'Agree', 'Disagree' or 'Don't Know' in relation to each statement. Then members of each viewpoint try to convince members of the other two groups to join them. Give a few minutes to each statement, then move on. Act as referee.

The statements:

- Blue for boys and pink for girls.
- Women and their friends are closer than men and their friends.
- Women and men have more similarities than differences.
- A man and a woman can never be 'just friends'. There is always sex involved somewhere.
- You can talk to women friends in a way you can't talk to men friends.
- Women are the equal of men.
- Women are treated equally to men.
- Adults treat girls differently to boys.
- Men are more violent than women.
- More is expected of boys than of girls.
- All this stuff about sexism is a fuss about nothing.
- Sexism, like racism, causes a lot of problems and unhappiness between people and should be got rid of as soon as possible.
- Women need to be looked after by men.
- Women should look after men.

(This exercise is taken from Davidson, N. *Boys Will Be . . . ?*, London, Bedford Square Press, p. 106.)

Just a Bit of a Laugh?

Aim: To raise issues about what constitutes inappropriate sexual behaviour around rape, sexual harassment, and abuse.

Materials: A set of stimulus statements, prepared using the statements below

Time: 30– 45 minutes

What to do:

Identify three areas of the room as 'Acceptable', 'Unacceptable' and 'Don't Know'.

Read out one of the statements to the whole group. Ask each boy to go to one of three areas in the room according to whether they find the statement acceptable, unacceptable or don't know.

Members of each viewpoint group take it in turns to say what has made them choose their position. It is their job to convince members of the other two groups to join them. This can be quite a lively session so that the facilitator needs to keep an eye on what is happening and be responsible for the pace of the exercise.

The statements:

- A woman is walking past a building site. Several men whistle and shout at her.
- A man at work making jokes about the size of a woman colleague's breasts.
- A man touching-up a woman in a crowded underground train.
- A group of young men staring at two women sitting together in a pub.
- A husband insisting that his wife has sex with him because it's 'his right'.
- A boy making a 'heavy breathing' phone call to a girl in his class for a joke.
- A father showing his son his porn magazines.
- A father showing his daughter his porn magazines.
- A judge at a trial saying that a man's rape of his step-daughter was 'understandable' because his wife was pregnant at the time and was not interested in sex.
- A man raping a prostitute.

(This exercise is based on Davidson, N. *Boys Will Be* . . . ?, London, Bedford Square Press, pp. 90, 96.)

Sexual Harassment Questionnaire

Aim: To raise awareness and promote discussion about acceptable male behaviour in relation to women.

Materials: Copies of 'Sexual Harassment — The Questionnaire,' prepared using the questions below

Time: 45 minutes

What to do:

Encourage all group members to complete the questionnaire. Emphasize that it is important to answer the questions as honestly as they can.

On completion of the questionnaires, ask the group members to join together in pairs or threes to compare their answers, and make any changes they feel is appropriate in their answers.

Bring the whole group back together to enable a general discussion to take place.

The questions:

Sexual Harassment Questionnaire

1. Do you ever whistle at women/girls?
2. Do you ever make remarks about women/girls so that they can hear?
3. Do you ever touch, grab, pinch, put your arm round girls without their permission?
4. If you have answered YES to any of the above questions — what encourages you to do it? What do you get out of it?
5. If you have answered No to the above questions (1–3) what has stopped you doing these things.
6. How do you think *most* women/girls respond to being whistled at or commented upon? (Put a tick by your answer.)

   - They enjoy it
   - They don't mind
   - They are embarrassed
   - They are annoyed

7. Do you think women who seem to enjoy or don't mind this attention are being entirely truthful? What else might they be saying?
8. Which of the following would you call sexual harassment? (Put a tick by your answers.)

- Wolf whistling
- Eyeing-up a woman/girl
- Making intimate remarks/comments
- Displaying Page 3 type calendars/pin-ups
- Unnecessary physical contact, e.g., deliberately brushing past too closely
- Touching-up
- Any others
- None of the above

9. Do any of the above occur at your school/college?
10. If you saw a girl looking uncomfortable about the way a boy was treating her, would you do anything about it?
11. If 'Yes' how would you help her?
12. What would you find difficult about doing this?

Chapter 5

Violence and Bullying

The Theory

Violence in Schools, Clubs and Colleges

For many students, everyday life in schools, clubs, and colleges is a violent experience. Along the corridor at break, in classrooms, in the toilets, behind the bike sheds — all of these places can turn out to be threatening and scary. When we talk of 'threatening' we're not just limiting ourselves to physical hurt but referring to a much more broad-based definition of violence that would include various violent and controlling behaviours like being punched, kicked, shown-up in front of friends, verbally abused, having your hair pulled, being sexually harassed, being teased, mocked and psychologically intimidated.

The Elton report on *Discipline in School* (HMSO, 1989), makes it very clear where the violence is coming from. It mainly comes from an aggressive masculinity that is partly condoned by a society that has got too used to some men being in the driving seat. The report says that '. . . our evidence suggests that the way in which some boys are brought up causes particular problems in schools. Some parents tolerate or even encourage aggressive behaviour.' Without wanting to totally swallow the implied comments about ineffective parents, or the 'dysfunctional family', the report is very sure about the problem being one of boys. Later in the report they take this further: 'It's quite clear from our evidence that the greater majority of pupils involved in disruptive behaviour are male. Boys are also far more likely to be involved in physical aggression than girls . . .'

However, we don't want to narrow our focus on the violence caused by bully-boy students, although it's often shockingly frequent. We also want to draw attention to a wider climate of masculine violence and brutality that some male teachers condone or even actively participate in. These linking threads between aggressive masculinities in both classrooms and staffrooms can be clearly seen in the overall, macho ethos of many colleges and schools. If you're doubtful about this then listen to the following three examples from students and staff:

> Nicky was a small, 11-year-old boy but a hard little nut at the same time. He knew which boys he could take on and which boys he

couldn't. So he always picked on a boy called Stuart who was seen as soft and a bit wet.

One particular day, Nicky went up to Stuart and demanded that he dropped what he was doing to tell him the time. Stuart shrugged and looked away. But Nicky, determined to get his own way, wrenched Stuart's shoulder and twisted his wrist around suddenly so that he could see the time for himself. Stuart let out a loud protest of pain and sat nursing his wrist for the rest of the period. The teacher hadn't noticed what had gone on.

A bullied Doncaster boy spent three days in a coma after trying to kill himself with an overdose. The mild-mannered, church-going 13-year-old boy had been picked on by four older boys who took his books and called him 'a queer'.

Here's what a rugby teacher said in the staffroom about one of his most awkward boy students: 'The young O'Brien is going the same way as the older one did. He was the only boy whom the staff actually asked me to hurt. "Get him on the rugby field" they said. "Really hurt him in a tackle!". So I did! He was like an angel after that. This kid looks to be the same — all mouth — until he's sorted out. Just give me the word!'

Schools, clubs and colleges are institutions where gender is actively forged. Gender isn't just reflected or expressed. They are places where a certain type of 'top dog' masculinity is made, celebrated and confirmed through daily acts of violence and bullying. Both Nicky and the rugby teacher are linked here in their tacit acceptance of a culture of aggressive manliness. They both expected to get their own way through determined acts of toughness and physical force, often at the expense of other more marginalized types of masculinity, like gay, bisexual or gentler boys such as Stuart.

Turning a Blind Eye to Daily Acts of Violence

Masculine violence and bullying are so much a taken-for-granted part of school/college life that they seem to be invisible to many teachers. There are perhaps three main reasons for this.

Firstly, daily school routines often normalize the violent behaviour of both staff and students to the people already existing within these institutions. One of the authors can remember the daily beatings, threats, sarcastic comments, clips around the head that went on so frequently in the life of a 1950s grammar school that he assumed that was a perfectly acceptable behaviour. Violent behaviour was so naturalized that he hardly noticed that it took place at all.

Secondly, some teachers turn a blind eye to masculine violence because they assume that the violence is an inevitable part of being a boy or a man. When you ask some teachers about this, they often reply 'Well boys will be boys!', or 'But that's what boys do isn't it?' The implication is that being a boy involves a 'natural' expression or an innate, aggressive drive or instinct that we are all stuck with for the rest of our lives.

The third area of blindness is linked to teachers' frequent denials of power and oppression in their own practices. Valerie Walkerdine (1990) has pointed out that the historical legacy of many teachers (however confusing and contradictory those legacies often are) is to see themselves as neutral facilitators, 'partners in learning — no power, no hierarchy, called by our first names'. This value-free, neutral fantasy means that for many teachers they can't bear to acknowledge the extent and the persistence of the daily acts of violence and controlling behaviours that go on in their classrooms.

Some teachers seem to remain oblivious to these daily acts of cruelty, as in the example of Nicky and Stuart above, or react with puzzled surprise when they hear about more extreme cases, as in the case of the Doncaster boy above, when bullied children have had to choose desperate measures rather than go on subjecting themselves to the daily brutalization.

Against Biological Arguments about Masculine Violence

Little can be done about this taken-for-granted state of affairs until we challenge the biological arguments about masculine violence. Violence isn't a 'natural' expression or reflection of men's innate, warrior/hunter instincts. It isn't just because of their hormones or genitals that many boys or men are violent, although they might be partly shaped by them. Instead, violent and controlling behaviour is a major part of the social processes that forge masculinities within a male-dominated society. Putting that another way, men and boys aren't violent because they have male bodies. They are violent in order to become more masculine. And it's certainly true that some masculine violence comes from a frustrated attempt to cover up or disguise a sense of personal inadequacy. As Vic Seidler (1985) says 'Violence is a sign not just of our strength, but of our impotence and frustration.'

Masculine violence is inextricably linked to the wider structures of male power and control in society. What this means, practically, is seen in men's assumptions of male entitlement and privilege. If they don't get their own way then they'll lash out, sulk or use more subtle, coercive behaviours. It's these everyday assumptions — that boys and men have a natural right to get what they want all the time, or to demand instant servicing (like in Nicky's bullying of Stuart) — that have to be challenged if we are going to do anything effective to counter this systematic battering and intimidation.

If we are going to do anything about this, however, a more precise targeting on who the violent bullies are is urgently needed. First we have to recognize that the majority of boys don't bully. It's only some boys who do on a regular basis. And these are mainly the dominant, heterosexual, 'cocks of the class, club or group'. These 'cocks' achieve their supremacy by actively putting down and marginalizing other more vulnerable forms of masculinity. Through placing themselves in opposition to anything unmanly (especially girls and gays) they define themselves as 'real' boys or men. So bullying isn't a randomly casual affair. Rather it's an integral part of making a manly identity for some boys and men.

The other necessary recognition is that boys mostly bully other boys, although girls are regularly knocked about, threatened and teased as well. (Girls bully as well but generally use subtler techniques of exclusion from the peer group and psychological intimidation rather than the more overt, physical violence that boys use.) Odd, weak or vulnerable boys bear the brunt of the 'cocks' brutality. They are often given demeaning nicknames that associate them with traditional femininity, passivity and softness. Despite developing strategies that deflect the bullying fists (like joking, verbal inventiveness, cheeking teachers in order to gain a more popular status for themselves, etc.), their school lives are often nightmarish. In schools they don't have a safe place to hide from the tongue lashings or the fists. Adult authority often turns a blind eye or even colludes with the 'cocks' against the weaker boys. So boys like Stuart are left to face a savage undermining (both physical and psychological) that would break even the sanest and most courageous of us.

Positive Challenges

Many schools/colleges just passively react to this 'hard case', bully boy culture. Or only give their serious attention to it when the daily acts of bullying occasionally flare up in extreme crises that can't be ignored. However, many hours of valuable pastoral time are already spent in picking up the pieces after the bullying/violence have taken place.

What we want to question here is why can't the valuable time, energy and resources now spent on clearing up the mess created by bullying be spent in a more preventive, pro-active approach that attempts to go the heart of the origins of masculine violence? A possible starting point is changing the invisibility of the problem to a more explicit, high profiled awareness about the destructive pattern of behaviour that teachers and students can do something about. Another way in is to challenge the avoidance of responsibility that often creates a smokescreen around the subject of masculine violence. We don't believe that masculine violence lies outside the grip of personal choice and decision making. We want to expose the camouflaging excuses many men and boys use in separating themselves from the full horror of their own violent actions, such as loss of control, temporary 'black outs', impulsive explosions, irrational rages.

The central question that informs these challenges and investigations is 'How can we work with boys and men in such a way that prompts them to begin to take charge of their own violent actions?' We believe that masculine violence is intentional, deliberate and purposeful. It comes from an attempt by men and boys to create and sustain a system of masculine power and control that benefits them every minute of the day. Any attempt to excuse the devastating results of this violence in schools and colleges by down-playing or trivializing it, is tacitly validating a system of brutality over other put-down forms of masculinity.

Many teachers would condemn masculine violence in its most visible form, like in football hooliganism. Perhaps it is time for them to start exploring the connections between the more explicit and dramatic forms of masculine violence in the world outside the school gates (like at the Heysel Stadium in Belgium) and what is going on, in a much taken-for-granted way, right under their noses every day of the school or college year?

A School Anti-Bullying Policy

We recognize that the problem of bullying in schools is partly about the condition of being masculine but we also want to acknowledge that bullying can also have strong racist overtones. It shows itself in the amount of aggression boys display towards each other. The death of Ahmed Iqbal Ullah at Burnage High School being an extreme example of racial bullying. It is recognized that girls can also bully each other, but that the problem of bullying among boys is very much more extensive than among girls (Olweus, 1978). The Elton report supports this view:

> It is quite clear from our evidence that the great majority of pupils involved in disruptive behaviour are male. Boys are also far more likely to be involved in physical aggression than girls. The difference is that the incidence of misbehaviour is much lower and that some of the anti-social activities typical of girls are much less noticeable than boys' aggression. Bullying illustrates this point. Research shows that boys and girls are involved in bullying. The difference is that boys are likely to use physical intimidation and violence; girls make use of more subtle techniques . . .

Bullying in schools is linked with the fierce push and striving of boys wanting to become more masculine. Schools are places where boys are made. They don't just reflect an innate aggressiveness. To become more manly, some boys are persuaded that they can only achieve this through force and intimidation. This shows itself in the competitive individualistic ethos which exists among the boys themselves and also with the masculine power structure that controls the school establishment. Askew (1989) quoted a teacher as saying that 'in order to get to the top you have to fight it out with your colleagues'. It is small wonder that boys notice this kind of example and the way society values competitiveness and winners, while at the same time forgetting losers. Boys see instances of bullying all around them. They experience it, collude with it and dish it out.

Some of them also deflect and resist it but all are in some way ensnared into a cycle of violence and aggression which pervades the school atmosphere to a greater or lesser degree.

It is important that the school community does not tolerate the oppression of one person by another and provides an alternative ethos based on caring and valuing. Our contention is that this will be unsuccessful without concerted action that critically challenges masculinity and power within the school. There is a mismatch when schools try to create caring environments based on mutual respect and personal growth without offering work programmes that ask males throughout schools to consider the way they are as boys and men.

The following guidelines aim to establish a whole school policy and they contain short- and long-term strategies involving the curriculum, the school organization and staff development training.

A School Policy Statement

A very effective preventative measure in relation to bullying is a school policy statement that states simply what the school values are. Such a document should be widely circulated to pupils, parents, staff, governors and the local education authority. It should also be clear in the document what action will be taken on breaches of the rules. Such action should be taken seriously and may include automatic notification of bullying incidents to parents and governors. This in itself could be a powerful deterrent for those inclined to aggressive, oppressive behaviour.

The School as a Community

One of the most effective ways of preventing bullying is perhaps to look on the school as a community where the aim is for each member to be responsible for his or herself and for the well-being of all others. Schools have begun to offer work programmes which stress cooperation, but this has been largely centred on academic learning experiences rather than towards social development. The value of democratically working towards a mutual goal repays the effort of making it a familiar experience for pupils since when social and emotional problems are tackled in this way, real changes in behaviour can be perceived. It should not be supposed that cooperative learning will automatically lead to cooperative behaviour, but it will be more likely to do so if the task for the students to deal with is rooted in their own social experiences, e.g., working on strategies for preventing bullying.

Gobey (1991) has worked in inner London schools with workshops looking at the complexities of bullying. His programme of activities is closely associated with the Neti Neti Theatre Company's travelling production of *Only Playing Miss* (1989). Other work involving dramatic structures and role play have been described by Herbert (1989) and Askew (1989).

Fostering cooperative learning will itself be more successful if the experience fits the general ethos of the school. If the school is hierarchical and competitive, then it will be out of sync with the aims of cooperative education. Well organized and developed schools' councils not only indicate a diminution of hierarchical control but can also take initiatives to tackle problems of real concern to students, e.g., bullying. Laslett (1982) advocates the setting up of children's courts to which pupils can bring complaints against their peers. Such experiments need careful monitoring in view of complaints that may be levelled concerning impartiality and, hence, value.

Ethos of the School

The ethos of the school was described by Dancy (1980) as 'the values, aims, attitudes and procedures of a school which inter-relate and which remains a permanent feature of the school.' He might also have added a phrase concerning social relations between all who work within the establishment. It is important in the struggle against bullying that a school climate be created where pupils can learn about and from each other in a constructive way. They might learn that when regular meetings of pupils are held to deal with conflict, they can tackle emotive issues, work out amicable solutions and see each other's point of view.

A caring, cooperative ethos can be created if the school looks seriously at 'the relationship between aggressive behaviour and school organisation, policies on discipline and teaching methods' (Askew, 1989). The Elton report (1989) also speaks of the futility of inappropriate punishment for bullies: 'punitive regimes seem to be associated with worse rather than better standards of behaviour', and again, 'avoid permissive or harshly punitive responses or aggressive behaviour particularly by boys . . . '.

A successful experiment at an inner-city school was chronicled by Caroline St John Brooks (1985). Robin Chambers of Stoke Newington School had created a 'telling school' which undermined the tradition of secrecy and breaking down the schoolboy code of honour. In his school it was clear that not to tell about bullying was a strategy invented by bullies to protect themselves and their activities. Bullying and racism were discussed openly and the macho swaggerers were made to confront their bullying behaviour.

Working with groups of teachers is essential. Workshops in which the seriousness of the problem of bullying can be discussed is an essential prerequisite of the establishment of a caring, valuing ethos.

Style of Management

All steps to counter bullying in schools will only be effective in a limited way if the quality and style of management in school is not wholly supportive. Three features of management style are of crucial importance:

- a consistent anti-bullying policy understood by everyone;
- clear communication of the aims and goals of this policy;
- a unity of purpose within a cooperative team.

The best policies will fail if the whole team are not pulling together in the same direction.

Bullying and Student Learning

Amid the teachers' crowded timetable of lessons and responsibilities, we think that every effort must be made to make real and personal contact with children. The quality of caring so displayed will help to give a child a real individual identity. Besag (1989) stresses the importance of a strong, stable relationship with an adult outside the family as a powerful factor in enabling otherwise very disadvantaged children to experience success which is a powerful influence in encouraging self-esteem and confidence. Children will be helped in this way to feel better about themselves and therefore will be less likely to be caught up in a spiral of oppression, either as a bully or victim.

In 1985 Carol Askew worked with a first year group at the Hackney Downs School in London. Her experience is worth re-telling for the pointers it offers in creating an atmosphere where it is more difficult for bullying to grow. Her practice was to share life stories and incidents during class time each day. This encouraged the children to be more honest with each other and had the additional effect of breaking down the power dynamics between pupils and teachers. Her emphasis was on personal regard for her students' strengths and the development of a mutual respect within the form group. It was made clear that if bullying and fighting occurred, then it was very much a problem for the whole group to solve. This development of honesty and openness and the idea of bullying being everyone's problem is shared by Gobey in the workshops he ran in 1989 (Casdagli and Gobey, 1990).

Bullying and Masculinity

Work in schools on bullying has tended to be from a liberal, personal growth standpoint and has been undertaken as part of personal and social eduction or pastoral initiatives. We are suggesting that a specific gendered awareness approach be highlighted to show the way violence and bullying in schools is an integral part of the social construction of masculinity.

Almost from birth, boys and girls are taught what is expected of them in becoming male and female. Much of the behaviour that boys regard as natural has in fact been learned from parents, relatives, adults and from other boys within the peer group. Adams and Laurikietis (1976) suggested that the myth of naturalness which boys operate on suggest that males are active, aggressive, independent and adventurous. They can cope with the world and are tough, ambitious and ruthless. There is an assumption around boys' behaviour that they have a natural right to get their own way.

This assumption of male entitlement and demonstrations of male power is closely related to how boys become bullies. Boys in groups knit tightly together to protect their power and privilege (Herbert, 1989). They think that something is wrong with boys who do not behave in their masculine kind of way, thus there is the striving to maintain a position where intimidation and bullying will not be a problem for them. Those perceived as weak are picked on by the cult of aggressive manliness on display. Positive self-esteem is flattened and withers as victims cower away from the insistent taunts of violence. Children are prevented from learning and from taking any positive nourishment from school life.

In the face of such pressure, we contend that the main focus should be on changing boys' conventional behaviours and that this should go alongside encouraging victims to become more assertive and confident. Our dilemma is the question that each boy might ask, 'What's in it for me to do this?' For boys this is probably a more difficult task than for men, since at least some men can learn the benefits of behavioural change and even relish the gains of less stress, better health and a greater emotional range. For boys, our challenge seems to affect them at the level of destroying their cherished identity. Our strategies aim to encourage boys to take personal responsibility for their own violence and bullying. In addition we aim to show boys that it is possible to take different choices as they move towards alternative masculine identities.

'Bullying the Bullies Doesn't Make Sense to Kids'

A harsh and punishing disciplinary system in schools is largely ineffective (Elton, 1989). But worse it can also be seen by pupils as violence directed upon themselves, so validating their own aggressive bullying behaviour which is meted out on the younger and more vulnerable students in the school.

Riley (1988) decided that there might be a link between disruptive behaviour in classrooms and bullying. It is easy to understand his thinking since he posits that disruptive behaviour is sometimes seen as a systematic attempt to unsettle and humiliate a teacher. The member of staff is then working in a stressed and frightening environment where it may be impossible to prevent the 'disruptives' from transferring their taunts to the more vulnerable children in a form of overt bullying.

To prevent this scenario from taking place it is vital that there is a whole school approach to classroom practices. Children are keen to pounce on laxity by staff and exploit it in their own interests. Many such problems can be dealt with if the teacher adopts a firm, good humoured and prompt response to an escalating problem. This approach may work in most areas, save where pupils disrupt simply because they see the teacher as an authority onto whom they can project feelings of anger, disappointment and fear.

Supervision

It is tempting to suggest that friendly, high level supervision of pupils will help to prevent bullying from taking place. In school this means teachers not being late for lessons since lateness gives an opportunity to the bored bullies to select a target for the attentions before a teacher arrives. Besag (1989) uses the term 'active vigilant supervision' to spot intimidating behaviour in its early stages. Ignoring incidents gives a tacit message to the bullies to continue in their activities.

We recognize how hard pressed teachers are. We see that the energies that they expend in helping children to learn being sabotaged by overtly aggressive behaviours. Children cannot learn because they are being intimidated and terrorized. We draw links between the difficulties children have in learning with the difficulties teachers have in responding to the demands of the National Curriculum and all that has come in its wake. If taking responsibility for bullying is tacked onto an increasingly big list of duties, then advances cannot be made.

The urgent need is for a re-think of whole school priorities so that masculinity and violence can become a part of the schools' response to the National Curriculum. Such an investigation by staff and students can provide the climate in which National Curriculum initiatives can prosper as the school becomes a safe and nurturing place where real learning can go on.

Selected Further Reading on Violence and Bullying

BEYNON, J. (1989) 'A school for men: An ethnographic case study of routine violence in schooling', in BARTON, L. and WALKER, S. (Eds) *Politics and the Processes of Schooling*, Milton Keynes, Open University Press.

BESAG, V. (1989) *Bullies and Victims in Schools*, Milton Keynes, Open University Press.

KIVEL, P. (1992) *Men's Work: How to Stop the Violence that Tears our Lives Apart*, Minnesota, Hazelden Educational Materials.

SHARP, S. and SMITH, P. (1994) *Tackling Bullying in Your School: A Practical Handbook*, London, Routledge.

SMITH, P. and SHARP, S. (Eds) (1994) *School Bullying: Insights and Perspectives*, London, Routledge.

OLWEUS, D. (1993) *Bullying in Schools: What We Know and What We Can Do*, Oxford, Blackwell.

Bullying Survey — Towards a Whole School Policy

Schools can conduct a survey of bullying within their establishment to discover the extent of the problem in their location. Here we offer some practical guidance based on one of the author's experiences of delivering workshops at conferences in Derbyshire to raise awareness about bullying. Central to the theme of the conferences was the concept of a whole school approach to tackle bullying.

Ways of Conducting a Survey

A.   *Questionnaire* — What do you need to know?
        Types of behaviour (received and perpetrated)
        By whom on whom (age/gender/group or individual)
        Where/When
        Pupils' perception of   • which behaviours are 'bullying'
                               • whether they tell
                               • who they tell
                               • feelings/comments
     Tips — Closed and multiple choice questions are easier to collate!
          — Anonymity encourages a truer picture.

If the word 'bullying' is used in the questionnaire be sure to have defined its meaning at the beginning. There are many definitions which vary slightly in emphasis. The important thing is that the staff agree on *their* definition and stick to it. Alternatively, phrase questions in terms of observable behaviours. A sample questionnaire offering a recent definition of bullying is laid out in DFE (1994) *Bullying: Don't Suffer in Silence*. The following questions are suggested:

'A pupil is being bullied, or picked on when another pupil or group of pupils say nasty things to him or her. It is also bullying when a pupil is hit, kicked, threatened, locked inside a room, sent nasty notes, when no-one ever talks to them and things like that.

These things can happen frequently and it is difficult for the pupil being bullied to defend himself or herself. It is also bullying when a pupil is teased repeatedly in a nasty way.

However, if two pupils of equal power or strength have an occasional fight or quarrel, this is not bullying.'

1.   Have you ever been bullied in this school?
2.   Are you being bullied now by someone in this school?
3.   Have you told anyone that you are being bullied?
4.   If you told someone, was it:

- a friend
- a family member
- someone who works at school

5. Do you think that they believed you?
6. Do you think that they will try to stop the bullying now?
7. Do you know that the school now has a special group that deals with bullying?
8. Do you think that it is telling tales to tell someone that you are being bullied?
9. Do you think that there are enough places in school where you can feel safe, away from bullying?
10. From the following list, please tick where you have been bullied:

    - classroom
    - corridor
    - toilets
    - playground at breaktime
    - playground at lunchtime
    - on your way to school in a morning
    - on your way from school in an afternoon
    - outside the school grounds during lunchtime
    - somewhere else? Please list

11. What has the bully done to you? Tick as many as you need to.

    - hit or kicked you/hurt you physically
    - spat at you
    - called you names
    - called your family names
    - taken things away from you
    - asked you for money
    - given you dirty looks
    - teased you so that it upset you
    - kept ignoring you
    - threatened to hurt you after school
    - pulled your clothes/damaged your things
    - written bad graffiti about you
    - anything else? Please list

12. Have you been bullied at this school by:

    - a boy
    - a girl
    - a group of children
    - anyone in the same form as you
    - someone older than you

13. From the following list, please tick which of these you felt after you had been bullied. You can tick as many as you want.

   - upset
   - frightened
   - angry
   - felt like not coming to school anymore
   - did not want to tell anyone
   - ill
   - felt I could not work properly
   - puzzled, confused, wondering why I had been picked on
   - felt like getting my own back
   - wanted to tell a friend
   - wanted to tell my family
   - wanted to tell someone who works at school

14. Why do you think that children bully other children?
15. What do you think that the school should do to the children who have bullied you?
16. Is there anything else you would like us to know?

   B. *Mapping-type questions* — i.e., looking at where bullying takes place in the school.
   C. *Drawings/Cartooning* — asking students to draw their experiences.
   D. *Discussion* — 1:1, Group or circle time in tutor groups of PSE time.
   E. *Pupil–pupil interviews* — using older students as peer counsellors. They may be easier to talk to than adults.
   F. *Observation* — by teaching/non-teaching staff.
   G. *Video observation*
   H. *Role play, puppet shows, theatre presentations*
   I. *Stories* — encourage students to read or write stories around bullying behaviour and linking these with what is happening inside and outside school.
   J. *'Telling' box* — encouraging an atmosphere in school where it is good to say what is happening.

After the questionnaire and/or other ways of collecting information have been completed and analysed, the extent of the problem of bullying will be known. School staff can begin the task of formulating, launching and maintaining an anti-bullying policy. At Etches School a group of committed staff including teachers, lunchtime supervisors and governors assessed where their resources and expertise could come from,

Figure 5.1:   *Bullying policy making*

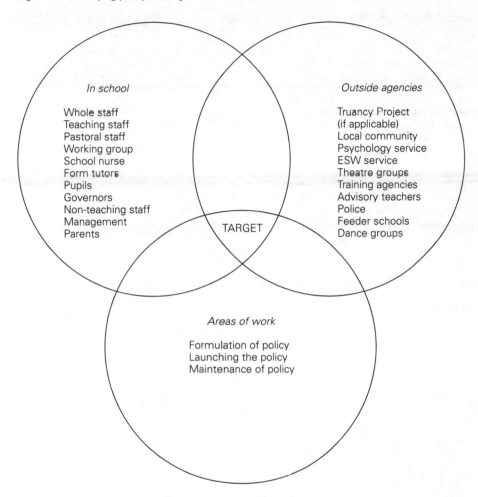

In school

Whole staff
Teaching staff
Pastoral staff
Working group
School nurse
Form tutors
Pupils
Governors
Non-teaching staff
Management
Parents

Outside agencies

Truancy Project
(if applicable)
Local community
Psychology service
ESW service
Theatre groups
Training agencies
Advisory teachers
Police
Feeder schools
Dance groups

TARGET

Areas of work

Formulation of policy
Launching the policy
Maintenance of policy

to produce a policy which would have sustainable roots. The Bullying Policy Making (Figure 5.1) suggests the re- sources within the school and the range of outside agencies which can be used to formulate, launch and maintain a whole school policy. The policy aims to provide a framework to improve the social climate of the school so that bullying activity is reduced.

Figure 5.2 offers an example of what a school might produce after working parties made up of some of the out- side agencies and in-school resources have consulted. The righthand side offers examples of what the schools agreed policy will be, while the lefthand column offers supporting systems and procedures which can help maintain the policy.

Figure 5.2: Example of policy statement and procedure: secondary model

Policy Statement	Supporting Systems/Procedures
We aim to make sure that our school is a caring community where our pupils are able to learn in a safe and happy environment. We strive to encourage an atmosphere of equality, cooperativeness and care. We all have a duty and responsibility to ensure that our aim is achieved.	• Prevention via whole school approach • Messages of collective responsibility, openness, telling, stressed via assemblies, tutor-time, PSE • Whole school projects/charity events, etc. • Whole school/year reward system, supporting positive *behaviours* • Clear reporting system with in-built support for victims/tellers
Any pupil who upsets another through physical violence, taunting, teasing, name-calling, threatening or ignoring, will be encouraged, and helped, to change their behaviour.	• Peer counselling • Common Concern Method • Group work or Individual programme (for bullies and victims) • Vigorous reiteration of policy • No blame approach
If the behaviour persists despite help, the parents and governors will be notified and details of the behaviour kept on file until such time as the behaviour stops.	• Parents notified by letter • Parents asked into school • Details and 'evidence' (witness reports, etc.) kept on file on 'charge sheet' for specified period. Reviewed (with governors and/or parents) — charge sheet removed from file — improvement praised. • Contract • Pre-exclusion contract • Involvement of Ed. Psych/Social Services/ESW
Pupils who still refuse to change their behaviour or who commit particularly violent acts against a pupil, will be excluded from the school to ensure the academic, social and emotional well-being of the other pupils.	• Fixed term exclusion • Permanent exclusion

In this model, work is undertaken with both bullies and victims. Counselling can help some of the bullies to empathize with their victims as well as looking at some of the personal problems which encourage the motivation to bully. Victims can be supported and encouraged to adopt assertive strategies which make them less vulnerable to the activities of the bully.

Of particular interest are the Common Concern and No Blame approaches to dealing with bullying behaviours (see Figure 5.2). The strategies are similar and further information on these approaches can be found in Bullying: An International Perspective, Chapter 8 The Common Concern

Method for the Treatment of Mobbing by Anataol Pikas who is the creator of the method. Alternatively the No Blame Approach — its written material, videos and workshops information can be obtained by writing to Lucky Duck Publishing, 10 South Terrace, Redland, Bristol, BS6 6TG.

One actual example of the general approach will suffice. David, pupil at a school in Derby, was able to report a group of boys who were bullying him. While David was supported by a member of the Rykneld Support Service (Staff in Derby secondary schools who support children with emotional and behavioural difficulties), the Head of Upper School saw the suspected bullies. With no suggestion to this group that David had 'grassed' on them, the teacher produced the following line of enquiry. The following questions and comments act as a guide:

- A statement to the group that she knows that David has been having a hard time and that other teachers have noticed.
- What have you noticed?
- What do you know about the treatment he has been subjected to?
- The dialogue continues to encourage the boys to understand what it would be like for David to be treated unkindly.
- What do you suggest we do about it?

  > Obtaining suggestions from the group for how things might be different for David in the future.
  > If we meet again next week you can tell me about what you have been doing to make life different for David.

- When the following meeting took place the boys were able to report that they had been kinder to David. Separately David was able to report that the taunting and aggression had been eliminated. He was much relieved.

Figure 5.3 shows a number of areas of work that can be considered, prioritized and acted upon. We suggest the topic 'Awareness Raising Among Pupils' to show the kind of ideas that can be generated to heighten pupil understanding (see Figure 5.4). Each of the areas of work can be treated in a similar way.

Figure 5.3: Bullying: action planning — a whole school approach

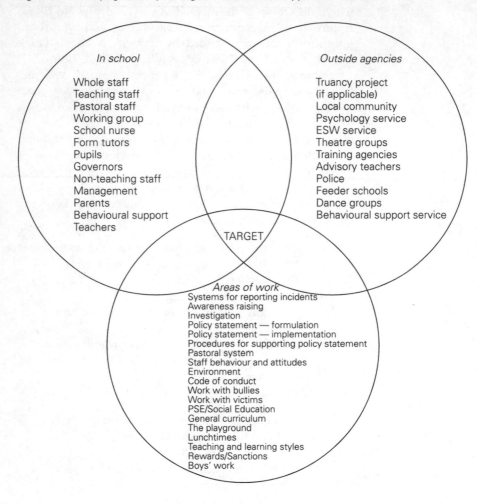

In school

Whole staff
Teaching staff
Pastoral staff
Working group
School nurse
Form tutors
Pupils
Governors
Non-teaching staff
Management
Parents
Behavioural support
Teachers

Outside agencies

Truancy project
(if applicable)
Local community
Psychology service
ESW service
Theatre groups
Training agencies
Advisory teachers
Police
Feeder schools
Dance groups
Behavioural support service

TARGET

Areas of work
Systems for reporting incidents
Awareness raising
Investigation
Policy statement — formulation
Policy statement — implementation
Procedures for supporting policy statement
Pastoral system
Staff behaviour and attitudes
Environment
Code of conduct
Work with bullies
Work with victims
PSE/Social Education
General curriculum
The playground
Lunchtimes
Teaching and learning styles
Rewards/Sanctions
Boys' work

The Session

I feel better at standing up for myself. (Student quote)

Using Psychodramatic Methods in the Investigation of a Bullying Relationship

I work with boys in a secondary school setting. The school is an inner-city comprehensive in Derby and has a school student population of different races. My concern and motivation around working with boys centres on the way social norms and peer pressure within schools conspire to produce a restrictive male stereotype as a norm. Boys are complex and contradictory and find it difficult to acknowledge their fears, insecurities, joys and happiness with others

Figure 5.4: *An example of a topic that can be used to maintain or top up the anti-bullying approach*

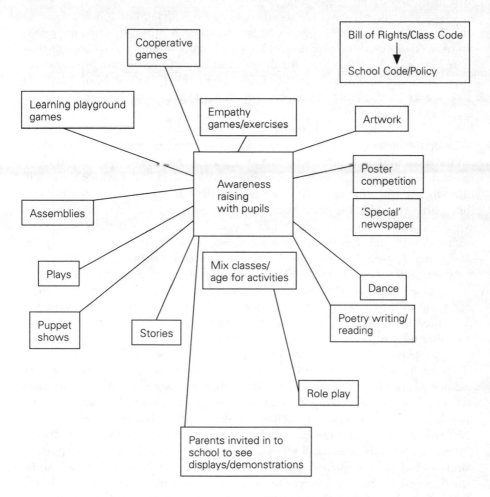

in their social group. There is a real fear of being seen as less than manly which will lead to taunts, teasing and physical intimidation. By such means the 'top dogs' in any year group police the boundaries of what is acceptable 'real lad' behaviour. My work with all boys' groups has been about building up an atmosphere of trust so that boys can begin to share their vulnerabilities, fears and gentler qualities without the ridicule that such self-disclosure would bring if it were expressed in corridor, street corner, playing field or changing room.

One of the topics that is prominent in boys' minds is bullying. It is unusual for boys of secondary school age to not experience some form of bullying during their school life, either as victim or bully. I feel it is particularly important for boys to look honestly at the bullying phenomenon and the desire to control and intimidate which is the function of bullying. After all, a lot of conventional masculinity is about power and control of others — particularly women and marginalized weaker or gay men.

My sessions with boys are about working on bullying but also encouraging the boys to show more of their feelings towards each other. It seems important to try to tie-in work on showing feelings with work around the feelings engendered by bullying. I was keen for the boys to begin to recognize what goes on in a bullying relationship, not only from the point of view of being paralysed into silence by the bully but also by beginning to recognize how much of the bully exists in all of them.

This particular boys' group has been together on other activities for about four or five weeks. I suggest that we do some exercises which will help them all to be less inhibited with each other. We stand in a circle and pretend to chew gum. I realize someone really is chewing gum and decide the whole thing will not work if that is the case. The gum goes in the bin. I am a little self-conscious but plunge in with the instruction to chew gum. I start exercising my jaws vigorously, the boys nervously follow my lead. 'The gum's getting bigger; it's more difficult to chew. Really work those jaws.' Two boys stop chewing altogether. I sense their shyness. I feel my own embarrassment. I move round to them and encourage them. We try other qualities of gum and continue to chew in a variety of different ways. They are enjoying the experience now. I tell them to throw their gum away but somehow it gets stuck to their fingers and then stuck to each other as the circle dissolves into a curiously stuck together mass of bodies. They like it. They say so. I am relieved.

Straightaway we move into other games of feeling. Walking as the leader does, each takes a turn to do a funny walk. Some are more expressive than others. We walk over broken glass, through raw sewerage and over hot coals with each of the boys taking the lead. With some groups we also moved around like kangaroos, monkeys and elephants, making appropriate noises. We had fun and shared a sense of enjoyment before moving into a very strictly controlled 30 second brainstorm in small groups. All the feeling words they could possibly think of had to be written down in that short time. On completion I asked the small groups of three to go away to plan a very short mime showing one of the feelings on their sheet. They were to perform it in front of all the others and then stay 'on stage' to receive guesses and comments about what was going on. On this afternoon all four groups spontaneously came up with scenarios which centred around violence, intimidation and fear.

As a group we discuss what is happening within the room, what has changed the mood of hilarity and shared enjoyment around feeling foolish together which came from the warm-up exercises. What has happened to the mimes which might have been — those centred on feelings of happiness, excitement, caring and love? 'It's easier to do ones about violence.' 'We're more familiar with that.' 'It's all around us anyway.' These three remarks sum up the chilling atmosphere which has descended. I sense that the boys wish it was not like this. I reflect back my concern and am greeted with shrugs of 'that's how it is'. 'What can we do about it?' My sense of eternal optimism revives and

I suggest that here in this room we can certainly look at other ways of coping with threats, intimidation and violence and that perhaps we can offer some advice on how to cope with all this within the school. We take leave of each other for this session with a final question about what word can be given to what has been described in the mimes and in the group's discussions which followed. For the first time the word 'bullying' was mentioned and acknowledged.

For the second session on bullying, I have decided to use the boys' own experiences of bullying in their lives to explore what is really going on in the dynamic that exists between bully and victim.

I have great respect for the psychodramatic method. I believe in its ability to provide insight, clarity of expression, a sense of being in another's shoes, and its capacity for integration of new 'behaviours' into participants' role repertoires. Above all, psychodramatic method is appropriate for enabling people to show and explore the life situations which are relevant to them. I felt that short dramatic role-plays using students' own bullying experiences would help new ways of functioning to be expressed, clarified and integrated into personal practice.

The boys assemble and we talk briefly about the last session. I suggest that we do some role-plays but that first of all it would be a good idea to get into pairs to talk about an experience of bullying which has happened to them or for which they might have been responsible. Such a warm-up produced a restlessness and a flight from the task which proved disruptive, but eventually most of the boys have something in mind however small.

The question 'Who wants to go first?' brings to the fore the most warmed-up boy in the group. It is Alan who is 15 years old, round faced, overweight and outwardly cheerful. He enjoys being the centre of attention but is anxious and fearful. He admits to the group that he is worried about what he is going to do.

I am going to facilitate the work Alan is going to do and as such I need to take care with him to ensure that he feels safe. We spend some time talking about trust, checking out what he needs from the other boys that will help him and also, of course, getting an understanding that it is really OK for me to help him. I tell Alan that my job is to look after him and that the bit of his world we will be looking at that afternoon will have my entire attention. I sense him become calmer. He calls me 'safe' and taps me appreciatively on the shoulder. I feel it necessary to tell him that whatever his story is he will have the central role but also have the experience of seeing what it will be like to play other people in his drama. In that way he will be able to understand what is going on in the minds of anyone else who is part of his story.

We have already defined our stage area. The only two people in that space are Alan and myself. I encourage Alan to tell me the background to the incident. He tells everyone about Steve Taylor who bullies him. It is not consistent bullying but it happens from time to time with varying intensity. It is bad at the moment. I suggest that he stops being Alan for a moment and becomes Steve Taylor instead. I take care that Alan changes position on the stage area. As director, I use the interview technique to find out information about Steve Taylor. Alan finds it difficult to stay in role but we persevere together. The dialogue goes as follows (I have simplified this slightly because there were times when Alan had to be reminded of the role he was playing):

Teacher as director (D): Hello Steve. Tell us something about yourself.

Alan (in role as Steve) (A): What do you want to know?

D: How old are you?

A: 14

D: How long have you known Alan?

A: All the time we've been at this school.

D: What is it about Alan that you don't like?

A: Well he's always messing about. He bugs me.

D: Is there anything you like about Alan?

A: Sometimes he's alright but he's always messing around. He doesn't show me respect.

D: You deserve respect then Steve?

A: Oh yeah — it's important. (As Steve, Alan puffs out his chest and tries to look hard and virile.)

I bring Alan back as himself and ask him to pick someone in the group to be Steve. He finds this difficult. I have to resist those who want to volunteer saying that it is very important for Alan to choose because he will know who is the right person. This doesn't stop Mark from lying on the floor begging to be chosen. I begin to wonder whether this is a good idea. I decide to persist. Eventually John is chosen. Immediately, without prompting, he starts to act hard and aggressive. I get him to sit down again and watch carefully because Alan is going to tell us the incident and create where it was in real life.

Alan tells us that the incident occurred on Monday after school. He was going home. He was on his own. He was going down the jitty (alley way) towards Bedford Street and there was Steve Taylor with two of his mates.

D: Who are the mates?

A *(in role as himself)*: Michael and Leon.

D: Are they important in what happens?

A: Yes, it just made it all the more difficult.

D: Tell us three things about Michael.

A: He's stupid, sometimes he's a laugh and he's a big friend of Steve Taylor.

D: What about Leon?

    A: He's the same — sometimes he can be a real idiot, other times he's alright. They both do what Steve says — well not all the time.

    D: Alan, pick two people to play Leon and Michael.

It was important for Alan to play or talk about the significant people in his drama since it was a way in which he was being warmed-up to dramatic action and also encouraging him to be in another reality as another person or object. This latter was to be important as part of the scene setting.

    D: Can you show us what happens in the scene?

Alan starts telling us again. I stop him and ask him to create the jitty. He tells of the narrowness and the high hedges on either side. I ask him to create the sense of narrowness. I suggest that he picks boys to be the hedges and that the sense of narrowness and height is accurately created. This emphasizes the importance of full scene setting. It not only helps to create the atmosphere in Alan's mind, but also means that the full scene is present when it might really be needed later in the drama.

I suggest that someone else becomes Alan for a moment so that he, Alan, can become part of the high hedge looking down at Alan in the jitty. This proves a little difficult but Alan, as the high hedge, was able to say that Alan was always a bit worried about it all seeming so closed in and there being nowhere to go.

Alan comes back to being himself and I ask him where Steve, Michael and Leon are in this scene. He says they are waiting at the end of the jitty and he thinks they are waiting for him.

    D: Show us what happens. Speak your thoughts as you enter the jitty.

    A: Walks casually towards the entrance to the jitty. He says he is feeling alright but as he turns the corner he thinks — oh dear, what's going to happen now? I've seen them here before — perhaps it will be OK. A bit of me wants to go another way but they'll think I'm scared. I can't stop now. Perhaps it really will be OK.

I stop the action and ask him who speaks first. Alan tells me that Steve does. I explain to Alan about role reversal so that he will become Steve and Steve will become Alan. I reverse them, encouraging Alan to say what Steve had said and done.

    A (in role as Steve):   Hey — look who's here. It's that twat. Let's get him. (He starts running towards Alan.)

I tell Alan to go back into role as himself. Steve repeats the words he has just heard Alan give him. Alan shows what happened next, and turns to get out of the way. I encourage him to tell us what he is feeling at this point.

> A: Oh god — they'll get me. I can't run. It'll just make it worse. Just turn away and run when you're round the corner. It's too late.

Steve catches up with him and starts kicking him. At this point I have to be cautious since there is a temptation on the part of the boys to really kick Alan. I slow the whole thing down to slow motion and allow kicks to just miss Alan's legs.

> D: What are you feeling now?
> A: I'm pissed off, frightened, I don't know how to get away. I hate him. What's he picking on me for?

With this question, I decide to role reverse Alan with Steve again.

> S *(in role as Alan)*: What's he picking on me for?
> A *(in role as Steve)*: 'Cos he's there, 'cos he's a fat twat, 'cos he's a pain, 'cos he cheeks me.

Alan *(in role as himself)* hears this again delivered by Steve.

> D: What do you want to do about this Alan?
> A: I want to stop it. It's not fair. I want to tell him to stop. (Alan is getting angry as he speaks and his finger starts jabbing away. He seems frustrated at his powerlessness.)
> D: This has been going on for a long time hasn't it?
> A: Yes
> D: What are Michael and Leon doing while you're being kicked?
> A: They're just there — laughing. I hate them too.

I suggest that Alan role reverses with one of them, and Alan picks Michael.

> D: As Michael, tell us what is going on for you while Steve is terrorizing Alan.
> A *(in role as Michael)* It's funny isn't it. I think everything's a laugh. Well I don't think so really — it's just that . . . what can I do? If I try and stop him he'll pick on me. I don't want that.

D: (*Brings Alan back to being himself.*) It's difficult being Michael and Leon isn't it?

A: Yes, but they shouldn't do it. It's him really. I really hate him.

I notice that Alan is becoming particularly enlivened. His hands and arms are twitching, his body and bearing seem somehow ready for action. I sense that he really wanted to express the frustration, fear and anger about being bullied. There was a real sense of 'this shouldn't have happened to me'. I offer him the opportunity to be angry with Steve and to tell him what he really thinks about what is happening to him. In so doing, Alan will be trying out a new form of expression in a real situation. I check out whether he thinks he needs any help. He assures me he doesn't.

We go immediately into the scene then and there while Alan is able to be angry with Steve and utilize some of his inner power to help him. I felt it important that he do two things here. Firstly to be angry and secondly to be clear about his anger being focused on Steve's behaviour — that is what actually Alan doesn't like and rejects. Alan proves able to be abusively angry. He rails vehemently at Steve with plenty of pointing, popping eyes and aggressive body stance. He finds it difficult to separate Steve from Steve's behaviour but shows a determined effort to be angry with the behaviours Steve displays which so hurt and frighten him.

When his anger has subsided, I ask Alan how he feels. He says that he feels much better: 'It feels good to say all that.'

D: Do you think that Steve really heard you?

A: He'd better have done.

D: Shall we find out?

I put Alan into the role of Steve and ask Steve to become Alan. The auxiliary (in role as Alan) is then encouraged to repeat some of the words and phrases he has just heard using similar tone and volume. He does so.

On completion, I interview Alan in role as Steve asking him what he is feeling: 'I can tell he means it. You can't ignore him.' Then I reverse Alan back to himself and ask Michael and Leon how they felt. They reply that they've never heard Alan like that before. All three, Steve, Michael and Leon, seem quietened by the experience. The rest of the audience, restless at first, have become rivetted and absorbed by the brief drama enacted for them. I suggest that we get back into a circle to look at experiences this has brought up for other people.

This sharing brings out others who have been bullied by persistent name-calling, violence, threats of violence or extorting money. Those who shared felt they couldn't do anything about it and wished that at the time they could have been like Alan. Alan joined in and said that he wished he could be like that with his older brothers and that they would listen to him. (The possibility of more work here?)

In the final minutes I try to focus on two aspects of bullying.

1 What do the group think bullies are really doing when they pick on people?
2 What do the group think is a good way of dealing with bullies?

I ask audience and players to draw on their experience of what they have seen this afternoon and other work we have done to suggest what it is that makes a bully? 'They've been bullied. Perhaps they have a hard time at home,' says Zaheer. 'I think they get threatened a lot. They learn that's how to get their own way. They're weak really.' I ask the boy who played Steve to see if he thought any of that would fit. He shared from his own life that he often called people names. He had begun to recognize that it was a way of making sure no-one thought he was a 'poofter or a queer'. John shared that it was easier for him to give money to people who threatened him because then he would be safe. S said that was rubbish, 'cos they just go on asking for more. You've got to stop it somehow.' 'Why don't we just beat up bullies?' I said. 'It wouldn't do any good. It doesn't make Steve Taylor any better', came the reply. 'What needs doing with Steve Taylor?' I ask. There are still those who want to beat him up so that he stops. Robert says that if you beat up bullies it just shows that beating people up works. I think this is brilliant and say so — the rest of the class respond. Someone says 'Don't forget bullies have got problems too.' 'Who can you take all this to?' I ask. There is some reluctance now to draw some obvious conclusions. It seems that no-one wants to be the first to say tell a teacher.

I summarize where I think we have got to. The group agrees that lots of bullies must have problems at home and they like power and want friends. The boys in role, Michael and Leon, acknowledge that they were there partly because they were worried what Steve would do if they went against him — so they were his mates.

The group understand that bullying, wherever it occurs, is wrong but I think part of them are still saying things like, 'So what if his Dad let's him — what can I do about it?' Someone breaks the deadlock with,

> He needs help. It's not just the one who are bullied but it's the bully as well. You've got to tell a teacher or a youth club worker or some-body.

> A teacher can talk to him to find out what it's all about — that might help or in any case it might stop people being bullied.

What can be done to try to make bullies feel better about themselves? First reactions were fairly negative here. Remarks about teachers talking to the bully were as far as the group would think. I decided to question the boy who had played Steve. What did he think was at the bottom of all this. It was a risky question and it might have fallen flat. 'Steve' said he needed decent attention so that he felt valued. He felt he was just covering everything up with the bullying. In conclusion I asked Steve how he would sum it all up — 'I need to be important in good ways. I just want a bit of proper attention.'

With this the bell went and no-one moved which was most unusual. I sensed that this had been a very valuable experience — above all it had been the boys who had done the work and made the connections. There had been a real interest and the whole session had not been troubled by disruptive, 'bored' behaviour which had sometimes been a problem in this group in the past.

Postscript

Approximately six months later I conducted a short interview with Alan about what he had held onto from the session we had done. He said that he now knew how to cope better with bullying. The most important thing he remembered from the work he had done was that bullies had problems too and that he realized that he provoked people like Steve Taylor. What Alan has done he says is to not act as silly as he now realizes he used to and also to hang on to the fact that he has some power and he doesn't have to put up with treatment like that. 'I feel better at standing up for myself.'

Classroom Strategies

Violence and Bullying

In our approaches to violence and bullying it is important to have a broad general sympathy for all who are bullied and also an understanding of what prompts bullying behaviour. But it's also important to point out that much of the work on bullying has been gender blind particularly around boys' involvement. What has been missed is the way in which boys use violence and bullying as part of the struggle to become more masculine in a male-dominated culture. It is about the way many boys try desperately to reassert power and mastery over events and others in a situation where they feel increasingly weak and vulnerable. It is not about violence as an inborn warrior instinct that boys can do nothing about. There is a link between power and vulnerability in boys' lives — about how they try to get their own way to counter their fears about their anxiety, dependency and a sense of their own weakness.

Our strategies encourage work on vulnerability, hence the exercises that help boys begin to acknowledge their own feelings and frustrations and feel supported in that. Other activities encourage boys to confront the aspects of themselves which use power games and controlling behaviour as an expectation of getting their own way at whatever cost.

129

Feelings Brainstorm

Aim: *To discover and name feelings.*

Materials: *Large sheets of paper and felt-tip pens*

Time: *5 minutes*

What to do:

In groups of four or five boys, ask them to write down all the feelings they can think of in a strict 30 seconds.

Count up how many feelings they have come up with.

Each group reads them out. Make sure everyone understands all the words.

Feelings Mimes

Aim: *To express and communicate feeling.*
             To practise recognizing particular feelings.

Materials: *None*

Time: *20 minutes*

What to do:

It is important to have done a feelings brainstorm first. Divide the group into pairs, certainly no more than threes. Each pair choses one of the feelings without letting anyone else know their choice. The idea is to prepare a mime centred on their feeling. Inevitably the mime will tell some sort of story, but the main aim is to show the feeling at the heart of the situation.

The pairs perform their mime, the rest of the group act as the audience. The audience has to guess the feelings on display. At the conclusion of the short performance, the performers receive the comments, guesses and suggestions from the audience.

Role Play

Aims: To explore one-to-one situations and behaviour.
            To find out what makes bullying behaviour.

Materials: Role-play cards, prepared using the statements below

Time: 45 minutes

What to do:

This work follows the work done on feelings. The group is to form into pairs to role-play one of the situations on the role-play cards. Here are a number of suggestions for presenting the message of each role play.

1. It is tempting to simply ask each pair to perform a short, snappy playlet with dialogue. This is always popular. It is fun, easy to understand, but does not make the audience think about what is really going on.

2. Miming key moments in the scene is interesting because it makes the actors choose exactly what they want to show. They have to focus very carefully on expression, posture and gesture. The whole story has to be presented in three or four still scenes, held in a freeze frame sculpt for a few seconds at a time. (A freeze frame sculpt is imagining that you are having your photograph taken and you are frozen into a picture of how you feel about each other or the group.) The audience has to work hard to guess what the feelings are that are being shown. They need to ask questions and really participate.

3. Groups could also mime the whole scene. Again they have to devise ways of showing status, age, sex, and relationships between the people. They also have to show the situation and the feelings. As in the frozen key moments (above) the audience has to get involved to find out what is happening.

4. An important variation of the mimes above is to perform the piece and have the problem identified. When this is concluded, ask a friend of either character to intervene and sort the drama out to some kind of resolution. The friend can bring speech into the drama to engage in dialogue with either or both of the parties to resolve the crisis that exists between them.

5. Key questions to ask as a summary of what has been done might include:

    • What is happening in all these mimes?
    • What makes each of them similar?
    • Do any of the mimes remind you of incidents that have happened to you or that you have witnessed?

- What word would you put on the type of behaviour on display in each scene?

The statements:

- An elder brother trying to get his younger brother to do his maths homework for him.
- A teacher ordering a boy out of the room for something the child didn't do.
- A boy in Year 9 getting a younger boy to give him money.
- A boy teasing one of his friends about the trainers he is wearing.
- A teacher and a boy who keeps on forgetting his homework.
- A boy who makes rude remarks in class to a clever girl who is sitting in front of him. She ignores him.
- A boy insisting that he and his sister watch the TV programme that he wants to watch.
- A boy in Year 7 telling his father that he daren't go to school because there are too many boys ganging up on him.

How Did You Feel? What Did You Do?

Aim: To get in touch with your own feelings in different situations.

Materials: Copies of 'How Did You Feel? What Did You Do?' sheets, prepared using the questions below

Time: 45 minutes

What to do:

Ask each member of the group to complete the questionnaires as honestly as possible.

On completion ask the pupils to find a partner with whom they can share some of the situations, experiences and feelings.

Come back together as a whole group to share any feelings and common experiences.

The questions:

1.   When was the last time that you were worried?
     How did you feel?
     What did you do?
2.   When was the last time that you were scared?

How did you feel?

What did you do?

3. When was the last time that you were really proud of something you did?

How did you feel?

What did you do?

4. When was the last time that you felt very sad?

How did you feel?

What did you do?

5. When was the last time that you felt very happy?

How did you feel?

What did you do?

6. When was the last time that someone came to you with their troubles?

How did you feel?

What did you do?

7. When was the last time that you were angry?

How did you feel?

What did you do?

8. When was the last time that you spent time with a small child?

How did you feel?

What did you do?

9. When was the last time that you cried?

How did you feel?

What did you do?

Friends and Enemies

Aim: To discover the give and take of friendship and the nature of enmity.

Materials: Paper and pens
              'Friends' and 'Enemies' sheets prepared using the questions below

Time: 50 minutes

What to do:

Ask the group to complete the 'Friends' and 'Enemies' sheets and to do the writing involved with it. On completion share the stories with a friend in a pair or small group.

A variation from writing stories of friends or enemies would be to perform a mime to illustrate the nature of your friendship and enmity or to set up a freeze frame sculpt to illustrate the same qualities.

The questions:

Friends

Which of the following statements about 'friends' do you agree with?

A friend is . . .

1. Someone I can be angry with and they don't stop being my friend.
2. Someone who is always on my side, whatever I do.
3. Someone who does what I say.

Write down what you want your best friend to be like.

Enemies

Which of the following statements about 'enemies' do you agree with?

An enemy is . . .

1. Someone I don't feel bad about hurting.
2. Someone I want to be friends with, who doesn't want to be friends with me.
3. Someone who is different — not the same as me.

Have you ever had enemies? Write down a short story about an enemy you have had.

Who Has the Power?

Aim: *To recognize our own power and acknowledge the nature of the power others have over us.*

Materials: *Paper and felt-tip pens*
'Who Has the Power' worksheets, prepared using the questions below

Time: *45 minutes*

What to do:

Group discussion about our own power. Ask each member of the group to describe their own power. Hopefully from this will come power of mind, body and personality.

Write about your own power. Tell the story of how powerful you are. Secure in the knowledge of your power, move on to look at who has power over you.

As a whole group discuss those who have power over you and how they use their power. Move on to answer the 'Who Has the Power?' question sheet.

Follow up any examples where students question the nature of the power that some people have over them. Use the group to provide support and assistance.

The questions:

1. Who has power over me?
2. What power do they have?
3. Do they use their power in a good way?
4. What power do they NOT have?
5. Look at question 4 again. Does anybody have that power over you?

How Does Bullying Make You Feel?

Aim: *To enable students to focus on the feelings surrounding bullying.*

Materials: *Use of bullying video, or bullying posters*
              Paper and felt-tip pens

Time: *50 minutes*

What to do:

Either use a commercially produced bullying poster or ask the boys to produce a poster which shows the impact of being bullied. Alternatively any of the videos available on bullying in schools could be used to raise awareness levels.

Whichever way you choose, ask students to form groups of three or four. Give out paper for a brainstorm. On one side of the paper write the word 'Bully', on the other 'Bullied'. Brainstorm words and phrases associated with the feeling of being bullied. Take two minutes. Then do the same thing for feelings associated with being a bully. Take two minutes.

Students use the brainstorms to share their own experiences of bullying and being bullied. This can be followed by a discussion on why people bully or get bullied including social situations such as racism, pressure to win or achieve, not to be seen as weak, etc.

Finally, the brainstorms and shared information from the discussions can be used to produce a group poem (in the original brainstorm groups) or a personal poem about an aspect of bullying.

Have You Ever?

Aim: To ask the boys to acknowledge personal experience of bullying.

Materials: Paper and pens
             'Have You Ever . . . ?' question sheets, prepared using questions below

Time: 30 minutes

What to do:

Give the boys copies of the 'Have You Ever . . . ?' question sheets. Ask them to complete the yes/no part of the questionnaire.

Ask them to pick the situation which most touches them. They can write about it in story form or alternatively the boys can form pairs to share each others' experiences.

The questions:

Have you ever . . .

1. sided with a group that was picking on someone?
2. sided with someone who was being picked on by a group?
3. teased someone younger than you again and again?
4. answered back at someone who was teasing you?
5. used force to get your own way?
6. stopped being friends with someone because nobody else was friends with them?
7. started being friends with someone unpopular?
8. sent someone to 'Coventry', i.e., totally ignored someone by not talking to them/blanked them?

Now choose the question you find the most interesting. Write as much as you can about how this question applies to you.

The Bully Circle

Aim: To share experiences of bullying situations to realize how powerful the group is.

Materials: None

Time: 45 minutes

What to do:

The bully circle needs plenty of preparatory work in the form of trust building exercises because good class trust is essential for this session. The classroom is organized into a tight circle of chairs. One of them is empty. In this chair sits a bully. He is not really there but he is going to exist in that chair in everyone's imagination. The facilitator/teacher asks everyone to focus on the chair and asks questions of this type:

- What does the bully look like?
- What sex?
- What size?
- What is the bully wearing?

Each question allows an opportunity for those in the circle to voice an experience of a real bully:

- What has this bully done?
- What happened?
- How did you feel?
- What happened next?

If the bully seems to be becoming a very big figure:

- Why are we afraid?
- How come he's so popular?
- Does he have any friends?
- What are they like?

By discussing these questions, it is possible that they begin to have to take group responsibility for the bully as a member of this group or a group of which they are a part.

Is there a way of solving our problem with this bully? Is there also a way of solving the bully's problem?

By now it is obvious that the bully's behaviour is not doing anyone any good. Thus strategies for dealing with the bully begin to be discussed.

- Is this problem too tricky to solve on our own?
- Can we get help from a teacher or parent?

In this way the discussion should hopefully begin to reduce the bully in size until he is just another member of their year group/or older. He is someone who has an image to aspire to.

The crucial stage of the bully circle arrives. The facilitator/teacher summarizes the problem and asks whether the group is going to leave it there. By this stage, the group should be very keen to do something about the bully. Encourage this mood by discussing what makes a bully and then offering advice about how a bully might change. What might you need to prevent you from being a bully?

(Most of the Classroom Strategies in this section are from the workshops accompanying the theatre presentation *Only Playing Miss* by Casdagli, P. Gobey, F. and Griffin C. (1990) and reproduced by permission of Trentham Books.)

Chapter 6

Media Education, Boys and Masculinities

The Theory

The Unofficial Curriculum

By the time [American] boys are eighteen, they have seen an average of twenty-six thousand television murders, a vast majority of them committed by men. (Myriam Miedzain, 1992)

School children in the industrialised countries spend an average of 24 hours every week watching television, nearly six hours listening to radio and music and three hours reading comics, newspapers, magazines and books. To these figures should be added cinema attendance and the increasing use of video. Roughly speaking, the 30-odd hours of weekly exposure to the mass media compares markedly with the 20-odd hours spent by children in the classroom. (World Communication Report, 1987)

These quotes and statistics show clearly how boy students' lives are deeply shaped by the media, particularly when schoolroom time is set against media exposure time. It's also important to recognize how television dominates other forms of the media. Neil Postman (1979) has convincingly argued that the media, and especially television, represents an unofficial curriculum. We believe that this secret curriculum is powerfully influential in providing a destructive masculinity training in the everyday lives of boys. This doesn't come about through accident. The media industry is tightly organized and it's big business. It makes a massive financial investment in researching and trying to expand its potential markets. It uses research evidence on consumers to target particular interest groups, like adolescent boys with Nintendo's promotion of video games like Streetfighter 1 and 2.

The Media as 'Macho Propaganda'

. . . the lads were surrounded by a macho propaganda more potent in its penetration of young men's hearts and minds than at any other time in history — they were soaked in globally transmitted images and ideologies of butch and brutal solutions to life's difficulties. (Campbell, 1993)

Young boys and men are growing up today in a culture of aggressive manliness. Their everyday worlds are bombarded by the superficially thrilling macho imagery of the Incredible Hulk, video games, Slasher films, fast car fantasies of the 1980's Peugeot 405 TV commercial variety where the car tears across dangerous country, leaving a charred trail of flaming cane fields behind it as a woman sings, 'Take my breath away'. There's also a tabloid press in Britain that often celebrates sporting heroes in terms of a fiercely militaristic/imperialist culture. English soccer players like Terry Butcher who put on a 'gutsy show' against Sweden in Stockholm in September 1989 — after having 13 stitches put in a head wound — are referred to as imperial warriors. Bobby Robson, the then England manager, commented on Butcher's performance in this way: 'People won VCs in the war for less than that. He was absolutely marvellous. It was a typical courageous performance that one expects from England skippers' (*Daily Express*, 7 September 1989).

This aggressive attack isn't just confined to the electronic and print media. It's also found in popular music, like in some rap music and Heavy Metal rock bands, like Led Zeppelin, Aerosmith, Thin Lizzie, Black Sabbath, Iron Maiden, etc. Here, on stage, male performers strut their stuff with 'jutting lips, fists forward in the air, back tilted forward, lower pelvis thrust out . . .' (Denski and Sholle, 1992).

Idealized, fantasy images of hypermasculine toughness, dominance and invulnerability are also seen in the action/adventure films of Stallone, Schwarzenegger and Mel Gibson. Even though the male stars are now engaged in softening their macho images, films like *Terminator* (James Cameron, 1984), *Lethal Weapon* (Richard Donner, 1987) and *Robocop* (Paul Verhoerven, 1987) invite adolescent boys to identify with their reassuring hard men/mechanical men fantasies (Campbell, 1993). These iron men heroes don't have dependency needs or awkward, unmanly feelings. Instead, they are proud to be pure men, without women or the threatening woman in themselves to confront. For example, Mel Gibson in *Lethal Weapon* (Richard Donner, 1987), on the brink of suicide, has only his manly pride in killing and shooting to cling onto:

Riggs (Mel Gibson):	I do it real good you know.
Murtaugh (Danny Glover):	Do what?
Riggs:	When I was 19 I did a guy in . . . from 1000 yards out . . . a rifle shot in high wind . . . may be 8 or even 10 guys in the world could have made that shot . . . it was the only thing I was ever good at . . .

No compassion is expressed here for his victim. There's no feeling for the act of killing another human being. Only boasting and competitive pride in the accuracy of his shooting are conveyed. The death of another human being is reduced to an emotionally distanced target practice. No wonder there are young boys out there who are learning, from a brutalized media, to detach their feelings from acts that damage and control other people's lives. Just think of the two 10-year-old boys who were responsible for the death of James Bulger, for example. There were probably many other reasons for James Bulger's death, but perhaps it's not too farfetched to see some kind of link between an aggressively macho media culture and the two boys' actions.

Although there isn't a direct brainwashing of boys' hearts and minds (more about that below), these pervasive models of traditional manliness in the media — constantly involved in fights, killings, car chases, acting hard and tough, and keeping cool — do act as a form of 'macho propaganda' working on the dreams, desires, pleasures and identities of adolescent boys, especially between the ages of 10–16.

Lacking any real economic power in the outside world (especially at a time of recession and unemployment), fearful of being thought of as unmanly, and often aware of their own physical puniness in contrast to the enticing promises of male authority and power in the media, many boys find these macho images and fantasies very appealing indeed. At a time of great insecurity and fear in their own lives, these boys dream about and passionately desire idealized models of strutting manhood that will reassure them about their future status as 'proper' boys and men. So these macho media images influence boys indirectly — at the level of their unconscious desires and pleasures.

For example, one of the authors can remember in the 1940s and 1950s in Britain how adverts for Charles Atlas body-building courses hooked up with his desire to have an ideal, manly body. The advert involved a contrast between a 'seven-stone weakling', a bully who scuffed sand in the 'weakling's' face and the bulging muscles of Charles Atlas. He felt weedy like the 'seven-stone weakling' and he desperately hungered, in a compensatory and protective way, for a Charles Atlas body that would defend him from being bullied by other boys. The advert played on his deep-seated anxieties and fears about being an inadequate boy and, as a result, he actually bought into the imaginary power promised by the idealized image of manhood, to the point of nearly filling in the form for the body-building course.

Confronting Gender Blindness

Boys and masculinities have traditionally been approached by media education as a taken-for-granted norm. The power- and gender-blindness surrounding boys and men has hidden them away from public view. It's only relatively recently, with the influence of feminist action and theory, that a more critical focus has emerged on the gendering and masculinizing of boys and men.

With this increasing gendered awareness, has developed the possibility of the social construction of boys and masculinities becoming a more explicit area of enquiry. In particular, the invisibility of white, heterosexual, middle-class boys and men is now in the process of being hauled into the light of critical scrutiny. The taken-for-grantedness of that privileged perspective is now being disrupted by the new emphasis on variety, difference and an awareness of the power relations between 'top dog' masculinities and more marginalized masculinities. The conventional notion of man equals human being has also been stirred up and shaken by the critical undermining of the seamless impression of unity, oneness and false universality. The hidden and more complex lives of black, gay, disabled and emotional men have begun to surface.

There's now an urgent priority to take these questionings further, and to more clearly contest 'macho propaganda' in the media. It's high time that critical media education work that interrogates and challenges these traditional models of manliness was developed more coherently and widely in schools, colleges and clubs up and down the country. The state of urgency comes from the power, pleasure and intensity of these images of enticement to speak directly to the unconscious desires of young, insecure males in this country. The immediate attractiveness of these macho heroes and stories — their dangerous, thrilling pleasures, their humour, their sense of heightened engagement — make the growing culture of aggressive manliness an increasingly dangerous threat to the lives of many boys and their victims, as the riots and disturbances of Bradford, Luton, Leeds and Sheffield can testify.

Deepening our Gendered Awareness of Traditional Models of Manliness in the Media

We can't go much further, however, if we don't deepen our gendered awareness of the usual ways men and boys are represented in the media today. Digging deeper means being more concrete and specific about what's wrong with these representations. To be clearer, we want to limit our focus on three, detailed media examples of 'macho propaganda' to give you a taste of what we mean. They are: beer ads; car advertising in magazines; and, male newsreaders on television.

Beer Ads

In a marvellously illuminating essay on beer ads, Lance Strate (1992) draws attention to the way the

> '. . . beer industry relies on stereotypes of the man's man to appeal to a mainstream, predominantly male target audience'. Although the immediate function of beer commercials and beer ads is to sell more beer, 'collectively the commercials provide a clear and consistent image of the masculine role'. He goes on to suggest the ads 'constitute a guide for becoming a man, a rule book for appropriate male behaviour, in short, a manual on masculinity'.

They do this by providing conventional answers to five, central questions about masculinity.

What kinds of things do the men do?

Beer drinking is represented as a key masculine activity, an activity that often defines masculine identity. It's rarely presented as an isolated activity but it's often linked to a variety of male occupational and leisure pursuits, all of which involve overcoming challenges.

Physical strength and manual labour are often stressed in these ads, as well as skill, patience and craftsmanship. In the business world, wit and competitive drive are also emphasized.

Beer is linked to the world of work in three ways: (a) in some commercials it's seen as the product of patient, skilful craftsmanship as in the 'Two barrels in the back of a taxi' ad by Theakston's best bitter, (b) beer serves as a reward for a job well done, and (c) beer acts as an indicator of the end of a working day.

In terms of leisure pursuits, men are usually seen being active in outdoor settings, involving some kind of danger or risk. In beer ads, men are frequently seen striving to gain mastery over nature, over technology, over others, often engaged in humorous horse-play and over oneself.

What kind of settings do men prefer?

Outdoor settings are most common in beer ads — usually natural, untamed environments that have to be conquered by men in order to survive. In this context, men are seen as rugged doers, adventurers and conquerors. Nature and animals are often associated with both masculinity and beer, like the wolf moving single-mindedly through inner-city decay towards its goal, in the Banks bitter 'Follow your instinct' ads.

The other major setting is the self-contained world of the bar. Inside the local pub is a popular setting in British beer ads, where 'real men' can bond with other men and find entertainment and excitement, often in a world without women.

How do boys become men?

In the world of beer ads, boys become men by earning acceptance from those men who seem to be already fully paid-up members of the male club. They do this through displaying their competence in doing the things that 'real men' do, like taking risks, meeting challenges, facing danger bravely and dominating their environments. After having proved themselves as 'proper men' they are then rewarded with beer. Take the Carling Black Label parody of an Australian lager ad, for example, where the young, male arrival from Britain has to face the challenge of the grinning monster spider in the isolated, shack toilet in order to gain acceptance and later defeat the older men's barroom challenge. Only, when he has earned his laurels, can he receive his well-earned reward.

Without any formal initiation rites to mark the transition from childhood to adulthood in men, beer-drinking often serves as a symbol of adulthood and manliness.

How do men relate to each other?

In beer ads men are mostly seen in groups. Teamwork, group loyalty and male bonding rank high in the list of traditional, masculine values. In direct contrast to this, men are rarely seen drinking alone, or in solitary pursuits.

Humour (joking, boasting, story-telling and good-natured insults), self-control and a refusal to show excessive emotion are some of the main qualities valued in men–men interactions. Gathering in groups gives men the support to act wildly and irresponsibly. The groups also provide a much needed audience to display and confirm one's masculinity.

How do men relate to women?

When beer ads do include women they are often there in the form of seductive challenges or sex objects. The presence of women also seems to threaten men with the loss of emotional self-control. To defend themselves against this threat, men must appear cool, detached and masterful around women.

In the most sexist beer ads, the secret of the seduction scene is persuading women to drink. The macho fantasy is that if a woman drinks she will lose her inhibitions and become sexually available.

In beer ads, women are rarely seen as active desirers, initiating action. Mostly, they are there as passively admiring onlookers to male action, or, at other times, posing as decorative sex objects. These male-defined women know their place and don't get in the way of male bonding.

Although beer ads have become more clever and sophisticated in Britain, involving complex parody, wit and often showing an ability to play with gender meanings (Boddington's beer 'Cream' commercials, June–November 1993), nevertheless Strate's argument (1992) is still richly suggestive. Try applying his critical understandings to beer ads like Castlemaine 4X, Carling Black Label, Banks Bitter, Murphy's etc and see for yourself how many of his points are still valid.

Car Advertising in Magazines

Car culture and advertising in the 1990s is a site where 'real man' fantasies and desires for power are played out, especially on the terrain of fast performance cars.

An ideology of virile, heterosexual manliness is to be found in the advertising used in some of the glossy car magazines. For example, in the September

1990 edition of *Car* there was an ad for the new Ford Fiesta RS Turbo that reads:

> How hot do you like your hatch?
>
> The XR2-i has deservedly made a name for itself as the most potent Fiesta on the road.
>
> Now it's about to be overtaken by a new Fiesta — the RS Turbo. With the combined muscle of a Garrett TO2 turbocharger unit and a 133 DIN Ps engine, the RS Turbo scorches from zero to 60 mph in 7.7 seconds.
>
> And you can push it (at any rate, on your own private road) to a top speed of 127 mph.
>
> In keeping with this hot-blooded performance, the styling is appropriately cool. Note the unique alloy wheels and the low profile tyres, the body-coloured bumpers and rear spoiler, the dark green moulding inserts and the bonnet extractor vents . . .

Here, the reader is bombarded by words with a physical attack. Words like 'hot', 'potent', 'muscle', 'scorches', 'push' assault the reader's attention. This car culture world is clearly a heavily gendered one where it seems natural to thrust and compete with vigour.

Looked at more closely, the links between fast performance car possession and the enticing promise of virile manliness are firmly established. The suggestion that car ownership (or symbolic ownership and conquest in terms of young, male joy-riders) entails a sexual and material power is loudly announced throughout the ad. The imagery of heat and strength are used as ways of associating the car's punchy performance with the masculine fantasy of full-blooded, heterosexual conquest. The implication is that your masculine potency (however shaky in reality) can be built and confirmed through your association with such a 'hot hatch'.

To deepen the resonance of this promise of virile sophistication, there are further references to physical strength ('muscle'), competitiveness ('overtake', 'push it') and individuality ('unique', 'distinctive'). And there's also an emphasis on the connection between socially assured forms of masculinity and detailed technical know-how about engines, and intricate facts about speed and performance and internal and external fittings.

Male Newsreaders on Television

The news media seems so matter of fact and neutral that we are hardly aware that it has been put together to favour male interests. We sit in front of our television sets every day and everything seems so natural and inevitable. But looked at more closely the male domination of the news media becomes clear.

That domination starts with the numerical superiority of men over women in the organization and production of the news media. Of top management positions in the US news media, 94 per cent are taken by men (Lee and Solomon, 1990). But it doesn't end there.

One of the central ways male supremacy has been able to perpetuate itself in areas like news media is through establishing a dominant definition of what counts as serious, hard news. This has been achieved in four ways:

1 *The visual frame of the male newsreader*

The calm, rational authority of male newsreaders on television is achieved through selectively limiting the visual frame to a 'head and shoulders image' (Holland, 1987). Viewers have come to expect 'serious' news to be public, rational and objective — a 'head and shoulders' knowledge, if you like. That visual frame has become a traditionally gendered one in that the visual image of the head and shoulders fit into the male-defined version of the news as rational knowledge within the public realm.

The appearance of assurance and power of the male newsreader has been built at the expense of marginalized women. The calm, authoritative, rationality of this masculine version of the news is defined in opposition to the traditional, gendered expectation of women as decorative sex objects to look at, who are emotional and who are mainly associated with the domestic sphere. (Within the 'head and shoulders' frame, the significant absence of women's bodies and legs have a disturbing resonance for many male viewers when women are reading the news.) As a result, women newsreaders, although their numbers have increased over the years, don't carry the same traditional authority and seriousness as male newsreaders do.

Women's right to be respectfully listened to is undermined by the tantalizingly hidden presence of their bodies and legs as traditionally sexualized beings. That's why women newsreaders, like Anna Ford, are systematically trivialized and cut down to sexist size through male responses like this:

> Could I suggest that Miss Ford cut out the frosty lipstick and shiny blush-on which makes my screen look wet and slippery.
> (A letter in the *Daily Express*, 5 July 1978)

2 *The choice of subjects*

News is only thought to be serious when it's about the world of hard politics. So a male-defined view of what is newsworthy means that the public world agenda of politics, industry, international affairs, economics and defence usually take precedence over the subordinated world of domestic/social issues. Domestic issues, like how do we bring up our sons, are seen as 'soft', associated with women, and so usually down-played.

What is being left out of the news are the everyday emotions, longings, desires, grief and loss of our lives. And also important questions like: how do men deal with the traumatizing shock of unemployment, compulsory retirement and homelessness? How do men deal with a world where the traditional security of being a breadwinner and pro-vider is being rapidly eroded? How do men approach housework and childcare in a world of changing partnerships and families? All these questions are being silenced or ignored.

3   *Commentators on the news*

The news media is interpreted by 'expert' commentators and it's done almost exclusively by men. The areas where women commentators appear are again, predictably, the domestic and social terrains, like health, education, caring concerns, religion, family and children. The high-status world of hard politics and international affairs is seen as the sole property of men.

But as Croteau and Hoynes (1992) make clear, we're talking about a certain type of man who has regular access to the major news media. The ideal, male commentator is an 'elite, white man' who isn't publicly critical of the social/political status quo. These men are likely to be 'government officials, professionals, or corporate representatives' and they also exhibit 'a high degree of machismo or toughness when inter-preting the events of the day'. Not for them the complicated social skills of negotiation, careful listening or conciliation. Rather, they believe in tough talking, consistently advocating 'brutal solutions to life's difficul-ties', as Beatrix Campbell has pointed out.

4   *The myth of objectivity*

The news media mainly sanctions a narrow, male-defined world-view through the myth of objectivity. News media validate their authority to speak for all of us through giving an impression of detachment, neutrality and impartiality. They want to remove themselves from the many clashes and collisions that occur over different values, interests and emotions in the actual world. In doing this they construct a privileged perspective for themselves based on the illusion that their viewpoint is more trustworthy and authoritative than anybody else's.

These myths of neutrality and objectivity are linked to a masculine world-view. Many men in the media and elsewhere have a vested interest in maintaining a certain level of abstraction and detachment in the public sphere. Their power and privilege is achieved through detached rationality being accepted as the only source of valid, serious knowledge. So men create an authoritative presence on the television screen though projecting an unruffled, unflappable image. As viewers, we see a formal jacket and tie, a head and shoulders world, and a grave, serious face. As Patricia Holland (1987) suggests, male newsreaders appear '. . . controlling and competent, grey-haired and unruffled'.

In practice, news media perpetuate these male myths through distancing themselves from emotionally committed, personal opinions, and calculating a spurious sense of balance between opposing viewpoints. They legitimize their own concealed viewpoints (white, elitist, patriarchal) though gaining confirmation from established authority and avoiding disruptively diverse viewpoints, in terms of race, class and gender.

The Changing Meanings of Masculinity

The overall picture is a bit more complex than we've made out so far. The images and meanings of masculinity don't just stay frozen for all time, but are very responsive to social and historical change. Even an established figure like Superman, in the comic books, is responsive to historical movements. Norma Pecora has commented that 'During each decade [in the USA], *Superman* comic books appeared to reflect the time: 1940s–1950s, isolationism and a quiet conservatism; 1960s, liberalistic and radicalization; 1970s, humanization; 1980s, political and social conservatism of the Reagan era' (Pecora, 1992).

Andrew Wernick (1987), in his essay 'From Voyeur to Narcissist' has also drawn attention to the historical shifts between the representation of men in the ads of the 1950s and the ads of the 1970s onwards. He shows the historical movement from the fixed family, male roles — breadwinner, provider — through to the current obsession with the 'single young exec, eternally in his thirties and dressed for success'. Alongside these movements has gone a shift from a version of masculine identity that defined itself through a traditional, heterosexist gaze (at women's legs for instance), to a changing and more fluid masculinity that itself can be defined as an object of desire.

As consumer capitalism in western, industrialized countries has tried to expand its markets, there has been a parallel attempt to open up traditional masculinity as a marketable object of narcissistic and other people's desire. To achieve these ends there has been a softening and feminizing of rugged masculinities as a way of constructing a masculine, consumer subject. Even an ad. for Nurofen (1994), a pain reliever, can feature a glossy, rippling man's back. It's one that's very much on display although he is also clutching his side in pain. Pain and pleasure are ambivalently intertwined here. This has given rise to fresh images of men who might buy a whole range of beauty care products, traditionally associated with women. Jan Moir, in an article in *The Guardian* (21 December 1994) comments that British men spent £212.6 million on aftershave and £145.1 million on fragrances and colognes in 1993. But extreme care has been needed. Many men are still frightened by the fear of unmanliness, in associating themselves with femininity. So in order to persuade men to buy these new products, a combination of old and new images of men have been brought together. The new images of men as sensitive and caring have had to co-exist with the reassuring, old images of 'real men'.

This mixture of softness and virility is seen clearly in the selling of men's fragrances and perfumes. Diane Barthel (1992) has wryly commented that, 'Men's fragrances need masculine-sounding names: Brut, Boss, English Leather, or Hero . . . They must convince the suspicious male that he can be both "romantico" and "virile".' Take the advertising promotion of Lynx, the men's body spray deodorant, for example. Making your body smell sweeter, a traditionally feminine activity, will only be considered by men if the product can also associate itself with manly virility. This it has tried to do through the phallic shape of the spray can (the screw top looks like a penile glans), the association of its name Lynx with a wild, ferocious predator and the TV commercials that have emphasized using the spray in a context of vigorous, sporting activity.

Along with this media focus on the caring, emotionally expressive 'New Man' (itself an invention by the media) has gone a much more conspicuous interest in men's bodies. Now the new rash of fashion and style magazines for men (*For Him, GQ, Arena, Esquire,* etc.) has given official permission to boys and men to take narcissistic pleasure in their own bodies.

However, under the glossy, slippery surface, men's social power and control are still very much there. Men's images are being modified to fit into the caring and sharing 1990s, that's what the media tell us, but institutional power inequalities remain much the same. New audiences are recruited in the black and gay communities but the structures of domination and subordination remain stubbornly there. Take two examples here. Black men have been targeted in body-building ads and their greater visibility looks promising but they are still being addressed in terms of the racist stereotype of savage, uncivilized beasts. One example focuses on black, working-class (unemployed?) masculinities in a muscle magazine called *Bodypower*. There's a bulging, black 'He-man' on the front cover. Black men are being invited to buy into the compensatory promise of being a powerful, muscle-rippling stud in a demoralizing social context where unemployment meets institutional racism. On the back cover (June 1991 edition) is an advert for 'hard core sports foods' that promise to improve 'big boys' bodies. A ferocious, Viking muscleman with his mouth thrown open in a snarling cry, wields an enormous axe that announces 'the big breakthrough' in body-building techniques. This ad is a deeply contradictory one. Black, British men are being denied self-respect and dignity through white racism. In circumstances where they are being hemmed in (economic powerlessness and dependency), some black men are turning to black macho behaviour — the association of the black, male body with toughness, force and aggression — as a way of recovering some kind of power and pride in humiliating conditions. The ad works on black men's desires for greater power and dignity in the real world. But they are sold a compensatory fantasy that brings together white racism (in the image of the savage, Viking beast) with aggressive, macho values.

Another advert uses a much more subtle approach. The Pioneer advert for Raleigh bikes (*Observer* magazine, 12 May 1991) 'for men and women', targets the new adventurous and independent desire in middle-class, white women produced by the second wave of the women's movement. This 'pioneer' spirit is set within the 'caring and sharing' ethos of the 1990s and a New Age environmentalist concern that seems to be blurring the traditional boundaries between 'masculine/feminine'. The scene is an inviting one. Two Pioneer bikes are propped against the large, stone blocks of a quiet, country place that offers a fine viewpoint over the dreamy surrounding woods and meadows. The two riders (a man and a woman) are in the middle of toasting the scene, perhaps for a reward for their physical exertion, with two glasses of wine, perched on the very edge of the stone blocks. They are celebrating their journey and the New Man is caught in the process of stealing the woman's hat and, jokingly, trying it out on his own head. The caption on the advert says, 'Share the pioneer spirit'. But beneath the surface impression of equality and sharing, the power relations of domination/subordination between the man and the woman remain the same as in a more traditional age. The New Man is in the old, supremacist position, standing up and looking down on the more passively seated woman. The only slight difference is that the man can retain his old privileges while, at the same time, enjoying the dissolving of some of the rigid boundaries between masculinity/ femininity both within and without. So here he can playfully try on the woman's straw hat. Superficially, the relations between men and women have been modernized and brought up to date but, structurally, the power imbalance endures.

Interrogating the Media: School Students as Active Meaning Makers

Sometimes the media is viewed in an over-deterministic way. It's falsely seen as an Evil Force exerting a massive, indoctrinating control over a faceless and gullible audience. What this leaves out is students' active, questioning struggles to make sense out of what they see in terms of their own social experience and usual ways of looking at the world.

Male students aren't just brainwashed by what they see, hear and read. They don't just swallow these media messages in a docile, passive manner but in fact play a very active part in creating meaning for themselves. This meaning-making process is a much more dynamic and participatory collaboration than having single, fixed meanings imposed on them from without. Meaning is made by students when they set up a dynamic negotiation that connects the special codes and conventions of the media messages *and* the psychological and social/ cultural baggage that they bring with them from their personal histories as viewers/readers/listeners (a varied mixture of gender, race, age, disability, religion, sexual orientation, etc.).

As a result, male students have a much more fluid and contradictory relationship with media images than is traditionally assumed. Recent media research has seen a developing awareness of diversity and difference in the ways students respond to media messages. There has been a broadening out of the range of meanings and pleasures different boys can get from the media. Just as *Dynasty* became a cult show amongst gay boys in the US, so it's not too far-fetched to imagine some heterosexual boys enjoying Julian Clary, or some finding pleasure and comfort in watching caring and compassionate male nurses like Charley and Ash in *Casualty*?

Male students also show the same kind of contradictory, diverse range of response in their customary ways of viewing television. Students know when to tune in and switch off their attention. They have much more control than we suppose over the quantity and quality of the programmes they let into their lives. Recent research into modes of viewing has drawn attention to these different ways of interacting with television:

> Periods of rapt attention rarely lasted for more than ten minutes at a time and the range of activities that children combined with their watching of television was remarkably wide, ranging from doing homework, building craft models, to singing, dancing, talking, jumping and fighting. (Fiske, 1987)

Therefore, any media education approach that wants to extend male students' critical understandings about masculine representations in the media, has to make positive use of what boys already know about the media (probably much more than adult teachers do!) and what they actually find pleasure in. It has to start from students' wry, half-mocking, ironic approaches to what they watch, listen to and read. And it has to acknowledge that most boys know the difference between tomato ketchup and real blood.

No amount of elegant, discriminatory work from teachers wanting to immunize their 'ignorant' students from liking 'rubbish' can force students to involve themselves with a media teaching programme if their everyday understandings about the media aren't positively validated. We have to start with the hidden resources and understandings that boys bring with them into the classroom. We have to learn how to work with these tacit pleasures and meanings, through inviting them into the classroom and respecting them. Then, at a later stage, we need to work on those understandings by introducing other ways of making sense of them. At this second stage, when enough confidence and trust have been built up between student and teacher, other ways of making sense of the students' initial impressions can be introduced. When the time is right, the teacher needs to bring in alternative, critical perspectives to unsettle students' common-sense assumptions.

A media education approach to men, boys and masculinities, if it is to be effective, has to focus on both these stages. After a pleasurable engagement stage, it has to try and build questioning conversations with students' taken-for-granted assumptions about conventional images of boys and men. This can only be achieved by introducing students to a fresh way of looking at these familiar assumptions. This fresh way of looking can be summarized as a critical, anti-sexist perspective on conventional images of men and masculinity.

Some Key Features of a Critical, Anti-Sexist Perspective on Traditional Manhood in Media Education

What needs to be questioned from the outset is the taken-for-granted assumption of male power and privilege in many media messages. There is often a power- and gender-blindness in the media that needs to be confronted. We can make a start by interrogating the dominance, competitiveness, false universality, aggression and taken-for-granted heterosexuality of traditional masculinity.

1   Challenging macho values in the media means unmasking the hidden norms of a men-on-top, male-defined world-view. Assumptions of male supremacy, that 'men are powerful and successful, occupy high-status positions, initiate action and act from the basis of rational mind as opposed to emotions, are found in the world of things as opposed to family and relationships . . .' need to be critically challenged (Fejes, 1992). Similarly, the representation of boys in the media also needs to be carefully investigated. Recent studies of child characters in the media found that boys were consistently shown as more 'active, aggressive, rational and unhappy' than girls (Peirce, 1989). Boys were also seen as engaged in traditional male activities, 'such as playing sports, going places, and making mischief, while the girl characters talked on the phone, read, and helped with the housework' (*ibid.*).

2   A critical approach to the media also needs to expose the false univer- sality and imaginary unity of conventional manhood. The unexamined habit of treating the male as the *real* human being (and women as some- thing else) often protects men and masculinities from being investigated. That needs to be changed.

3   The question, What is being left out and excluded in traditional media representations of men? is a crucial one. The overemphasis on a single, unified, fixed form of masculinity — white, middle-class, heterosexual — elbows out other more marginalized forms of masculinity, like gay, black, disabled, asthmatic and emotional men. More critical attention needs to be given to these diverse, excluded voices, as a way of chal- lenging the dominant, hegemonic version of masculinity.

In terms of looking closely at specific, media texts, the systematic absence of women, work and marriage/commitment in the lives of men is also an area that needs critical examination.

4   A critical focus on gendered narrative is worthy of attention. John Fiske (1987) in his book, *Television Culture*, contrasts gender-specific narrative forms for women and men. He looks closely at soap opera as a feminine narrative and contrasts that with the action/adventure form as a mas- culine narrative. Students need to follow up their own pleasures and curiosities in this area.

Feminine narratives, like soaps, are characterized as multi-track stories, with multiple characters and plots, and no endings. They stress dialogue, problem solving, especially in the area of social relationships, and intimate conversations. Pleasure for women viewers is seen as 'on-going and cyclical rather than climactic and final' (*ibid.*).

On the other hand, masculine narratives are goal-centred rather than relationship-oriented. They often work through single plots and a focus on a single hero, or a tightly knit hero pair or team. Story endings are closed and climactic. There is a strong emphasis on fast and furi-ous action (car chases, men running, fighting and killing, etc.), speed, aggression, ingenious technology (guns, tanks, armed helicopters and other instruments of destruction), and the hardened male body.

Dialogue is minimal, the 'determination to succeed replaces feel-ings, mechanical ingenuity replaces insight into people, and success in problem solving replaces the process' that is so important in feminine narratives (*ibid.*). No wonder there is a crisis in gender relations and in traditional forms of masculinity!

5 The taken-for-grantedness of the heterosexuality of the single male hero, in many media experiences, needs to be urgently interrogated. We need to question the way this 'Top Dog' version of masculine, sexual identity is achieved at the expense of other sexualities and sensual relationships, especially gayness and bisexuality. We need to keep draw-ing attention to the more contradictory forms of male sexuality that are being repressed in this overemphasis on cardboard cut-out, heterosexual figures with their fixation on performance, penetration and conquest.

6 More investigation is needed of the 'actual processes of reception' in-volved in men and boys responding to the media. We need to know much more about how adolescent boys, for example, use media images of masculinity to construct their own gendered view of themselves. We need to know the influence of peer groups on these responses, and how social contexts affect their responses. We need to know how far boys embrace, resist, negotiate, ignore traditionally gendered media messages that address them as 'real lads'. There is a lot of room here for small, school-based enquiries into some of these questions.

7 The importance of answering back to an offensive, sexist media mes-sage. Many more men and boys need to break ranks and dare to dis-agree, when confronted by media messages that are saturated with macho, sexist values. Voices of protest can make a difference, as the 1991 letter campaign against the overtly sexist Hennes lingerie ad proves. Here's the 16 April 1991 *Guardian* bulletin piece that explains how letters of protest did make a difference to the cynical sexism of the Hennes' advertising campaign:

> Letters can make a difference. Following more than 100 com-plaints to the Advertising Standards Authority about an ad for Hennes lingerie, it was announced last week that they have been ordered to withdraw it. The ad featured a reclining model

wearing only underwear and the copyline, 'Last year we ran an ad for Swedish lingerie. 78 women complained. No men.' It was promoted during December and January, and on January 23 *Guardian Women* reported on the situation, asking concerned readers to lodge their complaints with the ASA. The response was substantial, the results tangible: the authority has ruled that the campaign 'caused considerable offence to both men and women' and agreed that the ad mocked those who had complained about previous commercials.

And here's the original *Guardian Women* report that encouraged readers 'to lodge their complaints with the Advertising Standards Authority'.

Bare-faced cheek

Scantily clad, glamorous women sell everything from chocolate and cars to holidays. No surprise, then, that the Swedish-based chainstore Hennes should use a photo of a woman reclining in underwear in their advertising campaigns, both last year and this. They do, after all, sell lingerie.

What has provoked an outcry, however, are the copylines Hennes place with the photos. Last winter's ad read, 'This is what the au pair will be wearing this winter.' The Advertising Standards Authority received 34 letters of complaint. Rather than retreat from the flak, Hennes went on the attack. This winter the copyline was, 'Last year we ran an ad for Swedish lingerie. 78 women complained. No men.'

For a start, the ad is factually inaccurate: of the 34 complaints the ASA received, some were from men. But, more seriously, Hennes' reaction shows extraordinary cynicism in the face of ASA disapproval.

The ASA investigated the 34 complaints last year and upheld them. In its report on the case it concluded: 'From the number of complaints the advertisement had provoked (it was clear) that the headline had exacerbated the offence caused by the illustration.'

According to the ASA report on Hennes' response, they were 'taken aback by the adverse reaction to the poster ... the humorous headline was not intended to be deprecatory, but to diffuse the fact that the model was wearing lingerie.'

Hennes even claimed that 'as employers of a very high percentage of women at a managerial level, they were sensitive to the portrayal of women and were concerned to present both their products and women in a positive light.' In conclusion, the ASA requested Hennes to 'take greater care with both the portrayal of women and the use of innuendo in future advertisements.'

Hennes' response was to do just the opposite. In its winter advertising campaign, a copyline above a reclining girl reads, 'You think it comes from France, it comes from Sweden.' 'It' cannot refer to the two pieces of underwear, so must refer to the girl.

When told about this ad, Christina Sedwall, women's editor of Swedish paper *Upsala Nya Tidning*, expressed shock. 'As a Swedish women, I'm upset and angry that they use us as sex objects in this way. They wouldn't dare do it here.'

In Britain, however, the second poster campaign caused the greater stir. The line '78 women complained. No men' shows extraordinary contempt for women, presumably many of them Hennes customers, who bother to complain when an ad offends them.

A group of women in Brighton were so incensed that they organised a boycott of the Brighton Hennes' store during late-night shopping hours before Christmas. They distributed 2,000 leaflets, printed at their own expense.

An article five weeks ago on this page, referring to that Hennes' ad, provoked a number of letters from readers — men and women. Alex Stitt sent us a copy of his letter to Hennes: 'I do not like the feeling of complicity you are ramming down my throat in the conjecture that all men respond to beautiful women in underwear, that women should understand this if they are to keep up and any man who objects is a wimp.'

Emma Hayes wrote, 'Although I would never have complained about a photograph of a half-dressed woman, I would never, never sneer or seek to humiliate anyone who had, which is quite obviously the intention of this ad.'

The attractiveness of the lingerie illustrated 'disappeared under the weight of the irritation and offence I felt towards the arrogant cynicism of the advertising company.' She wrote that although she had been a customer of Hennes in the past, she would not shop there again 'and, listening to my friends, this is surely true of many, many women.'

Hennes' spokeswoman said the advert this year was intended to be 'humorous' and refused to comment further, though she admitted they had received complaints. To date 25 people have written to the ASA to complain.

If you too feel strongly about the ads' attitude to women, leave Hennes out of your next shopping trip. Or go one further: write to them and the ASA and let them know why.

Selected Further Reading on Boys, Masculinities and Media Education

FISKE, J. (1987) 'Gendered television: masculinity' in *Television Culture*, London, Methuen.
CRAIG, S. (1992) *Men, Masculinity and the Media*, California. Sage.
MIDDLETON, P. (1992) 'Boys will be men: Boys' superhero comics' in *The Inward Gaze: Masculinity and Subjectivity in Modern Culture*, London, Routledge.
NEALE, S. (1993) 'Masculinity as spectacle', in COHAN, S. and HARK, I. (Eds) *Screening the Male: Exploring Masculinities in Hollywood Cinema*, London, Routledge.
WERNICK, A. (1987) 'From voyeur to narcissist: Imaging men in contemporary Advertising', in KAUFMAN, M. (Ed.) *Beyond Patriarchy: Essays by Men on Pleasure, Power and Change*, Canada, Oxford University Press.
CAMPBELL, B. (1993) 'Strangers and conquerors' in *Goliath: Britain's Dangerous Places*, London, Methuen.

The Session

Manly Characteristics

Its the first session of the day and the group are meeting in the comfortable surroundings of the community lounge — soft furnishings and carpet! The group tend to drift in, coming from different tutor bases. I never feel sure that everyone is here. Today is no exception as I reluctantly assume that only eight will be arriving. No-one knows where the missing three are. Those present are eager to know what is going to happen. Throughout the life of this group there has been much comment about the pressures of having to behave in particular ways that do not encourage scorn and ridicule. Boys have said how they feel about that pressure and there have already been references to the way in which the media portrays men as behaving in stereotypically manly ways. Bold denials of the affect of these pressures doesn't prevent the boys from going to great lengths to avoid showing any signs that could be perceived as weak and unmanly.

I was also keen to work with these pressures because I had recently become aware of the phenomenon of 'blow-out'. This is a particularly cruel and vicious way in which boys test each other's 'manliness'. Groups of boys congregate together and, targeting one individual, they say all the most hurtful, humiliating and frightening things they can think of. Knowledge of the victim's life and circumstances is important. All known areas of difficulty or embarrassment are probed by the group. Nothing is left out in the barrage of taunts and insults. The object is to 'blow-out' the victim until he can't take it anymore and he breaks down or runs away from it all. When this happens the victim is laughed at and ridiculed and has to live with the embarrassment and shame of his humi-liation for days afterwards. The peer pressure to withstand the breaking point is enormous. Boys take pride in being big enough or macho enough to have survived. Status and respect has been gained by their ability to 'take it'. On the other hand life becomes particularly difficult for those who court the attention and are then not able to withstand the challenge.

To hear boys talk about what happens during 'blow-out' is to pick up the atmosphere around fear of failing, of not looking good in front of your mates and of not having the respect of others in the group. And so after the boys have emphasized the manly values necessary to survive a 'blow-out', I decide to encourage them to think more closely about these manly values — where they come from and who decides what they are.

I ask the boys to find a partner and give out sets of Masculine Stereotypes characteristics cards (see pp. 160–1). They are to arrange the characteristics/qualities cards under the headings of manly and unmanly. There are some quips around the group about under which heading some of them are placing the cards. I encourage them to use the blank cards to add other words or phrases. Among such cards I notice 'soft', 'cries easily', 'tough', 'loyal', 'sticks up for your mates' and 'good drinker'.

I had spent some time in the weeks leading to this session picking out small newspaper extracts in written or picture form which show men behaving in a variety of different ways. I want the boys to use their thinking about manly values and characteristics, to decide how many of the extracts show men behav-ing in manly ways. They don't want to do the exercise on their own. I question this, asking them to tell me the real reason and not say that it's boring or difficult. There is a silence which Martin breaks by saying that 'we might get it wrong'. 'What will happen if you get it wrong', I reply. There is some shuff-ling while the logic of the question and the inevitable answer emerges that even here the pressure to conform and to get it right for fear of ridicule is operating strongly. I ask what they need to be able to do this exercise. 'What about agreeing that whatever anybody does, they don't get the rip taken out of them', says Philip. The boys agree with much head nodding. I decide to pass a comment on how important this decision is for their process and progress as a group. They seem pleased and enthusiastically get on with selecting examples of men acting bravely or against the odds as manly, and rejecting stories of men raising small children or being involved in the care of plants and animals as unmanly.

We come together as a whole group to talk about what they have been doing. My initial question is to ask what messages they are supposed to get from magazines and newspapers about how men are supposed to behave? 'What do the magazines want you to think?' Martin comes in quickly with 'Well you've got to look the part whatever you might feel inside. You've got to look brave and tough on the outside.' The other boys agree with him. I ask what the newspapers and magazines are actually doing. Tim says he thinks that the stories are only interested in showing men in a certain way and 'you've got to be like that or they'll take the rip out of you'. The boys all agree that 'they' are all the other boys. 'Newspapers just tell you how you've got to be — it's the same in computer games even.' 'It's showing men being tough and heroes and that's not how things really are.'

During this discussion I had a sense of the atmosphere in the room softening and the boys becoming more supportive of each other. There was almost a sense of relief that guards could be lowered because all the boys felt very similar. Gareth and Neil explained how they

> had to act like everyone else and everyone else seemed to be acting like they were supposed to from films and things. It's the same with all this 'blow-out' stuff — it's just about being seen to be tough. You can't get away from it because that's how you've got to be. If you try and avoid it, it's difficult — you just get ripped apart later and you've got to pretend it's not happening.

In view of the pressures that boys experience I felt that we were on the verge of some real honesty here. I wondered aloud whether anyone could tell us of times when they have behaved in so called unmanly ways. There is silence as each boy waits for someone else to make a move. Martin volunteers to start as long as everyone has a turn and that 'we're not going to say any of this outside are we?' He wants to be sure about confidentiality and says that he is not going to repeat things to anyone else. There followed some banter about what would happen if anyone did say anything — a kind of lapse back into the world of macho posturing and threats. Finally, Martin feels happy that the group is with him and he told of the time when he daren't show anyone how frightened and upset he was when his father was severely burned in an industrial accident. He told us that his mother had told him that his father was in hospital with a bad hand injury. He couldn't believe it when he saw him and realized that he was so badly burned he could have died. He had been really upset and had tried hard not to show it.

The other boys sit silently as Martin speaks and comments are made about how his mother had dealt with it. They show their understanding of how it feels. Gareth was moved to talk about the time when his sister was killed — and how he wasn't allowed to cry about it. He spoke of how he really had to fight hard during a 'blow-out' to show that he wasn't weak — he had felt really dreadful inside and had been unable to sleep but he had told no-one. As he speaks there is a catch in his voice. The other boys notice and ask questions about Gareth's sister in an understanding and supportive way and create the atmosphere where he can talk about her openly. Tony is quite bothered about Gareth not being able to cry when his sister died but relates it to his own experience of being told by his father that 'only babies cry' and so

> I could only cry on my own or I was made fun of. I had a dog that died and I just had to pretend it didn't really matter and yet when I was on my own, I would cry a bit, but not very much. That's why I told you all earlier on that I didn't cry — 'cos that's how I've got to be. I've got older brothers who are just the same. I can't show them I get upset so I just bottle it up.

David told us that he pretended not to be bothered when his girlfriend packed him up. He just went round 'slagging her off' rather than letting anyone else see how hurt he was. This tragedy touched a chord with others who talked of doing something opposite, bad or outrageous just to stop themselves feeling upset. 'It helps it to go away — perhaps that's why I get into trouble a lot', was Philip's response. He went on to tell us about how difficult it was living at home because his parents were getting a divorce and he was in the middle of it all — he wished everything would be alright again. He feels angry about the whole situation but keeps it all to himself, but takes his angry feelings out on his little brother or messes about at school: 'There's nothing anybody can do to me that's worse than anything that's happening at home.' I ask if anyone could help him here. Gareth suggests that we could listen when times get bad — 'You could talk to me anyway cos I'm you're mate. You don't have to be on your own.'

When everyone has had a turn and been listened to, I ask how the boys feel about what they've done in relation to the images of masculinity which the media stories and pictures portrayed: 'Outside of here it's still really difficult — you don't want to be seen as soft and different.' 'It's very difficult to talk like this until you get to know people well.' I acknowledge these problems and the powerful pressure that they feel. I ask what was different about the session they have just experienced and what they can do in the future. The boys say they feel they can trust everyone here and that it will be easier to share things with each other in the future. As the bell goes it's Martin who seems to sum up what has happened, 'I think it brave to be able to say all this — it's just a different sort of bravery.'

Classroom Strategies

Media

What we need to emphasize in these strategies is that male students are active makers of meaning in their dealings with the media. Although they are surrounded by images of an aggressive macho culture they aren't simply brainwashed by them. They don't react in a docile passive manner to those images. In these classroom strategies we want to extend that active meaning making by encouraging the boys to enter a participating collaboration with what they see hear or read.

We need to move into this area slowly by looking firstly at stereotypes to encourage the boys to start noticing some of the pressures which impinge upon them. At a later stage we need to engage the boys in a deeper critical interrogation of some of these macho meanings and images — hence the work on newspapers and the investigation of the adventure–action story form in films.

Masculine Stereotypes (1)

Aim: To help boys recognize stereotypes of masculine behaviour.

Materials: 'Characteristics' cards, prepared using the statements below

Time: 15 minutes

What to do:

Ask the boys to work in pairs to organize the characteristics cards under 'Manly' and 'Unmanly' headings.

Get each pair to write down their lists in preparation for the next exercise. They might need to add other words to the two lists.

The statements:

weak	uncertain
strong	sure about it
courageous	knows it all
emotional	makes mistakes
keeping control	never makes mistakes
lone wolf	brave
frightened	innocent

Masculine Stereotypes (2)

Aim: To allow boys to look critically at newspaper stories and pictures about men and male characteristics.

Materials: A variety of newspaper stories and pictures about men

Time: 30 minutes

What to do:

Divide the boys into groups of 3 or 4 and give out examples of newspaper stories and pictures. They need to refer to their lists of 'Manly' and 'Unmanly' behaviours from the previous activity (Masculine Stereotypes 1).

As they look through the newspapers and pictures, ask them to decide how many of the examples show men behaving in a 'Manly' way.

Introduce the idea that the 'Manly' list is full of masculine stereotypes and that in real life most us have a mixture of qualities from both the 'Manly' and 'Unmanly' lists. The newspapers and pictures have more fixed and narrow ideas about how men are. Many daily newspapers use stereotyped ways of showing how men think, behave, feel or look.

Masculine Stereotypes (3)

Aim: To enable boys to look at the limiting effects of male stereotyping on their own lives.

Materials: A variety of newspapers, magazines, pictures
large sheets of sugar paper,
glue and scissors

Time: 45 minutes

What to do:

Ask the boys to individually, or in pairs, prepare a collage under the heading of 'The Typical Man'.

When the collage is complete, ask the boys to assess the messages of manliness that are being shown and answer the questions on the worksheet 'Manly Values.' (use the questions below)

When the worksheet is complete ask them to share their answers with a friend.

The questions:

Look at your collage together with your lists of 'manly/unmanly' values and answer the following questions as honestly as you can.

1. From your collage what are the main messages about the way men are supposed to behave?
2. How are these messages like your list of 'manly' values?
3. Do you think your collage shows a fair picture of what men are really like?
4. How do the images of men that you have cut out affect the way you behave?
5. What qualities that men show are missing in your collage or in your list of manly values?
6. Do you behave in so-called unmanly ways? If so:

    • How?
    • When?
    • Where?

What is Brave?

Aim:	*To build on work on masculine stereotypes by encouraging a critical review of newspaper coverage.*
Materials:	*Previous work on masculine stereotypes* *Photocopies of news stories of men acting in a brave and heroic fashion* *'What is Brave?' sheets prepared using the statements below* *Paper and pens*
Time:	*45–50 minutes*

What to do:

Make sure each boy has a copy of the news story, together with copies of the 'What is Brave?' statements. It will be helpful if boys work cooperatively in pairs for this exercise.

The statements:

What is Brave?

• Someone who admits he is wrong.
• Doing something you ought to when you're scared.

- Sticking up for someone when everyone is putting them down.
- Saying what you think when everyone else thinks differently.
- Saying 'no' when all your friends want you to say 'yes'.
- Someone who does something dangerous.
- Someone who takes risks.
- Someone who is never scared.
- Someone who carries on when things get tough.

1. Ask the boys to look through the news story treatment of this brave act. Encourage them to notice body posture and facial expression shown in any pictures accompanying the article.
2. In pairs the boys should decide together which of the 'What is Brave?' statements fit the story they are looking at.
3. When this is complete ask them to make their own list of alternative qualities that could fit the main hero of the story.
4. Now imagine that you were the hero of this story, what would your mother and/or father be saying about what you were doing?
5. What activities do you do that you consider brave?
6. Who do you want to notice what you are doing when you are acting brave?
7. How difficult is it to be a boy without being brave?
8. How do you honestly feel when you're not being brave?
   Enable the boys to get through as much of the worksheet as time permits but to make sure that enough time is left to allow some discussion of findings in the whole group.

Images of Men in Newspapers or Magazines

Aim: *To build on work on masculine stereotypes by encouraging a critical review of newspaper and magazine coverage.*

Materials: *Previous work on masculine stereotypes*
Photocopies of selected news stories to do with macho behaviour
Worksheet prepared using the questions below
Paper and pens

Time: *45–50 minutes*

What to do:

Give out copies of the news or magazine stories. It will be helpful if the boys work cooperatively in pairs in this exercise.

Enable the boys to get through as much of the worksheet as time permits but to make sure that enough time is left to allow some discussion of findings in a whole group.

The questions:

Images of Men

1. Bearing in mind your previous work on masculine stereotypes, make your own list of fixed, narrow and often untrue ideas about men that you can find in the story and in the pictures which may accompany it. When you have written your list share it with a friend.
2. Imagine that you've come from an alien planet. You're seeing what takes place on Earth for the first time. You understand the language, you already know about the basics of human life, but you don't know anything about the rules, habits, ideas and values that people who live on Earth take for granted. You don't know what the powerful, influential people look like. You don't know what kind of behaviour is approved of and what is considered brave, honourable and worthy.

    Imagine that you are reading the story for the first time. Write a report back to the people of your planet describing the kinds of male behaviour that are considered — clever, stupid, right, wrong, good, bad, honourable, dishonourable.
3. Select one of the macho behaviours you notice in this story. Act out a conversation between two of our visitors from an alien planet trying to understand what is going on.
4. Share with your partner something of what you discovered about macho values and the way they are reported.

Questioning Masculine Action Adventure Stories in Film and Television

Aim: To question macho values in the action adventure story form in films and television.

Materials: Video recorder, extract from popular action adventure film

Time: 50 minutes

What to do:

Select an action adventure film suitable for your age group. Choose a particularly lively, exciting extract of about 15 minutes in length.

Using the following checklist ask the boys to note examples of the following:

Fights
Killings
Car chases
Men running
Use of mechanical gadgets e.g., cars that do wonderful things, protective gadgetry like forcefields etc., sophisticated and fantasy weaponry.
Men firing guns of various kinds.

Ask the boys to share their lists with a partner and to give some thought to answering the following questions:

- What does this say about how men are supposed to behave?
- What kind of talking goes on in the film? See if the boys notice clipped instructions, barked commands, threats, insults, monosyllabic terse comments.
- How are the male figures in the film valued for what they do? How do they gain admiration and respect?
- How do the men in the extract solve problems?
- What do you think of this way of behaving, relating and communicating?
- How do you and people you know get on differently in your relations with other people?

Encourage the boys to reassemble as a whole group to share what they have learned about men in films and what that says about themselves.

Chapter 7

Language as a Weapon

The Theory

Building Male Power and Control

Although language is a way of making personal sense of the world and is also a means of bringing people closer to others, it is also a weapon in the mouths of many boys. Boys spar with language in their daily interactions in the classroom, corridor, sports field and street. They use language to keep others, particularly other boys, at a distance while also demonstrating and celebrating their own power and importance. Insults are the language weapon of control and they come in many forms, including sexual abuse, racist remarks and mocking humour. The weapon is being used to tell the receiver not to get too close — to back off.

On many occasions, one of the authors has noted boys who are known to be 'real good mates' engage in open hostility by means of words. The weapon most commonly used is the accusation of being gay which is tossed out in a variety of forms from 'poofter' to 'bum bandit'. The rejoinder is swift. Similar language is used together with physically pushing away the offending party to the accompaniment of an almost obligatory sneer of contempt.

Boys who speak and behave in this way in their teenage years have grown up as products of a culturally and historically specific language system. A system moreover which is highly influenced by gender, class, region and race.

From a gender perspective, the patriarchal framework creates a man-on-top language assumption which permeates social consciousness. This still seems to be relevant despite increasing unemployment, the rise of single parent families and the growing sense that work practices are rendering individual men's contribution to work as less important (Seidler, 1989). Language is at the heart of this struggle: while boys' use of language is influenced by the powerful frameworks and legacies of male supremacist history, they are at the same time, having to actively create new meanings to take account of altering social conditions.

Subtly and almost invisibly, language validates the taken-for-granted assumptions inherent in the dialogues and exchanges between people. And so language retains its unique position as a major means of building male power and control. As a striking example of this, imagine a martian coming across a marriage service and witnessing the form of words that operate as part of the ritual. The martian would notice a man and woman entering a church for the ceremony and emerging as man and wife. The man is untouched but perhaps now that he has a wife he has gained greater status and prestige. Perhaps also his power has been enhanced since he has gained a wife for whom society assumes him responsible. As a man he has acquired the status of being normal, whereas women are defined in deviant relation to the masculine norm. Dale Spender has defined this power and status relationship in terms of male and minus male. To be linked with maleness is to be associated with things that are active and positive: to be linked with minus male is not to have those qualities, that is 'to be decidedly negative and usually sexually debased' (Spender, 1985).

School settings provide a rich source of material which also shows how taken for granted our language uses are. We need to stand back a little and listen more clearly to what is really going on. Looking carefully behind the words and structures reveals a complexity of power relations controlled by subtlety of language.

The Language of the Corridor

Boys use name-calling to put down and regulate girls' lives (Lees, 1986). Girls earnestly seek to avoid being dubbed as a 'slag' but they find they can be derogatorily defined no matter what they actually do. If they engage in sexually permissive behaviour or they rebuff approaches they will still face the language of the boys who define girls in terms of male control of girls' behaviour.

It is not just women and girls who feel the power of male controlling language but also other boys who are perceived as not belonging to the ethos of 'top dog' masculinity. 'Top dog' boys are adept at 'keeping their end up' and appreciating the shared comfort and safety afforded by being steeped in the language of the male pack. There is risk and accompanying tension very close to the surface, however, because the pack's attention can swiftly turn on one of their number who slips from grace with a remark that calls into question pack norms and assumptions.

Thus boys use language as a shield to make sure other boys only see and hear what will be acceptable to ensure status as 'one of the boys'. To be seen as strong, cool and hard is very important for peer acceptance. Boys use sexist jokes and banter to not only define their relationships with girls but also as an ingredient of the mortar which binds them within the male club. To be strong and cool is to be accepted by the 'buddy boy' club as one of their own. So boys joke with each other, tell jokes in front of girls which are sexist and crude but with a seductive purpose. Among themselves there are much wilder examples of sexually aggressive banter and jokes. Such language displays a hostility towards women and girls but the boys laughter and shared enjoyment at these crudities helps to bind them together. The importance of this male bonding into a 'buddy boy' network justifies any inconvenience to girls who are the butt of the humour. Sexist jokes and banter are part of the mechanism whereby the order of gender domination is sustained in everyday life.

Boys also verbally abuse each other about a wide variety of things — about the size of sex organs, about a mother's imagined sexual activities and many others in a similar vein. The important thing for a boy is to be able to take it. If you can take it without getting upset you will be accepted. Jackson (1990) describes what lay in store for those who could not take it in his examples drawn from boys' dormitory life. The misery, degradation and sense of loss is graphically portrayed.

Being able to introduce a string of 'fucks' into normal language is another way of emphasizing status. Since such language is associated with an active thrusting virility, it is another way of demonstrating self as 'one of the boys'.

The greatest fear over not conforming centres on the area of sexual orientation. In this area in particular, boys must be seen to be openly, obviously and even rampantly heterosexual. Any sign of deviant behaviour will be pounced on by the pack who are your 'friends'. Boys find it necessary to continually state and re-state their position to ward off the biggest humiliation of all — the accusation of being gay. They make it clear to all and sundry in explicit terms that they are not 'queer' or 'one of those'. Any seemingly innocent remark about friendship will be prefaced by 'I'm not gay you know', or something in a similar vein. On a wider stage, the same vigorous denials are heard. Paul Gascoigne interviewed on the *Wogan* show (BBC Television) in the summer of 1991 determinedly asserted, 'I cry but I'm not a poofter'. Any signs of touching intimacy between friends will be shunned. Only acceptable touching will be allowed in the form of play fights, punches and slaps which bear no malice. The tragedy is that some boys even consciously avoid their friends for a period of time to further ward off the accusations.

So boys learn the coolness, defensiveness and strength which they see as necessary to survive and achieve in a male atmosphere. Being able to take the banter, the jokes and the jibes teaches them how to keep control of their emotions.

Language of the Classroom

In school settings this lesson has been well learned and reinforced. Children learn when to speak, when to remain silent and when it is possible to interrupt. All this helps to contribute to different outcomes for girls and boys.

The differences in communicative competence enables boys to dominate the classroom with a wide variety of attention seeking strategies. Boys tend to be more boastful — they will talk about how easy a test was while girls are more likely to express anxiety about their performance. This confidence shown by boys is also apparent in their participation in lessons. They call out answers and make lots of guesses, whereas girls listen more passively (Stanworth, 1981;

Spender, 1982). Girls notice this and comment on their perception of the boys seeming to know so much more than themselves (Salisbury, 1988).

Boys in group discussion situations reveal all the traits of not listening, which adult males in groups are noted for. One of the authors has been involved with anti-sexist boys' work at a comprehensive school in Derby. When group discussions were taking place, most of the boys found it very difficult to take turns. They each wanted to say their piece at the earliest opportunity. They would shout out their remarks, grabbing the space from the quieter boys whose contributions had to be specifically sought out. On many occasions the teacher had to specifically stop boys from talking until the person to speak had an audience who would listen to him. Contributions could not be very long, no more than one or two sentences, since the cocks of the group would soon be ready to interrupt again with their own agendas.

This behaviour was mirrored in mixed sex discussion groups where a minority of girls in the group were almost entirely silenced by the dominant use of space and sound by the boys in the group. In this case, the minimal girls' contributions or their lack of response was publicly despised by the boys. Thus the boys hog the space loudly and aggressively and then criticize the girls for their quietness and for 'just sitting there'. The boys groaned when girls made contributions or asked questions or just simply made rude comments about them.

The following incident pointedly demonstrates the way girls can be dismissed by boys. A 13-year-old pupil at the school had been sent to the school's 'sin bin' for unacceptable behaviour in class. He was being abusive to girls. He didn't know the names of most of the girls in his class despite the fact that he had been in the same group with them for two years. He said that he wasn't interested in knowing their names since, 'They're girls and that means boring'. The only contact he was prepared to have with them was via abuse and name-calling. Psychologically was he defending his fear of the 'girl' in himself? If he makes a rigid segregation between boy — the normal, the human being — then girls become the dangerous, invasive others.

Language of the Staffroom

Moving from the children in classroom and corridor to what goes on behind the staffroom door reveals an adult world in which much the same linguistic practices are going on in a broadly similar way. To make this clear, we need to look behind the everyday experiences of teachers, who, in various states of stress, view the staffroom as an uncertain haven. They rush in to look at notice-boards, mark books, consult colleagues and receive information. At the same time, some might also be jealously guarding their corners of personal space.

One of the authors has taught at a school where there was a corner of the staffroom occupied by longer serving male members of staff. It was their corner and attempts by others, particularly women, to sit in the area were viewed very suspiciously or even angrily. The tea- and coffee-making facilities were very near this corner and the presence of men in this area was intimidating. The male colleagues would be engaged in banter with each other around *Bilko* and *The Lone Ranger* (yes — even in 1992). There was also abundant talk of football, rugby and horse racing, together with the recounting of dirty jokes picked up in bars the previous evening. The atmosphere engendered by this activity made even the acquisition of break-time coffee something of a risky activity for many women on the staff.

Individual relations between the men in the corner and women members of staff were superficially good in terms of communication about teaching and departmental matters, but the men as a group were flexing their muscles and showing their power. Power gained here could be extended into other working groups, staff meetings and committees which were supposed to guarantee the smooth running of the school.

Perhaps a look at language patterns and the way men and women behave in conversations or in groups will help to throw some light on how men use language to maintain their power and view their position in the world. We are talking here about the language of male power which operates not only through the words themselves, but also in the paralinguistics — the use of the body and space — to give emphasis to the words used. This language helps men to impress, to hog the stage and to exercise dominance and control, but it also acts as a shield whereby men can hide their feelings and avoid the unsettling intimacy of real contact with somebody else. Both these processes are going on at the same time — men seeking and asserting their power which their masculinity grants them and hiding their feelings about self from public gaze. Fear of seeming vulnerable haunts them as it has done throughout their lives. And so men speak in a guarded, wary, matter-of-fact, generalizing and distant fashion.

Men defend themselves through a false impression of certainty. They speak for others under an assumption that men's knowing is the same as human knowledge. Man comes to mean human being and the habitual male style emphasizes the persona of the man as the expert, in full control of knowledge. He is factual and remote so that his own feelings of emotional messiness are not revealed. All this is set up in such a way that women's interests are under valued. It also sustains the division between public and private spheres which maintains the inequalities and power balance between men and women. Even in the telling of personal anecdotes, there may be much heartiness mixed with mocking irony and self-effacement, but whatever happens in the telling, the anecdotes will serve to shore up the manhood of the speaker. Keeping personal talk rational and objective will help them to keep the public world severed from the disturbingly private world of emotions.

Men also vie with each other to tell anecdotes which centre around superiority and aggression. Such talk encapsulates the dual way in which men use language for domination. Men mix an interactional domination in language use which emphasizes male agendas and male style with a heavily implicit assumption of superiority in a sexist way. It is as if men were saying, 'We use words while standing centre stage. You speak from a totally inferior, marginalized position.'

In schools the interaction between male and female teachers in mixed groups, both in formal and informal settings, provides evidence of all the linguistic tricks which keep men safe and in control (Coates, 1986). For instance men and women use questioning differently. Women often use questions to encourage the flow of conversation, whereas men treat questions as straight requests for information. Women are also much better at maintaining links between what one person has said and their own particular contribution. Men, on the other hand, are far more likely to ignore what has been said before to make sure they can say their own preplanned point. In mixed groups, women become irritated at having their contributions ignored, whereas men become bored at not having the cut and thrust of conversations played according to their own rules.

Women use conversations to discuss problems, share experience and offer reassurance. For men such disclosure of matters of a personal nature are not normal. Men make assumptions that inputs of a personal nature are requests for advice. Such advice is often given but frequently in the guise of an expert. Men rarely share anything of their personal selves on these occasions. Men also display loudness and aggression, particularly in all male groups. Shouting, threats, name calling and insults are all part of male verbal aggressiveness. For men such practices are part of the conventional structure of conversation. Women find such displays not only unconducive to conversation but also unpleasant.

Interruptions are a common feature of conversation. Women interrupt in a supportive way to encourage a speaker to continue: they act as active, encouraging listeners. Men's interruptions seem to have as the objective the seizing of a turn and denying the present speaker the right to finish. Not surprisingly, in mixed groups men tend to achieve conversational dominance so that women feel inhibited from speaking.

Conversations depend on the dual roles of speakers and listeners. Listening is a skill which women seem to value highly but men, on the other hand, seem to construe conversation as a competition where the aim is to be the speaker. Once again, this implies the male need to grab a turn to speak and then hold onto it. The result in all male groups is that a few men dominate the conversation while the rest say little. Listening is not a highly prized value in men.

Conversations in mixed groups leads to difficulties. Men see women's failure to speak as confirming their belief that the only worthwhile things are said by men. Women see men's behaviour as insensitive of their right to speak and listen. Not surprisingly, in mixed groups women speak considerably less than men and begin fewer conversations.

Thus the different styles of conversation in men and women work to disadvantage both sexes. Men organizing their talk competitively and decisively produces clashes with the supportive, tentative and cooperative style displayed by some women. In these circumstances women either do not challenge and remain silent, or adopt the same thrusting decisive and knowledgeable qualities displayed by the men. In both cases, women can easily be written off either as having nothing to contribute or for being too assertive and dominant. There is also no value in being tentative, exploratory or simply admitting ignorance since men will be equally unimpressed. All this prevents real communication and shared understanding. Instead the end product is that the competitive style of men dominates the proceedings.

It seems clear to the authors that a style which gives good attention and which is supportive and cooperative is important in all conversations and that there are some men who are unhappy about the unfriendly male environment which prevents expression of feeling. Both sexes, therefore, seem to be disadvantaged — men because they lack competence in the women's style and women because their style leads them to being dominated in conversations.

One casualty of boys' defensiveness is learning itself. In school, boys fail to ask questions and check things out for fear of being seen as foolish. It is important for boys not to lose face in front of the pack by acknowledging academic weakness. On the other hand, academic excellence is not prized by the pack. Boys often have attitudes at variance with learning, homework and conscientiousness. There is a supposed link between academic work and effeminacy in many boys. Thus far more boys than girls leave school without any formal GCSE qualifications — 18,000 boys to 10,000 girls (HMSO, 1991).

The picture of male failure is no better in the sphere of personal relationships. Levels of communication between boys exist on a superficially friendly level. One of the authors investigating the nature of adolescent male friendships discovered that even supposedly good friendships are not wholly trusted. Boys find it difficult to share their personal discomforts and fears with their best friends in case there is an abuse of friendship and intimate secrets, or trusted information becomes pack property. The price to be paid when this happens is exacted in taunts, ridicule or worse.

Gender identities are reinforced by the fear of ridicule. Weaker, more vulnerable boys, together with girls, can be marginalized and debased. Boys do this, adopting the posture of the cool, tough, hard knowing boy who seeks to shore up his fragile sense of identity in case he too becomes seen as weak. Boys buy into this image of rugged manly identity so that it becomes the persona with which to survive in the world. By necessity, girls have to be defined adversely in relation to this image so that the traditional qualities of caring and softness have to be shunned at all costs.

Social interaction between boys and girls does not flow naturally. It remains hindered by the gulf that boys find difficult to cross. Girls distrust the brashness and the sexual innuendo which the pack often display. Boys who might behave differently are prevented from doing so. Fear of losing their image in the eyes of other boys is an important aspect of their reticence. There also exists a fear of how attempts at a genuine relationship would be received by girls so long used to the norm of posturing and a sense of display which the boys show in their presence.

Selected Further Reading on Boys, Masculinities and Language

MOYER, B. and TUTTLE, A. (1983) 'Overcoming masculine oppression in mixed groups', in KOKOPELI, B. and LAKEY, G. (Eds) *Off Their Backs . . . and On Our Own Two Feet'*, Philadelphia, New Society Publishers.

TANNEN, D. (1992) *You Just Don't Understand: Women and Men in Conversation*, London, Rago.

LYMAN, P. (1987) 'The fraternal bond as a joking relationship: A case study of the role of sexist jokes in male group bonding', in KIMMEL, M. (Ed.) *Changing Men*, California, Sage.

SPENDER, D. (1985) *Man Made Language*, London, Routledge.

COATES, J. (1986) *Women, Men and Language*, London, Longman.

The Session

Putting Down Women

B9 are very noisy — they always are. I struggle a lot with teacher authority and control issues in this group. I so want them to exercise that sense of self-control which really enables them to listen to each other. I am filled with trepidation as I try to anticipate how they will be. It's the last lesson of the day. Will one of the 'trouble makers' be away? They enter in a fairly boisterous and rowdy fashion. They reorganize the seating and I sense some feeling of anticipation for what might be about to happen.

'Any questions from last time?' I ask optimistically. There have been some times when I have been happy to use what is around in the group as a basis for the work of that session. This time there is nothing forthcoming so I suggest that we all have a look at a short playlet (See the 'A Look at Language' playlet and reference sheet in the classroom strategies section of this chapter pp. 185–8.) Much uncontrolled excitement around competition for parts ensues. Eventually Richard, Zubair, Gareth and Paul are chosen to take the play into another corner and read it through together. I explain to the others that their job will be to note down anything which strikes them as put-downs of women as the play is read through. The players will then read it through again when anyone in the group will have the chance to shout 'Stop!' and explain why they have stopped the action.

Before the reading, there are some further attempts to flee from the task in the form of talk about the WWF (World Wrestling Federation) wrestling stars as Ali proclaims himself 'The Ultimate Warrior'. The rejoinder comes back that he means 'Ultimate Dick Head'. This results in some aggressive touching between Ali and Safid which is ritualized into arm wrestling. Others start arm wrestling as well. I struggle to keep a semblance of order. I am deluding myself. I am not optimistic about this session.

The reading of the playlet starts, the listeners scribble down their points.

The second reading begins and there is enthusiasm for calling 'Stop!' There were many surprises. Ali was the first to pick out that the woman was 'over there with kids of course'. There was much vocal support for joint parenting and that it was wrong for children just to be with their mothers. Zaheer mentioned how important his father was to him. Only Richard noticed the reference to 'pin money' as being an undervaluing of women. He took the lead in suggesting that lots of women went to work: 'If my Mum didn't work there's lots of things we couldn't do in our home.' The boys question each other around the importance of both parents' incomes. Mark was put out because only his mother worked and her wages were vital.

There was a chorus of 'Stops!' for the put-down references to a wife going to college and becoming a 'woman engineer'. There was a general agreement for 'Why can't women go to college?' 'He's just being stupid. There's nothing to stop women becoming engineers.' In fact Richard went on to point out that he didn't think it was necessary to say *woman* engineer. 'Why not just engineer?' Asad thought it was really sexist and was just making out that women were really thick.

'Birds' produced the next 'Stop!' Ali said that it seemed degrading. They all admitted that they had referred to girls in this sort of way and even in this discussion Gareth told Ali to 'stop being a woman'. When Richard, Paul and Zaheer turn on Gareth and question his remark, he retires into silence briefly. I pose the next question, 'How do women feel about being referred to in this brainless way as birds or hearing men sneered at as "women"?' Richard suggests, 'They get bogged down with it.' Paul adds, 'They might think they're not good enough.'

Suddenly there seems to be a real shift in this group. Led by Richard and Zubair, they make a link between women not feeling good enough and the way men treat women. 'Look here,' says Richard, 'these things are important'. There's a reference here to 'what's your wife's little sideline?' (he refers to the play). 'How are women going to feel if that's how their work is treated?' 'Blokes don't get the same hassle', says Zubair. There was general consent for the view that it was easy for women to feel degraded and abused. The only dissenting voice was Gareth who said he didn't like any women and that 'the only good thing about women is bedding them'. That brought a chorus of disapproval down upon him which only had the effect of driving him to become more entrenched in his views around women. Certainly, Gareth was left in no doubt that he was very much out of step with the others.

'You can see where women get it from,' Paul remarks. We listen expectantly as he goes on, 'Here — the boys can go out and play — be on their own — sort of being adventurous and the girls are supposed to go upstairs and play with dolls. There's no wonder some of them don't do things.' The boys see this state of affairs as being really sexist. 'There's no reason girls can't play football. Miss G [a member of staff] does and she's really good. They just don't get a proper chance.' Apart from Gareth there is general agreement for Richard's remark.

On conclusion of the play, I ask if they notice anything else that's not been mentioned. This brings out that it's not fair to say that only women cook and three of the boys go into boasting over their own culinary expertise. Richard then shouts out, 'The women haven't got any names.' The boys notice that throughout the play the women are referred to as 'the missus, the wife, birds and women'. 'They don't seem to be people at all,' says Zubair.

We move on to feminize all the male references in the play. The boys do this in fours and then one group reads through the play again. There is some vocal over-feminization as they make the changes. This is seen as amusing until I ask what effect such behaviour and mimicry might have if there were women witnesses of what they were doing. I sense that they realize they were going 'over the top'. One group reads their revised play. Others comment on how peculiar it feels. 'It doesn't seem natural, it feels wrong,' remarks Sukhbinder. I throw in 'Why should it be natural for women? Can you feel some of the uncomfortableness that they feel?' 'It will make me more careful about what I say and how I behave.' Richard's remarks receive nods from most of the boys. Gareth is keeping quiet.

The bell goes and I sense that the ending has been rushed. I am sure that out of the session some new seeds have been sown but I have lingering doubts. Obviously we need to work more on how women must feel at the constant marginalization they experience. I take note that the best way of doing this is to have the boys monitor their actions around the girls in the school. Only then perhaps will their ability to spot sexist put-downs be converted into their own practice.

As a postscript to this session, I was heartened the next day when two of the boys, Zubair and Richard, came to me to tell me that they had walked home together talking about the session, that Richard had taken time to talk to his mother about her experiences of sexism and that more amazingly still they had both noticed how women get 'lost' when they marry since they lose their names!

Classroom Strategies

Continuing or Challenging Sex Stereotypes?

The way language is used around the school can play an important role in either continuing sex stereotyping or challenging it. The discriminatory effects of language use assume an air of invisibility in the school setting as the continued usage of sexist terms becomes a fact of existence for those going through the school system. It is not easy for girls to grow in a school atmosphere which actually renders their whole sex invisible. Schools not only have a high proportion of important jobs performed by men but the very titles indicate the inevitability of the office holder being male. Hence the use of the term Headmaster rather than Headteacher is still very common in many schools. Books and worksheets stress men's achievements. Man is a generic term and reinforces the idea of masculinity as a norm. By such means, girls are distanced from a sympathetic link with the work. Their experiences with men and maleness encourages women to defer to men in all situations with a corresponding lack in self-confidence, self-esteem and life management skills.

Boys are also damaged in this atmosphere of male universality. It encourages too many boys to make assumptions of superiority over girls. This concept of power-over gets in the way of normal exchanges between human beings as equals. It leads to an inability to communicate, a sense of self-estrangement, a feeling of being cut off from others and a deep sense of unconnectedness. It also encourages boys to become the men who control, who take charge against the odds, to be the rock on whom all can rely, and above all not to show the weakness and insecurity they feel inside. How many boys quail at this prospect and secretly long for a different way of relating.

Looking at and challenging language use in the classroom is very important. What do children actually hear, in what social context and what expectations are they exposed to? Are women and girls neglected or put down by the language used in staffroom and classroom? Are male and female pupils addressed differently? Despite changes in atmosphere surrounding equality issues, there are still schools that call boys by surnames and girls by their first names, just as girls and boys still line up separately to enter rooms. One of the authors attended a conference in Wimbledon in the summer of 1988 entitled 'Different Sex, Different Future', where the name badges given to the 6th form participants had initials for boys and first names for girls. More recently at an inner-city comprehensive school in Derby, he has witnessed examples of boys being asked to sit next to girls as a punishment for the boys' boisterous behaviour. At the same school there are examples of male teachers referring to girls as ladies in such a way that reinforces how the word is used by men to control women's behaviour. There are also the male teachers who assume that it is OK to make remarks about women's sexuality. One glaring example of this occurred at the time of the 1991 'Children in Need' appeal. A girl came into the maths class with her face painted as a clown. She went round shaking her bucket for contributions. When finished she received a parting shot from the teacher which was 'next time show a bit more leg'. What, too, of the careers teacher who persists in referring to young women in responsible positions, other colleagues and members of the Careers Service, as lasses? Despite a position on the Equal Opportunities Committee of a prominent teachers' union, he sees nothing wrong with these sort of references, asserting that, 'It's not the language but the practice which is important'.

Our contention is that the language is all important in whatever form, be it spoken or written. Hence we would offer strategies for looking at language at various levels.

1   *The language of the institution* — how the school can be encouraged to discontinue sex-biased terminology and thus challenge continuing sex

stereotyping. This concerns all official documentation that goes to parents, pupils and staff. It is also relevant in the way pupils and staff are expected to address each other. For instance, is it alright for some staff to be addressed by their real or imagined marital status, Miss, and for others to be denoted by the term Sir?

2   *The tone of assemblies often expresses the ethos of a school.* Are such meetings geared to the interests of all pupils? Are areas of concern traditionally associated with women seen to be as equally valued by the school as those more often associated with boys? Above all are those who deliver assemblies, be they staff or pupils, roughly in the same proportion as their numbers in the school? Who gets praised, rewarded or reprimanded and what implications are there for sex bias in the way this is done?

3   *Classrooms — the written word.* Are text books and worksheets checked for their sexist assumptions in the way they portray men and women in biased and stereotypical ways, either by means of language or in the illustrations used?

4   *Classrooms and corridor — the spoken word.* Are staff careful in the way they address pupils? Do they make sure that assumptions about boy-specific and girl-specific behaviour and expectations are not perpetuated? It is also important that the school has a disciplinary procedure to effectively challenge sexist abuse wherever it occurs — between pupils and by pupils to staff. Is it still practice for staff to refer to girls by their first name and boys by their surname? Staff awareness over the unspoken messages that they give to classes of students by giving too much attention to one sex at the expense of the other should be monitored.

5   *Exercises and classroom strategies to raise awareness among pupils.* We would like the boys with whom we work to begin to question the injustice that is done to women in a male dominated society. Boys also need communication skills to enable them to function more cooperatively in mixed groups.

Man is Everywhere

Aim: To show how powerful language is.
             To demonstrate how words can exclude half the population.

Materials: Large sheets of paper and felt-tip pens

Time: 30 minutes

What to do:

Each boy has a sheet of paper and a selection of felt-tips.

Ask each of the boys to draw or write the first thing that comes into their heads when some of the following phrases are read out.

- Mankind
- Man conquers space
- Fireman
- Caveman
- The best man for the job
- The wise men of the island
- The newsman interviewed the star
- The Business Man of the Year
- The man in the street
- Man overboard!

Ask the group to come together in a large group to discuss what they have done. What do they notice about their pictures? What is missing? What is important about what they have done? What effect might this exercise have on their future thinking? What is being left out when one dominant person has the 'natural' right to speak for others?

(This exercise is based on Slavin, H. (ed.) *Greater Expectations*, p. 71, Living and Learning Ltd.)

Equal and Opposite?

Aim: To look at the way male/female word opposites assume very different values in relation to gender.

Materials: A copy of the list of words (see below)
Dictionaries
Thesaurus

Time: 15–20 minutes

What to do:

Divide the large group into small groups of three or four. Each small group needs to appoint a spokesperson to make notes.

Each group is given a thesaurus, dictionary and list of words.

Ask each group to decide what each of the words mean in everyday language. Check in the dictionary that the definitions are correct. Consult the thesaurus for synonyms.

When each group has finished ask them to share their definitions. One important question for the whole group to discuss is: 'Why do supposedly equivalent words have different meanings?'

The words:

Equal and Opposite?

patron	matron
master	mistress
host	hostess
waiter	waitress
Lord	Lady
actor	actress
husband	wife
landlord	landlady
bachelor	spinster
wizard	witch
call-boy	call-girl

(This exercise is taken from Slavin, H. (ed.) *Greater Expectations*, p. 73, Living and Learning Ltd.)

Man on the Wall

Aim: To show the false universality of 'Man' as a generic term.

Materials: A4 Paper and felt-tip pens

Time: 30 minutes

What to do:

Draw a brick wall on a sheet of paper. Copy it. Keep one wall blank but write the statements below on the other, as graffiti.

Give out copies of the graffiti-ridden wall and the blank wall. Ask the group to each re-write the male terms to make them sound as if they mean females as well. Write the new versions on the copies of the blank wall.

Come back together as a large group. Share what has been produced.

Suggested questions to supplement this exercise:

- Can you think of any other words or phrases which use male terms but which are supposed to include women as well?
- Does it matter when women's identities get lost by using such words and phrases.
- If someone said to you that it was OK to use these male terms, that they were just more familiar and convenient, what would you say to them?
- Why does it sound ridiculous to say 'Who's going to woman the phone?' or 'Let me have the mistress copy'.

The statements:

Caveman
Chairman
Fellow-men
Mankind
Man-made
Craftmanship
Workman
Mr & Mrs Albert Hand WOZ 'ere
Manpower

Reading between the Lines

Background: *This exercise is best attempted after some preliminary work on sexist language. Try 'Man is Everywhere' (pp. 177–8), or 'Man on the Wall' (pp. 179–80) first.*

Aim: *To allow boys to practise changing sexist statements into non-sexist statements*
   To help boys identify sexist assumptions in written language

Materials: *Copy of the worksheet 'Reading between the Lines', prepared using the statements below*

Time: *30–45 minutes*

What to do:

Divide the group into threes — certainly no more than four.

Ask each group to talk about each of the following statements and *agree* about what an acceptable alternative should be so that they are no longer sexist.

Re-assemble in a large group to share what has happened. Discuss the changes each group has made.

The statements:

Example	**Alternative**
Mary Wells is a highly successful woman advertising executive.	Mary Wells is a highly successful advertising executive.
As a mammal, man breast-feeds his young.	
Stefan Edberg is one of the best tennis players in the world today, and Steffi Graf is one of the best women players.	
Male nurse	
Mr Pearson owns a hairdressing salon with his wife, an attractive blonde, who mans the telephone.	
She has mastered the art of . . .	
Mrs Lennard, mother of four, was one of the speakers at the conference.	
Mr Jones runs a garage in partnership with his wife.	
The stalls at the Autumn Fayre need manning.	
Mr Dale sent for the master copy of the timetable.	
The man in the street.	
I'll have my girl check that.	
The men and their wives.	

(This exercise is taken from Slavin, H. (ed.) *Greater Expectations*, pp. 76–7, Living and Learning Ltd.)

My Little Chickadee

Aim: *To discuss the way men's language usage portrays women and girls in a negative way.*
           To find out how these negative appreciations influence men's treatment of women.

Materials: *Copy of the 'My Little Chickadee' sheet (prepared using the statements below) listing common expressions associated with women*

Time: *30 minutes*

What to do:

Ask the large group to divide into groups with 3–4 participants in each.

Give out the 'My Little Chickadee' sheets and ask each person to read through the list.

Ask each person in each group to pick one word or phrase which catches their eye. Taking turns, tell each member of your small group what women would find offensive about your word or phrase.

Ask the group to come back into a large group. Each participant is now to pick another word or phrase. Then, taking on the character/role reverse with a girl or woman they know, *speak as that girl/woman* and say exactly why you find the word or phrase offensive. (For this part of the exercise, encourage an appropriate expression of feeling by the 'girl/woman' who is speaking.)

As a conclusion ask the whole group why some words/phrases were not chosen.

Discuss the general effect of these and other terms on girls'/women's views of themselves and their value to men and society.

The statements:

Hen pecking	Just like a woman
She's a perfect little lady	Woman driver
Wine, women and song	Girl watching
That's not lady-like	Sex pot
Loose woman	Flat as a board
My little princess	Boy, is she stacked
Girl talk	What a pair of legs
Dumb blonde	Playmate of the month
Just a housewife	She goes all the way
The little woman	She's so cute when she's mad
A woman's place is in the home	She's really bright for a woman
Stand by your man	You've come a long way, baby

Men Talk Seriously, Women Just Gossip

Aim: *To look at the myths and realities about the way men and women commu-nicate.*

Materials: *Paper and pens*

Time: *30 minutes*

What to do:

Ask the large group to form into small groups with 3—4 participants.

Explain the rules of brainstorming — stressing writing anything which comes to mind without self-censorship.

Ask half of the small groups to brainstorm the words and phrases which describe women talking. Ask the other half to brainstorm the words and phrases used to describe men talking.

After five minutes ask one of the groups brainstorming women talking to join with a group which has been dealing with men.

In these enlarged groups discuss any similarities and differences in the two lists.

Come back into a large group and encourage the group to share what they have discovered.

Discussion points at this stage:

- • What are the myths about women's communication?
- • Why do these myths exist?
- • What are the myths about men's communication?
- • What makes it important for men to make out that women gossip?

Listening (1)

Aim: *To encourage a more cooperative listening style.*

Materials: *None*

Time: *30 minutes*

What to do:

Divide the large group into smaller groups of four.

Ensure that each small group is sitting so that they can see each other.

Give each small group a topic to talk about for 10 minutes.

Apart from the person who starts, everyone else in the group has to give a summary of what the previous speaker has said before being allowed to contribute.

After 10 minutes re-assemble in a large group and — keeping the same rule — discuss what it feels like to discuss in this way.

- What makes it different?
- What are the advantages of behaving like this in a group?
- What do you find uncomfortable about working in this way?

As a variation, when in the small group — make sure each group has an object/ a tally stick. Group members may only speak if they have the object/tally stick in their hands.

Listening (2)

Aim: *To encourage a more cooperative listening style.*

Materials: *Instruction cards*

Time: *15 minutes*

What to do:

Ask the boys to choose a partner. Instruct the pairs to divide into 'A's' and 'B's'.

Ask the A's to talk for 3 minutes on a given topic. Make sure that the topic ensures some emotional involvement, such as 'My memories of early childhood'.

B's task is to be silent for the 3 minutes and then repeat the main points of what has been heard as accurately as possible.

A then feedbacks on how well B has performed the task.

Listening (3)

Aim: *To allow the boys to feel the difference between attentive and inattentive listening.*

Materials: *Instruction sheet, prepared using the instructions below*

Time: *30 minutes*

What to do:

Ask the group to form into pairs. One to be A, the other to be B.

Give B the instruction sheet which he is not to show to A. The instructions make clear that B is to not maintain eye contact while A is talking and to engage in other activities that show B to be as inattentive as possible.

Some **instructions** you might use are:

- count in your head backwards from 100
- look at your watch
- fidget
- interrupt with irrelevant comments
- tie shoe laces

Ask A to talk for 3 minutes about 'The worst thing about being my age is . . .' B follows the instructions of inattention.

At the end of the 3 minutes, ask the pairs to talk about how it felt not to listen and not to be listened to.

In the whole group ask the boys to come up with some ideas that will improve listening and being heard. Write up their ideas as a classroom brainstorm. Hopefully these will include:

- making eye contact
- leaning forward slightly
- minimal encouragement — head nods, noises indicating agreement e.g., mmm!
- asking questions (not too many).

In pairs again, give the boys the opportunity to experience being listened to more attentively. Give them 2 minutes each on anything they would like to talk about.

Give an opportunity to feedback to each other how it felt to be listened to.

A Look at Language

Aim: *To take a critical look at the way men's language and assumptions devalue and control women's lives.*

Materials: *Copies of 'A Look at Language' playlet (see below)*

Time: *50 minutes*

What to do:

Ask for 4 volunteers to read through the playlet. Allow them to decide who will play which part and run through the short piece.

With the others explain the purpose of the session. Give out paper and ask them to jot down anything which they hear which puts women down.

When the group is clear about the task ask the readers to run through the play. Give everyone time to write down what they can.

Ask the readers to run through the play again and ask anyone in the group to call 'Stop!' when they notice a put-down. Encourage the person who has called 'Stop!' to explain why and encourage group discussion at this point.

Any points not picked up can be added by the teacher. (A reference sheet has been included as a prompt.)

The playlet:

A Look at Language

(A group of people are standing around eating and drinking at a family gathering.)

Jim: Hi Ray, hello Les — how's the missus?

Les: She's gone to put the kids to bed — it doesn't half take her a time these days. She's full of herself though at the moment since she got a job to give her bit of pin money.

Jim: Mine's the same — she's getting a bit uppity — she thinks she can go to college and get GCSEs. I've told her she's got no chance. I mean I ask you, she's doing maths and science — it's a joke. The best bet is she says she wants to be woman engineer. The whole thing's a real joke — anyway let's forget that and have another drink.

Les: Do you want another one Jim?

Jim: Too right I do.

Gary: What about the birds?

Jim: They'll be alright, they're busy fiddling about in the kitchen. If we disturb them now we'll never get anything to eat — you know what women are like.

Ray: What's your wife's little sideline then, Gary?

Gary: She's a postman.

Ray: That must be difficult, how does she manage the bag — not much fun for you either if she's out at funny times. How do you manage in the mornings?

Gary: Bloody difficult it is, I can tell you. I'm getting fed up with it — I just hope the novelty wears off soon.

Jim: That reminds me — hey you kids, clear off and play somewhere. You girls go upstairs and play with the dolls' house; boys get outside and kick a ball about — watch the traffic though. Let's all have a sit down.

Ray: Hey Jim, this chair's hopeless — aren't you going to fix it.

Jim: I'll get round to it when I've time — it's been difficult though. Mind you, you should hear the amount of nagging I've had to put up with from the wife — real GBH of the ear hole.

Les: This is good this is, isn't it — a chance to relax is all I need. Oh good, the ladies have done their stuff — let's eat.

The reference sheet:

A Look at Language

The missus	Denotes marriage. Women tend to be referred to by their marital status, men are not. Women usually take their father's name at birth, and their husband's name when they marry. There is no legal requirement for this. Ms is an acceptable alternative. Also objectifies a woman — she doesn't have a name.
With the kids of course	Implies that women should be with the children as a matter of course.
She's been a bit uppity	'Uppity' is a word sometimes used for women who try to step into positions that are traditionally seen as male roles.
Pin money	Assumption that the money earned is extra, and not a valuable contribution to the family budget.
Thinks she can get her GCSE's — no chance — maths and science	Women are often belittled for trying anything intellectual, academic, technical or scientific.
Woman engineer	Why 'woman'? We don't specify 'man engineer'.
Birds	A derogatory term for women, objectifying them and grouping them all together as pretty, cute and brainless. Throughout the scene women are never referred to by their names.
They're busy in the kitchen	Assumes that women will automatically be found in the kitchen preparing food.
You know women	Is a generalization of women's behaviour, implying that all women behave in a certain way and that it is understood they do.
Little sideline	Again, a belittling of women's behaviour, implying that all women behave in a certain way and that it is understood that they do.
Postman	Why do we go on using male terminology? Postwomen, post person, post officer or letter carrier would be alternative terms. They may sound strange at first, but nobody thinks baker, butcher, carpenter

	and builder should be bakeman, butchman, carpentman or buildman.
Girls — dolls house	Certain playthings have become traditionally female or male.
Boys — football	Why shouldn't all children be encouraged to play with a range of toys?
In the bedroom *In the street*	Girls are often protected, whilst boys are allowed the freedom to explore. All children need both at different times.
You should fix it, Bill	Men are traditionally seen as practical, but they are not necessarily comfortable in this role. Women generally are not expected to know how to fix things.
I know, you're right. My *wife's been nagging . . .*	The point is agreed with when a man makes it, but it is regarded as nagging when made by a women. Classifying a statement as nagging diminishes both the problem and the person.
The ladies	Puts women into a particular category again and labels their role, rather than recognizing them as individuals.

(This exercise is based on Dixon, H. and Mullinar, G. (eds) *Taught Not Caught*, pp. 63–5, Living and Learning Ltd.)

Chapter 8

The Ideal Manly Body

The Theory

Macho Values Embedded in Boys' Bodies

The traditional conception is that everyone has to be Arnold Schwarz-enegger . . . [which] probably lead[s] to some violence, unhappiness and things like that if they [boys and men] don't meet the standards. (Alex, from Gerschick and Miller, 1994)

Macho values aren't just made and carried around in boys' heads. They are also a part of boys' bodies. Boys spend a great deal of time learning to make their bodies more manly through 'forceful and space-occupying ways'. They do this through the everyday practices of learning to walk with their shoulders and their chests thrown out, through practising the virile strut, through developing power in their upper bodies, through hardening and toughening their arms, legs, chests, and through learning to look mean.

As Bob Connell (1983) says, 'What it means to be masculine is, quite literally, to embody force, to embody competence'. The processes of learning to 'embody force' mean puffing up your own body through exercising power over girls and unmanly boys. Turning their boyish, infantile bodies into manly bodies means learning to associate their physical presence with power and privilege. It also means learning to expect privileged treatment in their relations with other people and the outside world.

Therefore in challenging macho values we also need to recognize the importance of the making of boys' bodies — how they are formed, their relations with other people, and how dreams and desires are used by boys in making themselves more manly in their bodies. We want to make teachers and students more aware that the gendering of boys' bodies isn't just a 'natural' and 'normal' process but socially shaped through a great amount of time, energy and institutional support being spent on their development.

Self Images and Boys' Bodies

Our experiences of our bodies are central to our self-images and how we socially relate to other people. Especially for adolescent boys for whom other sources of traditional, masculine authority and respect (like economic power, fatherhood, or adult sexual relations) are only distant invitations. That means they're particularly concerned about a compensatory, body image and bodily sense of male power. One bodybuilder, looking back on his reasons for starting to pump iron, has commented that: 'I don't know. I guess I wanted some size. I was, you know, real skinny' (Klein, 1990).

Adolescent boys are often haunted by fears of appearing weak, short and 'skinny'. Lacking adult, male status they often put a great deal of energy and time into masculinizing bodywork (sporting activities, exercise, bodybuilding and martial arts) as a way of countering the dangerous threat of effeminacy or unmanliness. That can lead to an obsessive pursuit of the idealized, macho body.

Damaging Patterns

As the introductory quotation, above, points out, considerable damage is done through the chasing after this Arnold Schwarzenegger-type body. This damage takes place on two main levels; the pursuit of the idealized, macho body keeps boys and men on the hook, toeing the conventional lines of male supremacy over girls and women, and, second, the dominating culture of the idealized, macho body oppresses and severely limits many boys who perceive their bodies to be weak and unmanly.

Let us give just one example of this second form of boys–boys, men–men oppression. Boys and men with disabilities are stigmatized and marginalized as failed boys in this dominant culture of the macho, aggressive body. As Robert Murphy (Gerschick and Miller, 1994) comments, 'For the male, the weakening and atrophy of the body threaten all the cultural values of masculinity: strength, activeness, speed, virility, stamina, and fortitude.' Those boys who can't measure up against the traditional standards of the dominant body-culture begin to perceive themselves as inadequate, failed boys and, as a result, are often put down and marginalized. A great deal of personal unhappiness and psychological damage result from this marginalization. Many boys restlessly strive to achieve an illusory body-ideal and in this way their own rights to define their masculine identities for themselves are eroded. Insecure boys, often desperate for bodily approval in the terms of the dominant culture, internalize the ideals of heroic masculinity — physical strength, sporting prowess or athleticism, independence and sexual virility/performance. In doing so, they severely restrict their own lives as well as damaging other people.

All of these damaging, social pressures are shown very clearly in the life history of Jerry, a 16-year-old disabled boy in the US, who has juvenile rheumatoid arthritis (Gerschick and Miller, 1994). Viewed from the perspective of the ideal macho body, Jerry's awkward walking (he is only able to walk for short distances and this requires a great effort from him) makes him feel self-consciously vulnerable: 'I feel like I look a little, I don't know, more strange when I walk,' he said. His constant sense of having to measure his own masculine inadequacy in relation to the ruling norm comes through clearly: 'I think (others' conception of what defines a man) is very important because if they don't think of you as one, it is hard to think of yourself as one or it doesn't really matter if you think of yourself as one if no one else does.'

Also Jerry has been made to feel sexually emasculated and physically unattractive: '[The girls believe] I might be a "really nice person", but not like a guy per se . . . I think to some extent that you're sort of genderless to them.' He's trapped in the double bind often confronted by disabled men; he urgently wants to prove his strength and independence because his conventional manhood is undermined but he also craves, perhaps unconsciously, for support, relationship and intimacy:

> If I ever have to ask someone for help, it really makes me feel like less of a man. I don't like asking for help at all. You know, like even if I could use some, I'll usually not ask just because I can't, I just hate asking . . . [A man is] fairly self-sufficient in that you can sort of handle just about any situation in that you can help other people and that you don't need a lot of help.

Jerry, like other vulnerable and subordinated boys and men, is actively contributing to his own limited existence. Through self-censorship and self-surveillance, he is cutting himself off from behaviours and relationships that he perceives as unmanly. The irony is that in doing so he is estranging himself even further from his longings for loving relationship and intimacy.

What Boys Say about the Ideal Manly Body

When we ask boys to define the ideal manly body, they often do so in a mood of embarrassment, characterized by shy mental and physical shufflings as they play with the question in their minds. When they realize our seriousness in asking the question, there seems to be three primary bodily ideals that often crop up.

The first quality which emerges is a certain ruggedness which is found in upper body strength. Boys should have a muscular, broad shouldered and broad chested frame, tapering down to a narrow waist with a flat stomach. Boys also aspire to well-developed biceps, firm muscly legs and a shiny, tanned skin. To supplement these bodily qualities are the all-important facial features of good-looking face with noticeable cheek bones and a chin which provides a firm but not prominent jaw line. Ears should not be too big, the teeth must be white and the eyes clear and prominent.

Parallel with this visual noticeability of adolescent male perfection is the need for physical fitness — the need to simply be in good, physical shape so this brawn and strength can be applauded by the peer group. To have a sense of self-worth or well-being, the shape must also suggest the promise of physical stamina with an energetic and vigorous use of the body. One of our group, on being questioned about his physical shape, was insistent that his body building was just 'something to do'. Further inquiries revealed that he was pleased to be seen as strong and fit. He showed us his biceps and the size of his fist. He was also keen to demonstrate his strength in arm wrestling with his friends. Other boys also want to be recognized for their virile bodies, but they often have these aspirations without the commitment to the bodily exercise which becomes a feature of the lives of many older adolescents and young men. Much of the interest in the stars of American wrestling rings or the 'beef cakes' of the film world stems from the fact that such men are exaggerations of how the boys would like to be.

Boys take anxious pleasure in the process of becoming masculine. Each small landmark leading towards manhood is carefully noticed and internally recorded. Developments like height, chest and shoulder size, the lengthening of the penis, the growth of hair on face, legs and in the pubic region, all become objects of detailed scrutiny. All are part of the internal anxiety around becoming more and more manly. Particular triumphs exist around shaving. One of the authors' son was very pleased to announce to his mother and father that he was shaving every two days. He glowed with the pleasure of simply being able to relate this fact since he knew that this made him seem more manly compared with those of his peers who were worrying about when they are even going to start shaving. Thus each growth landmark is seen as a triumph of virility to record against the gnawing anxiety of not measuring up in the eyes of the group norm. The hoped for result will be the imaginary pay-off of becoming increasingly attractive to girls and also being looked up to by less fortunate, less well-endowed boys within the peer group.

Those who are looked up to, wield the power within the world of juvenile manhood. They are the cocks who invest a ruling, dominating boyhood with power over more marginal, vulnerable masculinities — the boys who are not cocks. Yet all this is based on a social fiction of achieved and completed masculinity. The illusion is that somehow masculinity can actually be achieved, when in fact masculinity keeps boys on the hook of aspiring to a fantasy which is unattainable. It is the process of becoming manly that, in boys' eyes, defines what masculinity is. But it is a cruel hoax since even boys in the 'cock group' have continually to prove their status as cocks and reassert its force in their lives.

Fantasies and Desires about Ideal Bodies

The power of group fantasy about what constitutes a 'real boy' affects boys' relationships to their own bodies. Some live in an optimistic world which suggests that time and natural growth will fill their bodies out appropriately. Different rates of growth and development cause deep anxieties for many boys who see themselves as very small compared with their seemingly more grown-up and developed peers. Boys who do not shape up to the group constructed ideal are filled with a fundamental distrust of what they actually have which does not lead them to a positive acceptance of their own bodily resources. Instead of being satisfied with what they already have as something personal and unique, the boys' self-esteem is eroded.

Many boys have fantasies, projecting the adventurous, brave and heroic part of themselves into competition with real or imagined difficulties in which they alone can be triumphant. Boys also make use of their heroes, so that although the boy can't actually be like Arnold Schwarzenegger, he can use his hero's imagined qualities to get normal peer group acceptance.

Boys also use strategies to bolster their fragile sense of self when seen in competition with the rugged male ideal. This can also be defined as flirting with the tough lad culture or ingratiating themselves with the more fortunate 'top dog' element within the peer group. With the jokes, the banter, the posturing and the exaggerated stories, boys attempt to guard themselves against being found out. They are covering-up the undervaluing and distrust with which some boys view their self-image. Indeed, some boys' images of themselves are so full of self-hatred that they find it impossible to talk about. It is a forbidden zone where to let other boys into the world of internal doubt would risk the fear of ridicule and the possibility of being excluded. Thus boys who cannot compete in physical terms and who desperately fear being ignored, ridiculed and left out, actually leave themselves out by a deliberate process of detachment, separation, and dissociation. They come alive in the impersonal routines of such activities as video and computer games. To sink into such activities means there is no need to fear personal contact, no risk in personal interaction. They keep control by living in sealed off compartments of self.

What Can We Do?

In the 1990s, boys and men look around at the constructions of masculinity as seen in society today. They notice that the changing patterns of the working world do not define masculinity so obviously any more. Previous generations have defined masculinity simply by the jobs that some men did: miners, building workers, firemen. The physical strength involved in these jobs spelt them out as men's jobs. Of course, it is still possible to think in male terms about some jobs, but so many occupations are no longer so physically demanding that men can be defined as real men within them. This may explain the recent increase in popularity of bodybuilding. The rise may be connected with this decline of masculine status through work and the desire to fulfil a compensatory, symbolic achievement through the body. Thus the construction of masculinity in the body means becoming a kind of 'Mr Muscle' since other occupational identifying strategies are increasingly lacking. No matter what job the adolescent male goes into, he hopes no-one will mistake him for anything other than a real man.

The other point here is that heterosexual boys and young men are increasingly being encouraged to enjoy the spectacle of their own bodies. The media surrounds them with narcissistic images of young men's bodies on display. What with hair gel, earrings, aftershave, body deodorant, pony tails — boys' bodies are there to be preened and gazed at, as never before. But there are dangers in this growing preoccupation with their own bodies. Any hint of too much softness, effeminacy or homosexual desire has to be fiercely denied in this heterosexual reassertion of masculine pride in a dangerously uncertain world.

This tension is caught in the world of advertising. Heterosexual men can wear perfume, aftershave, deodorant but usually in a defensive context of active virility that protects boys and young men from the charge of being too soft, a 'woman' or a 'poofter'. Take Chanel's 'Egoiste' ad, for example, circulated in most colour supplements towards the end of 1994. The young, athletic man is literally boxing his own shadow (his repressed, 'feminine' self?). His softer self who wants to wear the perfume is in conflict with his pugilistic, public self. But the ad demonstrates that muscles and fists and a proud heterosexual activity can co-exist (however turbulently and contradictorily) with a softer, more displayed version of the masculine self.

The destructive effect of the pursuit of the ideal male body seriously harms the relations boys have with each other, and is also possibly damaging to their own self-image as a result of the self-loathing at not 'matching up'. It is important that the concept of the group's norm as the only worthy body image for boys is challenged. It is worth demonstrating that so many boys are unable to achieve the ideal body but are nevertheless influenced by those in the ruling/ leading cock group whose attitudes build distrust of more vulnerable bodies. This internal hatred at not shaping-up well enough leads to a self-imprisonment by the more vulnerable boys who are held by this ideal fantasy which holds the symbolic promise of the idealized self which will match the 'demands' of the cock group.

Strategies which offer some hope of making boys question their commitment to the ideal frame include working on the question, 'What does the ideal body help me to do?' Boys can be encouraged to ironically comment on the real life functions of some of the excess of muscle which they aspire to and spend so much time creating and worrying over. Also illuminating, would be the knowledge of what girls actually want of the boys they are attracted to. Boys might be surprised to know that there is a mis-match between what boys think girls will like and what in fact girls do find attractive. A survey of 56 girls at a Derby Comprehensive school certainly highlighted muscles and upper body strength as important, but the overdeveloped ideal was simply seen as ugly. Waists should be slim and legs should not be too developed in a muscular sense. Boys should walk 'like a male model on a cat walk' and the rigid male strut is not applauded at all. Girls are also very clear about what they look for within this frame. Qualities of being understanding, approachable, sensitive, kind and romantic, figure prominently in girls' expectations. All of these are not accorded a high profile in the way boys would portray themselves to other boys.

Above all, the pleasures to be gained from a variety of body images should be stressed. Boys don't have to be hooked in on the level of striving and straining to be more like *Rambo* or 'Mr Perfect'. It is fine if a boy is small, neat, slim and delicate. We are very keen for boys to accept and value what they have and appreciate it in a real spirit of celebration.

Selected Further Reading on Boys' Bodies and the Ideal Manly Body

JACKSON, D. (1990) 'Falling apart: Men's bodies and masculine identities' in *Unmasking Masculinity*, London, Routledge.

CONNELL, R.W. (1983) 'Men's bodies' in *Which Way is Up?*, Sydney, Allen and Unwin.

GERSCHICK, T. and MILLER, A. (1994) 'Manhood and physical disability', *Changing Men* **27**, Winter.

MORGAN, D. (1993) 'You too can have a body like mine: Reflections on the male body and masculinities', in SCOTT, S. and MORGAN, D. (Eds) *Body Matters*, London, Falmer Press.

McGRATH, R. (1988) 'Looking hard: The male body under patriarchy', in FOSTER, A. (Ed.) *Behold the Man: The Male Nude in Photography*, Edinburgh, Stills Gallery.

SIMPSON, M. (1994) 'Big Tits! masochism and transformation in bodybuilding' in *Male Impersonators*, London, Cassell.

MISHKIND, M. *et al* (1987) 'The embodiment of masculinity: Cultural, psychological and behavioural dimensions' in KIMMEL, M. (Ed.) *Changing Men*, California, Sage.

The Session

The Importance of an Ideal Body

I would like to encourage boys to think more seriously about their bodies. Boys seem to have such an investment in the importance of an ideal body. I had already been told about the admiration for Arnold Schwarzenegger and other heroes of the big screen. I was also aware of the attraction which WWF (World Wrestling Federation) wrestling has in the eyes of boys who are devotees of the 'grunt and groan' wrestling world. What is the fascination? What is the attraction? What will having an ideal body within the peer group of 14 year olds really mean? Would boys be able to share bodily insecurities with other boys and be able to learn from each other? Could all this be done in an atmosphere of trust and respect? The answer came in two important sessions with two different groups. Both sessions were flawed but contained some positive and rewarding work.

Class 09 were coming into their seventh session. It was early January, a bright day, and just after lunch. Boys came in breathless and restless. They seem to slump and also to be irritatingly more interested in what had been going on at lunchtime than in what might be happening over the next 70 minutes. I decide to just 'go for it' — getting straight into the work by asking them to stand up and look at each other. I ask, 'How do you feel about your bodies?' There is much embarrassment around this. I want to get at what they have just been doing with their bodies and for them to actually share what that really felt like? Steve decides to sit down while he and Jagvir engage in some idle banter, with prodding! On inquiry they tell me that they are messing about because they are worried. They decide that it is quite brave for them to have said this. I agree with them. Scot and Chris have been playing football but they find it very difficult to actually say how their bodies felt while actually playing the game. As Chris said, 'You don't think about how you feel when you're doing it.' It seemed extremely difficult to articulate even a sensation of bodily pleasure.

I decide that they will fill in the 'How Do You Feel about Your Body?' sheets. On completion I ask each of them to pick a part of their body and to become that part. In a dramatic sense they are to role reverse with a part of themselves. It was not something they were used to doing and certainly required much direction on my part. I then pose four basic questions with lots of variations in the form of encouragement:

- What does part x do for the rest of your body?
- What type of person do you think your owner is?
- What sort of shape do you think your owner wants to be?
- How does he want to be seen by the rest of the group and those outside?

So the structure here is to use an externalized, though important, part of self to say things that may not be revealed or shared by the boy in role as himself.

The boys seemed surprisingly keen to try this. Jagvir volunteered to go first and became his back. The group all listened as he told us, 'I hold Jagvir up, I keep him erect, but I bend him when I feel like it.' Jagvir's back went on to say that, 'Jagvir thinks his body is good and glamorous' and that 'he has a good physique which could be a bit fragile.' It was difficult to get him to say more about what 'fragile' meant — perhaps it was enough for him just to have hinted at being vulnerable. The other boys were quiet while Jagvir wrestled with his embarrassment about doing this. They were tolerant of his shyness, his asides, his hand waving, his laughter and his sincerity. He chose to show how he wanted to be seen by the rest of the group by posing. He showed in his stance that he wanted 'a bit of a broad chest'. Shazad asked him what would happen if he didn't get one — Jagvir's impressive reply was, 'nothing, I'll still be me'.

There was competition about who should go next — eventually it was Shazad who had chosen to be his legs. 'I support him. If I wasn't there he'd collapse. He's a physical person. He's athletic and it's very important that I [legs] am here. He's not very happy at the moment because he's only of average build. What he would really like is muscular legs, chest and big, broad shoulders and biceps.' Shazad posed by sticking his chest out and his shoulders back to try to give himself the breadth that he wanted.

Chris' comment on what he had seen so far came through his own work. Chris chose to be his hands, saying, 'Chris is normal and there is nothing greatly different about him. He's not interested in being big and broad — he is who he is — he is Chris.' He was quite determined about this and his ideal body sculpt just showed him posing in as natural a way as he could.

Scott chose the same body part but found it very difficult to be his hands. Despite encouragement from the rest of the group, he wasn't able to do it. He was able to say that he didn't want a broad chest and shoulders. 'But you're always watching wrestling,' said Mathew. More promptings from the group revealed that he would like to be 'a bit like one of the wrestlers'. Scott was very shy about this and I felt that he did well to overcome his shyness.

Abid and Mathew are both very small in stature. Abid was very concerned about being tough. If he was tough, he wouldn't get pushed around. His sculpt saw him drawing himself up to emphasize his height. He really did want broad shoulders and a broad chest. However incongruous he appeared in his words and action, though, there was no attempt to belittle Abid. The same response was true for Mathew who having chosen his feet to speak for him said, 'He's a nice person, he gives me clean socks, he keeps me warm and looks after me. He wishes he was taller but doesn't want broad shoulders. He's not bothered about being tougher.' Again there was no attempt to minimize or laugh at what Mathew had said, although Mathew is the 'clown' of the group. Generally, he finds a lot of things difficult and gets confused easily, but this time the whole group were with him as he struggled with the task. There was a willingness to volunteer support by means of suggestions.

It seemed appropriate to acknowledge what the group had shared by demonstrating that sharing in a frozen sculpt. They chose to get everyone in contact with each other's nominated speaking body part. This was done really well without any of the embarrassment which creeps in. The 'freeze' was held and acknowledged with thanks to each other.

About a fortnight later, I had thought of the idea of actually having boys draw their ideal male bodies and then follow that by drawing their own as they are now. The idea was that on completion everyone in a group could share the gap which existed for them between the ideal and reality. In the session, four of the boys were absent and there was a lot of fuss about not being able to draw, with some sheepish comments about whether the figures had to be drawn with clothes on or not. In truth there was something of a hubbub which only re-solved itself when everyone had paper and pencils. There was much looking at what each other was doing and some sniggering around the drawing of genitalia. When the drawings were complete, the boys found a partner with whom to share what their drawings were saying about themselves.

Like a lot of pairs work with 14 year olds, they need a bit of encourage-ment to stay on the task rather than drift off into talk about anything else or just simply indulge in a desire to mess about. Of course, the material is difficult and dangerous to talk about. The boys know that they are in the world of the chance injudicious remark resulting in ridicule from the group and, above all, the group's long memory of perceived indiscretions. I make a point of visiting each of the pairs and hear what they have to say to each other. Anwaar, who is slight, wants a broader body. Part of him says this doesn't really matter but he would just like it. He wants bigger arms, a broader chest and even uses the words 'Incredible Hulk-ish'. 'It feels normal not to be like that because all my life I've been living like this.' He gestures to his small thin body. 'But I have daydreams about being a hero.' Azzar listens in respectful silence. He takes his cue from his partner's level of sharing by acknowledging that he too wants more muscles. He thinks muscles make him look tougher and more attractive and, also, with such attributes he wouldn't be shy.

Paul shares that he would like to have the bigger arms, more muscly chest, legs and broader shoulders. He goes into his desire for an ideal physique but then takes it away by saying that he isn't really bothered about it at all. A little questioning about this revealed that Paul would like to be taller. His eyes lit up at this because 'He is a little bit upset, not really upset', about not being tall. His partner, Darren, is really into the idea of having the broad physique. He is disappointed about being thin and slender. He says that it is very important to go bodybuilding but meanwhile he admits to daydreaming about being big and tough.

Lee, John and Parminder worked in a group of three. Lee, who had drawn a very hairy, ideal person, decided that he didn't want to be hairy at all. He admitted that it was one of the occasions when he wasn't really listening. It is very difficult to get Lee to talk — he just smiles a lot. I think he says things either to please or to give himself a quiet life. He just wants to be medium and thinks he has achieved this. John, on the other hand, drew himself as being fat. He was reluctant to talk much about this, just letting his picture speak for him. He did speak with a real sense of urgency about being a lot taller with more muscle. He shared this feeling with Parminder. Both boys also have daydreams about being more adventurous and heroic and of feeling more secure in the stronger, more vigorous bodies that time will grant them.

Something active was needed and continuums are always good for encouraging dialogue and debate. Two ends of the room became polarized as non-ideal body and ideal body. The boys were asked to place themselves where they felt they were in answer to the question, 'How far are you away from an ideal manly body?' Most of the group (six boys) positioned themselves at the non-ideal end, indeed there was competition around who should be nearest the wall. It was surprising to find John who was worried about his weight putting himself a little way down the continuum, indicating some degree of attainment of an ideal male figure. Lee placed himself very close to the ideal end of the continuum. The boys then talked among themselves as to why they were in the position they were. Similar responses came up as had been revealed in the pairs. Certainly the ideal would make them seem stronger, smarter, older, tougher, and 'looking like a gentleman'.

At that point, I changed the continuum to reflect the ideal 14 year old. Suddenly the continuum was peopled throughout its length as only Paul and Anwaar stayed as non–ideal 14 year olds, with the other six standing at various stages of idealness. The boys were to hold their position and talk to the person nearest to them about what being an ideal 14 year old would do for them. When they had done this, each shared from their position on the continuum and showed again how important an appearance of strength and tallness would be. This time other dimensions emerged like brains, good eyesight and just looking more grown-up.

I brought the boys together in a whole group. The question I wanted them to share in the group is, 'What would being ideal protect me from now?' Paul shared his dislike of being called shrimp: 'No-one would call me names. I would be bigger and taller.' He even stood up on his stool to demonstrate how tall he wanted to be. Anwaar is sick of being called 'werewolf' because he happens to have bushy eyebrows which join together. This provokes a real life piece of name-calling between Anwaar and Parminder. Anwaar's sense of frustration is triggered and he becomes angry. I want him to be angry with Parminder, to tell him what his unkindness actually makes him feel. I facilitate so that both parties can hear each other. They agree to a truce in name-calling and threats for at least a week. We check the following week and both Anwaar and Parminder say they have not broken the truce and that they are listening to what each other feels. They are heartened by this, and so am I.

John also mentions name calling. He thought that being ideal would stop people from calling him fat. Azzar's concern is his glasses. He is sick of being 'vision express' and 'four-eyes'. He is also taunted with his height and referred to as 'Daddy Long Legs'. Being ideal would protect him too. No-one gets at Lee since he makes people laugh. Five of the group confirmed this. He likes being a joker. Parminder thought it protected him from being called names. I encourage the group to check this out with Lee who, in a rare moment of self-revelation in the group, acknowledges that being the class joker does protect him and keeps him safe from taunts.

I encourage the group to conclude the session by sharing appreciations of what they have heard about each other. How will it affect behaviour, both within and outside the group in the future. There is a general feeling expressed that it has been good to hear what each other said, that they didn't realize how strongly each other felt or how important the ideal 14 year old was in their minds. They felt that they had really shared something. They would now be more appreciative of each other and, because they were aware of each others' frailties, they could be happier as they were without striving for ideals which may not be important. That was true in the group but it still felt different and more frightening outside the group with other boys.

Classroom Strategies

Ideal Manly Body

The central organizing focus of this section is on the critical contrast between idealized fantasies about male bodies and actual bodies. The strategies encourage boys to become more explicitly aware of how they masculinize their bodies through embodying force and superiority over girls and unmanly boys. Particular emphasis is given to visual exploration of bodies as a way of challenging the traditional visible presence of boys, i.e., looking at the preoccupation with the over-development of boys' upper bodies, the suggestion of rugged manly presence, the shoulders, the strut and the whole persona of 'Don't mess with me I could be hard and dangerous!'

How Do You Feel about Your Body?

Aim: To help boys talk about their bodies.

Materials: 'How Do You Feel about Your Body?' sheets, using questions below
    Pens

Time: 45 minutes

What to do:

Ask the boys to complete the 'How Do You Feel about Your Body?' sheets.

On completion ask the boys to share in pairs what they have written down and to help each other identify a particular body part that he would feel comfortable to talk about in the group.

Taking volunteers in turn ask the boy to role reverse with the chosen part of his body, e.g., the boy will speak as if he were his legs.

Encouraging questions might include the following:

- As the chosen part, what do you do for the rest of the body?
- What type of person do you think your owner is?
- What sort of shape does your owner want to do?
- How does he want to be seen by the rest of the group and those outside?
- What is X (boy's name) doing when he feels bad about his body?
- What is X (boy's name) doing when he feels good about his body?

Sometimes groups have wanted to conclude this exercise by making a group sculpt to show the different body parts linked together but demonstrating the importance for each person of their bodies as a whole.

The questions:

How Do You Feel about Your Body?

Which part of your body:

    Is most pleasing?
    Is most upsetting?
    Are you most aware of?
    Is most ignored?
    Do you like best?
    Do you like least?

Would you most like to alter?

Is most attractive?

Is least attractive?

What activities make you feel good about your body?

What activities make you feel bad about your body?

Body Contrasts

Aim: *To encourage boys to explore the feelings about the differences between an ideal manly body and the reality of their own.*

Materials: *Paper and pencils*

Time: *45 minutes*

What to do:

Boys are encouraged to take paper and pencil and draw their ideal manly body. Some coaxing may be necessary around those who say they can't draw. It is important to stress that being able to draw a generalized ideal shape will be enough.

On completion of the drawing the boys can be instructed to take a separate sheet and draw their own bodies as they see them now.

Ask the boys to go into pairs with their drawings. The following questions have proved useful.

- What do these drawings say about yourself?
- How much of the Ideal Manly Body do you hope to achieve?
- What will be important about having a more developed body?
- What will having an Ideal Manly Body protect you from?
- Can you share anything about how difficult it is to be the shape you are now?

Alternatively or in addition the use of continuums can be encouraged. Select two sides of the room as ideal and non-ideal manly bodies. Ask the boys to place themselves along a line between the two points that express where they feel they are now. Ask them to speak to someone near them in the line about why they have taken up their particular position. Similar questions to those above can be used.

The continuum idea can also be used to explore ideal and non-ideal perceptions of a particular age group.

Drawing My Body's History

Aim: To help boys explore how their bodies have been made rather than just taking them for granted.

Materials: Very large role of paper, felt tips

Time: 45 minutes

What to do:

(i)   Give each boy enough paper so that a partner can draw round his outline.
(ii)   Each boy labels the outline of his body in terms of what has happened to different parts. They need to date the happenings. e.g., broken arm 3 years ago.
(iii)   With the partner share what they have identified, i.e., breaks, scars, etc. Helpful questions which boys could consider are:

- How have their bodies changed since they were little?
- Can they identify any significant growth points?
- Do they over-use or under-use certain parts of their bodies?

(iv)   Display all the bodies and encourage boys to mingle and share each other's work.

Photographs of Boys Growing Up

Aim: To help boys explore what they are learning while changing from boys to young men.

Materials: Photographs of themselves as children aged

(i)   Three to seven years old.
(ii)   Eight to eleven years old.
(iii)   Twelve to fifteen years old.

The photographs can be solo, any sorts of group or team.

Time: 45 minutes

What to do:

Help the boys reflect on the development shown in their photographs.

In pairs encourage the boys to talk to each other using the following suggestions:

- How do my photographs show I have physically changed as a boy?
- What were the important feelings connected to those changes?
- Helpful areas to concentrate on are:

  Height
  Size
  Hairiness
  Muscularity

- Encourage the boys to notice the contrast between childhood softness/pudginess and adolescent firmness.
- What were the main influences on their changes through the years e.g., immediate family or media images?
- Which image of themselves do they most like/dislike? — Why?

Towards the end of the session ask the group to re-assemble as a whole group to share what they have learned about themselves.

Chapter 9

School Sport and the Making of Boys and Men

The Theory

Gritting their Teeth and Ignoring the Pain

One of the authors' memories of playing school sport at a grammar school in the 1950s brings up many of the key connections between sporting activities and the building and confirming of manhood. This account focuses on the author's experience of playing scrum-half in a school rugby match. There are historical differences between then and now but there are still many common features.

> Our opponent's forwards were much stronger than us that day and I remember the pack breaking through our defence with the ball at their feet. For a brief moment the ball broke loose and I fell on it, curling my body around it so that only my own forwards could get at it. It was a really daft thing to do and nothing to do with courage. I just unthinkingly conformed to the warrior norms of the game. That is what you were supposed to do when playing school rugby, wasn't it? At all costs you had to defend the citadel against invaders. You had to detach your body from your head and feelings to be heeled and brutalized. To save the team, the platoon, the male club, you had to pretend that all the bruising didn't hurt. Or you had to pretend it only hurt a bit, but you could bear it. That was the name of the game, wasn't it?
>
> The opposing side's forwards tore at me, screwing their boot studs down into my buttocks, trying to kick me off the ball, but I clung onto it till my own team mates had got back behind me and managed to scramble the ball into touch. The warrior ethos — displaying courage and bravery, and not deserting my post while under heavy enemy fire — only became clear to me much later.

There is often an exhilarating energy in school sport for many boys. Even, at times, a repressed sensuality and sense of drama. But alongside that energy and fierce movement boys also learn what it is to be a 'real boy' in our culture. As we can see from the extract above, boys learn about the necessity of hardening their bodies, accepting violent confrontations as a 'normal' way of life and splitting themselves off from their feelings. To play sport in an appropriately manly way, boys have to prepare their bodies for physical clashes and jarring crunches. Through this, they often develop a clenched determination to win at all costs by gritting their teeth and ignoring their hurt and often confused feelings about what they're doing to themselves and others.

The language of school sport for many boys is the language of warfare — 'Hit them hard today, lads!' All the talk is of combat, battles, seeing your opponents as the enemy, and military conquest. There is a gladiatorial type of imagery of sparring and grappling and not deserting your post. The results of this sport-as-warfare approach is often to normalize aggressive competitiveness in the lives of many boys. This overemphasis on battling and winning is re-warded by becoming a member of the male club. Or, rather, an illusory fantasy of recognition and acceptance is offered to all boys who, like me in the rugby match, are striving to conceal their fears of unmanliness through heroic, sporting performances. I stupidly defended the honour of my rugby team through stop-ping my opponents' forward dash. And through the emotional and physical bruising and brutalization, I tried to prove that I was man enough to be taken seriously by the buddy-boy peer group.

School Sport as a Masculinizing Process

As Bob Connell (1982) suggests, boys don't express their innate manliness through sporting activities; they make themselves into 'real lads' through regu-larly repeated sporting practices. School sport isn't just an innocent pastime, but a heavily gendered, masculinizing process that builds a 'top dog' model of mas-culinity to aim for and live up to in many boys' lives. This model of masculinity suggests that it is natural and normal for boys to crunch together and compete to achieve a robustly virile manliness.

In order to achieve this fantasy state of heroic virility, boys have to learn to go for aggressive performance, success, superiority over women, emotional stoicism, physical strength and goal-directedness in their sporting activities. However, they often learn to do this at the expense of their capacity to act as human beings. Their abilities to relate to other people, to feel for others, to trust, to cooperate, to link together their bodies with their hearts, are all dam-aged and severely limited by such sporting practices. Connell (1982) offers a telling example from his investigations into schooling and gender relations in Australian education. The emotional and social damage is clearly visible in his portrait of Brian Andrews, a boy who goes to a 'ruling class', all boys school in Australia.

Brian Andrews, for instance, the son of a company manager, is being comprehensively trained as a competitor by his family and his school,

There is a fierce push behind his involvement in football. Unfortunately, he is still physically small and consequently last year ran into a series of injuries, culminating in concussion. It took an anxious teacher getting on the phone to Mr Andrews before Brian, to his chagrin, was put down to a lower grade, playing with smaller boys. Asked what he would most like to improve about himself, his answer was 'to grow bigger physically'. (p. 93)

This continual straining to be bigger, stronger, harder, more successful in their sporting behaviour keeps many boys on the hook (one of the authors can even remember one small, talented, 15-year-old boy in a Lancashire comprehensive being rejected after a trial for a first division football club and being told that they might want to look at him again if he could grow a few inches). It's this haunted pursuit of an illusory masculinity that puts so much pressure on boys like Brian. The fear and the shame of failure is always there for boys like him, the flip-side of winning and success. The message is that you're not a 'real boy' if you can't measure up to these manly values in physical and cultural terms. Try as hard as he could in that culture of winners and 'big boys', Brian is savagely confirmed as an unmanly 'short-arse' who has been relegated to play with the smaller boys. It's that sense of culturally learnt personal 'inadequacy' and 'incompetence' that often drives boys like Brian to have to go on proving themselves that they're really okay in other spheres like work, sex and car driving.

Part of this driving pressure also comes from the fathers. Some fathers want to live through their sons and this often allows them to have a second chance at the kind of sporting career they never had in their own lives. The father urges on his son. The son tries to live up to those inflated expectations. And the frequent result of these interactions is that the culture of aggressive competitiveness is perpetuated.

However, not all boys buy so heavily into these masculinizing processes. Other boys develop their own subtle strategies of non-compliance and resistance. They feign illness over a long period of time, lose their kit, ask if they can do some alternative activity, forge notes, invent excuses for not going into the shower, develop preferences for other sporting activities like field events in athletics, such as high-jumping, putting the shot or throwing the javelin. There are also boys who have the inner confidence (and sometimes emotional bravery) not to pretend that they are harder than they look, who often refuse to fit in to manly expectations from sports teachers, fathers or other boys. They can show that the occasional enjoyment of challenges in sport doesn't necessarily have to be linked with the compulsion to beat others or win at all costs. Other sport or non-competitive games (see Is There an Alternative? pp. 209–14) can be enjoyed in a different kind of spirit — more relaxed, playful, experimental, even irreverent. There is also a class dimension to this non-compliance. In ruling class schools there is often a much greater, competitive pressure to conform to the public school ethos of gaining manliness through sport. But in more working-class institutions, sometimes the distance between middle-class cultural values and working-class boys' world-views results in some of the boys defying or sending up officially approved sporting activities. However, even more complexly, class rebellion can also trap some working-class boys into using sport as an aggressively manly way of getting back at a middle-class cultural authority that puts them down.

Black boys also often have a contradictory relationship to school sport in Britain today. Their attempts to develop a balanced perspective on sport as an occasionally enjoyable part of their lives are often interrupted by the narrowing assumptions and expectations of a racist, colonial discourse. Within this warping framework, black boys and men are still often seen as mere bodies — sensual, athletic and highly sexual. The black, sensual body is defined in opposition to the imaginary white man — intellectually superior, civilized, stoical, emotionally detached. The practical result of this shaping of the black, sensual 'other' is the reinforcing of racism through everyday sites like the school playing fields and the school gym. Black boys who show any potential at all in the sports arena are often prematurely channelled into sports as a career because of the white male domination of the more professional and educational routes out of a state of powerlessness and poverty. Of course, for some black youths success through sporting activities is an important part of the building of a more positive self-esteem and we ought to respect and encourage that, as long as we don't believe that that success isn't a direct reflection of the innate, physical strength, instinct and rhythm of all black boys and men. That racist assumption should be replaced by a more informed choice about alternative life chances and possibilities, rather than sport being seen as one of the only escape routes from the black economic ghetto.

School Sport as a Male Sanctuary

Locker rooms, changing rooms, showers, team baths, pavilions are all male sanctuaries. They allow boys to build up a closely bonded sense of male peer group solidarity. This sense of manly bonding (often expressed through horseplay, dirty jokes and banter) is produced through the segregation from and exclusion of women and girls. There is often a hearty guffawing, male camaraderie in such places that revels in sexist sniggers and innuendoes and keeps some boys' spirits up through the false bravado of the pack. However, boys also have to watch their backs in such places, for the next witty jeer might suddenly turn on them as the object of its humour. Mock fighting, wet towel flipping, horseplay in the showers or communal baths offer boys an acceptably violent form within which they feel able to express some of their need for closeness, and the need to touch and hug other boys without being ripped apart as a 'Poofter!'

What these divisions and exclusions add up to in the end is to deepen boys' fears of the 'feminine' inside themselves. A defensive, buddy-boy team culture helps to give boys the safety and reassurance of the pack to assert their manliness in direct opposition to girls, women and gay men. So male sanctuaries act as buttressing forces in boys' lives where they seem able to police the boundaries between their always fragilely held virility and unmanliness. As a result, many boys hold themselves together by using sport as an exclusively male preserve. 'Hard' parts are asserted through sporting activities and 'soft' parts are split off from the 'hard' bits and disowned.

The Gendering of Boys' Bodies through School Sport

School sport doesn't just play a part in shaping boys' emotional and social lives. It also locks many boys into an aggressively virile culture through the masculinizing of their bodies. Boys are born with male bodies (biological characteristics) but quickly develop a gendered sense of masculinity in their bodies through the social meanings and relations they meet in a world that is organized in the interests of male power.

Building a sense of masculinity in boys' bodies means physically embodying the power and authority conferred on them by a men-on-top culture. Practically, that means boys learning to hold and to relate to their bodies in a particular way. They learn to detach their emotional lives from their bodies and to manage that split through hardening and brutalizing their bodies. Indeed, some boys even view their bodies as objects of force to gain power over other boys.

Through these processes many boys lose touch with their bodily limits and often develop a destructive, mechanical relationship to their bodily health and well-being. Also this automated response is often seen in relation to others, as shown in contact on the playing field and in sexual relations. Their own emotional responsiveness to others becomes deadened as they learn to impose the demands of their conscious wills on themselves. In short, in order to qualify as properly masculine, some boys learn to deny their emotional and bodily needs. There is often a lack of connectedness as boys become more detached from their own bodily signals.

The physical embodying of masculine power often means boys taking on a virile strut and swagger. It means carrying your body in such a way that other boys have to watch out for themselves when they walk past or play against you. Peter Shilton, an ex-England goalkeeper, once said that when he faced a penalty kick he tried to make his body appear to swell in size so that it looked, to the opposing side's penalty taker, that it occupied the whole space of the goal. Similarly, that's what many boys are learning in playing rugby, cricket, football, all the year round — to suggest the menacing promise of power through the way they hold their bodies.

Through constant tackling, kicking, throwing, yelling, jumping, lunging, running hard, boys tauten their muscles, put an arrogant hardness on their faces, throw out their chests and hold themselves firm and upright in an attempt to intimidate their opponents. They learn to walk taller than they actually are and their eyes scowl rather than hint at any suggestion of human warmth or humour that might be interpreted as 'softness'. Perhaps what they need to feel about themselves is that they are taller and harder than girls. Many boys are trying to embody superiority over girls and gay men. They hold their bodies in a firmly decisive way that hopefully marks them off from an imaginary girl. Through banishing their own physical sensuality and grace they identify themselves as 'really' masculine. And by doing so they betray their emotional selves and deny the full reach of their bodies' potentialities.

Watching Sport

Both on the television and the football terrace, sport offers boys images, models and fantasies of what it is to be a 'proper' man today. Growing boys are surrounded by images of sporting success, triumph and honour that are closely tied to assertions of manly virility. Practically, they show boys what to strive for and how to behave as a boy or a man.

As the erosion of traditional masculine values goes on, sport has become one of the key sites where boys and men can establish and validate their manhood. This happens both at a physical level, on the school soccer pitch, but also at a symbolic/ideological level as well, usually through being a sporting fan, being a spectator, watching sport on television and reading about it in newspaper reports. The newspaper reports on Terry Butcher (in Chapter 6, p. 140) illustrate what we mean. Battlescarred and bleeding from a head wound, Butcher's heroic actions offer ideological models of manliness in boys' lives. And boys don't just copy these models, they are incited to emotionally identify their desires and longings in terms of these heroic fantasies.

Boys' consent to these ideological models is often secured through dominant codes of manliness, defining and controlling what it is possible for a boy to think, imagine and long for when considering boys' and men's sporting behaviour and relations. As a result, some boys are often over-impressed by the masculine show and display of force, toughness, emotional stoicism, hardness and the ruthless determination to win what they see in front of them and which is often endorsed by the social and cultural values they find around them. These tough displays sometimes offer compensatory fantasies for boys who feel helpless and powerless in their everyday lives. In these conditions, some boys can invest a great deal of suppressed passion, emotion and drama in the fantasies of achievement and mastery represented by their favourite, sporting stars. That is why a straight, critical debunking of boys' sporting heroes often backfires. Any criticism of their heroes is seen as a threat to the boys' *own* masculine identities. So any educational work in this area needs to be handled with sensitivity and complexity.

Is There an Alternative?

The rigid disciplining of boys' bodies to create winning machines is achieved at a great personal cost. In order to stand a chance of winning, many boys begin to toughen themselves up, cutting themselves off from the fully expressive range of their own bodies. All physical qualities that might be viewed as 'feminine' are disowned, or approached with defensive banter. Aesthetic grace, relaxed playfulness, gentle movement, sensual flow, all are shunned through the pressing fears of being branded 'soft', 'sissy', or 'poofter'. So what can be done about this? There are at least four areas of school sport in which positive alternatives are emerging:

Mixed Games

> I used to think girls couldn't play football. But we've been playing in the field just now and we've been letting girls play. It's been more fun. It's surprising how good the girls are. I thought they'd be rubbish. But they're really good. (13-year-old boy student, a Derby Comprehensive School)

The competitive, manly ethos in school sport (especially in traditional team games like football, rugby and cricket) can only be sustained in a tightly segregated, school regime. This splitting off of a boys–only sphere from a girls–only one is now being challenged by girls and women, both inside and outside school.

Many more schools are exploring mixed games options as girls and women, in the outside world, have become more active in participating in games traditionally considered exclusive, masculine spheres. In football, for instance, where there has been a 50 per cent increase in female players in Britain over the past two years, women are demanding that they are taken seriously. These changes are also being felt in schools where, as the above quotation proves, some boys are having to re-think their condescending assumptions about gender and sport.

A mixed games approach offers expanded possibilities to both girls and boys. Girls can claim a fairer share of the PE/sport resources and time allocation traditionally given to competitive team games for boys. And boys can start to break out of the narrow funnelling into a limited range of sports activities. Practically, what this means for boys is the opportunity of experiencing a wider choice of activities and, often, a different approach to taking part.

The obsessive pressure to win at all costs only seems to thrive in all-boys clashes. As we have seen from the 13-year-old boy student's comment, a more playfully relaxed attitude to sport is often possible when the sides are mixed. Of course, this varies with individual boys and girls, but generally the drift is towards greater enjoyment in the process of playing, having fun and sharing skills.

The time has come for a developing range of alternative, mixed options and mixed gender groupings for both girls and boys in school sport. This urgent need for a broadening out of traditional, school sport has been backed by the

National Curriculum proposals for Physical Education 5–16, Welsh Office, August 1991. It states, very clearly, in the section on Sex and Gender that 'a broad and balanced programme of physical education, sensitively delivered, can help to extend boys' restricted perceptions of masculinity and masculine behaviour'.

Working Towards a Balance between Cooperation and Competition in School Sport

The unresolved tensions between PE and school sport, cooperation and competition are still major blockages that prevent many boys from developing a fuller, healthier approach to their own bodies. The wider concerns of PE (often emphasizing a more cooperative method of playing) for the physical, psychological and social well-being of the student are often in open conflict with the more limited sports focus of heroic performance in team games.

This emphasis on manly performance through team games is very much an historical legacy. The over-concentration on school sport as an arena where 'muscular manliness' can be built and confirmed (still there in some male PE teachers) is partly inherited from the English public school/imperial ethos of manliness of the period from about 1870 to 1914. Watered down and considerably changed, competitive team games nevertheless still carry with them something of that compulsive concern for manly character-building through sport that Charles Kingsley and Thomas Hughes popularized in the second half of the nineteenth century.

The results of these past movements still linger on. In practice, what this means is that a reasonably balanced spread of PE activities, involving a more equal emphasis on cooperation and competition, is blocked because of competitive team games having more than their fair share of time, money and space in the PE curriculum. In order to redress this lack of balance, a greater awareness of the value of cooperative games needs to be developed in PE departments through staff development training schemes. Also, other PE activities that encourage personal challenges rather than over-concentration on beating opponents, urgently need a place in a more balanced curriculum.

What we are arguing for here isn't the usual condemnation of traditional, competitive games. We still want many boys to be able to extend their physical skills and coordination through playing soccer, rugby and cricket but we also want a greater variety of cooperative games options to be built into PE programmes. We want programmes that more explicitly acknowledge these positive diversities amongst boys. We're recommending programmes that cater more for the different abilities and interests of boys so that the majority of boys aren't coerced into proving their manhood on the sports field. These new games or cooperative games can be best explored through following up some of the references at the end of the chapter, see p. 214.

Dance for Boys

The recent National Curriculum proposals ('Physical Education 5–16', Welsh Office, August 1991) make a strong case for the educational value of dance for boys as well as girls. They see it as a way of extending the often stifled, expressive reach of boys' bodily activities through supple flow and rhythmic sensitivity, as well as fierce, physical energy. The authors of the proposals see wide-ranging opportunities in physical education in . . . 'challenging body images, sex stereotypes and other perspectives which limit the choices and achievements of children with disabilities and of both girls and boys'. They also see dance for boys as an integral, compulsory part of a National Curriculum for Physical Education.

But without an accompanying attempt to re-educate the conventional, manly values and assumptions of many male PE teachers (one who was overheard by one of the authors protesting that he would rather stack shelves in Sainsbury's than have to confront the terrors of teaching dance to boys!) and the homophobic attitudes of many boy students, it's unlikely that these suggestions for change will be readily taken up. There are still so many fears and anxieties in men and boys that would provoke resistance to these future schemes.

The central, blocking fear is the fear of unmanliness. The historical legacies of single-sex segregation and the persistence of traditional stereotypes in physical education create a negative climate for new learning and experimentation. As a result, school dance and movement are usually seen as threatening, unmanly behaviour. With mocking jibes flying around, like 'sissy', 'girl' and 'poofter', many men and boys feel that they can't afford to lose face in public. In this way, gender polarities are sustained that cramp many boys' potential to relate to their bodies in more fluid ways. However, the overall picture isn't totally bleak. It's much more contradictory than that with some promising initiatives emerging around the country. There are subtle cultural shifts that are changing the habitual relationship between masculinities and dance. Some of these cultural movements can be seen in films like *Fame*, *Flashdance*, *Dirty Dancing* and *Strictly Ballroom* and rock videos featuring Michael Jackson and Prince, and the increasing importance of black youth culture to these movements.

Given this background of gradual shifts and changes, it is now more socially permissible for 'real lads' to participate in dance. Some of that is still pushy and thrusting disco dancing against a background of pulsing beat or rap music but, nevertheless, there are signs that new combinations of strength and grace are being explored, like in Leroy's dancing in *Fame*, where there's a mixture of 'sexy masculinity with half-balletic, half-gymnastic movement'. There's a mounting sense that some of the old, rigid gender divisions are in the process of being eroded. What we have instead, in some cases, are much more elusive and androgynous figures like Prince who, according to Suzanne Moore (1991) 'slithers between hetero and homosexuality, blackness and whiteness, masculinity and femininity'.

Some of these promising developments can also be found in educational approaches to dance. To illustrate this in greater detail, I'd like to focus on the work of one dance teacher in a Nottinghamshire comprehensive school.

Boys and Dance: Redhill Comprehensive School, Nottingham

> It's fun! It's exciting and it keeps you fit. (16-year-old male student, Redhill Comprehensive)

The dance teacher at Redhill Comprehensive has had considerable success at encouraging older male students (14–16) to take part in dance activities. She has done this by rejecting the ballet version of dance (with its high art/effeminate associations) and concentrating more on contemporary dance — a cross between jazz dance, aerobics/gymnastics and a more creatively expressive dance. She believes in crossing gender boundaries through mixed dance groups where boys can be given alternatives to traditional gender stereotypes. She says, '. . . you can expand the male power bit into something quite graceful. Power is there but controlled, graceful, nice to look at. Not losing your identity but being able to appreciate other kinds of movement . . .' Traditional assumptions about gender identities still linger on here but there is also a movement towards change. Boys can express themselves through dance and movement without losing their male self-respect. In these mixed groups, some boys can learn that they can 'float and glide' as well as demonstrate forceful movement.

The dance teacher also runs a dance club on Tuesday lunchtimes every week that is able to attract 'twelve football team members . . . macho lads who turn up regularly', as well as girls. She sells her dance club to boys through emphasizing the club's commitment to pleasure and enjoyment. In doing this, she also stresses the twin notions of fitness and bodily awareness. She draws attention to the injuries games players often have and, as a way of avoiding them, she focuses on the need for physical suppleness and a personal responsibility for your own bodily limits, '. . . if you're aware of what your body is doing . . . how its limitations are . . . then you're not going to get those sort of injuries.'

Her approach to dance for boys is based on an awareness of the restrictive choices for boys. She feels that dance offers further options to all boys and helps them to break out of their imprisoning fears of unmanliness: 'I want to give boys alternatives. Not all boys want a gun or a bike. Not all girls want a doll.' Perhaps that's why some boys feel they can enjoy themselves in her groups without losing face. They can be there because dance is 'exciting and it keeps you fit', as one 16-year-old male student commented.

School Sport as Personal Challenge

So many boys are led to believe that they haven't achieved anything in school sport if they don't measure themselves against an opponent or win something.

This often leads to a narrow preoccupation with goals and outer victories, at the expense of inner processes and quieter, more gradual personal discoveries. But there are other ways of approaching school sport, like some of the social relationships to be found in long-distance or marathon running. Here little emphasis is laid on winning. It's much more the personal challenges and personal journeys through which the athlete goes that are important. So, for example, Janie Whyld (1983) comments that '. . . in the 1981 London Marathon, the two leading runners . . . made a point of finishing together, holding hands. Spectators regularly show as much interest in and support for those in weird garb, and those who collapse under the strain but crawl to the finishing post, as those who finish first.'

There are many boys who hate the humiliating, pressurizing climate of team games but who enjoy getting involved in personal challenges. At the moment, some PE curricula are neglecting the different needs of these boys. These boys need to be acknowledged and encouraged through designing PE programmes that offer more choices for them. They need to be trusted (through careful, personal negotiation) to organize their own personal targets where they can match themselves against their own personal best achievements rather than straining to beat the enemy. These alternative activities can be found in gymnastics, solo rowing, swimming, dance, ice skating, athletic jumping and throwing events, orienteering, outdoor pursuits, climbing, sailing, canoeing, as well as running. In these activities, these boys can often find their own comfortable levels without any comparative pressure being brought to bear on them. In these more relaxed and positive circumstances, the boys who aren't any good at conventional sports can find some real enjoyment and satisfaction in going at their own pace in exploring their bodies. The results, in terms of confidence building and positive self-esteem, can often be surprising to themselves and their PE teachers. Overcoming 'difficult personal odds' through personal challenges in school sport can turn out to be significant educational journeys for all kinds of boys who have a great deal to offer but who won't be cheered off a football or cricket pitch. Their hidden needs ought to be catered for in a PE programme that looks upon itself as broadly balanced.

References for Cooperative Games

FLUEGELMAN, A. *New Games and More New Games*, Dolphin Books, Doubleday, New York.

MASHEDER, M. (1989) *Let's Play Together*, Green Print, an imprint of the Merlin Press Ltd, London.

ORLICK, T. (1982) *The Second Cooperative Sports and Games Book*, Pantheon Books, New York.

ORLICK, T. (1978) *The Cooperative Sports and Games Book*, Pantheon Books, New York.

WOODCRAFT FOLK (1989) *Games Games Games*, Woodcraft Folk, London.

Selected Further Reading on Boys, Sport and Masculinity

WHITSON, D. (1990) 'Sport in the social construction of masculinity', in MESSNER, M. and SABO, D. (Eds) *Sport, Men and the Gender Order*, Champaign, US, Human Kinetics Publishers.

MESSNER, M. (1992) *Power at Play: Sports and the Problem of Masculinity*, Boston, Beacon Press.

KIDD, B. (1987) 'Sports and masculinity', in KAUFMAN, M. (Ed.) *Beyond Patriarchy*, Canada. O.U.P.

SPRINGHALL, J. (1987) 'Building character in the British boy: The attempt to extend Christian manliness to working-class adolescents 1880–1914', in MANGAN, J. and WALVIN, J. (Eds) *Manliness and Morality*, Manchester, Manchester University Press.

MESSNER, M. and SABO, D. (1994) *Sex, Violence, Power in Sports: Rethinking Masculinity*, California, The Crossing Press.

MAJORS, R. (1990) 'Cool pose: Black masculinity and sports', in MESSNER, M. and SABO, D. (Eds) *Sport, Men and the Gender Order*, Champaign, US, Human Kinetics Publishers.

Chapter 10

Boys' Well-being: Learning to Take Care of Themselves and Others

The Theory

Traditional Models of Masculinity

One of the most traditional models of masculinity that is presented to growing boys is Action Man. Either dressed as a footballer, cricketer, olympic athlete or as an underwater explorer, a treasure hunter, a space explorer or a soldier in combat gear, Action Man strides through the outer world as if he owns it. He looks continuously outward to the world of public adventure and glory. Indeed, Action Man is so caught up in the act of looking outwards, gaining power and doing things to others, that he never has any time to look downwards and inwards. Never looking closely at himself: his own life — feelings, relationships, bodily experience — is muffled in secrecy.

Many boys in our schools and clubs are trying to be like Action Man. They are brought up to only value what they do, rather than who they are. Looking downwards is seen as a sign of weakness and something to be avoided at all costs. So, gradually, over the years they cut themselves off from all that troubling messiness down there. They would prefer to soldier on, hiding themselves away in being busy, and not have to bother about taking responsibility for their lives, in terms of their own everyday survival, health and the quality of their relationships. In this way, yet another generation of boys and men are brought up who don't know how to look after themselves and others.

The social and emotional costs of this splitting and self-estrangement in boys and men are to be found in men's and women's lives everywhere you look. First, in the masculine sphere, the most wasteful and painful example of this lack of emotional/bodily responsibility is in the startling rise in young men's suicides. The suicide rate among men under 25 has risen 74 per cent in the past ten years. But the costs are also to be found in the number of accidents, alcohol-related illnesses, men in coronary care units, the emotional neediness of so many men in relationships and the disturbing number of homeless men on the streets and in night shelters. In the feminine sphere, the emotional and childcare/housework load that is dumped on so many women because of these splits and inequalities often creates a domestic power imbalance of an exacting 'double shift' for working women. These inequalities are maintained through a rigid, gender polarity that traditionally views girls and women as operating within the narrow and unfair realm of the private and domestic, and boys and men positioned within a much more privileged sphere of heroic action within the public. The fixed divisions of this gendered equation (below) have to be broken down if we are to see change.

> *Feminine/Private–Domestic/Nurturing, Caring vs Masculine/Public/Doing/ Controlling*

What breaking down these polarities means, in working in an anti-sexist way with boys, is moving away from the fixed idea that only girls and women can really look after things, and boys and men can only *do* and be looked after. Crossing gendered boundaries is what we're after, and challenging the deceptive, biological explanations that these qualities of caring or daring are born with us in our genes. But first we need to make more visible the roots of the problem.

What Prevents Boys from Looking after Themselves?

Boys as doers and makers:

> When you went out with the kids it was to do something specific — like go scrumping or play football. I mean, you never sat and talked. (Ruffell, 1989)

Many boys spend a great deal of time being encouraged, by parents, teachers, instructors, 'to do something specific'. Compulsive activity in the public world becomes so much a taken-for-granted part of being a boy that they don't notice what they're missing out on. They're so busy making and doing that they never just sit around and talk, or have a chance to share what's going on in their emotional lives.

Boys get into the habit of pushing themselves so hard that they lose touch with their emotional and bodily limits. They learn to treat themselves as objects, denying their emotional needs so that they can pursue feats of bravery and daring in the public world. Sometimes they split themselves from their emotional selves and distance themselves from the realm of the unmanly (i.e., the nurturing, domestic sphere). This splitting and unconnectedness in boys' lives often has disastrous results. Some boys have become so numb to their own emotional and bodily needs that they have no idea of how to survive by themselves without being looked after. And that increased burden of emotional responsibility falls again on girls and women.

Expecting to be serviced by girls and women

In a social world of unequal gender divisions, many boys soon learn that they don't have to look after themselves. They still look to women and girls to pick up the pieces after great surges of energy out there in the public world. Clearly, many women won't put up with it any longer, and some boys and men are struggling to break out of these stifling boxes. However, many boys and young men still assume that women and girls will do the everyday chores of caring and nurturing for them. Producing clean socks and underwear for the next morning, cooking, ironing, cleaning, hoovering, shopping — all these urgently necessary, 'hidden' acts that hold everyday life together for all those boys and men are assumed to be women's work. Too frequently, women are still having to take overall responsibility for keeping the domestic show on the road, despite minor changes.

In expecting to be sorted out by women/girls, boys rob themselves of personal skills and resources — domestic crafts — that are needed by any person who wants to take charge of his life. Many boys hand over their inner resources — the intricate skills of knowing how to soothe and nurture yourself — to their mothers, grandmothers, aunts and sisters through the processes of being looked after. Boys who have robbed themselves like this will always have problems in growing up to be more fully developed, rounded human beings. So many of them remain emotional babies, half expecting women to rescue them when the going gets rough.

These domestic role imbalances are not only unfair to women/girls but are severely damaging to boys. Boys who have been brought up to shun the 'unmanly' survival skills of domestic and emotional responsibility will always be susceptible to injury, accident and illness. Often, they would prefer to disown their own pain and distress and soldier on by gritting their teeth and keeping the door firmly shut on their private lives until they crack up or are, often literally, picked up off the floor by women. So what we urgently need in many more schools, clubs and colleges are programmes of work, often in Personal, Social and Health Education courses as well as Technology, Biology and English and Media studies, that help boys to take domestic and emotional responsibility and not to regard this as an inferior woman's realm.

Living on the edge

> . . . we're going to have to confront the facile, universal equation of masculinity with risk taking. Masculinity means always going for it, taking no prisoners, living on the edge. (Kimmel, 1991)

One of the authors recently watched two boys playing the 'I dare you to . . .', 'Chicken' game on a main road. The boys were lingering in the road as cars swerved around a corner towards them. The art of the game was to force the approaching car to brake and then to put yourself out of danger with a cool, swaggering style. Not to hurry too much but to move out of the way with a leisurely arrogance. One of the boys was trying to do just that. He was putting on a cheeky casualness that masked his fear as he tried to give an appearance of strolling away from the car at the last minute.

This proving of masculinity through living on the edge, through playing

'Chicken' with your life, is a central part of learning to become a 'real lad'. The despising of personal safety and the more 'feminine' values of continuing nurturance are crucial to this definition of 'real lad' masculinity. 'Real lads' are deliberately careless about their lives. Through their risky bravado they attempt to distance themselves from the world of femininity/domesticity/caring. They often welcome dangerous actions where they can get a buzz out of displaying just how wild and hard they are — as the young bikers who clashed with the police on a Coventry estate in May 1992 bears out. That's why a wide range of games and activities that manufacture excitement — from cheeking the teacher in front of your mates through to biking and joy-riding as well as excessive drinking, smoking and taking drugs — are important in enabling boys to identify themselves as part of the club of 'real lads.'

Also these manly acts of living on the edge can't just be done in isolation. They need the confirmation and approval of the male peer group. As one ex-joyrider admitted, 'Stealing nice cars is just showing off, its showing face to the other guys, showing they're bad. . . .' 'Showing face to the other guys' means putting manly status and pride above the priorities of looking after yourself and others. As a result, many boys' search for a daringly brave face cuts them off from taking emotional and domestic responsibility for their own lives. Take young men's approach to alcohol for example. How can many young men keep to a sensible limit in their drinking habits when drinking as a social event among boys and young men is mainly seen as a test of 'real lad' status? How can young men develop the personal understanding and self-acceptance to stop at 2–3 pints, two or three times a week, when there is a great pressure on them to prove that they're one of the lads by demonstrating that they can hold their drink? What we desperately need are other forms of being boys and men that aren't so tied into macho pressures to perform — particularly driving fast and drinking heavily.

The invisibility of boys' bodies and their emotions

Despite a recent media interest in the narcissistic male body, many boys' bodies still remain invisible to them. Generally, they expect their bodies to take care of themselves: because the traditional male gaze is focused on the distant horizon, male bodies are kept out of sight. The assumption is that their bodies will just keep on churning away by themselves, without any special help or attention. As a result of this taken-for-grantedness, many boys learn not to value their bodily needs and experiences. They get so used to imposing the demands of a strict, rational control on their bodies that they often feel disconnected from them. So, many boys grow up in a stunted way that makes it difficult for them to listen to or take care of their bodies through health or illness. For many boys the problem is exacerbated because they see their bodies as the functional carrier bags that carry around their pulsing brains. Middle-class boys, particularly, are encouraged to live through their heads. They detach themselves from the vital rhythms of their bodies and impose their rational goals, plans and deadlines onto these subtle and varied flows. And this disowning of bodies is also reinforced, socially, by the mind/body divide in Western cultures.

On another social class level, some working-class boys strive to harden and toughen up their bodies, in an attempt to embody the force and superiority that's expected from a driving, heterosexual virility. From one angle, this would seem to make their bodies more visible to them, but the process of holding themselves in such a way as to display strength and power often deadens them to the full and varied flow of their bodily responses. The rigid disciplining of their bodies (perhaps a preparation for the estranging manual labour they might meet up with, later, under Western capitalism) cuts them off from a more self-monitoring awareness of what's going on in their bodies. So what we have, in some cases, is the development of a self-destructive, mechanical relationship to their bodily health and emotional well-being. (See the more detailed arguments in Chapter 9 'School Sport and the Making of Boys and Men'.)

The central question for an anti-sexist programme focused on working with boys in this area is, 'How can we encourage boys to break through their denial of their bodies and begin to take seriously something that often remains invisible to them?' Many boys go on denying their feelings and bodily experiences because they learn, very early on, that being concerned about the state of their bodies is seen as effeminate whinging and not to be encouraged. Instead what is socially condoned is the manly habit of keeping going while under pressure. The traditional, macho ideal is soldiering on against all the odds and closing your ears to the disruptive messages (often full of pain and emotional distress) that are coming from your body. It's in this kind of a way that boys learn to detach themselves from what they're feeling and cover up by developing the competitive individualism needed for the lonely hero. As potential heroes they learn emotional denial and self-sufficiency at the expense of becoming vulnerable to others. They learn to scorn the idea of letting others in to support them. They even seem to prefer individual isolation to the supposed loss of status in seeking help.

Finally, as a result of such alienating habits, some boys lose touch with their bodily limits and edges. They become so distant from their bodies that they almost become numb to exactly what it feels like to drive your body too hard and for too long. The persistent goal-directedness blinds many boys to the creeping sense of tiredness and exhaustion in their bodies so that they can no longer hear or understand what their bodies are trying to tell them. In this way, gender plays an active part in the construction of boys' and men's illness. Some boys actively participate in their lack of emotional and physical well-being because their resources for understanding and looking after themselves have been eroded over the years.

Key Points of Development within an Anti-sexist Curriculum for Boys

Men's (and boys') lives are often precarious because they are always living out the dilemma between being 'exceptional' and being 'worthless'.

> These are two sides of the same experience. Both grow out of deep distrust and hatred of self, so that we cannot trust our natures or feel good about ourselves unless we know that we are 'successful'. It is only by keeping on proving ourselves that we avoid the feelings of worthlessness. (Seidler, 1991)

Many boys find it difficult to take responsibility for themselves while living in a school or family culture that overemphasizes winning and success. Often, they're so busy proving that they're somebody special, as a way of covering up and countering a fear of helplessness and impotence, that they don't develop the self-awareness and survival skills necessary to look after themselves. Indeed, taking charge of their own lives can only really begin when there is enough self-worth to build upon.

Useful, anti-sexist work with boys in this area needs to challenge this self-estranging distrust. We urgently need to find new ways of working that help boys to reconnect themselves to their feelings and bodies, and to the skills of everyday survival. That means not identifying so much through doing and controlling but more through listening to their suppressed needs and wants. Some of the key areas of development in this field are:

Working towards a Greater, Emotional Expressiveness in Boys through Discussion and Small Group Work

Broadening out boys' feelings range by creating space for them to get to know denied feelings, e.g., fear, bewilderment, sadness, frustration, tenderness, closeness, warmth. In doing this a challenge is mounted to the narrow funnelling system of traditionally accepted emotions in boys/men, like anger, rage, violence, rather than a wider flow of feelings.

Assertiveness Skills for Boys — Not Putting Down Girls, Learning to Communicate Wants and Needs, and Not Always Getting Your Own Way

Learning the difference between assertiveness, submissiveness and aggressiveness.

Learning How to Make and Keep Relationships, Particularly with Boys

The competitive rivalry between boys is often so fierce that boys spend much of their time guarding their backs when they're together. In this wary, defensive climate, many boys don't know how to make contact with each other.

Traditionally, boys meet on the basis of sharing an obsessive interest or hobby (sports, music, bikes, collections, etc.), or boasting about an ambition or achievement. They don't know how to communicate in closer ways about uncertainties, fears or failures because of the cheery, brave face facade they feel they ought to keep up in public. Through the years they learn to put self-defence before disclosure, or learning to understand other people's needs and concerns.

So there's a need for classroom strategies that encourage boys to work together rather than against each other. They need to learn how to open up more about themselves and take the occasional risk of being vulnerable in groups rather than keeping their guards up. Also they need to break down their isolated individualism and learn how to be supportive and responsible for the emotional well-being of other boys.

Learning to Look After Your Own Body

Work needs to be developed in this area that introduces a more sharply focused gender perspective on Men's Health and Well Man clinics, and then adapted for a younger age group. The key issues here are:

1 Understanding how your body works and getting to know its different moods, rhythms, needs.
2 Gaining a more precise knowledge of the limits and boundaries of your body, so that you don't have to dump that responsibility onto somebody else. Learning to recognize your body's own specific warning signals when you've been pushing yourself too hard.
3 Learning to recognize the contrasts in your body between your bodily signals of tension, illness and exhaustion and your bodily sense of emotional/bodily well-being.
4 Learning to relax and know how to release pressure on yourself.
5 Taking responsibility for your sexual behaviour. Learning to convert 'uncontrollable urges' into shared choices. Learning to distinguish between sex as performance and sex to make contact. HIV/Aids education. Safer sex practices. (see the chapter on 'Boys' Sexualities'.)
6 Develop the inner courage to seek help about difficult feelings and bodily experiences when you need to. Find out what help is available from counsellors, doctors, alternative medical practitioners, self-help groups. Don't see seeking help as a form of weakness, or 'feminine' helplessness to be avoided at all costs.

Learning the Skills of Everyday Survival, Especially in the Home

Boys are so often dependent on women (mothers, sisters, grandmothers, aunts) that they never learn for themselves the domestic skills of ordinary, everyday survival. They are always half expecting a woman to sort them out, so they never seem to develop the motivation to learn these urgently necessary skills.

These traditional, gendered expectations of boys and men need to be confronted. Why is it that many boys know how a car works, but they don't know how to operate the washing machine? Why can't boys cook simple and satisfying meals for the family and themselves, rather than just relying on *Pot Noodles*, chips, pasties or meat pies? Why can't boys iron their own shirts effectively? Why can't they shop sensibly and with some awareness of the comparative costs involved, and other people's tastes, without just grabbing hold of the first special offer they come across in the local supermarket?

These are all questions that need to be seriously asked if an adequate anti-sexist approach is to be designed that explores ways of encouraging boys to look after themselves. Learning housework skills, childcare work and learning to cook must be at the centre of that kind of approach. Promising beginnings have been made in schools like Hackney Downs' 'Skills for Living' course, developed in the 1980s. Now we need to build on those brave, starting points and extend the range of that work. There is an even greater need for those kind of everyday life skills for boys and young men. It's because so many boys learn to look down on those skills as 'girls'/women's' work that an increasing number of them end up in night shelters, leaning heavily on women or even taking their own lives.

Selected Further Reading on Boys' Well-being

ASKEW, S. and ROSS, C. (1984) *Anti-Sexist Work with Boys*, Manchester/Hackney Downs School, London E5, Equal Opportunities Commission.

BRUCKENWELL, P., JACKSON, D., LUCK, M., WALLACE, J. and WATTS, J. (1995) *The Crisis in Men's Health*, Community Health UK (6 Terrace Walk, Bath, BA1 1LN).

MEN'S HEALTH ISSUE *Health for All by the Year 2000 News*, London, Faculty of Public Health Medicine of the Royal College of Physicians, Winter 1994, No. 29.

HARRISON, J., CHIN, J. and FICARROTTO, T. (1989) 'Warning: Masculinity may be dangerous to your health', in KIMMEL, M. and MESSNER, M. (Eds) *Men's Lives*, New York, Macmillan.

ILLMAN, J. The Curse of the Stiff Upper Lip, *The Guardian*, 7 June, 1991.

SABO, D. and GORDON, D.F. (1995) *Men's Health and Illness: Gender, Power and the Body*, California, Sage.

The Session

Showing Respect for Each Other

The first two sessions with a new group had been difficult. There were only seven boys in the group but all of them had behavioural problems which were apparent throughout the school. Most of the boys had low attention thresholds, finding it difficult to concentrate on activities for very long at a time. The last session had been particularly difficult. The weather was hot, it was the last period before lunch and there had been a marked reluctance to have anything to do with a worksheet! Instead, the session had been characterized by a wide variety of disruptive activities, centred mainly on quite outrageous put-downs and a general sense of animosity between certain individuals in the group. I had felt powerless and anxious. The crucial question was how I could help these boys to value themselves better so that they might more easily be able to give voice to their respect for each other. Perhaps a strategy that would allow feelings to be aired and acknowledged in a less direct way would help this process along.

I was drawn to a game called 'Aeroplane and Control Tower'. One boy is the aeroplane, another is his control tower. The object of the game is for the control tower to guide the aeroplane around an obstacle course without crashing. The aeroplane is blindfolded and a crash is a serious banging into part of the obstacle course. The only way that the mission is considered successful is when all the planes get back to base. I emphasize the group solidarity factor that is vitally important. When it comes to each boy's turn to be the plane, the others need to be aware of the boy's flight through the obstacle course and encourage his safe landing. The boys enjoyed creating the course, using their imagination to fix tables and chairs in various ways to create tunnels, slopes, step-ups and tight corners! They looked pleased to view their creation!

'Who wants to be blindfolded first?' produced offers to be control tower. We explore a little about what is stopping someone being the plane. Various excuses about not being bothered came out. One boy admitted that he didn't know whether he could trust anyone. Another said he didn't want to do it at all. I assured him there was no pressure and that he could change his mind if he wanted to. Certainly the trust factor seemed to be at the heart of the difficulty of volunteering. 'What advice would you give to the control tower? What must he remember?', I ask. Ivan says, 'He mustn't get hurt — it would be dangerous.' There is nothing here about the aeroplane mustn't crash — just a concern for another person in the group. Others agreed that it could be dangerous if not done properly. Immediately a volunteer emerges — it's Gareth who has quite a close friend in this group. He is keen and enthusiastic, not normally noted for his apprehension. He turns to me and says, 'I'll be alright won't I?' I throw the question to the rest of the group. Ray who is to be the control tower says he'll do his best; others say they'll watch out for him. I am not entirely sure but Gareth is encouraged and I know that I can always step in.

As the 'flight' begins the level of interest is high. The control tower (Ray) can decide where the plane (Gareth) can go — there is no fixed circuit. Ray realizes very quickly that he has to give very precise instructions as early in the flight some near crashes occur. The other five in the group are closely in attendance — they make encouraging noises and offer hands and arms in close support when some precarious points are negotiated. There are some sharp intakes of breath and some debate about whether minor bumps with table legs constitute a crash or not. The tension in the room increases as the flight nears its completion. I tell Gareth he can take off the blindfold. He is full of it — 'Where was I going, when . . . ?' 'Did I really go under . . . ?' 'It was scary when the table rocked and I was feeling my way across the chairs.'

Gareth's first flight made it easier for the others to volunteer and the same degree of commitment to each other's safety was expressed throughout. The control towers varied their routes and made interesting changes to what they expected their planes to do. There were some crashes but no plane crashed completely (i.e., more than two big ones!). The whole flight of planes successfully completed the mission. Sometimes in other groups when I have played this game, controls have deliberately made fun of their plane by making them crawl on the ground in open space, pretending it is a low tunnel, when in fact no obstacle exists.

There needs to be sufficient time to have a closing circle to evaluate what has been happening. I bring them together with about 20 minutes to go. I ask them how it felt to have played the game. All the boys agree that it was good and different. They want to do it again next time. I wonder how it was different from the last session we had. They agree that it was much better and that they 'did it properly' this time. We explore what that means. How did it feel to leave the room at the end of the last session? Ivan says he felt angry, fed up and bored — the others agree. Robert said he wasn't going to come again if Clint was there. He said that he'd only come today because the alternative was maths. 'So what made today different?' I ask again. 'We got on with each other; we didn't mess around or doss about.' 'How will you feel about leaving at the end of this session?' I continue. 'I feel good — I feel better about everybody,' said John — a feeling echoed by the others.

I wonder aloud what feelings they remember noticing in themselves during this session. 'Worried, anxious and kind', emerge spontaneously, together with 'feeling a bit scared'. I ask what stopped them from feeling a bit scared? 'I just thought he [the control tower] wouldn't mess me about and that everyone else wanted me to do it right. You said things, you helped, I just felt that I could trust you all.' 'You', meaning John, who had been Clint's control tower, 'were crap at first 'cos I had to keep stopping suddenly but you got better though.'

I ask them what they think they learned from all this as a group? Ivan started the reply by saying that you had to give very careful instructions. 'No it's more than that — it's about caring about what happens to everybody else. It feels better when no-one acts daft. I felt as if I cared what happened to everybody. I feel as if I know people a bit better and I don't have to be stupid to get respect here.'

Classroom Strategies

Learning to Look after Self and Others

Boys Well-being

In turning themselves from boys into men, boys often learn not to look after themselves. They learn that nurturing and caring are 'feminine' activities whereas boys are expected to be deliberately irresponsible about their well-being in the public world. They also learn to actively seek the mother figures who will service all their needs and interests. The tensions that arise as women become increasingly and understandably reluctant to do this cause tension, stress and domestic violence.

The classroom strategies here deliberately challenge this gendered division of labour. Instead, boys are invited to learn about the skills of everyday survival — by cooking, cleaning, learning to monitor their own feelings and bodily limits. So one of the things they are learning in these everyday skills is to become more responsible for their own well-being and not to depend on women.

Aeroplane and the Control Tower

Aim: *To encourage boys to show and acknowledge care and concern for each other.*

Materials: *A classroom with enough furniture to create an obstacle course*
             Material for use as a blindfold

Time: *45 minutes*

What to do:

Ask the group to create an obstacle course in the room using the available chairs, desks, tables.

Explain that all the group are going to take it in turns to be the plane (blindfolded) and the control tower who will guide the plane round the obstacle course and bring it safely into land.

To win or succeed all the planes have to land safely. More than two noisy collisions with any part of the obstacle course constitutes a crash.

While one control tower and plane go round the course the rest of the group need to be supportive and encouraging of their colleague's efforts.

When all have had a turn, ask the group to come together as a whole to talk about their feelings during the exercise. Try to elicit a group consensus so that the good feelings engendered by this exercise can be translated into the culture of their work together.

So You Say that You Help Around the House

Aim: To encourage an appreciation of the wide variety of jobs which need doing in our homes.

Materials: 'So You Say that You Help Around the House' sheets, prepared using the statements below
Paper and pens for brainstorm
Housework – Homework sheets, prepared using the questions below

Time: 50 minutes

What to do:

Divide the class into groups of 3–4. Brainstorm in groups the variety of household tasks. Decide how often they ought to be done and how much time they take. As a small group discuss how well you could do all the household tasks. How important is it for you to be skilled at such jobs?

Give out the 'So You Say that You Help Around the House' sheets. Ask the boys to complete them individually.

When the worksheets are complete ask the small groups to get back together again and share the results of what they have done. Have them focus particularly on the question 'Why is it important for me to be able to do work around the house?'

In a whole group share the general feeling of the group about this activity. Give out the Homework – Housework! sheets.

Additional exercises in this theme could make use of Darren's Day and Family Housework. Both worksheets can be used to emphasize boys' responsibility in the world of housework.

The statements:

So You Say that You Help Around the House

This is the work that you want to do in the house today:

Making breakfast	Tidying up
Washing up breakfast	Ironing
Washing up lunch	Getting up
Washing up tea/dinner	Making dinner
Making the beds	Shopping
Dusting	Cleaning windows
Making lunch	Washing clothes
Hoovering	Going to bed

Show how you would organize your day.

The questions:

Housework – Homework

Choose a housework task to do as homework. When you have done it, answer the questions below.

What did you do?
How long did it take?
Do you usually do this job?
Did you find it difficult?
Did you have any help?
Did you enjoy doing it? Why/why not?
Is this a job you could carry on doing?
What job will you try next?
Your comments:
Parents'/guardians' comments:

Additional exercise:

Family Housework

Two adults and two children live in a 3-bedroomed house which also has a kitchen, a bathroom/toilet and two living rooms. There is also a hall and staircase.

Give the adults and children names and divide up the housework so that everyone gets some free time. Don't forget to make it fair.

Additional exercise:

Darren's Day

One of the children in the house is called Darren. Write a story or draw a cartoon about Darren's day. Include his share of the housework.

To Make a Meal

Aim:	*To encourage the importance of being able to consider the value of healthy eating.*
	To cooperatively make a balanced dish.
Materials:	*Worksheets 'To Make a Meal'*
	'Planning Your Meal' sheets
	Ideas for the worksheets are included below
	Any simple recipe books (optional)
	Paper and pens
Time:	*Two sessions, each 90 minutes*

What to do:

Produce a worksheet that enables boys to consider what a balanced meal should include. Below is a suggested outline for a worksheet:

1 Meals need staple fillers:

> Brown bread — with lots of fibre and some protein
> Rice — with fibre and some protein
> Potato — with fibre.

    What makes fibre and protein important for us?

2 In addition to a staple filler a meal needs:

> Some vegetables or fruit
> Some fat
> Some protein

    What is important for our health about having these in our meals?
    What happens if we don't get enough fibre and protein?
    What happens if we eat too much sugar or fat?

3 Produce a sheet which lists different foodstuffs together with an explanation of what else they provide:

> e.g., fish (protein)
> cheese (protein)
> butter (fat)
> onions (vegetable)
> chicken (protein)
> peas (vegetable-protein)
> cucumber (vegetable)
> lentils-dahl (protein)
> eggs (protein-fat)
> lettuce (vegetable)
> mine (protein-fat)
> apple (fruit)
> broccoli (vegetable)
> carrots (vegetable)
> banana (fruit)
> orange (fruit)
> beans (vegetable-protein)
> tomatoes (vegetable)

    What other foodstuffs could they include?

4 Ask the boys to work in pairs and write down three examples of a different balanced meal using each of the staple fillers. Encourage them to share their ideas with another pair.

5 In the new group of four they are going to plan and make a meal. This is where some simple recipe books may be useful.
    Produce a worksheet in three sections that lists:

Ingredients
How to make the meal
Cleaning up jobs

Ask the boys to cooperatively decide what they are going to make and to write down who is going to bring which ingredients and perform the associated tasks. Encourage them to allot the tasks so that everyone is equally involved in every stage of planning, production and clearing up.

6   It is a good idea to take photographs of finished meals before they are consumed.

7   Before the end of these sessions ask the boys to come together as a whole group and discuss how it felt to do this task and its potential importance in their lives.

Time for a Snack?

Aim: *To help boys make an informed choice about some of the things they eat.*

Materials: *'Time for a Snack?' information sheets*
'Time for a Snack?' worksheets (see ideas below)
Paper and pens

Time: *45 minutes*

What to do:

Ask the group to form into threes and to brainstorm the snack foods that form part of their daily diet.

On a separate sheet ask the same groupings to divide up the snacks into those generally good for them and those that are harmful in some way. Ask them to jot down the healthy and unhealthy properties of each selection chosen.

Give out the information sheet which each small group can compare with their own work.

Ask the boys to come together as a whole group and open a discussion along the following lines:-

1.   What's difficult about what I've just discovered about snack foods?
2.   What are the implications for how I view myself if I fill myself full of stuff that is harmful to me?
3.   'We are what we eat.' What does this say about what I think of my body?

In a conclusion give out a worksheet prepared to help boys summarize their thoughts around snack foods and to make considered decisions about future eating habits.

The following questions/statements should suffice:

1. When I feel like a snack I eat any one of the following foods/drinks because ....
2. Sometimes I might allow myself to eat/drink .... because ....
3. I will certainly eat/drink less of .... because ....

Chapter 11

How Boys Become 'Real Lads':
Life Stories about the Making of Boys

The Theory

Born or Made?

Boys aren't born 'real lads', they are made through a long process of learning. The problem is that this learning is often so taken for granted that it is usually invisible to most of us. If boys are going to take greater charge of their lives, then that learning urgently needs to become more visible to them. In schools, clubs and colleges, we need to offer courses and learning approaches that encourage a growing awareness of that invisible learning and, at a later stage, the taking of alternative choices about their developing gender identities.

The most useful way of introducing this investigative approach to the making of boyhood is through critical, life story work in schools, clubs and colleges. Adequate time, support and space need to be given over to this work so that boys can begin to recognize the value of their life experiences. Instead of deferring to other people's experiences (teachers, heroines and heroes, and other grown-ups), students can learn to build confidence and trust in the processes of how they have been put together as boys.

Boys are often more prepared to open up about the problems and contradictions of traditional manliness through the emotional commitment of their own personal stories about growing up masculine. These stories are especially meaningful to them because they affect the daily flavour and running of their lives. It is the electrical charge of stories that they recognize have something to say about their lives that really motivates them — stories like Ronald Fraser's one about his lack of contact with his father and about the day his father threatened 'to get my mother's curlers to put in my hair which was as shamefully long as a girl's'. Or the stories about sex education lessons in school: 'The only sex education I had was about worms and that's very confusing because they can be both male and female, whatever they choose.' Stories like these can provoke interest and curiosity in many reluctant boys.

Also a collaborative approach needs to be taken if this life story work is to stand a chance of developing. Competitive individualism can get in the way of a project like this. Instead, what is needed is relaxed, supportive exchange through paired work, which is then moved outwards towards a wider group and exchange. This can feel like a safe way to start a sometimes risky exploration. It breaks up the savage hierarchy of the boys' peer groups (where many boys fear being mocked and shown up in public) and offers the more positive possibility of working together with trusted friends. This context of support and safety can also generate the incentive to make visible to another person fleeting scraps of memory, story incidents, and shadowy images that can be turned into effective life story work.

Teachers have an important part to play in making the context safe enough to encourage that kind of emotional sharing. It won't happen all at once but, given a teacher with some personal feeling for this kind of work, it can develop. What needs to be looked at carefully before work of this kind can begin are the group rules and the pecking order within the boys' peer groups. The group rules need to be negotiated but the most useful ones that we have found are:

1 No mocking or ridiculing of any other member of the group.
2 No interruptions or negative comments while somebody else is speaking.
3 Respect other people's contributions as you would like others to respect your stories.

The pecking order issue is more delicate but makes sure that boys work with somebody they can trust or, failing that, who will make some effort to behave by the group rules.

The educational value of life history work is that it can challenge the familiar common sense of a 'boys will be boys' approach. Turning a blind eye to the regular swearing, thumping, calling, horseplay, attention-seeking behaviour and occasional lashing out usually comes from the assumption that boys often act in this way because of their biology. But life history work can question these normalizing assumptions about boys. It can scrape beneath the false bravado to expose the daily routines and rituals that have built up these assumptions and hidden fears, uncertainties and anxieties, which many boys feel about not coming up to expectations.

For this to happen, teachers need to stimulate a deliberate stock-taking approach in the students to their own lives. Boys need to expand their ability to occasionally stand outside the dulling habits of their lives, look around and carefully ponder some of the key awakenings and turning points in their lives (like the first time they were told that 'Big boys don't cry', or began to realize what was expected of 'real lads'). Sharing and exploring these moments with other students can create de-familiarizing perspectives on some of the processes that make them feel they have to strive to be more manly than they actually are. Through continuing attempts to grapple with, question and contest their common-sense assumptions about being boys, some of them can begin to dismantle the 'masculine mystique' and learn how they have become masculinized themselves.

Really valuable life history work with boys is achieved when students are motivated to go beyond the literal surface of their personal stories and make sense of them *in a critical light*. Rather than seeing their customary behaviours as a 'natural' expression of the fact that they are biologically boys, a sharp probing of these habits and routines can reveal how these behaviours have been learnt through the years. Can they remember when they learnt to hold their bodies in a particular way? When did they learn the virile strut? Or can they remember when it became more important for them to impress the cockiest, male peer group rather than to look towards themselves or even their parents for advice and guidance? Then a careful teasing out of why they learnt to do such things would put them on the road of viewing their life histories in a critical light.

Making Critical Life Story Work

The process of making critical life story work in schools, clubs and colleges is a complex process. Perhaps the most useful way of working here is to build a gradual progression through three, linked stages.

Developing a Personal Commitment to Your Own Stories

Having the chance to recognize your own life stories, and to view them as a valid form of knowledge. Building confidence in the power of your own stories and learning to value them: 'They're important because they're mine.'

Making Your Stories Strange to Yourself

Stepping outside the habitual familiarity of your life and starting to see it, in glimpses, from the outside, or partly inside and outside at once. That means taking a martian perspective on some of the incidents from your life that you know very well. Ask, why do boys do what they do? What would appear strange if seen through the eyes of a visitor from a different planet? What do you notice about boys' actions, facial expressions, interactions with other people, the groups they go around in, the way they carry their bodies, their voices, the noise they make, what they look at? What about yourself? What might appear strange?

Developing a Sense of Yourself as Masculine

This is a difficult, demanding stage that needs to be sensitively negotiated with individual students. Only when a student is ready, and this approach becomes appropriate, can this stage be fully entered. But a whole class/group approach is out of the question.

A good place to start is to investigate their emotional investment in key life stories. What made these stories significant for them as boys growing up? How far did these stories give them a developing sense of themselves as a particular kind of boy? Artistic, hard, tough, intelligent, caring, brave, sensitive, honest, bullying, lying, competent, dependable, emotional, friendly, responsible, warm, loyal? Are any of these stories about specific moments when they deliberately made a decision to be different from other types of boys or girls, or decided to mark themselves off from others? They might find that these key moments are also influenced by other shaping forces, such as:

1 Your detailed personal history, e.g., early relationships with your parents, brothers and sisters, family life, place, religion, etc.
2 Class — how did you see yourself in relation to other families and children from other homes? What differences did money, or the lack of it, make to you? Did you feel powerful and confident or ignored and put down because of your home background.
3 Race — how did your racial and ethnic background affect you as a growing boy? How did that racial background shape your masculine sense of self, for example, did you feel on top of the world, or excluded, silenced, marginalized?
4 Sexual orientation — have you always taken it for granted that heterosexuality is the only 'normal' kind of sexuality? Or have you felt stifled or uneasy by having to fit in to conventional heterosexuality? How has that affected you as a growing boy?
5 Disability — how was your developing sense of yourself as a boy influenced by your own awareness of being able-bodied or disabled?

Selected Further Reading on Boys' Life Story Work

HUMPHRIES (1984) *The Handbook of Oral History: Recording Life Stories*, London, Inter Action.
DEVLIN, P. *et al.* (1995) *Sinews of the Heart: A Book of Men's Writings*, Nottingham, Five Leaves Press.
ABBOTT, F. (1993) (Ed.) *Boyhood, Growing Up Male: A Multicultural Anthology*, California, The Crossing Press.
SPENCE, J. (1986) *Putting Myself in the Picture: A Political, Personal and Photographic Autobiography*, London, Camden Press.
JACKSON, D. (1990) *Unmasking Masculinity*, London, Routledge.
MORGAN, D. (1987) *It will Make a Man of You: Notes on National Service, Masculinity and Autobiography*, Manchester, Department of Sociology, University of Manchester.
SPENCE, J. and HOLLAND, P. (1991) (Eds) *Family Snaps: The Meaning of Domestic Photography*, London, Virago.
HALL CARPENTER ARCHIVES (1989) *Walking After Midnight: Gay Life Stories*, London, Routledge.

The Session

Putting on a Brave Face

With R10 I am using the school's community lounge. The room is quite large with a small kitchen area in one corner. We are going to use a circle of soft seated chairs in one corner. It is 8.50am and the room is bright with winter sunshine. When I first met this group three weeks ago, I had anticipated trouble. Among the boys were two or three real characters including one boy (Clive) with whom I had experienced many problems in his younger years at school. I had been responsible for sending him to the school's 'Sin Bin' (Room 20) on a number of occasions. Although I had cleared the debris of the past in an earlier session, I was still mindful of the unpredictability of most of the boys, particularly Clive.

Today the boys enter quietly. They sit down without fuss or comment. One boy, Roger, has missed the first three weeks of these sessions. He has missed the group warm-ups which have been so important for the settling cooperative process with which this group is beginning to work. I ask Roger what he needs to know about what we have been doing so far. He seems unsure what to ask so I invite members of the group to tell him what has been important for them so far. Dean says, 'Well we're not doing sex yet in case you thought we were.' Steven offers a cautious, 'It's been worth coming, you do things differently here,' and Ben offers, 'We've been talking about how we are. It's like making it easier to talk to each other.'

I decide to use the 'First Times as a Boy' sheet this lesson (see p. 239). I ask the boys to tick the statements on the list which mean something to them and then share what lies behind the ticks with another person. It has been my experience that boys will do all manner of things rather than do the task as set. This morning it was different and I noticed that all the pairs were talking about 'first times'. There were mixtures of animation, engagement and excitement on display. Coming together as a group all were invited to share their experiences. Two of the 'first times' stood out for all the boys. They were, 'the putting on a brave face rather than admitting pain' and 'learning to jeer at something they were afraid of'.

Leon volunteered to share first, and he spoke of his fear of the dark when he was 7 years old. He was frightened of going upstairs, imagining that some 'things' were going to 'get' him. He also didn't like skating but rather than say he was scared of going fast, he just said that he didn't like skating. 'It's shameful if I say I don't like going fast.' Nadim said that he felt like that when he fell down some steps at school. He had laughed but inside he could have cried because he had hurt himself. Above all he had felt the pressure to cover up his real feelings. Other boys really relate to these experiences. Tim had fallen flat on his face and even a teacher had laughed. Tim had pretended it didn't matter and covered up his hurt and anger. Clive told a particularly scary story about someone meddling with his BMX bike so that a wheel fell off as he soared off a ramp at speed. He had come down to the ground in a mess of bike and body, landing really heavily. He felt a lot of pain and dizziness but made sure that all his friends saw his violent anger rather than the pain of being hurt. Steven told us how he had fallen out of a tree when he was 11. He broke his arm but felt an enormous pressure to get up and 'laugh his head off'. 'It was really killing inside, but I kept saying it's nothing even though my arm was flopping around all over the place. I just said I'd got to go home for tea and it was only then that I showed how painful it was. I didn't want my mates to see I was a wimp or something.'

I wonder about the atmosphere of conformity but within that a question begins to emerge about the competitiveness of what I am witnessing. What lies behind some of the tinges of humour which appear in the telling? I reflect these thoughts back to the boys. They seem quite shocked. I sense the anger in Nadim's reply, 'I've never admitted things like this before and it seems as if you think I'm making a joke out of it.' I assure him I'm not trying to put down anything which has been said — that I am genuinely pleased that they can share things with each other like this. I explain my tendency to be cynical.

I ask them about some of the more difficult 'first times' they might share with each other. Ranjit spoke of his fears of ordinary things like when he was very small he was frightened of the toilet flushing when it was dark. He thought some things were going to get him. This revelation brought a number of similar stories which went largely unresolved and unheard when the terror was around. For most boys it was the first time that these fears had been heard by others apart from their parents. Steven was relieved because he almost thought he had been alone in his terror about his cupboard under the stairs.

'What other things are difficult to share?' I ask. Dean reckons that 'things about sex' are the most difficult. Other boys wonder what he means. 'Well, like wanking' stumbles out. He pushes on, 'Well, it's like difficult admitting it but everybody does it.' 'Have you ever shared what it feels like?' I ask, 'Have you ever said what it made you feel like discovering masturbation for the first time?' This is an enormously difficult area but I am reminded of the question in the 'Man's World' game — 'What was it like the first time you came?' Some of the boys share the tingling, electric sensation that just made them want to do it again. The boys seem to be appreciating each others' difficulties in communicating their feelings. I realize they are helping each other, the smiles are of embarrassment but understanding.

Once again the conversation turns to talk of tears, and fears of being seen as weak. Stories of having to be strong about a grandfather's death and about only choosing to cry alone when a grandmother died begin to encourage the boys to notice what they are missing. I ask them what has made it alright to share so much this morning. They point out that no-one has laughed at anybody else, they've all had similar experiences: 'It's like you can trust everyone and they won't go and tell anyone else.' The boys admit to a sense of relief about what they have done. Dean told us a story of ten boys recently spending the night in a shed in an isolated area with no lights. He now realizes that all those sleeping out were scared of the quiet and what might happen. It was dark and cold and the talking went on and on. He realizes that the boys (himself included) who kept on telling the others to shut up and go to sleep, were really just doing it to keep the noise going. For his part any recognizable noise helped him to stop feeling frightened. He realizes that none of them in the shed could admit fear. 'Now I'll realize I'm not the only one who's scared, I'll know that someone else is feeling the same way — it's not just me! If this happens again, perhaps I'll be able to say but it will be really difficult.'

Classroom Strategies

Life Stories

The danger of doing masculinity work is that it might just become another conventional subject. The positive learning potential of life story work with boys is that it often provokes a personal engagement with the subject. When boys realize that the subject is about themselves, they often come alive with their willingness to take part. Bridges can be built between their own worlds and the worlds of school learning. Their everyday knowledge and emotional baggage can be linked to what teachers bring with them to present in the classroom. If the session involves showing a Stallone or Schwarzenegger film this can be linked to the way in which boys do daring, risky things in their own lives like 'chicken' games or daring deeds like being the first in the group to jump into the river (story from Dean, aged 13). Through this emotional engagement with their own lives boys can also become more aware of the social processes that turn them from boys into men.

Life Journey Maps

Aims: *To make some progress in answering the question 'What has made us into the boys we are today?'*

Materials: *Large sheets of paper and felt-tip pens*

Time: *Two sessions, each 45 minutes*

What to do:

Give each boy a large sheet of paper and a felt-tip pen. Ask the boys to use the whole area of the paper. Discourage spidery, little drawings done in one corner! Then encourage the boys to follow the directions below.

    (i)   Working by yourself, make a map of your life journey as a boy, showing all the masculine things you have learnt on the way, e.g., learning to speak in a particular kind of a way, learning to appear more manly than you are, learning to hold your body in a special way, learning to do your hair in a particular way etc.

   (ii)   Begin with your birth and continue the time-line to the present day. On this line show the key influences and special stories involved in the making of you as a boy.

  (iii)   Some of these key moments might be significant personal events, or incidents, stories, relationships, sights, places, people, characters, what you saw on the television, what you read or overheard etc. But only select the moments that say something about your growing up as a boy.

  (iv)   After you have finished, choose one other boy to share your life journey maps with. Take it in turns to explain your maps step by step and point out the main details. You are in control of exactly how much you want to share.

Come back into the whole group. Do any boys want to share what came up for them? Are there any common patterns, new ways of looking at things, important themes that you want to bring up in the whole group?

First Times as a Boy

Aims: *To discover the importance of 'first time' events in boys' lives.*
               To share their significance as landmarks of emerging masculinity.

Materials: *Copies of 'First Times a Boy' sheet, prepared using the statements below*

Time: *45 minutes*

What to do:

Give the boys 'First Times as a Boy' sheet. Read through some of the examples given on the sheet so that the boys understand the significance of the statements.

Working in pairs encourage the group to make a list of their own first times as boys and then share with each other. Encourage a critical attitude towards the messages which some of the 'first times' present in the way boys construct their lives and attitudes.

Alternatively, the first times may be written on flip chart paper and each pair can circulate to read each other's efforts. A whole group sharing can then be encouraged, viz:

- What are the messages of these first times for me as a boy?
- What impact are these first times having on my development as a boy now?

The statements:

First Times as a Boy

- The first time I discovered sewing wasn't for boys.
- The first time I realized my sisters were different at school.
- The first time I discovered a boy's voice had to be deep rather than his own.
- The first time I realized that boys were expected to talk about girls in a certain way but also realized that some of those girls were our sisters and best friends.
- The first time I saw myself as a titch against the menacing height of the other boys.
- The first time I measured myself against other boys and found that my hands were delicate and soft rather than just my own.
- The first time I learned how big penises ought to be by peeing in urinals with other boys and glancing anxiously around.
- The first time I learned how small and smooth and soft and unhairy I was by having to take showers in the changing room after the match.
- The first time I gave a friend a mock punch rather than a hug.
- The first time I jeered at what I was scared of.
- The first time as a boy I put on a brave face to cover up my hurt.

Boys' Toys

Aims: To examine boys at play and discover the hidden messages of favourite toys.

Materials: A collection of toys

Time: 45 minutes

What to do:

Encourage the boys to bring in toys with which they played at different times in their lives. This needs to be approached sensitively since there is a lot of denial around discarded toys. It is amazing how many long forgotten toys can be discovered and brought in — particularly if *everyone* takes part!

Once assembled the toys can be sorted into the different stages of boys' lives.

- very young   (0–4)
- infant   (4–7)
- primary   (8–11)
- early secondary (11–13)

After the toys have been sorted, divide the boys into groups of 3 or 4. Ask the boys to take toys in turn, and tell stories to show how important they were in that boy's life. What do they think the hidden messages were in the toys they played with?

A dramatic structure can be used whereby the boys role reverse with a toy of their choice. They speak from the role of the toy and spell out the messages that they gave to their owner. This structure can also provide insights into the owner's character and much valuable emotional sharing between boys can be achieved in this way.

Family Photographs

Aim: To use family photographs to look at the messages about the way boys grew up as boys.

Materials: Individual collections of photographs

Time: 45 minutes

What to do:

The boys have previously been asked to bring in family photograph albums or a few selected photographs.

Divide into groups of 3 or 4. Ask the boys to take it in turns to tell the stories that are associated with the photographs. (Remind them to talk about only those photographs which have something to say about the way they grew up as a boy.)

Encourage them to look through and pick out examples like:

- A sulky expression on your face after a run-in with Dad.
- Pictures taken with particular male friends or relatives.
- Some sort of sports photograph.
- Pictures taken with particular toys.

- Pictures where you notice the types of clothes you are wearing.
- Pictures showing your relationship with girls/women.

Almost any picture can be interesting but those which allow some significant information about the special ways boys grow up masculine are particularly interesting here.

How I am a Boy

Aim: To encourage boys to be aware of the shaping forces in the way they are growing up masculine.

Materials: Copies of Being a Boy by Julius Lester (see below)

Time: 50 minutes

What to do:

Ask the boys to look through *Being a Boy* by Julius Lester.

Get them to pick out the sections or sentences that rang a special bell for them — those that say to them 'that happened to me', or 'I was like that'.

Ask them to get into pairs to share what they have discovered.

Ask the boys to start making their own small anthology on key turning points or awakenings in their own life journey as a boy. They could write about and make cartoons on those selective, autobiographical moments that say something about them as a developing boy. (For example, the incidents from *Being a Boy* — where he chronicles his illuminating failures — '. . . a record of a childhood spent falling from bicycles, trees, the tops of fences, and porch steps; of tripping as I ran (generally from a fight), walked, or simply tried to remain upright on windy days.')

Open up a general discussion of what emerged for each boy during the exercise. Encourage the boys to tell stories of their childhood and what stands out as important to them in growing up as a boy.

The story:

Being a Boy

As boys go, I wasn't much. I mean, I tried to be a boy and spent many childhood hours pummelling my hardly formed ego with failure at Cowboys and Indians, baseball, football, lying, and sneaking out of the house. When our neighbourhood gang raided a neighbour's pear tree, I was the only one who got sick from the purloined fruit. I also failed at setting fire to our garage, an art at which any 5-year-old boy should be adept. I was, however, the neighbourhood champion at getting beat up. 'That Julius can take it, man,' the boys used to say, almost in admiration, after I emerged from another battle, tears brimming in my eyes but refusing to fall.

My efforts at being a boy earned me a pair of scarred knees that are a record of a childhood spent falling from bicycles, trees, the tops of fences, and porch steps; of tripping as I ran (generally from a fight), walked, or simply tried to remain upright on windy days.

I tried to believe my parents when they told me I was a boy, but I could find no objective proof for such an assertion. Each morning during the summer, as I cuddled up in the quiet of a corner with a book, my mother would push me out the back door and into the yard. And throughout the day as my blood was let as if I were a patient of 17th-century medicine, I thought of the girls sitting in the shade of porches, playing with their dolls, toy refrigerators and stoves.

There was the life, I thought! No constant pressure to prove oneself. No necessity always to be competing. While I humiliated myself on football and baseball fields, the girls stood on the sidelines laughing at me, because they didn't have to do anything except be girls. The rising of each sun brought me to the starting line of yet another day's Olympic decathlon, with no hope of ever winning even a bronze medal.

Through no fault of my own I reached adolescence. While the pressure to prove myself on the athletic field lessened, the overall situation got worse — because now I had to prove myself with girls. Just how I was supposed to go about doing this was beyond me, especially because at the age of 14, I was four foot nine and weighed 78 pounds. (I think there may have been one 10-year-old girl in the neighbourhood smaller than I.) Nonetheless, duty called, and with my ninth-grade gym-class jockstrap flapping between my legs, off I went.

To get a girlfriend, though, a boy had to have some asset beyond the fact that he was alive. I wasn't handsome like Bill McCord, who had girls after him like a cop-killer has policemen. I wasn't ugly like Romeo Jones, but at least the girls noticed him: 'That ol' ugly boy better stay 'way from me!' I was just there, like a vase your grandmother gives you at Christmas that you don't like or dislike, can't get rid of, and don't know what to do with. More than ever I wished I were a girl. Boys were the ones who had to take the initiative and all the responsibility. (I hate responsibility so much that if my heart didn't beat of itself, I would now be a dim memory.)

It was the boy who had to ask the girl for a date, a frightening enough prospect until it occurred to me that she might say no! That meant risking my ego, which was about as substantial as a toilet-paper raincoat in the African rainy season. But I had to thrust that ego forward to be judged, accepted, or rejected by some girl. It wasn't fair! Who was she to sit back like a queen with the power to create joy by her consent or destruction by her denial? It wasn't fair — but that's the way it was.

But if (God forbid!) she should say Yes, then my problem would begin in earnest, because I was the one who said where we would go (and waited in terror for her approval of my choice). I was the one who picked her up at her house where I was inspected by her parents as if I were a possible carrier of syphilis (which I didn't think one could get from masturbating, but then again, Jesus was born of a virgin, so what did I know?). Once we were on our way, it was I who had to pay the bus fare, the price of the movie tickets and whatever she decided to stuff her stomach with afterward. (And the smallest girls are all stomach.) Finally, the girl was taken home where once again I was inspected (the father looking covertly at my fly and the mother examining the girl's hair). The evening was over and the girl had done nothing except honour me with her presence. All the work had been mine.

Imagining this procedure over and over was more than enough: I was a sophomore in college before I had my first date.

I wasn't a total failure in high school, though, for occasionally I would go to a party, determined to salvage my self-esteem. The parties usually took place in somebody's darkened basement. There was generally a surreptitious wine bottle or two being passed furtively among the boys, and a record player with an insatiable appetite for Johnny Mathis records. Boys gathered on one side of the room and girls on the other. There were always a few boys and girls who'd come to the party for the sole purpose of grinding away their sexual frustrations to Johnny Mathis's falsetto, and they would begin dancing to their own music before the record player was plugged in. It took a little longer for others to get started, but no one matched my talent for standing by the punch bowl. For hours, I would try to make my legs do what they had been doing without effort since I was nine months old, but for some reason they would show all the symptoms of paralysis on those evenings.

After several hours of wondering whether I was going to die ('Julius Lester, a 16-year-old, died at a party last night, a half-eaten Ritz cracker in one hand and a potato chip dipped in pimiento-cheese spread in the other. Cause of death: failure to be a boy'), I would push my way to the other side of the room where the girls sat like a hanging jury. I would pass by the girl I wanted to dance with. If I was going to be refused, let it be by someone I didn't particularly like. Unfortunately, there weren't many in that category. I had more crushes than I had pimples.

Finally, through what surely could only have been the direct intervention of the Almighty, I would find myself on the dance floor with a girl. And none of my prior agony could compare to the thought of actually dancing. But there I was and I had to dance with her. Social custom decreed that I was supposed to lead, because I was the boy. Why? I'd wonder. Let her lead. Girls were better dancers anyway. It didn't matter. She stood there waiting for me to take charge. She wouldn't have been worse off if she'd waited for me to turn white.

But, reciting 'Invictus' to myself, I placed my arms around her, being careful to keep my armpits closed because, somehow, I had managed to overwhelm a half jar of deodorant and a good-size bottle of cologne. With sweaty armpits, 'Invictus', and legs afflicted again with polio, I took her in my arms, careful not to hold her so far away that she would think I didn't like her, but equally careful not to hold her so close that she could feel the catastrophe which had befallen me the instant I touched her hand. My penis, totally disobeying the lecture I'd given it before we left home, was rigid as Governor Wallace's jaw would be if I asked for his daughter's hand in marriage.

God, how I envied girls at that moment. Wherever *it* was on them, it didn't dangle between their legs like an elephant's trunk. No wonder boys talked about nothing but sex. That thing was always there. Every time we went to the john, there *it* was, twitching around like a fat little worm on a fishing hook. When we took baths, it floated in the water like a lazy fish and God forbid we should touch it! It sprang to life like lightning leaping from a cloud. I wished I could cut it off, or at least keep it tucked between my legs, as if it were a tail that had been mistakenly attached to the wrong end. But I was helpless. It was there, with a life and mind of its own, having no other function than to embarrass me.

Fortunately, the girls I danced with were discreet and pretended that they felt nothing unusual rubbing against them as we danced. But I was always convinced that the next day they were all calling up their friends to exclaim: 'Guess what, girl? Julius Lester got one! I ain't lyin'!'

Now, of course, I know that it was as difficult being a girl as it was a boy, if not more so. While I stood there paralysed at one end of the dance floor trying to find the courage to ask a girl for a dance, most of the girls waited in terror at the other, afraid that no one, not even I, would ask them. And while I resented having to ask a girl for a date, wasn't it also horrible to be the one who waited for the phone to ring? And how many of those girls who laughed at me making a fool of myself on the baseball diamond would have gladly given up their places on the sidelines for mine on the field?

No, it wasn't easy for any of us, girls and boys, as we forced our beautiful, free-flowing child-selves into those narrow, constricting cubicles labelled *female* and *male*. I tried, but I wasn't good at being a boy. Now I'm glad, knowing that a man is nothing but the figment of a penis's imagination, and any man should want to be something more than that. (Lester, 1974)

The Extra-terrestrial

Aim: *To encourage a critical look at the way boys do the things they do and what this means for the way boys learn to be masculine in this society.*

Materials: *None*

Time: *45 minutes*

What to do:

Explain to the boys that they are going to examine their behaviour through different eyes. What better than through the eyes of extra-terrestrial creatures who can look down on human interactions without any preconceived notions of norms of behaviour.

Encourage the boys to look at some of the day-to-day incidents in their lives which they know very well.

In role as a martian get the boys to ask Earth boys why they do what they do. What are these daily taken-for-granted behaviours that appear strange to this visitor from another planet? What is strange or questionable? What might a martian notice about boys' actions, facial expressions, ways of getting on with other people, the groups they go around in, the way they use their voices, what they look at, the way they carry their bodies, etc.? What might appear odd to a stranger who didn't already know about those things?

Ask the boys to make a list of the things a martian would find the most strange. Then to choose one or two and write two versions of the incident; (a) as seen through your eyes; and (b) as seen through a martian's eyes.

Is He Man Enough?

Aim: *To look at the influence of family sayings on the making of boys/men.*

Materials: *None*

Time: *45 minutes*

What to do:

Ask the boys to make a collection of family sayings, catch phrases, proverbs, jokes and anecdotes that are connected to memorable events and happenings that they experienced as a boy growing up. The sayings should have something to say about the making of boys/men. Examples might include:

> 'We're going to make a man of him.'
> 'Is he man enough to . . .'
> 'Real men don't . . .'
> 'Are you a man or a mouse?'
> 'Boys will be boys.'

In pairs or in small groups of 3–4, ask the boys to look at the statements, sayings, jokes, etc., which they have collected. They need to talk about the effect the sayings had on their development. The following questions are offered as guidelines.

- What were you doing when you heard and reacted to the messages like those above?
- How difficult was it to do things differently in the light of not wanting to disappoint family expectations around you being a real boy?
- What happened if you didn't come up to the expectations contained in the saying.
- What might you have chosen to do without this pressure to conform being placed upon you.

Help the boys to share as much as they can so that the myths around 'Is he man enough?' can be exposed.

The Facts of Life

Aim: To consider the role of finding out about the facts of life in the shaping influences of how boys become 'real lads'.

Materials: Sex Education Anthology (see below)

Time: 45 minutes

What to do:

Ask the boys to read through the 'Sex Education Anthology'.

Ask them to record how they found out about the 'facts of life'. When they have written their accounts, ask the boys to join into small groups (3–4) and to share their stories of discovery.

Still in groups. Ask the boys to look critically at what they were told and how they found out about the facts of life. What do they think was missing in the information they were given? How has what they were told affected their relationships to girls/women, and their attitude to expectations around sexual activity?

As a whole group, open a discussion on male expectations and male entitlement around the area of sexual activity. How important are the behaviours and attitudes of other boys in their approach to sexual activity?

Sex Education Anthology

Question: Did you have any sex education in school or home?

My dad sat me down at the age of eleven to tell me the facts of life and basically said, 'If a woman's got a hole, you cork it up'. That was his sex lesson and it wasn't at all what had been going on in my head.

Seeing the way he treated my mother, and the way women were generally treated in our community, gradually made me think that this wasn't how I felt. Also the men in our community were very, very macho and I knew I couldn't live up to that. If people ever discovered what I really was then I'd get rejected anyway by the community, so I felt I should reject it before they had the chance to reject me. (Kyriacos Spyroy)

No, none at all. The only sex education we had in school was when we did the rabbit in biology and the teacher just threw it in at the end of the lesson [laughs], 'And that's how we have babies'. It was really peculiar. I remember when I was at primary school, somebody told me how babies are born and I wouldn't believe them. [Laughs] I said, 'No, you're lying.' (Zahid Dar)

I was sort of a wimpish person while at school, and was mocked as effeminate since a very early age. I never had a proper sexual education so I tried to find out everything by myself. I once asked my sister to explain it to me, and she told me in very crude terms, using a fork and a cup. I was so disgusted. I couldn't believe it. She was really amazed that I was so shocked, and told me, 'You must talk to our father or our mother.' But my father was too busy gaining money and had left all the education to my mother, who gave me a book written by a priest which was so full of metaphors that I didn't understand it at all. My whole sexual upbringing was really a mess. By eleven, I had my first awareness in sexual things. In Brazil this is an incredibly late age. People develop sexually there very early. (Eduardo Pereira)

At thirteen I was told the facts of life by my mother and stepfather, which was an interesting experience. My stepfather gave me good practical advice — you know, if you go out with a whore make sure you wear a rubber. It was a very male-chauvinist viewpoint and I guess he must have told my mother that he had told me the facts of life, because the next night she decided to sit down and tell me her version of it. The two had nothing to do with each other. Hers was around the satisfying of the woman, making love and being affectionate and tender. My stepfather hadn't told me any of this. (Todd Butler)

One day, my dad decided that I'd reached the age when he should give me a talk about the facts of life. He said that sometimes I might find I'd got an erection when I woke up in the morning. But an erection to me was a building! So I said, 'What do you mean by an erection?' He said, 'Well, your penis may go hard.' And I thought, 'Oh, that's an erection!' He told me that this was perfectly natural, that boys quite often played with themselves and when they did they produced this sticky fluid. It was a nice feeling, so maybe they did it again and again. All boys did it and I wouldn't come to any harm.

The funny thing was that I'd never done it before, so, the very next day when I was alone in the house, I lay on the bed and masturbated. I thought, 'This is fun.' So I promptly started and went at it like mad for the next two or three years. Needless to say, I never told my dad that he started me doing this! (Bernard Dobson)

The only sex education I had was about worms and that's very confusing because they can be both male and female, whatever they choose. I remember a boy that I really fancied in my last year. I remember him making an arrangement with a girl that they would go on Barnes Common one night and he would fuck her. I mean, I used to stand there and listen to them — it was amazing. That was sex education. But it was very exciting to learn that way. (David Ruffell)

Chapter 12

Playing War

The Theory

The Warrior

The warrior is the most extreme example of virile manhood — the ultimate in power and ruthlessness. A machine without feelings — muscular, agile, capable of instant decisions to kill, maim, destroy.

The warrior-killer is the clearest expression of the emotional and social processes that shape aggressive masculinities. It is a defensive masculinity that's organized around the splitting off and denigration of conventional femininity. The processes are the splitting off of feelings from bodily action;[1] the inadmissibility of empathy; the cultivation of physical strength as a supreme virtue in itself; the celebration of insensitivity to brutality; the glorying in being 'hard'; the acknowledgment of physical strength as the ultimate arbiter of conflict; the celebration of male bonding in action.

The warrior is man *par excellence* whose reflection is celebrated in all forms of the media. All 'boys' clubs' prepare for and lead to this ultimate male club. The nearer an individual man approaches this warrior status, the more importance he is accorded by society, the more self-important he feels. Collectively, this warrior pattern is at the heart of patriarchy. The individual man achieves glory by the willing prostitution of his body for war, masked as for the greater good. It is the war or threat of war that is repeated every generation which has maintained this for millennia. With world wars and mass conscription, the tighter the net of aggressive masculinity draws. The logic of war runs like this: the threat of war creates a need for warriors. The warriors' mentality creates war.

The set of ideas above we dub the 'John Wayne syndrome'. Below is one example from real life showing the lure of joining the military machine, its offer of prestige and total security in one's masculinity, bounded by the forced containment of emotions. Why do men like Pete buy into this tempting mixture? Pete was a submariner whom one of the authors met while doing voluntary work at a psychiatric hospital. Why did he buy into the tempting mixture above?

> Military life could give Pete a sense of being valued which had been missing in his childhood. His father had also been in the Armed Forces

and was a hard task master. Punishment for misdeeds or not doing things the right way was swift and harsh. Pete wanted to please his father but felt inadequate and fearful around him. It was an uncertainty about 'shaping-up' in his father's eyes and this was further exacerbated by not being able to express feelings safely. Negative feelings of anger were punished; softer, gentler feelings were ridiculed. By his father's treatment of him, Peter was becoming aware of the equation: toughness equals manhood. The uniform was a badge of attractive, rugged masculinity. It marked him out. It made him feel special and it gave him an importance and an appeal in women's eyes. The status, recognition and skills which the Navy could provide also offered the promise of responsible employment after military service. After all, a military man was cool under pressure, trustworthy and, above all, controlled. He would have an air of outer control to match the rigorous control exercised from within. This is the controlled masculinity which gains respect and rewards within the working world.

For all the above reasons Pete was attracted by the type of rugged masculinity which the Navy offered. It is the type of rugged masculinity which is lauded in newspapers, literature and on TV and cinema screens. There is a long tradition of warrior heroes displaying compassion and action. The recruiting material feeds into that promise. So boys like Peter have grown up with Richard the Lionheart, Lancelot and Robin Hood and have at times identified with twentieth-century celluloid creations from James Bond to Rambo. He became familiar with the concept of the good, courageous warrior man who thwarts evil doers by all violent means necessary. The message is that it is OK to be a warrior man using violence in the cause of good to overcome evil because this is what real men are all about.

Pete could easily buy into these heroic fantasies by actively espousing the John Wayne promise of warrior power and status. It was the perfect antidote to all his childhood insecurity. He might have agreed with the words of Phil Caputo speaking of the lure of the US Army in the 1960s. He enlisted because he wanted 'the chance to live heroically . . . I saw myself charging up some beach head like John Wayne in *Sands of Iwo Jima* and then coming home a suntanned warrior with medals on my chest.' Gerzon (1982) wrote of the John Wayne syndrome as an 'explicit if unwritten code of conduct — a set of masculine traits we have been taught to revere since childhood'. These traits include being hard, ruthless, tough, unemotional, competitive, eager to seek out danger and thwart evil doers. Pete felt that this was what the Navy could give him and he would 'be somebody'.

Pete also spoke with pride of the other qualities which the Armed Forces seek to instil into their recruits and which permeates the whole functioning of a successful, harmonious, military machine. It is precisely because these admirable qualities are inextricably intertwined with warrior ones that the cocktail is so powerful and hard to resist.

In reality what the Navy encouraged in Pete was a kind of phoney status. Here was an expression of masculinity which it was deemed fit to show to the world. It gave a sense of self-worth which was shored up by the conformity to the military ethos. Who he really was, the feelings which threatened his warrior status in his own eyes and those of his naval peers were distrusted and pushed down. Once out of the Navy, he was lost. He was stripped of the authority framework where the external routines, rewards and rituals of Naval life made him feel safe.

In truth the cracks in his manhood were apparent long before he left the Naval service. The routine, the boredom, the inability to show feelings, the sense of confinement as a submariner had lured him to the twin attractions of drinking and womanizing at all available opportunities.

Drinking large quantities of alcohol helped reinforce the camaraderie of the male club and also blotted out the memories of horrific visions on the battlefield. In Pete's case this was the Gulf War clean-up operation and his being brought face to face with the reality of this so-called clean war of precision bombing of purely military targets. He witnessed the lie and still has nightmares about the thousands of dead bodies which lay rotting under the desert skies in the two months he was involved in this operation. He also drinks so that the images retreat from his consciousness. He feels that there was never anyone to talk to about his feelings of sadness and revulsion.

This failure to communicate, to acknowledge and express his feelings led to relationship problems with women. This, together with his failure to attract any sort of job other than 'I hit people' as a nightclub bouncer, led to bitterness and disappointment. Drinking binges led to the gloom of overwhelming depression, suicide attempts and treatment on an acute ward of a psychiatric hospital.

Warrior Values

The military system is the patriarch under whose influence and discipline a man emerges. Boys become men because being a man is equated with finding discipline. Since the army is an institution where men are shouted at, rigidly controlled and disciplined, that experience in itself is a kind of hardship ritual, a kind of male rite of passage in pursuit of maturity. It is not surprising that recruits buy into the masculinity–warrior equation and talk of the slow insidious pressure of the routine and organized brutality of military life that means 'you found you were capable of doing much more than you ever anticipated you could do' (Lifton, 1974).

In warfare and preparation for warfare, this conformity and comradeship exacts an awful price — the loss of value in self. Thus from as far back in history as the Gilgamesh story, an ancient heroic epic, comes the price that men pay for the male bonding and camaraderie which war provides (Starhawk, 1987). Gilgamesh says, 'Do not speak like a coward.' In military terms it is essential to ignore your feelings because cowards are not to be trusted, do not make good comrades. From Gilgamesh to the present day what has changed?

In talking about his problems to me, Pete spoke with awful clarity of the necessity to hide his feelings during his nine years in the Navy. If he showed weakness or hints of fear then this would be rigorously punished by various unpleasant activities which would pull him back into line. One such degrading and humiliating practice to remind comrades of their duty was to part fill a bath with water and then for everyone in the section to urinate and defecate into the water. The offending sailor was then thrown in and held there. This 'regimental bath', as it was called, was not an experience to be repeated and was powerfully influential in ensuring conformity. It was unspoken and well learned: 'Don't show your feelings — learn to shut them off' (Pete, 1992, oral communication).

Stouffer *et al.* (1949) spoke of the proof of manhood that a soldier fulfilled in combat: 'Courage, endurance and toughness, lack of squeamishness when confronted with shocking and distasteful stimuli, avoidance of displays of weakness, reticence about emotional or idealistic matters.' Such values would be tested in time of war. There could be no failure. The cult of masculine toughness has to be continually reworked and re-affirmed. Any feelings of tenderness, aesthetic feelings or emotional messiness are pushed down and not revealed, resulting in emotional numbness. To be hard and to function properly as a soldier, empathy with an opponent must be repressed so that in war time faceless enemies can more easily be slaughtered like the Vietnamese who were dismissed as Gooks throughout the period of the Vietnam War. One veteran of the war told of a time when he and members of his unit fired indiscriminately into a Vietnamese village simply for fun because it was New Year's Eve. Next day the villagers brought out seven small packages that were the seven little children who had been killed. This is a testament to the emotional splitting from feelings to enable barbaric acts to be carried out.

Heterosexuality and Military Manhood

To guard the sense of masculine heroic toughness, softer, gentler feelings and emotional complexities are cut off and assigned to women and lesser men. Such men in contemporary ethos would include those who are gay, who can be dismissed as 'poofters', or artistically creative men who are dubbed 'wimps'. The patriarchal system which stresses men's superior status is used to keep men striving to be unlike women — and hence good soldiers. The term 'Women' actually becomes an abusive epithet that can be hurled out at any man who fails to act like a 'real' man. Use of obscenities which refer to women's bodies, sexualities or both are also very common. It is as if the next worse thing to the enemy is a woman. It seems that the whole ethos of military life is in someway based on the denigration of women. Indeed, in the USA, the Marine Corps' slang for any women who isn't the wife, mother or daughter of anyone present is 'Suzie'. It is short for Suzie Rottencrotch.

Naming equipment by women's names further reveals the function that objectifying women has for confirming male values of dominance and power. Bombs and guns have women's names but are used by men to achieve their military ends. Another example is the way the joystick (control lever but also slang for penis) controls the movement of an aircraft feminized by its nick-name. Thus the first atomic bombs dropped on Japanese cities from aircraft were given women's names. A picture of Rita Hayworth was stencilled onto the first atomic bomb exploded on the Bikini atoll in 1946.

The denigrating use and abuse of women in military terms is perhaps only understandable in terms of the threat that women pose in encouraging feelings of love and affection which threatens a chink in the men's armour. Men are afraid of the feelings that women arouse in them, both because they are disgusted by them and because they feel unable to cope with the intensity of feeling so aroused. Love and affection may at the same time trigger feelings of fear of loss which may create the urge to flee rather than fight. One group of service men representative of so many perhaps are the F1–11 pilots from Upper Heyford in Oxfordshire who published a pamphlet called the *Gambler's Song Book* (Smith, 1989). These pilots of the nuclear fighter bombers set down these songs which are essentially their private feelings as a particular group. The two main concerns are sex and war, but throughout the gross and obscene imagery there runs the theme of intense loathing and objectification of women. Here is an example of a common military cadence count.

> I got a gal in Kansas City
> She's got gumdrops on her titties
> When I get back to Kansas City
> Gonna suck those gumdrops off her titties.

Such objectification, humiliation and abuse of women pales alongside the content of the *Gambler's Song Book*. Titles like 'Ghost Fuckers in the Sky', 'I Fucked a Dead Whore' and a particularly obscene piece sung to the tune of 'These Foolish Things'. All the songs punish women in some way. In some, the punishment is death and decomposition: it is the women's punishment for stirring up pleasurable feelings. In some ways women who are seen as deserving to die in these songs are transformed into the image of death itself. Women seem to have taken the place of a distant, unknowable enemy and indeed in some senses it is clear that women are the enemy.

The pilots are part of the macho swaggering heterosexual culture in a military establishment that constantly asks them to re-assert and prove their masculine identity. The songs demonstrate the strong links which exist between killing and fucking and serve to keep at bay suggestions of emotional dependency on women. Military life emphasizes an aggressively heterosexual version of masculinity. Gay men are excluded on the grounds that their 'severe personality defect will impair morale and discipline' (Williams and Weinburg, 1971). Thus, in the USA military discipline stresses the close connection between the phallus and the cultural construction of male supremacy. Recruits are instructed to grasp the rifle in one hand while his other hand grasps his crotch. In unison the squad will then shout rhythmically and with correct gestures for:

> This is my rifle
> This is my gun
> This is for pleasure
> This is for fun.

This is the powerful reminder that the military ethos works through the links between the penis and power.

Connell (1989) points out that 'at any given moment some forms of masculinity will be hegemonic — that is most honoured and influential — and other forms will be marginalized and subordinated.' Thus in contemporary Western society the 'top-dog' hegemonic masculinity is very much associated with aggressiveness and capacity for violence. Men split themselves off from their feelings almost as if there is a ground swell of collective personal resentment towards the caring, sensitive part of themselves. Vigorously suppressing those feelings, denying them, railing against them, they turn their attention to those men who they imagine display the feelings they most disown. Chiding, undermining, baiting and beating are the ingredients of a homophobic response. By such means men can locate their capacity to be unfeeling and cynical. The Armed Forces know the value of desensitizing their personnel. Reports from the Gulf War revealed the showing of *Slasher* and hard core pornographic films before US fighter pilots went on missions. The same procedure was used in Vietnam so that soldiers can perform warrior acts of deadly cruelty and callousness.

Schooling and Warrior Values

How do warrior values influence boys' lives at school? As a child between the ages of 7 and 10, I was deeply immersed in the culture of the Wild West via films, comics and television. Along with my male friends, I owned toy guns and tried to be quick on the draw like my Western heroes. I stood in front of mirrors, pouted, sneered and 'drew' as fast as I could, I was a 'law man', a survivor and a killer in our make-believe battles which transformed the waste ground near my home on the outskirts of Derby into the frontier land of the Wild West. We also played war games as British soldiers overcoming our German and Japanese opponents: images of whose treachery and deviousness had also been picked up from comics, film and television. Oral machine gun noises, sounds of grenades and gun and rifle shots produced by 'caps' punctuated the air as we played for hours on end, day after day.

All this activity and action was reinforced by my devouring of a regular diet of adventure and war stories provided by comics like *Eagle* and *Lion*, together with *Wizard* and *Hotspur*. They were filled with heroic stories of good over-coming evil as the 'baddies' got their due reward by coming to a particularly messy end. I played and read because the games and stories could be thrilling and exciting. It was also important because I played with other boys and could be accepted into the warmth of the boys' club.

I knew the games weren't real. When I shot someone there were always too many arguments about who was 'dead'. The whole of the play had an excitingly unreal feel around it. Indeed, at times I could be non-committal, indifferent and mocking about my participation in the play. But the stories, games and TV programmes also had a very real value for me as I flitted in and out of this fantasy escape from everyday reality. As a severe stammerer as a child, I often had feelings of insecurity and inadequacy together with a sense of frustrated anger. When I was feeling low, it was easy to summon up one of the heroes of the Wild West or John Wayne himself and live out one of their fantasies in my head — to be fully immersed in the emotional identification with my hero and his sense of justice. It gave me a feeling of power and strength together with a promise of my grown-up sense of competent manhood in the future.

What do I carry around with me from those far off days? I still harbour a deep sense of identification with an underdog who deserves to triumph against all the odds. In a more sinister way I am still attracted to toy guns and the new and sophisticated sounds of death they are capable of making. It is as if a part of me is drawn to the comfortable feel of those plastic weapons while at the same time being repelled by them.

My work with boys in the 1990s reveals many similarities with what is really going on for boys in their world of violent play, and what was happening for me almost forty years ago. The difference is that more than a generation on, the images are more violent, virulent and real. Today, images of war and destruction are all around in war and violence toys, on television and cinema screens, on videos and in comics and computer games.

As far as war toys are concerned, the most basic piece of equipment is the gun and two very important points need making about guns. Firstly, most guns are actually for killing people or living things and toy guns are imitations of these. Secondly, there is a correlation between the real world of violence and the world of play. It seems that the link has been around for a very long time. The following quote is from a toy maker who was talking to Henry Mayhew in 1851:

> In war time, bless you, that was the time for my business. There was
> a demand for guns then, I can tell you! I sold eight then to one that

I sell now, though the population's increased so. These pistols, which I get 1s 6d a dozen for now, I had 3s 6d a dozen for then. I remember the first botched-up peace in 1802. I can just recollect the illumination. My father (I can hear him say so) thought the peace would do no good to him, but it didn't last very long, and the toy-gun trade went on steadily for years — with a bit of a fillip, now and then, after news of a victory; the grand thing for the trade was the constant report that Bonaparte was coming — there was to be an invasion, and then every child was a soldier. Guns did 'go off' briskly at that period — anything in the shape of a gun found a customer. Working people could then buy plenty of toys for their children — and did buy them too. (*Morning Chronicle*)

It is apparent that the demand for war toys is stimulated by real conflicts. Indeed war toys enjoyed a boom at the time of the Falklands/Malvinas conflict, and during and after the Gulf War, in the form of appropriate toy soldiers, military models, planes, guns and games. The illustrations on the packaging present boys with a very clear message. The pictures are of men fighting, thus suggesting that this adult male gender role is an acceptable one for boys to aspire to. The language, too, stresses words like 'action', 'assault', 'attack', 'battle', 'combat' and 'strike' since it is only by such means that the 'ruthless forces of evil' can be overcome. The simple solution is force — no alternative means for resolving conflict is considered.

I always used to assume that Action Man was simply an acceptable doll for boys to play with. It was a slow realization, and typical of the insidious manipulation of the market by toy manufacturers, that the main emphasis of Action Man was military — all the clothes in the sets available were uniform. The model was moulded and jointed so that military postures could be created. The hands were made to accommodate toy rifles and machine guns. One of the features of play with dolls concerns their encouragement of caring for others. Unfortunately, within the Action Man concept the intention is all about killing and none at all about caring.

Although Action Man was deleted from the range after 1985, the Action Force figures rapidly assumed enormous popularity. There are a number of teams of characters that are linked together by a story line. One example will suffice. One of the teams is known as 'The Enemy' — the 'deadly and feared enemy of the world' — who are intent on world domination. The figures are in red and the writing on the vehicles looks suspiciously Russian in character. What irresponsibility on the part of the manufacturers in a nuclear threatened world to create such images and clear messages. Throughout this whole range, danger, disaster and menace threaten from every quarter and the only solution is to be found in the justified use of the deadliest of military hardware. It is little wonder that politicians and press could so easily convince people that the only solution to Saddam Hussein was the unleashing of weaponry of deadly and precise sophistication.

Wherever you look there is massive aggression and violence. 'Goodies' and 'baddies' are clearly defined. The good are clean cut, rugged and bright in image and dress, while the bad look repulsive and are dressed in dark colours — particularly black. He-Man from the Masters of the Universe range illustrates this well. He is big, very broad and muscular, blond and white. He is very obviously a super hero and the righter of wrongs. His most feared opponent is Skeletor who looks shifty and evil simply because he looks Japanese. This fuels the racist equation of Japanese or other foreigners being used to imply evil in much the same say as 'Red' Indians were always shown as creeping about in a sly fashion in the old Wild West myths.

Children of all ages seem to watch a variety of cartoons. Many of them have the theme of good versus evil on a galactic or inter-planetary scale with the destiny of the world at stake. One of the most popular in recent years has been Transformers where the heroic Autobots battle against the evil Deceptions with all manner of technical wizardry involved as instruments of death. But, in some ways the most sinister figures are provided by real people who appear in films and in television series because then the identification with heroes can be even greater. The best example in recent years has been *The A Team*. *The A Team* have a clean image since they are on the side of good and justice. Indeed they champion the oppressed. There is an appealing atmosphere of humour and violence with the accent very firmly on violence. There are all manner of shootings, bombings, explosions and wild car chases. Those who are bad always lose but there is never any sign of blood, pain or dead bodies which would be the inevitable result of such horrific violence. The simplification of good versus evil in these programmes has appealed even to very young children with the result that there have been nursery and infant schools where so called 'A Team' games had to be banned from playgrounds because children were being physically damaged.

Older children and teenagers choose to buy into cult heroes like Rambo played by Sylvester Stallone or Terminator with Arnold Schwarzenegger. Such films and characterizations of macho, militaristic viciousness hold a promise of excitement and power. Sometimes I notice boys with *Rambo* or similar videos and they will freely acknowledge the way they buy into the promise of strength and manliness that they portray. They acknowledge the unreality of much of what they see but the identification at a moment of insecurity and inequacy in their lives means that they buy in to a compensatory sense of virility and power. It is almost as if they are saying 'I can be hard and tough too'.

War comics work within a similar value system which sees good triumphing over evil and against the odds. The drawings and the imagery stress the violence, virility and strength as the stories build to a climax of excitement while the hero demolishes the evil-doers. The most persuasive writers and illustrators skilfully provide an authenticity which grounds the story in the believable so that boys' imaginations can be held.

The most recent phenomena are the hand-held computer games from firms like Nintendo and the Game Boy range. They have particular appeal for young teenage boys. Jason may be typical. He is 13 and spoke to one of the authors about his fifty-two hand-held games all costing between £24–£30 each. He told me that all of them except one contained lots of fighting and violence. Jason likes them because they are adventures which can have many different endings so that 'they are better than reading books'. The heroes include names like Hu-Man, Wonder Boy, Mega Man, Psycho Fox, Spider Man and others. Stories involve rescuing princesses and destroying various dragons, humans and creatures of evil with laser guns and other sophisticated weaponry. According to Jason there is something about being actually inside the game that gives it its excitement and sense of adventure. This state of excitement reflects those delicious moments of virtual experience where he experiences killing things but knows that 'it's not for real so it's OK'. Chasing this fleetingly tangible sense of near reality, he is exploring the area of consciousness that lies between external reality and the world of imagination.

Boys like Jason carry around computer games and magazines and eagerly devour their contents. One such magazine is Mean Machines. The January 1992 edition has page after page that includes some form of violence, be it ancient cartoon warriors wielding clubs with metal spikes to high power laser destroyers and fiercesome tank-like creations. The message is one of overwhelming male power with women as helpless and in need of rescuing by dominant, powerful men.

Laser Quest is a new amusement chain with branches in towns and cities throughout the country. It seems to have tremendous appeal because for a short period of time the participant can be clad in a form of protective armour with circles (targets) on front and back and equipped with a laser gun. In a darkened room, complete with obstacles, you then fire at people similarly clad and equipped, scoring points for every time you 'kill' someone. Points are scored for the number of kills. In the world of make-believe the participant is firing at and 'killing' real people. Laser Quest outlets act like a magnet to many boys. It is another example of the making of masculinity. Armed with their lasers, boys are 'zapping' the enemy, reducing other boys to targets, objectifying and taking particular pleasure if there are girls there to be hit. They are task orientated. The only thing that matters is the score at the end of the time allowed. They are demonstrating power and control over others by means of skill with their weapons.

The image of killing people who do not die provided by the Laser Quest experience has also been graphically illustrated on our television screens with the selective news reporting of the Gulf War. Many boys were avid followers of the news during that troubled time. Here they could see footage of the latest sophisticated bombers and weapons systems in action. They could see the warrior values of courage, heroism and duty extolled on the screens as the newscasters and war correspondents spoke endlessly of the precision bombing techniques. Slow-motion camera work was used on a number of occasions to show bombing so sophisticated that only military establishments were hit, leaving the people of Iraq 'safe'. The lie is given to this in later statistics of thousands dead and the eye witness accounts from such as Pete, the submariner (see p. 250). It was almost as if the lessons of the computer games were being retold. Here, carried out before the boys' eyes, was the reality of a clean, surgical war — a war without dead bodies. The final push into Kuwait by the Allied Forces was reported as receiving no resistance from Iraqi troops who just gave in or ran away. It told nothing of the slaughter, the death and destruction which left thousands of Iraqi soldiers buried alive or left to rot in the hot desert sun. Such images seriously trouble Pete's mind as he wrestles with his depression in a Nottingham psychiatric hospital acute ward. He knows the reality of war, of precision bombing and of newsreaders' lies. He knows that violence in all its forms really does mean death.

Boys' Responses

One of the authors was doing role-play mime work on feelings with a group of boys. Almost all the mimes included scenes of aggressive, violent behaviour. The boys' response was that aggressive feelings were the easiest to show: 'We are more used to that than anything else. You've got to be able to look after yourself and show you're hard.' The range of war toys, films, cartoons, comics and games seductively ensnares boys to behave in dehumanized, aggressive and war-like ways and to value physical strength, power and violence. Although it is well appreciated that the images they see are not real, it is inescapable that violent scripts are inevitably transferred imitatively into play. In such situations, boys are less likely to develop meanings for themselves; to work out for themselves why and how things happen; to decide for themselves what is real and not real; or to face that they are in full control of what goes on in their play. While playing they learn early to shut off from the sensitive and caring feelings, particularly in the company of other boys.

Boys are not just brainwashed by their involvement with war toys, war comics, computer games and films, they are very much aware of the stories and films as escapist entertainment. They have a complex attachment to them — partly wanting aspects of them to be true, while another part is resistant and distrustful. They sense the larger-than-life quality of patriarchal culture and posturing that is on display but they also need to survive in the boys' world. This is why boys willingly bow before a conspiracy of almost unconscious rules of conduct. Out of situations in their own lives where they feel inadequate and insecure, boys buy into the symbols of hegemonic power which are on display all around them. They give their consent to the dominant meanings and what is socially permissible to think and believe in. The unconscious rules of conduct, so bought, means that caring and sensitivity will not be on display while other boys are around, but that expressions of unfeeling callousness and hardness will be.

Boys can move back and forth between the imaginary and the real world. Sometimes everyday reality is boring and the escape is enticing. Winnicott used the expression 'play space' to define the space boys might use to keep out the adult world of inconvenient pressures and retreat into the safety of active participation in fantasy. They are responding to an invitation to identify. It doesn't happen automatically but is a powerful choice to make when a boy feels inadequate, vulnerable or is filled with self-doubt. Such self-doubt might surround fears around achieving fully formed masculinity: 'Will I shape up?' is an important question in adolescent boys' minds. 'Have I got the physical strength to meet the rigorous demands of expected manhood?' The films, toys, stories, computer game fantasies all serve to give a promise of future competence. The dreams are important rehearsals for manhood.

Note

1 The public display of the highest virility exactly mirrors its private peak, i.e. in 'fucking' where hardness (literally), insensitivity and emotional splitting are also the essential underpinning of sexual behaviour to women.

Selected Further Reading on Playing War

DIXON, B. (1990) *Playing them False*, Stoke, Trentham Books.
DAWSON, G. (1990) 'War toys', in DAY, G. (Ed.) *Reading in Popular Culture*, London, Macmillan.
CONNELL, R.W. (1989) 'Masculinity, violence and war', in KIMMEL, M. and MESSNER, M. (Eds) *Men's Lives*, New York, Macmillan.
MIEDZIAN, M. (1992) *Boys Will Be Boys*, London, Virago.
GERZON, M. (1982) *A Choice of Heroes: The Changing Face of American Manhood*, Boston, Houghton Mifflin.
DAWSON, G. (1994) 'Playing at soldiers: Boyhood phantasies and the pleasure-culture of war', in *Soldier Heroes*, London, Routledge.
SMITH, J. *Misogynies*, London, Faber.

The Session

Threats of Violence

I had been concerned for a long time about the level of aggressive language between boys in the school environment. I constantly overheard threats of death and serious beatings. I would sometimes shudder at the glib way the 'You're dead' message came out in the way of a casual daily rejoinder. Like other threats of violence it was a taken-for-granted, easily forgotten way of communicating between boys. Sometimes it was just words in the air, at other times it was the prelude to one of the semi-planned fights between two boys which would take place after school. The afternoon of such an event is filled with that air of anticipation as so many other boys become vicariously excited by the prospect of the scrap ahead. Sides are taken, the followers congregate as the crowd grows, urging combatants on in this strange atmosphere of fascination with violence. All too soon it's all over, one of the fighters is beaten and shamefully gives in or the fight is stopped by outsiders (teachers).

What has the fight been about? Sometimes it is about girls, at others it is more about the round of jibes and insults getting out of hand. Insults around members of families provoke the most hostility so that references to mothers as prostitutes can trigger the excuse to deliver a beating. It makes the aggression justified.

In previous sessions the group had worked on questionnaires about violence and debated boys' attachments to violent acts and we had also investigated attachment to heroes and male heroic qualities. I now wanted to make a link between the boys' involvement with an atmosphere of violence with male participation in wars. I had collected pictures of dead soldiers lying where they fell. The pictures were from many different sources but most were from conflicts which have taken place since 1939 and were not white, euro-centrically based. I wanted to use some of these as the focus for the day's session.

The boys enter the room with an air of anticipation. They had enjoyed the debate last time which had encouraged them to think about violence more deeply. We have a little time for a kind of check-in. I am interested to know what the boys' experience of violence has been since the previous week. Have they felt angrily aggressive towards anyone? Have they been physically violent? Have they witnessed violent acts? One boy reports that he had been head-butted in the face on his way home from school. He said that it was his fault since he had said things about the other boy's mother. The assailant was also much bigger than he was and he acknowledged that it had been a silly thing to do but 'it was only a joke'. How many times have I heard this? How did he feel about what happened to him? 'I don't feel very good about it, but it was my fault. I shouldn't have said anything'. There was an atmosphere of acceptance of brutality as a way of sorting out problems or of punishing someone else for wrong-doings. Another boy reported that he had been beaten up by his brother and we discover that he has taken it out on his younger brother who 'bugs' him. He feels his elder brother picks any excuse to have a go at him so in a way he just passes it on and he knows he does. Another boy reports jibes about his family, which have been directed at him. He won't actually tell us what the remark was but it was bad enough to justify seeking revenge and punishment of the offender: 'Some things you don't ignore.' He had gone out of his way to smack the guilty person. I wonder aloud at the link between this personal response and the way governments go to war for justified reasons. I ask what happens when governments do this. The boys talk about people being killed or badly injured or mentally damaged and that buildings get wrecked. I suggest that we are going to have a look at what this might mean in human terms for people's lives.

I ask the group to have a look at the selection of photographs of dead soldiers from a recent conflict. I have chosen the Gulf War because it had such a marked impact on the life of the school with its significant Muslim population.

There are just four photographs, two from each side of the conflict. I pose a variety of questions:

> *How old is he?* A variety of ages are suggested, but the boys are surprised to learn that one of the soldiers was in fact only 17. There is an air of it being impossible to imagine that they would be involved in a war in two years' time.
>
> *What has he got in his pockets?* Someone shouts condoms, some laugh, others look rather witheringly at their colleague who has made the remark. 'Chewing gum, sweets, money, keys, a wallet, photographs.'
>
> *Whose photograph would he be carrying?* 'It's probably his mother.' 'It would be his mother and his girlfriend — or his father.' What about if he's got any children — not the young one but the others? 'Perhaps he has got children.'
>
> *So who loved him then?* 'Well all those people would — he's never going to see them again is he?' The atmosphere in the room has become quiet and quite sad.
>
> *What was he doing before he put the uniform on?* 'Do you mean what job he'd got?' 'That one was probably at school, the other ones could have been anything. He could have been a car mechanic or worked in a bank or anything — perhaps he had a shop.'
>
> *What were his values or what did he believe in?* The group had some difficulty with this until they began to relate it to their own lives. One of the Sikh boys suggests that he believed in God, others agree with this. Most of the boys just think that he wanted to live and have some fun in his life.
>
> *What about this man's childhood — how did he play as a child?* 'He'd play all sorts of running about games, he might have played computer games. I bet he played football.' 'I bet he'd got brothers and sisters — perhaps they all played.' The boys get into the swing of it all and suggest holidays, camping trips, learning how to smoke, going drinking, all the sort of activities that belong to their own lives.
>
> *What do you think attracted this man into military service?* The boys think he might have had to fight and suggest he was fighting for his country. There was a split opinion here in that some boys seemed to take on the notion of duty to fight and that the country was worth fighting for. Others totally reject this and say that no way would they fight — they didn't want to end up like this (pointing to the photographs). 'But it's your duty to fight when your country needs you. I want to join the army anyway,' says Kevin. 'You might have been in the Gulf War and ended up like this,' replies Steve 'Look what you'll have missed.'
>
> *What do you think this soldier wanted from his life?* 'If he wasn't married, perhaps he would want to be, and have children and a job and just do what everyone else does. At least he'd have had the chance.'

I ask them what they've heard or read about the value of dying for your country. Some have seen films which stress the duty of laying down your life for others and things like that. It's not for Steve, though, he can't imagine anything worse. Because we had done some work in this group about being in other people's shoes, I ask them to role reverse with the person in the photograph and just ponder on whether it was all worth it. They get into pairs and have a dialogue with each other as two dead soldiers, whose names the boys invent. I move around eavesdropping these fragments of conversation and pick up an extraordinary sense of empathy. The boys have slipped into role and using their imagination they speak of the terrible loss which they have suffered and what an impact that is going to have on other people's lives. Martin slips out of role to realize how awful it must still be for his neighbours whose son was killed in Northern Ireland, 'We've just forgotten about it — but I bet they'll never forget.'

The boys join back together again as a group. Spontaneously Martin says, 'It doesn't matter what side you're on, it's the same. It's like everyone has the same sort of dreams about living and it's just been take away.' Greg says that he has a real fear of fighting. He doesn't like going out at night because of the area he lives in. He can't imagine being in the army and being forced to fight. The rest of the group take him seriously. There are no jibes about being a wimp. The boys start to tell stories of things they have heard or read about when people who get into fights often end up as dead as the people in the photographs. They agree that sometimes things just get out of hand. They recognize the fights they see or get involved with are really about nothing very much. I wonder whether anything they have done this morning will affect their desire to get involved with fights. Steve suggested that, 'It makes you think more, but sometimes there'll be times . . .' His voice trails off and there is a short-lived silence until Kevin, who seems quite emotional, said, 'Really I wish there was no fighting at all — it would just be a better world'. It seemed like a good note on which to finish.

Classroom Strategies

The Glorification of War

In class one day, Scott called Abid 'thick'. Abid responded by calling Scott's mother 'thick'. The scene was set for an escalation of abuse which in different circumstances may have led to violence. I have often witnessed the stages of this escalating, confrontative behaviour. It starts by name-calling, progresses through more extreme abuse until 'male pride' is seen as threatened. Heads jutting, shoulders pulled back, bodies and arms twitching in readiness, erstwhile friends become implacable enemies in the heat of the moment. The arm is thrust forward. At first it's a shove and the response is similar but then, in a tangle of bodies, flaying arms and flying feet, the two combatants hurl into each other with all the venom appropriate for the erupting anger and injured pride.

If we are serious about reducing these incidents of male violence then work on conflict resolution is essential. The fights in the playground cause excitement and fear for the combatants but also encourage the rush of excited onlookers to view the action. All this sense of thrill and intensity of interest can be viewed on a more public and global scale. In sport, boxing and wrestling offer institutionalized violence which attracts massive money and prestige. In boxing, the violence is brutal, dangerous and degrading. In wrestling, particularly appealing are the stars of American wrestling with their impressively masculine names — Hulk Hogan, Sergeant Slaughter and the Undertaker. Their activities are eagerly followed. Boys applaud the moves. They imitate them. They carry plastic models of these heroes around with them. Eyes light up when wrestling magazines are pored over. Although the bouts are choreographed, the action appears as vicious and violent. The posturing is copied in the playground.

On a global scale, the rush to glorify violence was graphically displayed at the onset of the Gulf War. The war received the kind of attention from boys which showed how they were gripped and riveted by the justness and the glorification of the conflict without any sense of what it was really to mean in human terms. The link between maleness and the glorification of war was made very forcibly to me on the day the Gulf War broke out. The landlord of the local pub had been in the army for many years. He was upstairs when a representative from the brewery called. He came down reluctantly to greet the visitor with the words, 'What are you doing here now — I've got a war to watch.' With excited eyes he went on to say the TV screens showed that, 'We were giving them hell.' I found it all very chilling. He was very much the male soldier at that moment vicariously living the excitement of protecting his sense of injured male pride at the hands of the vicious dictator so far away. The bully had been cruel, unthinking and out of order in the world playground. He had to be sorted out.

Along with other programmes in this book the crucial point of understanding for boys lies in the appreciation of these flashpoints which provoke violence as being part of their maleness. What is it that makes it difficult for a boy to turn away or ignore taunts or insults directed at himself and family? What is this pride which promotes the virtue of being hard and tough at the expense of any more sensitive emotions? What is it about being tough and not soft that is so important for boys? What is it about hiding fear in fights which is so important?

Learning to be a real boy has meant that much of the capacity for empathy, caring and gentleness has been lost at the surface. It is so often determinedly not present in interaction between peers, lost behind the hard exterior or the jokes and the banter which obscure any expression of real honesty and truth in relationships.

In pursuit of conflict resolution we offer a course which emphasizes putting 'becoming a real boy' under the microscope of critical thinking. As a boy what am I really doing? Who am I trying to impress? What am I hiding? What is stopping me from showing other boys what I am really like? What makes it important for me to have to fight this person? Work on conflict resolution, promoting empathy, deglorifying violence and war will help boys to look critically at their layers of learned manhood and reveal other qualities at the surface. They may try new behaviours, new qualities of sharing and understanding in the company of other boys before the stultifying weight of learned manhood becomes very difficult to shift.

We advocate three ways of working in school settings to help influence boys' attitudes and behaviour towards manly aggression. The three areas are:

1   Conflict resolution by such means as listening skills exercises, avoidance of put-downs, cooperation, seeing situations from someone else's point of view.

2   Reinforcing boys' empathic and caring feelings towards children by an active participation in a child development programme which emphasizes real contact with babies and small children. By encouraging a greater connection with life-giving as they learn the qualities of being a nurturing father, this would tend to diminish the need for excitement, power, and the gang mentality which leads to fighting and ultimately to war.

We are firmly of the view that boys' involvement with child rearing will be of enormous benefit in reducing the incidence of male violence (Miedzian, 1992). Despite all manner of educational initiatives, boys and child care is still an area where boys are conspicuously absent. Boys seldom opt for child care at GCSE level, but more importantly schools seem to have very little interest or inclination in promoting boys' involvement with babies and very small children.

Think of the benefits. It would help boys find the qualities of empathy and caring which are often absent in the company of other boys. A boys' group playing with babies and responsible for their care for a period of time each week is an important social learning experience. There will be initial awkwardness, ignorance and embarrassment but each boy's learning and growth in this area will be publicly visible to all the other boys. It is an important shared, male experience. It would also encourage boys to think of themselves as future nurturant fathers with greater awareness of the importance and responsibilities of fatherhood. Picking up these skills of a nurturing father would have the added advantage of making life easier for the mothers of their own children since some sense of real equality around child care will become possible. Knowledge of child development also helps boys to know the value of praise and encouragement in a toddler's life. It also prevents misunderstandings around children who get smacked for activities and actions over which their development gives them little control.

One of the authors has seen in his family life the value of a boy being actively involved in child care. His own son (now 18 years old) has been uncle to seven small children who have been born at various times since he was 9 years old. His skill and understanding of babies and small children has made him a much loved and trusted figure among this young generation. He is proud of his expertise and his friends look on admiringly as he tackles the varied jobs associated with baby care. I feel sure that part of his capacity to care, to show kindness and to empathize is founded on his close connection with the life-giving process. He has less need of the excitement, power and camaraderie of the male club which seeks expression in rowdy behaviour, aggression, gang fights and ultimately warfare. For a detailed look at what we think is possible in relation to schools, boys and child care please consult the section on Fathers and Sons (pp. 274–91).

3   Challenging the Rambo and John Wayne role models of tough, dominant males ready to fight at any pretext because 'that's what being a man is all about'. It is important to look critically at the notion of bravery and heroism, to make some connections around inner and outer strength and learn to share feelings within the male group.

    In this section we would also draw attention to the exercises in the section on bullying in this book (pp. 104–38). In addition, we recommend a variety of cooperative activities where boys work with each other rather then competitively. (See the School Sport section pp. 204–15).

Boys from a very young age learn from violent cartoons, television shows, films and war toys that conflicts get resolved through fighting and wars. It is our contention that there needs to be a cross–curricula input involving work in the history, humanities or social studies departments which will encourage critical thinking around the received truths about involvement in war. Isn't it time to help boys who are attracted to the dominance and power of demagogic figures such as Hitler, to think through and experience the very real consequences in human terms of such leaders' policies? Isn't it time to challenge the notion that British involvement in war has been seen as invariably right, both politically and morally? Isn't it time to look at the concept of patriotism and fighting for your country? Doesn't this whole notion arise from the fear on the part of politicians that without it men would be far less willing to fight and die in wars?

    Nationalistic history courses legitimize the role models of John Wayne and Rambo. They teach boys that being tough, dominant and ready to fight at the drop of a hat is what manhood is all about. Those who buy into this idea are more likely to commit acts of violence at home and in the streets. When countries go to war to protect or achieve economic and political goals then why is it not acceptable for boys to resolve disputes in playground fights, or for rival gangs fight it out in territorial gang warfare?

    We recommend teaching programmes which emphasize critical thinking. We would like issues of war and xenophobia put under the microscope to enable the legitimization of violence to be seriously questioned. Boys who have already looked at conflict resolution will be less inclined to look at the willingness to fight as a proof of manhood. They will be less likely to view the only proper patriotic response to international conflict as belligerence.

We do no more here than offer some pointers and ideas. Recent war zones may be the most potent and relevant sources of information for a start to be made. Such wars which would be of relevance for boys in British schools would be the Vietnam, Falklands and Gulf wars. Hence our approach is to look behind the media coverage of the 'enemy' and view the people, whether Vietnamese, Argentinian or Iraqi/Arab. Questions which might be asked include:

- Who are these 'foreigners'?
- What are their communities?
             living conditions?
             clothes?
             work places?
             religious traditions?
             values?
             child-care arrangements?
             sources of entertainment?
- How fundamentally different is all this from our own lives?
- How do their lives match with the information that newspapers, television and politicians wanted us to know?
- What sort of things did the government and media leave out?
- Was it easier to fight and kill because of what the government and media said?

Another way into discovering common values, and one of the most poignant, is to look at pictures of the dead, preferably from both sides of the conflict. Taking pictures of dead soldiers, one from each side, we suggest that the following line of enquiry is helpful.

- What would be in this soldier's pockets?
- How old is he?
- What was he doing before he put on the uniform in which he died?
- Who loved him?
- Who did he care for?
- How did he play as a child?
- What were his values?
- What attracted him to military service?
- What made him want to fight?
- What did he want from life?
- How is that different from you? (See the Session p. 261)

By such questioning, boys will be able to make links with the quality of their own lives and to develop some understanding of their commonality with the dead soldier on the battlefield. This is the springboard for the simple message that war is not a Ramboesque adventure. There is no glory in war.

Am I a Good Listener?

Aim: To show the effects of good and bad listening on the potential for positive, non-aggressive relationships.

Materials: Sets of Speaker and Listener cards, prepared using the instructions below

Time: 45 minutes

What to do:

Arrange the class into two halves in two concentric circles of chairs, the inner circle facing outwards and the outer circle facing inwards. This means that the boys will be sitting opposite each other.

Get agreement as to which of the circles will speak first and which will listen. Give out the instructions to all the speakers and the listeners (use instruction cards 1 first).

At the end of the two minutes, get the speaker to share with the listener how they felt. What did the speaker want to do with the negative feelings he has experienced because he has been ignored? Encourage honesty in the exchange.

Now ask the pairs to swap roles. Even though the speaker now knows what to expect, allow them to have the experience. The sharing at the end of the two minutes is important.

Give out the second listener card. Again the one to the speaker can encourage anything of interest to be talked.

At the conclusion of the two minutes, share how difficult the experience was. Encourage honesty in the expression of feelings around really being listened to.

A variant might be to have students in either of the circles to move one or two places to the left to ensure different partners for each repetition.

When both activities have been completed, re-assemble the group into one circle. Encourage a discussion on good active listening. What makes some boys bad listeners? What flare-ups or incidents have occurred because there has not been good listening. Is listening well a way of avoiding conflicts? How can good listening help to resolve conflicts that have already started?

The instructions:

Instructions to the listener (1)

Show your partner that you are not listening to him.

Suggestions:

> look away
> turn round
> yawn, fidget, shuffle about
> interrupt
> tie shoe laces
> anything else which shows you are not listening.

Instructions to the listener (2)

Show your partner that you are a good listener.

Suggestions:

> keeping eye contact
> nodding
> making encouraging noises as he speaks
> repeat key things he says but without interrupting.

Instructions to the speaker

Talk about any subject of your choice for 2 minutes.

You might choose:

- The best film I ever saw
- What I think about a favourite 'soap'
- My favourite football team
- An idea of your own.

Sticking Up for Yourself in a Non-aggressive Way

Aim: *To heighten boys' awareness about how remarks and the way they are delivered make others feel.*
     To show techniques for making your feelings clear and diffusing angry confrontations.

Materials: *None*

Time: *45 minutes*

What to do:

> 'You've lost my pen — you're a stupid, thick jerk.'

> 'You're a stupid, thick jerk yourself. Who do you think you're talking to you thick prat.'

Take an incident like the one above and ask the boys the following questions: When has this sort of exchange happened to you? Think of a time when you were involved in that kind of verbal conflict. Try to remember it from what was said first right through to its conclusion. Where were you? What were the words, gestures and actions used? How did you feel at the time?

When everyone has got a story, ask them to choose a partner and decide who is to go first.

Role play the first boy's scene as accurately as possible. It will be necessary for the partner to be shown how to stand, what to do and say. Rehearsal time is important. When you have finished sit down with your partner and tell him what you are feeling. What did you feel like inside? What did you feel like doing (hitting, walking away, sulking, crying, getting revenge, feeling devalued, feeling all bad, couldn't care less)? What could you say to the person who has abused you instead of just answering back in the same way?

Help each other to find the words. For example: 'When you call me stupid and thick I feel hurt and angry.' Repeat your sentence, get it right, feel it inside.

Do the scene again. This time don't throw back the insults. Stay calm say your sentence, keep eye contact, speak up, look positive and open. If he isn't listening properly say it again until you think he is beginning to listen.

Sit down with your partner and share how this experience felt. Were you less likely to get into a slanging match that might lead to violence.?

Repeat the whole exercise to give your partner the opportunity to experience his situation.

Bring the whole group back together. Begin a discussion based on 'What I have learned about being a boy from this exercise is . . .'

Who Wants to be a Hero?

Aim:　　To encourage boys to examine the effect of media heroes on their lives.

Materials:　Large sheets of paper and felt-tip pens

Time:　　45 minutes

What to do:

In a whole group introduce the idea that the boys are going to look at media heroes. Ask for the names of media heroes that spring to mind. What makes them attractive to the boys?

Allow only a very short time for this initial investigation of heroes before dividing the group into small groups of 3 or 4. Give each group a large sheet of paper and some pens. Give them 2 minutes to brainstorm the words Heroic Qualities. Ask them to write down all the heroic qualities associated with their heroes that they can think of.

In pairs, share with a partner:

- Who is your hero?
- What does your hero do?
- What makes him important to me?

In whole group, discuss:

What did you share together?
Is being able to fight well the characteristic of a hero?
In what situations is your hero important to you?
How do you feel when he is upfront in your mind?
What sort of adventures do you have in your head when your hero is upfront in your mind?

There is scope here to break off into written story telling or role plays as an alternative way of telling their fantasy stories.

Conclusion in a whole group. Consider the following question: How well would your fictional hero get on in real life?

Put-downs and Put-ups

Aim: *To consider the effect on this group of boys if everyone put each other down? To model the behaviour of putting boys up.*
    To show how affirming behaviour fosters self-worth and makes conflict less likely.

Materials: *Flip chart, paper and pens*

Time: *45 minutes*

What to do:

In small groups of 3 or 4 brainstorm all the words you consistently hear which are put-downs.

In the small group ask the boys to take it in turns to say how these words make them feel. Ask them to tell of a time when they have been put down. What did they feel? What did they do? Encourage honesty because boys will often have a wide disparity between what they felt and what they actually did. Questions which might help include:

- What made you laugh it off/say you didn't care?
- What stopped you saying you didn't like it?
- What would have happened if you had been upset?
- What is it that makes you say, even now, that none of these words bother you?

Encourage the belief that this is a place to experiment with new behaviour. Ask the boys in the small groups to take it in turns to make affirmations of each other. 'What I like about you 'x' is . . .'

Try to get them beyond the relative ease of calling someone 'a good mate'. What makes him a good mate? The other common affirmation is to dub someone 'a good laugh'. Encourage them to say what that phrase really means.

Bring the group together as a whole group. Ask: What did it feel like to have good things said about you? What makes it important to be told that you are well thought of? What are boys like who don't get good affirmations in their lives? Did anyone feel feelings of hostility when you were put down? How do you feel now? What lessons have you learned about conflict and fighting from this exercise?

Chapter 13

Fathers and Sons

The Theory

Being a Good Father

I have very negative memories of my father . . . my image of my dad is the one who was never there.

I didn't see much of my father, he worked long hours and was often away. I was much closer to my mother because she was around more and was always there — and oh I wish I could have done more things with my dad. I would have really, really liked that. The memories of being close to him are so sketchy.

Such memories emphasize the sense of absence and distance which boys feel when reflecting on the quality of the fathering they have received. Fathers and sons seem to be trapped in a cycle of estrangement in which a sense of image plays a large part. Credibility in the eyes of other men has determined the way fathers view their responsibility towards small children and babies. Fear of losing face by seeming soft in the eyes of other men helps to limit men's nurturing capability around their children. Oakley (1979) in her study of new mothers discovered that one-third of their husbands saw their babies for less than half an hour per day. Fathers squeeze child care into their available time. She suggests that it is more acceptable for partners to help their wives, 'provided that he doesn't help too much', since then his masculinity will survive.

Conventionally, strength, silence and being in control are the hallmarks of being a good father. Men are described as being unable to express their emotions (Farrell, 1974), competitive (Lewis, 1978), brutal in the way they use their muscular strength (Soloman and Levy, 1982), and incapable of showing intimacy, apart from during sexual contact (Fasteau, 1974). As sons grow older so men's distance and conformity to what is perceived as manly behaviour makes it difficult for them to show real affection for their sons. Andy Rashleigh (1984) writes:

If he washed us in the bath as opposed to my Mum doing it, it was not a loving wash. It was very much, 'That's your wash and that's it.' It was very formal. His formality was the thing which was very peculiar.

In his work with boys, one of the authors hears that fathers never hug their sons. Hugging, kissing and shows of affection will make boys soft. Fathers thus deprive themselves of this healthy, nurturing contact with their sons and boys begin to feel the sense of being physically deprived of their father's love. Love and generosity become entwined in phrases like, 'You're too big for a hug but I'll buy you a bike'. As years go by, fathers only touch their sons during back slaps, hand shakes and occasional play wrestling.

One of the authors meets men in psychotherapeutic circles who deeply regret the sense of distance that they experienced from their fathers in their growing and adolescent years. Such fathers encouraged strength in their sons by not showing their own frailties and by reminding their sons of their responsibilities as boys and men. How many boys have been encouraged not to cry or, worse, scorned for showing tears? Ronald Fraser (1984) has humiliating memories of a father trying to make him into the son he wanted long before he even went to school. He remembers 'the morning when, exploding with rage, he rushed to get my mother's curlers to put in my hair which was as shamefully long as a girl's.'

Fathers buy into the myth of sons being an extension of themselves as they wish to be seen by the world. How many readers are familiar with the father taking interest in a son's sporting activity? Trevor Cherry (1984) had a father who spent four nights a week playing football with him from the age of 6 or 7, but when he got to his teenage years he felt suffocated by his father's attention, wanting to be with other boys rather than forever having his father looking over his shoulder. Cherry's father is typical of many fathers who stand on football touchlines urging their sons to adopt the hard physical attributes of the professional game. Winning is all important and enjoyment of physical activity is secondary to that end. Fathers pursue a second career or a career they never had through their sons. They shout, they jeer, they ridicule in an effort to get their sons to play hard, to show toughness and not to show pain.

Fathers are reluctant to show too much affection for their sons in case it encourages them to be homosexual. They are also critical of sons who form what they see to be a too close attachment to their mothers. One of the authors was ridiculed by his father as a 'pansy' and 'Nancy boy' for expressing what he regarded as a healthy love for his mother. Corneau (1991) suggests that homosexual orientation depends less on the attachment to the mother than on the search for a missing father. Fathers' distancing behaviours may therefore be counterproductive in that direction.

Attitudes to homosexuality in the male culture are invariably hostile. It probably has more to do with a refusal to recognize homosexual or homo-erotic impulses in ourselves and a desire to repress them and put them down. The fear is deflected from within onto the stereotypically perceived traits of homosexuality seen in others. Boys from a young age shy away from shows of affection with their peers and even from their own fathers. The cry of 'I'm not queer/ gay or a poofter' is heard frequently and on a daily basis even in junior schools. It is a self-perpetuating and self-supporting cycle — an avoidance of intimacy dance.

Boys who have fathers who are ill or damaged in some way, be it by alcoholism, drug addiction or other disease, know the power of the condition to cause distance, unreliability and need. They keep sons in a state of permanent insecurity.

The cycle of father–son estrangement does mean that boys grow to learn to applaud qualities of independence, pride, resilience, self-control and physical strength. All of these are worthy qualities for sons and daughters alike. But for boys, the learning and example goes beyond these to stress competitiveness, toughness, aggressiveness and power. Boys grow to appreciate that it is these latter qualities which provide the silence and the distance between them and their fathers. Fathers who call their sons 'poofters' or who encourage them to *prove* they are not weak in the face of taunts from others are encouraging their sons to fight back. A combined collective paternal pressure to have sons to be proud of, in a vigorous 'real lad' kind of way, yields large numbers of boys who are swayed by the same pressure — so they all fight back. Boys continually talk in violent terms. Examples of 'You're dead' or 'I'll rip your head off' or others, fall from boys' mouths on a daily basis in response to real or imagined injuries to pride. Are fathers with their 'stand up for yourself' advice teaching that violence is a normal, appropriate and necessary behaviour of power and control?

What lies between fathers and sons is power. This distance shows itself as a real separation, characterized by a sense of heaviness and a retreat from each other. Fathers and sons come together when the latter's emerging values are in accord with their father's. When that doesn't happen the relationship breaks down and there is a gulf which is difficult to bridge. Boys want closeness but fathers do not understand their sons. Sons do not understand their fathers. Topics are never discussed because of the emotional embarrassment that creeps in between them. Fathers and sons stand apart from each other in tongue-tied silence.

What are the origins of distance and absence in boys' relationships with their fathers? Some traditional myths lie at the heart of men's inability and reluctance to fully participate in the lives of their children. Strength, silence and being in control is socially condoned behaviour for men and nurturing is an unmanly activity. Men expect women to be naturally maternal and creative with babies and children. This attitude was well illustrated in the recently successful film *Three Men and a Baby*. The father who is left with his child rings his mother to attempt to manipulate her into taking the baby off his hands. 'You know what to do with babies,' he says. Her reply, 'I had to learn it like you're going to have to,' suggests that men have conveniently got this natural inclination towards looking after children wrong. Both sexes have to learn this skill and men like women can acquire appropriate nurturing and parenting behaviours with practice and commitment.

This gendered division of labour provides rigid walls between public and domestic spheres. Fathers with their emotional involvement in work, money and status inhabit the public sphere. Mothers have the domestic sphere with its association with traditional, 'natural' femininity providing the nurturing and intimacy that children need. Fathers choose to cross the wall in their own terms. My interviews with boys on their relationship with their fathers suggests that fathers assume that by being a provider they are showing their love and sense of caring for their children. It is their money that provides for their children's needs. Sons learn that their father's work limits his active participation in child-care activities and accentuates the gender divisions in family life. Pollock and Sutton (1985) suggest that fathers pick and choose their particular forms of involvement as it suits them: 'They play rather than carry out the more mundane tasks. They select what they do and the commitment they feel they are willing and able to make; mothers are left with the rest.'

Alice Rossi (1984) points out that since child bearing temporarily confines · the mother and distances her from employment, she is more likely to be the primary carer in the early months. Bill and Newby (1976) suggest fathers' views of child care as being more natural for women makes sure that parenting styles develop 'in a manner which is consistent with the existing ideological hegemony' of men dominating women and that this inherent sexism around child care is very convenient for men who do not want the daily difficulties of looking after children. Many sons will notice the lack of active, participative parenting by their fathers and yet notice the disproportionate way they try to exert power in child-care decision making. Sons will grow to learn at first hand the nature of power imbalances in couple relationships.

Fathers are also victims of their own history. Andy Rashleigh writes:

> My relationship with my father reminds me of his relationship with his Dad. His father was a Petty Officer cook in the Navy and he had six children. When we sat at the dinner table nobody said a word. My father could talk but he was very formal on occasions. I think he felt there was a certain way we had to be brought up. My Dad had very clear ideas about the sort of things men do. He was very strict about things like that. (1984)

One of the authors can trace the quality of his own fathering back through learned patterns of behaviour emanating from a great grandfather. If children do not experience a close bond with their fathers then the skills and expectations around fathering will be lacking. It is a cycle of deprivation which revolves thus: I don't know what good fathering is because I did not get it from my father. I am uncertain and fearful about being a father because of this experience. My message becomes: don't get too close; devolve responsibility onto mothers; and take refuge in being the strong, silent type who rules from behind work, newspapers, television, pubs and cars — a world apart from the everyday reality of family life and also, if I could recognize it, an existence lived so far away from my body.

Where does this leave boys' sense of self as boys? How does it help them to learn about the type of boys and men they are becoming? In exploring the world of masculine identity with groups of teenage boys it has become apparent that the boys are grappling with a model of masculinity which they find difficulty living up to. Boys live with the way their fathers ebb and flow within the structure of family life. Of course, there will often be times of fun and connectedness for some boys but they also notice the shields that their fathers construct. They experience the lack of intimacy with a man who seeks refuge in a public image of distanced masculinity. Boys know that this sets their father apart from the everyday reality of family life but that it is somehow the way fathers are supposed to be. They notice that all this allows them to avoid speaking and that the associated silence and strength are a way of avoiding entering into relationships. They also notice how many avoid inhabiting their bodies and how strength and toughness can prevent even such things as minor heart attacks from being acknowledged. (I note here the well publicized case of Graham Souness' undetected heart attack prior to April 1992.)

Boys learn from their fathers that conformity to an ideal masculine image will keep boys safe in the world. Safe from the taunts of other boys as they march in step with each other in pursuit of a kind of unconscious image of what being a 'real boy' means. Taking their cue from their fathers they learn to live out the 'top dog' hegemonic masculinity which finds favour with other boys and men.

Positive father images are very important. When such images are lacking, the emptiness in boys' lives often stirs up the need in them to look for strong heroic figures to identify with.

Good fathering would allow the son to unite and reconcile opposing elements in the boy's psyche. It is a father's humanity which shows a boy a world which is not a world of extremes but one in which opposite feelings and attitudes can have free play, can exist side by side and be reconciled. When boys become too attracted to heroes, too attached to the inner voice which has doubts about virility, sense of personal competence and ability, then the boys return to the hero. The hero feeds the substandard male and covers the wounds of inadequate fathering.

The hero also serves to shore up the father's absence in the boy's lack of internal structure. Less than adequate fathering means boys' ideas are confused. He has trouble in goal setting, deciding what is good for him and identifying his own needs. Boys who have negative or less than satisfying images of their fathers make every effort to structure themselves from outside. They build shields. Sometimes the shields take the form of macho aggressive posturing and verbal epithets tossed out to impress and challenge so that there is no glimpse of the vulnerability that lies within. Admiration of physical exercise through body-building creates a shape that presents an imposing figure to the world. Sometimes it is enough to share conversations about the value of a tough, rugged exterior. Others work hard on their bodies by vigorously working with weights. Building an external structure compensates for the weaknesses felt within.

Some boys express some confusion about their sexual identity and spend their lives in pursuit of sexual thrills, either real or surrogate, via the medium of pornographic materials. Boys learn the crude, direct masculine language of sex which serves to distance themselves from their own unacknowledged, undiscovered feelings around intimacy. There has been no model in their lives to help them lift the lid of their Pandora's Box which contains the full range of their own intimate sexuality.

For other sons the need to be admired is dominant. They crave for the attention and accolades afforded by their peers. They enjoy being the centre of attention. They know the way to attract and keep attention is by constantly being in tune with prevailing societal values around emerging, dominant, heterosexual masculinity. Conversely, the more fragile a boy feels internally, the more likely he is to try building an outer shell to hide this fragility. By outward compensations boys assert their distance from their need for love and understanding, their desire to be touched and their need to love and be loved is embarrassingly pushed aside. It is hard for them to own these feelings because to own them opens up their vulnerability. The mark of absent fathering is reproduced in a fragile masculine identity in sons.

Breaking the Cycle

What do men need to do to embrace the concept of good fathering? If men are to fully participate in the lives of their children, then they need a place in the emotional development of their sons as a nurturing and actively caring father. It means breaking the cycle of deprivation, alienation and estrangement which is the sons' experience of fathers who live behind the shields with which they shore up their masculine identity.

Taking care of sons physically and emotionally doesn't mean simply imitating a maternal model. Fathers can be just as nurturant, responsive, affectionate and active with their children as mothers are. Fathers expose their sons to all these qualities but also to a unique distinctiveness in smell, warmth, deeper voice and rough and tumble qualities. Doing things together, making things, sharing time, being honest, appreciating strengths, acknowledging weaknesses, all help the father and son bond to grow. Fathers and sons showing affection through childhood by hugs and cuddles encourages a son's sensitivity and feeds the boy's need to be touched and appreciated.

According to Lamb (1976), well adjusted children come from families in which the father is an active, involved parent. Good fathering enables the transfer of identification from mother to father to take place more easily. There will be less pitched battles between mothers and sons over a son's desire to prove himself man enough. Psychologically good fathering enables the parental double function to be well served. It is a reference point for a child of the same sex and also the focus of desire for a child of the opposite sex. Thus, if well grounded, this allows a son to feel desire and love for the mother which in later years is translated into desire for women and not fear of them.

Giveans and Robinson (1985) quote a North Californian father who lovingly summarizes the fathering role he has undertaken:

> It is truly an experience to be a parent. I feel sorry a lot of times, when I am involved with things with my kids, for the fathers that just miss out on a lot of this — especially in the early years. Children grow so fast and before you know it those moments are going to be gone. A lot of fathers have never gotten in there and been able to have feelings or know the children when they are young. A lot of fathers are afraid of small babies — other than holding them. As I get older and my kids grow up, I will have a lot of nice memories looking back on their childhood — remembering them as babies and pre-schoolers. It's not an easy job, it's hard work. It is, however, a chance to get in there and do something and see things from a side that a lot of men never have seen.

How can such fathers be encouraged? How can new fathers share these experiences and delights? By means of father groups, father and child workshops, volunteering attendance at nursery groups, enrolling on child development courses and participation in family camp projects. In all these ways fathers can interact with each other informally and they are themselves helping to dispel traditional myths surrounding their roles as men and fathers. Men are also demonstrating to wives, teachers, children and the community their willingness to contribute not only to their own lives but to their families and society as well.

The Social Costs

The social costs of traditional masculinity are clear. Traditional masculinity subordinates women and 'lesser' men. In the family, on the streets or on the battlefield men are continuously engaged in efforts to dominate. Rape is one of the fastest growing crimes and it is men who provoke and sustain war. In short, traditional masculinity is life threatening. Men and boys need to actively and urgently consider their place within this power and control model and to make active, nurturing fathering a top priority in their lives. Only in these kinds of ways can macho values be effectively challenged.

What value will society place on active, nurturing, paternal behaviour? The price will be boys who can accept their vulnerability, who can express a range of emotions and learn to ask for help and support in appropriate situations. Good fathering fosters gentleness, cooperation and communication with an emphasis on finding non-violent means of resolving conflicts. Finally, by accepting attitudes and behaviours which have been traditionally labelled feminine as part of themselves and necessary for full human development, homophobia and misogyny will be reduced.

Selected Further Reading on Fathers and Sons

MORRISON, B. (1993) *And When Did You Last See Your Father?*, London, Granta Books.
JOSEPH, J. (1985) *Father/Son Book*, Bethesda, Maryland, Pandemonium Books.
HOYLAND, J. (1992) *Fathers and Sons*, London, Serpent's Tail.
CORNEAU, G. (1991) *Absent Fathers, Lost Sons*, Boston, Shambhala.
SEIDLER, V. (1988) 'Fathering, authority and masculinity', in CHAPMAN, R. and RUTHERFORD, J. (Eds) *Male Order: Unwrapping Masculinity*, London, Lawrence and Wishart.

The Session

Bringing Fathers into Focus

I had been watching the BBC showing of a programme on the 'Wild Men' weekends — the idea of about 150 men coming together for the Robert Bly experience of connecting with their 'inner wild man'. While we hold some considerable reservations around the work of Robert Bly, particularly the anti-feminist stance in his work, some of the work encouraging men to relate to each other is positive and valuable. One of the activities in the film was men bringing their fathers (metaphorically) into a circle and talking to them. It was like the empty chair exercises of gestalt therapy. I felt that I could do this or something like it with the boys' groups. We had often talked of fathers. They had always been present in our work. Boys had often told of playing rough and tumble with their fathers. They had spoken of their father's admired qualities and their physical contact with them. I thought it was time for these important men to be brought more sharply into focus. It was to be both a celebration of fathers and an opportunity to tell fathers what they weren't doing — to be happy, joyful, sad, angry or disappointed. The risk was whether 15 year olds could actually do this in front of other 15 year olds. I decided to try it first with my most mutually supportive group.

'What are we going to do today?' asks Mark. 'Well when we've given up on all the banter and mock abuse that is flying around we'll ask everyone how they've been doing since last week,' I reply. The humorous banter about relationships with a particular girl subsides. I had already decided to build into the boys' stories about their week some questions about what they have been doing with their fathers since we last met. All the boys share something of their week but fathers don't seem very prominent in the account and in at least three cases were almost entirely absent. The boys tell me that fathers work too much, that they've got no time and are tired. I reflect that all this will be useful to pick up on later if any of the boys get stuck with their fathers.

'Well we're going to bring your fathers here so you can talk to them.' This brings more confusion and everyone talking at once as the boys speculate on how this is to be done. The noise level is high. Order has to be restored and eventually I can explain that each of the boys is going to imagine that their father is seated on a chair facing them. This will be the opportunity to say whatever they like to this man. I explain that if they find it difficult to talk to an empty chair they can pick someone to be their father who can be the silent focus of their attention. I have decided that at this stage the exercise will be one way only. This is to be a son telling his father what he thinks of him — a celebration of his presence, regret for what is missing or a mixture of both — concluding with a sense of what each son feels his father has given him about being a man. (How has your father contributed to the way you are as the boy you are?) I conclude by emphasizing that if we don't get that far or if it is too difficult for anyone then it doesn't matter: 'If you can only manage one sentence to your father then maybe that's enough but give it your best shot for your own sake.'

Mark tries a new avoidance strategy. 'What are we doing this for anyway?' he asks. I choose to throw this question onto the group. I appeal to them for an answer. There is silence until Kevin says that it sounds interesting to him and he wants everyone to have a go. Steven thinks sharing feelings about fathers will 'help us all to share about other things'. I ask that they try this to feel the effect of some real contact with each other in a common area rather than existing at the level of endless superficial banter.

Kevin is keen to go first. He places his empty chair and begins to talk to his father. All is quiet as he regrets the fact that his father no longer lives with him. 'I hated it when you went away and I resent it that we can't go to the park or go shopping or do any of the things I really wanted to do with you.' He goes very quiet for a few moments before continuing. 'Bournemouth is so far away and I don't see you very much. When I do it's all over so quickly.' He breaks off and stops. There are tears in his eyes and his head is down. I ask him what he wants from us. He doesn't answer but I turn towards him. He wants comfort and I hug him. I gesture the rest of the group to come closer as well. They all put a comforting hand or arm onto Kevin. We sit in silent support of Kevin's sorrow at his loss. He doesn't want to do any more and we move on.

Kulvinder wants to celebrate his father. He speaks of his father's strength, their daily contact, his encouragement and shows of physical affection. He loves his father to hug him and he concludes with his love for his father. He beams with shy pleasure.

Like Kevin, Mark is also the child of a 'failed' marriage. He is currently on his second stepfather with whom he has a good relationship, but he still sees his real father. He has a room at his father's house in a village near Derby. He does not use it much. He tells his father that he misses him 'but there doesn't seem much to say when we meet'. He is sad when he says 'talking on the phone just isn't enough'. I suggest that there is some anger in his voice. He agrees and raises his voice to tell his father that the phone is a poor substitute for his father's real presence. Mark's ambivalence and shyness comes out as he alternates between this sadness and anger and a jokey rubbishing of what he is doing. I encourage him to stay with his real feelings. He becomes serious and shares that 'not living with his father is really hard because I've missed a lot, like Kevin. I know how he feels'. I suggest that they sit nearer to each other for mutual support. They briefly put their arms round each other.

We move on to each of the other boys. Steven is able to speak of his pride and love for his father. He needs quite a lot of prompting for this, not just from me, but from the other boys. His shyness is quite endearing. 'Oh go on just say what you really mean', was one of the ploys Mark used to get him to acknowledge his real feelings. Shayaz finds any personal work difficult. The group knows this and was sympathetic to his faltering, single sentence appreciation of his father.

Time was pressing and after I had shared some of my feelings for my father, we shared how the lesson had felt. Kevin's remark 'I feel much closer to everyone' seemed to sum up the feeling behind the smiles of appreciation as the bell went. I was conscious that no one had talked about the messages their fathers had given them about how to be a proper boy and mentally put that on the agenda for another time.

Classroom Strategies

Significant Men

Boys' lives and development are undoubtedly influenced by significant men. More commonly the most significant man is the boy's father who is physically present in his life. Where death, divorce or desertion has occurred the father figure may still be powerfully present in conversation or anecdote. The way a mother talks about the absent father and the respect she may or may not have for him is crucial in forming negative or positive images around masculine behaviour. Boys may also have other significant father figures in their lives who have a powerful influence on their upbringing. Such men include stepfathers, grandfathers, uncles and older brothers.

Boys find it difficult to talk about or acknowledge the influence their fathers or father figures have had and are having on their sense of male identity. Work on fathers can prosper best in an atmosphere of trust. Even then the diffidence around looking at personal relationships means the work requires sensitivity and patience. Ways in are to work on male heroes and admired men in the media. Talking about qualities that are displayed by these men can bring comparisons with men with whom boys come into contact in their daily lives. Regularly sharing values around fathers makes it easier to develop a full session on paternal influences later in the life of a group. Such a session can look at celebrating the nature of the father–son relationship or begin to question what is missing. It is important to look at the messages that boys are being given by fathers so that boys can look critically at the influences that helped forge their attitudes and behaviour.

The difficulty of actually starting a dialogue about fathers revolves on the centrality and invisibility of Dad's behaviour. He is both a father and a father figure. Boys struggle to get any further than that in critically examining the effect of their father on their lives. It is even more difficult to untangle fathers when part of their mystique and what they show of themselves to their sons is an expectation of uncritical acceptance of their own behaviour. The unaccountability, the refusal to acknowledge mistakes or be questioned exaggerates the uneasiness of any dialogue to assess paternal influences on sons. Talking about personal relationships, showing or reciprocating feelings, is not something they have done with their fathers. They haven't seen their fathers doing this with anyone else either, so that boys' skills in this area may be correspondingly limited. It is one of the things that boys and men don't do. It is part of being a man to develop a sense of personal unchallenged autonomy. Boys notice their father's sense of independence or at least their use of the language which proclaims independence. Their fathers know the answers. Even when they are fallible they seldom admit it and give the impression of expecting to be deferred to on any matters they think are important. Boys with this example of fathering can be very powerfully influenced to adopt the same 'real man' strategies. Alternatively, they can recognize the damaging effect of these qualities and work hard to discount and reject them in their own lives. Either way the process of personal confrontation with the image of their fathers is fraught with difficulty.

As an example of what can be achieved I want to briefly go through my relationship with my father and the influences that he had on me. In so doing here will be certain key questions and ideas which drive the investigation onward and which can be used with any group work on fathers. It is a good idea to try this exercise yourself or with a friend before using this loose structure with boys.

What Messages about Being Male Did I Get from My Father?

I picked up my father's sense of distance, that distance that sets males apart from other people. He always seemed uncomfortable in company, particularly with people who were clever. He was deferential to authority figures and keen to do the right thing in their company. I knew my father was shy and insecure but he was certainly going to exert his authority and his rights in the company he knew best — the family. Thus, for me, I saw him asserting his male control of the family. It was he who had the right to make decisions. Any decisions that were made would undoubtedly be carried out. There was a general assumption that he was in control and if things did not go as he wanted then his visible annoyance and irritation were justified. If his needs as a man were not being met, he would make the lives of other family members miserable. It was not part of being a father to reveal his insecurities. It was far better to bluff it out, cover up, and to do things without needing to ask for help. If men were to appear in control and infallible then my father was going to be a front runner.

My impression of my Dad, in his youthful years, is of a man who felt that it was unmasculine to show and share feelings. His behaviour made sure that his family were kept at a distance. All his pleasures have seemed to be solitary ones — those which in human terms could not communicate back. And so all his life he has been a stamp collector, and a keen railway enthusiast. He has enjoyed books, mainly thrillers, war stories and biographies. He watches television selectively, enjoys sport and has also made woollen rugs! Permeating all this has been his love of organization, 'a place for everything and everything in its place'. As a child I knew that men were efficient, invariably right and never likely to admit they were wrong. I have since realized that his shyness and his frustration, which got in the way of being a 'real man', were covered up and he boosted himself by putting down minorities. Hence, the household was 'treated' to his scorn of black people, minority groups of any kind, and women. His misogyny came out in his scorn around women's capabilities, with his wife and my sister the target of his anger or humour. In the face of this pressure, he has been indulged and pacified largely because of my mother's desire for a quiet life. She has compromised and given in for the last 55 years of their married life. As children we were encouraged to do the same. I think I was able to reject a lot of my father's behaviour as unacceptable because I was very close to my mother. Even though she had learned to 'keep a still tongue in a wise head' around him, she was more vocal on his shortcomings around me. She did not want me 'turning out like him' at any price.

What Did You Do with Your Father? What Messages were there about Being a Boy in What You Actually Did Together?

I began by trying to recall all the things that I remember about my contact with my father. They are listed below with appropriate comments and messages.

1   *He played football, cricket and table tennis with me.* The contact of this kind was not very great. I think I sensed that he was playing with me as a chore and that because I wasn't very gifted he soon lost interest and I felt dumped. My father had been a good local sportsman and had even played county table-tennis. I suppose I owe my father my love of cricket. I can remember seeing him play when I was only about five. He was a bowler and I can 'see' him bowling in my mind's eye as I

write. I wanted to be like him. He once umpired a game I played in when I was about thirteen. I so wanted to succeed but failed miserably with the bat. He didn't say anything to me afterwards and that really hurt.

2   *He took me to watch Derby County FC in the mid-50s.* In those days, football games were watched almost exclusively by men so this was a very important male club to be in. I became aware of my father's dogmatism in this area as he gave opinions to people who stood nearby. They didn't argue back because he was their boss at work!

3   *He took me to his workplace.* This was British Rail offices with their large, double, dark brown, wooden, sloping desks and tall stools and an atmosphere that was all men in suits and ties organizing something very important, like a railway. These were the men who had the power over the movement of the speeding trains that passed to and fro near our home. If my mother had not been a charismatic teacher and champion of women's rights, I would not have failed to be impressed by British Rail, run by men with women confined to service duties.

   One day, while at his workplace on Derby Station, he took me to the naming ceremony of a steam locomotive. This was in 1953 when I was 8 years old. I remember it well — 45509 Derbyshire Yeomanry. I became an ardent trainspotter. Dad bought me my first Ian Allen ABC of Locomotives (London Midland Region). I was rapidly being inculcated into the world of machines, objects, timetables and numbers. I loved it.

4   *I remember our very limited closeness.* My father was not a very demonstrative man — shy, uncomfortable and unsure around children. He gave all that sort of thing up to my mother. I have three memories only of our closeness. I can remember sitting on his knee once and him reading a comic to me. It was nighttime and I enjoyed his size, his smell and the roughness of his stubble. Similarly there were occasions when he would carry me 'up the wooden hill' (stairs) to take me to bed. I also went in the bath with him as a child. I can remember this once when we played rowing games singing things like 'Row — Heave Ho'. I remember this well because it is one of the very rare occasions when my father seemed to have fun or laugh without it being at someone else's expense. Regretfully, I have no memory of him playing with any of my toys with me. The only memory here is about toys which got in the way and caused his anger.

All my play and childhood experiences were conducted against the background of a very marked stammer. I was not perfect and he lacked patience with me. He mortified me with expressions like 'What's the bloody fool on about now?', if I would not get my words out when trying to tell him about something exciting that had happened. And I soon picked up the 'boys don't cry' messages if I came in crying after having fallen over. I hated his scorn so I learned to grit my teeth and be very determined when faced with childhood pains, scrapes and grazes.

What Do You Want to Say to Your Father about His Influence on You?

What I am very keen to tell my father is that I appreciate how tough it was for him with his own father. I know that my grandfather created a vigorously controlling atmosphere; that my father was the subject of very critical, heavy-handed treatment from a man who ran the childhood home like a tyrant. All this had a powerful influence on Dad and he has kept himself safe and protected by behaving as an imitation of his own father. Just as his capacity for showing sensitivity, caring and kindness was badly dented, so my sensitivity and gentleness were a threat to him. I think I touched something that was missing in himself which he could not cope with. And so he spent time pushing away those qualities and exaggerating the authoritarian father qualities. In so doing he pushed me away since I was a threat to his sense of manliness. My wish for my father is that he could have got closer to me and had fun with me. Instead we developed a relationship where, because he found it almost impossible to acknowledge and accept what I was, I just rejected his values and, indirectly, him as a person.

My sense of rebellion and rejection came out through music. I have a picture of a scene in our house in Derby. I am in the sun lounge, it is late afternoon and the record player is playing Chubby Checker's *The Fly* at full volume. My father enters the adjoining dining room. He has just returned from work. I expect he has had a hard and trying day and his anger and irritation is directed firmly onto me and *The Fly*. He shouts and raves at me and uncharacteristically I am angry and annoyed as well. The 17 year old and the 51 year old face each other in hostility and anger. I love the idea of being a rebel. I love Rock 'n' Roll and the excitement of the generational gap which is epitomized between my father and me. I use the loudness and the excitement of the music to assert the part of me that wants to be heard and acknowledged. I screen the pain of not being noticed, encouraged or knowing that I was loved by him. I was caught between the real fear of his rage and the excitement and invigoration of my own pleas to him.

This incident has seemed to epitomize my relationship with my father. My image of him is of him sitting stiffly in *his* chair. He always sat alone by choice. He sits there clutching at the newspapers which protect him from the invasion of his own space. He sits vulnerable, isolated and cut off. He has built his shield which keeps him distant from me who just wanted him to be able to share himself. He never did and I just got angry, scornful and rejecting. Cynically, I owe him a great debt for showing me how not to be a man — but I love him and wish that I could have loved him more.

Talking About Fathers

Aim: To encourage boys to talk freely about their fathers.

Materials: None

Time: 45 minutes

What to do:

The following questions can be used as part of a structure to enable boys to talk about their fathers. In no sense is this a complete package to be attempted in one session. The questions can be used sparingly to encourage boys to talk as much as they are able at any one time about their father's influence upon them. Depending on the size of the group we would recommend work in pairs with a trusted friend before any sharing is done in a large group.

The questions:

- How would you describe the ideal father?
- What is your earliest memory of your father?
- Do any of the following words describe your father?

dominating	sexist	weak
fun to be with	loving	authoritarian
ill	racist	bullying
kind	brave	
dependent	aggressive	
caring	courageous	
scornful	violent	

- How does your father show you he has any of these qualities?
- What is/are the quality/qualities you most admire in your father?
- What quality/qualities in your father do you find the most difficult to live with?
- What messages are there about being male in what you have observed your father doing? What is there in his interests or his behaviour which tells you how to be a boy?
- What sort of things do you and your father do together?
- What messages are there about being a boy in these activities?
- What activities would you never do together? What messages about being a boy does this reveal?
- What does your father do to keep you safe in the world of men? Does

that have any implications for you? Does it make you feel uncomfortable with yourself and how you really want to be?

- Does your father encourage you in activities or actions that you don't really feel comfortable with?
- How are you like your father?
- How do you want to be different?
- What part of your father do you love/value? What would you like to say to your father about the part of him that disappointed you, that does not give you what you want?
- Do you have any influence on your father? How much of you and your ideas does your father adopt? How do you feel about this?
- Does your father share his feelings with you? Those feelings which come from the sensitive areas of his life? His fears, his sensuality, his uncertainties about being a man?
- If you were a father, how would you be with your children, particularly your son(s)?

Fathers

Aim: To enable to clarify the influence of their fathers on their sense of being male.

Materials: 'Fathers' work sheet, prepared using the questions below

Time: 50 minutes

What to do:

Issue the 'Fathers' work sheet to each student to be worked on individually.

When completed ask the boys to work in pairs and to talk through their answers.

Come together in a whole group to share what they have written or talked about.

It is important for the teacher/group worker to be aware of the messages about masculinity and to draw out this learning from the boys' responses.

Offer a round of 'messages to my father' in which each boy can acknowledge the influence of his father on his life — positive or negative, or a mixture of both.

Conclude with a round of 'how I am like/unlike my father' and 'how that makes me feel'.

The questions:

Fathers

1. What is your earliest memory of doing something with your father?
2. What is the quality you most notice about your father? Tick those in the list below but add others if you need to.

dominating	caring
fun to be with	sexist
ill	loving
dependent	racist
kind	brave
scornful	aggressive
weak	courageous
someone whose word is law	bullying

others:

3. How does your father spend his time — work, interests, hobbies, etc?
4. What do these activities/interests tell you about the best way to be a boy?
5. What have you and your father done together during your childhood?
6. What things did you do in your childhood which your father did not approve of?
7. What were the messages about being a boy which you picked up from the things you did with your father and those he disapproved of?
8. How are you like your father?
9. How are you different from your father?
10. How will you treat your own sons?

Empty Chair

Aim: *For groups who have 'gelled' and who trust each other, this 'empty chair' technique enables boys to get in touch with their feelings around their father.*

Materials: *None*

Time: *45 minutes*

What to do:

Ask each boy if they can bring their father into the room so that they can talk to him. Sometimes it is easier if a boy picks someone else to be his father so that he actually has a person physically present to speak to.

Encourage each boy to talk to his father. Ideas, like the ones below, can be used as a stimulus.

- What I must appreciate about you is. . . .
- What I wish you had done with me is. . . .
- I think you messed up on me because. . . .
- I'm glad you were always there because. . . .
- What I most hated about you not being there was. . . .
- I'm glad that. . . .
- I wish we could have. . . .
- What you taught me about being a man is. . . .

Sometimes asking straightforward questions of the father can be answered by the boy himself. This is a role reversal technique which relies on the boy at some level knowing the answers his father would give. If you feel brave enough this is a most insightful activity. The boy as himself may be interested in finding out from his father the answers to questions like:

What makes you such a good father?
Where were you?
What stopped you getting closer to me?

To get the answers to such questions the boy role reverses with his father. He actually swaps chairs or position and answers as if he were his father. The boy may then reverse back to himself and continue the dialogue as more material becomes accessible to him.

Bibliography

ARKIN, W. and DOBROFSKY, L. (1978) 'Military socialisation and masculinity', *Journal of Social Issues*, 34, (1), pp. 151–68.

ARNOT, M. (1984) 'How shall we educate our sons?', in DEEM, R. (ed.) *Co-education Reconsidered*, Milton Keynes, Open University Press.

ASKEW, S. (1989) 'Aggressive behaviour in boys: To what extent is it institutionalised?', in TATTUM, S. and LANE, D. (eds) *Bullying in Schools*, Stoke, Trentham Books.

ASKEW, S. and ROSS, C. (1988) *Boys Don't Cry: Boys and Sexism in Education*, Milton Keynes, Open University Press.

BARTHEL, D. (1992) 'When men put on appearances: Advertising and the social construction of masculinity', in CRAIG, S. (ed.) *Men, Masculinity and the Media*, US, Sage.

BELL, C. (1979) *Becoming a Mother*, Oxford, Martin Robertson.

BESAG, V. (1989) *Bullies and Victims in Schools*, Milton Keynes, Open University Press.

BEYNON, J. (1989) 'A school for men: An ethnographic case study of routing violence in schooling', in WALKER, S. and BARTON, L. (eds) *Politics and the Processes of Schooling*, Milton Keynes, Open University Press.

BROD, H. (1987) *The Making of Masculinities*, US, Allen and Unwin.

CAMPBELL, B. (1993) *Goliath: Britain's Dangerous Places*, London, Methuen.

CANAAN, J. (1991) 'Is doing nothing just boys' play?', in FRANKLIN, S., DURY, C. and STACEY, J. *Off-Centre: Feminism and Cultural Studies*, London, HarperCollins.

CAPUTO, P. (1977) *A Rumour of War*, New York, Ballantine.

CASDAGLI, P. and GOBEY, F. (1989) *Only Playing Miss*, Stoke, Trentham Books.

CHANNER, D. and CHANNER, G. (1992) 'Boys against sexism', in SEIDLER, V. *Men, Sex and Relationships*, London, Routledge.

CHERRY, T. (1984) in ROBERTS, Y. (ed.) *Man Enough*, London, Chatto and Windus.

CITY OF LEICESTER TEACHERS' ASSOCIATION (NUT) (1987) *Outlaws in the Classroom: Lesbians and Gays in the School System*.

COATES, J. (1986) *Women, Men, Language*, London, Longman.

COCKBURN, C. (1991) *In the Way of Women*, London, Macmillan.

CONNELL, R.W. (1983) 'Men's bodies', in *Which Way is Up?*, Sydney, Australia, Allen and Unwin.

CONNELL, R.W. (1987) *Gender and Power*, Cambridge, Polity Press.

CONNELL, R.W. (1989a) 'Masculinity, violence and war', in KIMMEL, M. and MESSNER, M. (eds) *Men's Lives*, New York, Macmillan.

CONNELL, R.W. (1989b) 'Cool guys, swots and wimps: The interplay of masculinity and education', *Oxford Review of Education*, 15, (3).

CONNELL, R.W. *et al* (1982) *Making the Difference*, Sydney, Australia, Allen and Unwin.

CONNELL, R.W. *et al* (1985) 'Towards a new sociology of masculinity', *Theory and Society*, 14, (5), September.

CONNELL, R.W. and KIPPAX, S. (1990) 'Sexuality in the Aids crisis: Patterns of sexual practice and pleasure in a sample of Australian gay-bisexual men', *Journal of Sex Research*, 27, pp. 167–98.

CORNEAU, G. (1991) *Absent Fathers, Lost Sons*, Boston, Shambhala.

COX, P. (1989) 'Male order: The issue of gender in the secondary school', in LOWE, R. (ed.) *The Changing Secondary School*, London, Falmer Press.

CROTEAU, D. and HOYNES, W. (1992) 'Men and the news media: The male presence and its effects', in CRAIG, S. (ed.) *Men, Masculinity and the Media*, California, Sage.

DANCY, J. (1980) *The Notion of the Ethos of a School Perspectives, No. 1*, University School of Education, Exeter.

DAR, Z. (1989) 'Sex education', in HALL CARPENTER ARCHIVES *Walking After Midnight*, London, Routledge.

DAVIDSON, N. (1990) *Boys Will Be . . .* London, Bedford Square.

DEAKIN, G. (1988) 'Male sexuality', *Nursing*, 26, pp. 961–2.

DENSKI, S. and SHOLLE, D. (1992) 'Metal men and glamour boys: Gender performance in heavy metal', in CRAIG, S. (1992) *Men, Masculinity and the Media*, California, Sage.

DFE (1994) *Bullying: Don't Suffer in Silence*, DFE.

DIXON, B. (1989) *Playing Them False*, Stoke, Trentham Books.

DOBSON, B. (1989) 'Sex education', in HALL CARPENTER ARCHIVES, *Walking After Midnight*, London, Routledge.

EASLEA, B. (1983) *Fathering the Unthinkable*, London, Pluto.

EASLEA, B. (1987) 'Patriarchy, scientists and nuclear weapons', in KAUFMAN, M. *Beyond Patriarchy*, Canada. OUP.

EASTHOPE, A. (1986) *What a Man's Gotta Do*, London, Paladin/Grafton.

ELLIOT, M. (ed.) (1991) *Bullying: A Practical Guide to Coping for Schools*, London, Longman.

ELTON REPORT (1989) *Discipline in School*, London, HMSO.

ENTWHISTLE, D. and DOERING, S. (1981) *The First Birth: A Family Turning Point*, Baltimore, John Hopkins University Press.

FARRELL, W. (1974) *The Liberated Man*, New York, Random House.

FASTEAU, M. (1974) *The Male Machine*, New York, McGraw-Hill.

FEIN, R. (1978) 'Research on fathering: Social policy and emergent perspective', *Journal of Social Issues*, 34, (1), pp. 122–35.

FEJES, F. (1992) 'Masculinity as fact: A review of empirical mass communication research on masculinity', in CRAIG, S. (ed.) *Men, Masculinity and the Media*, California, Sage.

FISHER, N. (1991) *Boys About Boys*, London, Pan.

FISKE, J. (1987) *Television Culture*, London, Methuen.

FRASER, R. (1984) *In Search of a Past*, London, Verso and NLB.

GERSCHICK, T. and MILLER, A. (1994) 'Manhood and physical disability', *Changing Men*, 27, Winter 1994.

GERZON, M. (1982) *A Choice of Heroes*, Boston, Houghton Mifflin Company.

GILMORE, E. (1990) *Manhood in the Making*, New York, Yale University Press.

GIVEANS, D. and ROBINSON, M. (1985) 'Fathers and the pre-school age child', in HANSON, S. and BOZETT, F. (eds) *Dimensions of Fatherhood*, California, Sage.

GOBEY, F. (1991) 'A practical approach through drama and workshops', in SMITH, P. and THOMPSON, D. (eds) *Practical Approaches to Bullying*, London, David Fulton.

HANDY, C. and AITKEN, R. (1986) *Understanding Schools as Organisations*, Harmondsworth, Penguin Books.

HEARN, J. (1987) *The Gender of Oppression*, Brighton, Wheatsheaf.

HERBERT, G. (1989) 'A whole curriculum approach to bullying', in TATTUM, D. and LANE, D. (eds) *Bullying in Schools*, Stoke, Trentham Books.

HODSON, P. (1984) *Men: An Investigation into the Emotional Male*, Ariel Books.

HOFFMAN, I. (1977) 'Changes in family roles, socialisation and sex differences', *American Psychologist*, 32, pp. 644–57.

HOLLAND, P. (1987) 'When a woman reads the news', in BAEHR, H. and DYER, G. (1987) *Boxed In: Women and Television*, London, Pandora Press.

HOMANS, H., AGGLETON, P. and WARWICK, I. (1989) *Learning About Aids*, Churchill Livingstone.

HUMPLEBY, J. (1990) 'Work in Hillocks Primary School', in WHYLD, J., PICKERSGILL, D. and JACKSON, D. (eds) *Update on Anti-Sexist Work with Boys and Young Men*, Whyld Publishing Coop.

INGHAM, M. (ed.) (1984) *Men*, London, Century Publishing.

JACKSON, D. (1990) *Unmasking Masculinity*, London, Routledge.

JARMOLINSKY, A. (1971) *The Military Establishment*, London, Harper and Row.

JONES, C. (1985) 'Sexual tyranny: Male violence in a mixed secondary school', in WEINER, G. *Just A Bunch of Girls*, Milton Keynes, Open University Press.

JOSEPH, J. (1985) *Father/Son Book*, Bethesda, Maryland, Pandemonium Books.

JUKES, A. (1993) *Why Men Hate Women*, London, Free Association Books.

KAUFMAN, M. (1987) *Beyond Patriarchy: Essays by Men on Pleasure, Power and Change*, Toronto, Oxford University Press.

KIMMEL, M. (1987a) 'Rethinking masculinity: New directions in research', in *Changing Men*, London, Sage Publications.

KIMMEL, M. (1987b) 'Issues for Men in the 1990's', in *Changing Men*, Winter/Spring 1991.

KLEIN, A. (1990) 'Little Big Man: Hustling, gender narcissism, and bodybuilding subculture', in MESSNER, M. and SABO, D. *Sport, Men and the Gender Order*, Champaign, Illinois, Human Kinetics Books.

LAMB, M. (1976) *The Role of the Father in Child Development*, New York, John Wiley.

LASLETT, R. (1982) 'A children's court for bullies', *Special Edition* 9, pp. 1, 9–11.

LEE, M. and SOLOMON, N. (1990) *Unreliable Sources*, New York, Lyle Stuart.

LEES, S. (1986) *Losing Out*, London, Hutchinson.

LEES, S. (1993) *Sugar and Spice*, Harmondsworth, Penguin.

LESTER, J. (1974) 'Being a boy', in PLECK, J. and SAWYER, A. (eds) *Men and Masculinity*, New Jersey, Prentice Hall.

LEWIS, C. and O'BRIEN, M. (eds) (1987) *Re-Assessing Fatherhood*, California, Sage.

LEWIS, R. (1978) 'Emotional intimacy among men', *Journal of Social Issues*, 34, (1), pp. 108–21.

LEWIS, R. (1986) 'What men get out of marriage and parenthood', in LEWIS, R. and SALE, R. (eds) *Men in Families*, California, Sage.

LEVINE, J. (1976) *Who Will Raise the Children?* New York, J. B. Lippincott.

LIFTON, R. (1974) *Home from the War*, London, Wildwood House.

LITEWKA, J. (1977) 'The socialised penis', in SNODGRASS, J. (ed.) *For Men Against Sexism*, Albion, Times Change Press.

LLOYD, T. (1985) *Work with Boys*, National Youth Bureau.

LYMAN, P. (1987) 'The fraternal bond as a joking relationship', in KIMMEL, M. (ed.) *Changing Men*, California, Sage Publications.

MACKAY, W. (1985) *Fathering Behaviours: The Dynamics of the Man-Child Bond*, New York, Plenum.

MAHONY, P. (1985) 'A can of worms: The sexual harassment of girls by boys', in MAHONY, P. *Schools for the Boys?* London, Hutchinson.

MAHONY, P. (1985) *Schools for the Boys?* London, Hutchinson.

MAYHEW, H. (1969) 'Mayhew's London: Being selections', in QUENNEL, P. (ed.) *London Labour* and *London Poor*, London, Hamlyn.

McKEE, L. (1982) 'Father's participation in infant care: A critique', in McKEE. L. and O'BRIEN, M. (eds) *The Father Figure*, London, Tavistock.

MEADE, C. (1987) *The Him Book: Ideas for Men Looking at Masculinity and Sexuality*, Sheffield City Libraries.

METCALF, A. and HUMPHRIES, M. (1985) *The Sexuality of Men*, London, Pluto Press.

MIEDZIAN, M. (1992) *Boys will be Boys*, London, Virago.

MILLER, S. (1983) *Men and Friendship*, Gateway Books.

MORGAN, D. (1987) 'Men, masculinity and violence', in HANMER, J. and MAYNARD, M. (eds) *Women, Violence and Social Control*, London, Macmillan.

MORGAN, G. (1986) *Images of Organisation*, London, Sage.

MOORE, S. (1991) 'Getting a bit of the other — The pimps of post modernism', in *Looking for Trouble*, London, Serpent's Tail.

OAKLEY, A. (1979) *Becoming a Mother*, Oxford, Martin Robinson.

OLWEUS, D. (1978) *Aggression in the Schools: Bullies and Whipping Boys*, Washington DC, Hemisphere.

OLWEUS, D. (1993) *Bullying in Schools: What We Know And What We Can Do*, Oxford, Blackwell.

PARKE, R. (1979) *Fathers*, Cambridge, MA., Harvard University Press.

PECORA, N. (1992) 'Superman/superboys/supermen: The comic book hero as socialising agent', in CRAIG, S. (ed.) *Men, Masculinity and the Media*, US, Sage.

PEIRCE, K. (1989) 'Sex-role stereotyping of children and television: A context analysis on the roles and attributes of child characters', *Sociological Spectrum*, 9.

PEREIRA, E. (1989) 'Sex education', in HALL CARPENTER ARCHIVE *Walking After Midnight*, London, Routledge.

POLLOCK, S. and SUTTON, J. (1985) 'Fathers' rights, women's losses', *Women's Studies International Forum* 8, (6), pp. 593–599.

POSTMAN, N. (1979) *Teaching as a Conserving Activity*, New York, Delacorte.

RASHLEIGH, A. (1984) 'Extract', in ROBERTS, Y. (ed.) *Man Enough*, London, Chatto and Windus.

RILEY, D. (1984) 'Gender and parenthood', *American Sociological Review*, 49, pp. 1–19.

RILEY, D. (1988) 'Bullying: A study of victim and victimisers within one inner-city secondary school', In-service BEd, Inquiry Report, Crewe and Alsager College of Higher Education.

ROLAND, E. and MUTHE, E. (1989) *Bullying: An International Perspective*, London, David Fulton.

RUFFELL, D. (1989) *Walking After Midnight* (His Life Story Included), HALL CARPENTER ARCHIVES, London, Routledge.

SALISBURY, J. (1988) 'Born to lose', unpublished M.Ed Dissertation, Nottingham University Library.

SEIDLER, V. (1985) 'Fear and intimacy', in METCALF, A. and HUMPHRIES, M. (eds) *The Sexuality of Men*, London, Pluto Press.

SEIDLER, V. (1989) *Rediscovering Masculinity: Reason, Language and Sexuality*, London, Routledge.

SEIDLER, V. (1991) *Recreating Sexual Politics*, London, Routledge.

SHARP, S. and SMITH, P. (1994) *Tackling Bullying in Your School: A Practical Handbook*, London, Routledge.

SHOR, I. (1987) *Critical Teaching and Everyday Life*, Chicago, University of Chicago Press.

SLAVIN, H. (ed.) (1986) *Greater Expectations*, Learning Development Aids.

SMITH, J. (1989) *Misogynies*, London, Faber.

SMITH, P. and SHARP, S. (eds) (1994) *School Bullying: Insights and Perspectives*, London, Routledge.

SOLOMON, K. and LEVY, N. (eds) (1982) *Men in Transition: Theory and Therapy*, New York, Plenum.

SPENDER, D. (1985) *Man Made Language*, London, Routledge.

SPENDER, D. and SARAH, E. (eds) (1980) *Learning to Lose: Sexism and Education*, London, Routledge.

SPYROY, K. (1989) 'Sex education', in HALL CARPENTER ARCHIVES *Walking After Midnight*, London, Routledge.

STANWORTH, M. (1983) *Gender and Schooling: A Study of Sexual Divisions in the Classroom*, London, Hutchinson.

STARHAWK (1987) *Truth or Dare*, New York, Harper Row.

STORDEUR, R. and STILLE, R. (1989) *Ending Men's Violence to Their Partners*, London, Sage.

STARRATT, R. (1990) *The Drama of Schooling/The Schooling of Drama*, London, Falmer Press.

ST JOHN BROOKS, C. (1985) 'The school bullies', *New Society*, 6th December, pp. 262–5.

STRATE, L. (1992) 'Beer commercials: A manual on masculinity', in CRAIG, S. (ed.) *Men, Masculinity and the Media*, US, Sage.

STOUFFER, S. *et al.* (1949) *The American Soldier Vol. 2: Combat and Its Aftermath*, Princeton, NJ, Princeton University Press.

TATTUM, D. (ed.) (1993) *Understanding and Managing Bullying*, London, Heinemann.

THOMPSON, C. (1987) 'A new vision of masculinity', in ABBOTT, F. (ed.) *New Man, New Minds*, USA, Crossing Press.

TRENCHARD, L. and WARREN, H. (1984) *Something To Tell You*, London, Gay Teenage Group.

TUC (1983) *Sexual Harassment at Work*, TUC.

WALKERDINE, V. (1990) 'Progressing pedagogy and political struggle', in *Schoolgirl Fictions*, London, Verso.

WEINER, G. (1985) 'Equal opportunities, feminism and girls' education: introduction', in WEINER, G. (ed.) *Just a Bunch of Girls*, Milton Keynes, Open University Press.

WERNICK, A. (1987) 'From voyeur to narcissist: Imaging men in contemporary advertising', in KAUFMAN, M. (ed.) *Beyond Patriarchy: Essays by Men on Pleasure, Power and Change*, Canada, Oxford University Press.

WHITBREAD, A. (1980) 'Female teachers are women first: Sexual harassment at work', in SPENDER, D. and SARAH, E. (eds) *Learning to Lose*, London, The Women's Press.

WHYLD, J. (1990) 'A short history of anti-sexism work with boys', in WHYLD, J., PICKERSGILL, D. and JACKSON, D. (eds) *Update on Anti-Sexist Work with Boys and Young Men*, Whyld Publishing Co-op, Lincolnshire.

WHYLD, J. (1983) *Sexism in the Secondary School Curriculum*, London, Harper and Row.

WINNICOTT, D. (1971) *Playing and Reality*, London, Tavistock.

WILLIAMS, C. and WEINBERG, M. (1971) *Homosexuals and the Military: A Study of Less than Honourable Discharge*, New York, Harper Row.

WISE, S. and STANLEY, L. (1987) *Georgie Porgie: Sexual Harassment in Everyday Life*, London, Pandora.

WOOD, J. (1984) 'Gropin towards sexism: Boys' sex talk', in MCROBBIE, A. and NAVA, M. (eds) *Gender and Generation*, London, Macmillan.

ZILBERGELD, B. (1980) *Men and Sex*, London, Fontana.

Index

academic learning, 25–7, 109, 172
Adams, - 111
advertising, 13–14, 42, 142–5, 153–6, 194
Advertising Standards Authority (ASA), 153–6
aggression, 92–6, 104, 221, 250, 260, 262
AIDS, 3, 13, 42, 49–51, 73–7, 222
alcohol, 13–14, 142–4, 219, 252
A'levels, 31
alienation, 220
alternatives in sport, 209–14
analytical skills, 12
anti-bullying policy, 108–13
anti-sexism, 152–6, 220–3
Armed Forces, 250–5, 263
Askew, Sue, 6, 90, 108, 109, 111
assemblies, 23–4, 177
assumptions, 1–2, 35, 48, 112, 233
    attraction, 64
    harassment, 93, 96
    language, 166–7, 170–1, 176
    sexuality, 50–1, 54, 65–6
    sport, 207
    violence, 106
attention-seeking behaviour, 1–3, 26, 32, 168–9
attentions, unwanted, 86–92
attraction, 64
Australia, 205–6
authoritarianism, 18, 28, 32, 53
authority, 10, 22–3, 32
avoidance strategies, 43, 107, 282
awareness, 5, 11, 51, 107, 213
    curriculum, 12
    identities, 9
    outsiders, 60–1
    survival skills, 221
    traditional models, 142–8

beer see alcohol
behaviour, 49–52, 89, 109

Bemrose School, 34
Besag, V., 111, 113
biology, 11, 106–7, 217, 234, 248
bisexuality, 67
Bly, Robert, 281
bodies, 46, 95, 170, 219–20, 222
    harassment, 86–92, 89, 96
    ideal, 189–203
    media, 141, 149
body language, 45
body-building, 190–3, 278
boredom, 18
Bottomley, Virginia, 51
Brooks, Caroline St John, 110
brutalization, 204–5, 208, 253
Bulger, James, 141
bullying, 90–2, 104–38, 267
Butcher, Terry, 140, 209

Campbell, Beatrix, 2, 147
capitalism, 21, 22, 148, 220
career choices, 4, 27, 36
Careers Service, 176
caring, 41, 44, 54, 62, 260
    advertising, 149
    conflict resolution, 265–8
    fathers, 287
    media, 147
    school ethos, 109, 110
    teachers, 111
    well-being, 216–31
cars, 144–5
celibacy, 67–8
Chambers, Robin, 110
changing rooms, 207–8
chastisement, 24
childcare, 147, 158, 266–8, 274–91
    fathers, 274–91
    well-being, 216, 223
Children in Need, 176
children's courts, 110
cinema see media

classroom strategies
  bullying, 129–38
  caring, 225–31
  emotions, 222
  fathers, 283–91
  harassment, 93, 96–103
  ideal bodies, 199–203
  introduction, 15, 16
  language, 175–88
  life stories, 238–49
  media images, 160–5
  playing war, 264–73
  sexuality, 55–85
classrooms, 35–6, 168–9, 177
clothing *see* dress
collaborative learning techniques, 34,
    232–3
collusion, 36, 104–9, 147–8
communication, 221, 222, 261–2, 280
community, schools as, 109–10
competition, 21, 31–2, 51, 243
  bullying, 108
  language, 171
  media, 140
  relationships, 221–2
  sport, 210, 211
computer games, 139, 193, 258–9, 260
condoms, 3, 49, 72–6, 248
conflict resolution, 265–8, 270–1
confusion, 41–2
Connell, Bob, 6, 44, 189, 205, 255
containment policy, 3
contraception, 49, 72–6
control, 1–3, 45, 48, 51, 149
  bullying, 108, 121–2
  fathers, 276, 284–5
  language, 166–7, 170
  secondary schools, 18
  support staff, 28
cooperation, 31, 109, 211, 267, 268, 280
corridors, 167–8, 177
counselling, 22–3, 31, 116–17
courts, children's, 110
crisis, sense of, 39
critical analysis, 234–5
Croteau, D., 147
culture, 18–19, 27, 144–5, 212
  critique, 2, 6, 12
  heterosexuality, 15
  homosexuality, 275–6
  ideal bodies, 190
  intimidation, 11
  media, 141, 152–3
  mind/body divide, 220

school, 10, 29–31
  sexuality, 41
  sport, 205, 206–79, 209
curriculum, 7, 37–9, 55, 220–3
  hidden, 11–12, 35
  masculinist, 25–7
  official, 12–13
  unofficial, 139

dance, 24, 212–13, 244–5
Dancy, J., 110
daughters, 95, 101
Davidson, Neil, 5
Deakin, Gordon, 46
decision-making, 50, 65, 107, 284
dehumanization, 47
denial, 220
design of curriculum, 7, 15
detachment, 41, 45, 193, 208, 220
determinism, 2, 6, 150
disability, 190–1, 235
discipline, 10, 22–3, 112–13
  bullying, 104, 108, 110
  disruption, 18–19
  military, 255
  support staff, 28
  violence, 104
diseases, sexually transmitted, 3, 49–52
disruption, 1–3, 15, 18, 32
distancing, 45, 141, 274–9, 284–5
divorce, 283
domestic violence, 50
drama, 26
dress, 25, 30, 91

Education Reform Act, 50
education work, 4–6
Elton report, 104, 108, 110
embarassment, 53–4, 64
  playing war, 266, 276
  sexuality, 40–1, 46, 49
emotions, 21, 27, 38, 41, 216–17
  detachment, 41, 45
  development, 221
  distancing, 141
  fathers, 276, 279
  invisibility, 219–20
  life stories, 235
  masculinity, 112
  outsiders, 57
  responsibility, 3, 5, 51–2
  sport, 208–9
  warriors, 250, 253, 254–5
empowerment, 4, 56

entitlement, 48–9, 112
  biology, 106
  harassment, 91, 96
  sexuality, 54, 72
equal access approach, 4–5
Equal Opportunities Committee, 176
Equal Pay Act, 4
Etches School, 23, 25, 27–9, 37
  bullying survey, 116
  careers education, 36
  competition, 31
  science, 33
ethnicity, 12, 235
ethos, 29–31, 110, 177
  military, 254
  public schools, 206–7
  sport, 210, 211
exam results, 4, 32, 34
exclusions, 3, 28, 36
expectations, 33
experiential learning, 28

fantasy, 18–19, 30, 45, 50
  harassment, 88
  ideal bodies, 192–3, 199
  media, 140
  sport, 205, 209
  warriors, 256, 261
fathers, 158–9, 174, 232, 274–91
  childcare, 266
  life stories, 244
  pornography, 95, 101
  sex education, 247–9
  sport, 206
  warriors, 250–1
fear, 141, 172, 212, 236–8, 253
  harassment, 94–5
  peer-group pressure, 56–61
  sport, 206
feelings, 122, 130, 132–3, 135, 221
  fathers, 284, 285
  fear, 56–61
  harassment, 91–2, 97
  ideal bodies, 200–1
  life stories, 236–8
  military, 254, 255
  sexuality, 41, 44, 54
  sharing, 282
  showing, 24
  warriors, 253
fellings, harassment, 89
feminism, 3–6, 15, 32–4, 141–2
films *see also* media, 140
Fiske, John, 152

food, 35, 228–31
fragmentation of identities, 7, 8
Freud, Sigmund, 66
Fuller, - 26

games, 210–11
Gay Pride marches, 42
GCSE exams, 31, 172, 266
gender work, 4–7, 13–14, 55–6, 208–9
gender-blindness, 141–2, 152
genitals, 47–8, 106
girls
  caring, 217–18
  empowerment, 4
  ideal male bodies, 194
  life stories, 243–4
  mixed games, 210–11
Girls into Science and Technology, 4
Giveans, D., 280
Gobey, F., 109, 111
governments, 262
governors, 50, 109, 116
graffiti, 11, 12, 88, 179–80
green issues, 12
guidelines, anti-bullying, 109–13

Hackney Downs School, 5, 111, 223
harassment, 3, 5, 11, 20, 86–103
  classroom, 26
  relationships, 35
headteachers, 18, 29, 87–8, 175
health care, 49–52, 147, 208, 218, 222,
  228–31
Hearn, Jeff, 5–6
Herbert, .G., 109
heroes, 140, 250–1, 256, 267, 278
heterosexuality, 3, 10, 15, 50, 253–5
hierarchies, 10
history, 2, 4–6, 267
HIV awareness, 73–7, 222
Holland, Patricia, 148
homework, 172
homophobia, 20, 24, 38, 212
  fathers, 280
  military, 255
  sexuality, 40, 42–4
homosexuality, 67, 275–6
honour, code of, 110
hormones, 2, 106
Hoynes, W., 147
Hughes, Thomas, 211
humanities, 33, 267
Humpleby, Jan, 91
Hussein, Saddam, 257

identity, 7–9, 213, 232, 279, 283
  bullying, 107, 112
  mythology, 71
  ridicule, 172
  sexuality, 43, 45–6, 49, 55–6
  sport, 209
ideology, 2, 18–19, 140, 144–5, 209
inadequacy, 206
individualism, 222, 232
initiation rites, 144
Inner London Education Authority,
  5
insecurity, 9, 10, 141, 142, 284, 285
inservice training, 10, 16, 30, 37–8
institutions, 10–11, 18–39, 19–22
  aggression, 105
  harassment, 88
  language, 176–7
investment, 139
invisibility of fathers, 284

Jackson, Bullmoose, 46
Jackson, David, 168
Jackson, Michael, 212

Kimmel, Michael, 49
Kingsley, Charles, 211
Kinsey, A.C., 66

lads *see also* real men, 232–49
Lamb, M., 279
Lame Duck Publishing, 118
language, 11, 12, 36–7, 39, 166–88
  fathers, 284
  harassment, 87
  military, 254
  objectification, 47
  playing war, 261
  sexuality, 49, 52–5, 62, 66–7
Laslett, R., 110
Laurikietis, - 111
leadership, 10
league tables, 32
learning, 1–2, 31, 34, 232
  bullying, 111, 112–13
  cooperation, 110
  language, 172
  sex, 40–5
  unmanly, 3
Lees, Sue, 9
legislation, 4
lesbianism, 68
Lester, Julius, 242–6
life stories, 232–49

listening skills, 169, 171, 183–5, 266,
  269–70
Lloyd, Trefor, 5
local education authorities, 109
Local Government Act, 50

Mahony, P., 3, 90
management, 10, 110–11
marginalization, 3, 8–9
  homophobia, 38
  ideal bodies, 190
  schools, 23, 27, 30, 35
  women, 175
marking, 19
Marland, 55
marriage, 166–7, 175
masculinist curriculum, 25–7
masculinity, 2, 7–10, 148–50
  bullying, 111–12
  traditional models, 216–20
matriarchy, 37
Meade, Chris, 5
media, 42, 139–65, 160
  harassment, 87–8
  heroes, 271–2
  sexuality, 40, 54, 55
  warriors, 251, 255–61
Middlesex University, 50
military manhood, 253–5, 263
mind/body divide, 220
misogyny, 20, 30, 37–9, 40, 280, 285
mistakes, acknowledging, 284, 285
mixed games, 210–11
mixed-ability groups, 10
Moir, Jan, 148
Moore, Suzanne, 212
mothers, 24, 174–5, 248, 262
  absent fathers, 283
  childcare, 274
  language, 168
  life stories, 243, 244
  media, 158–9
  sons, 275–7, 279, 285
Murphy, Robert, 190
music *see also* media, 140, 287
mythology, 71–2, 183, 276

narcissism, 148–9, 193–4, 219
National Curriculum, 23, 25–7, 31, 113,
  211–12
nationalism, 12, 267
needs, 221, 222
Neti Neti Theatre Company, 109
New Man, 149–50

New Right, 42
newsreaders, 145–8, 259–60

Oakley, A., 274
objectification, 47, 254
objectivity of media, 147–8
orgasms, 45, 46
outsiders, 57–61

pain, 204–5, 243, 275, 286–7
paperwork, 19
parents, 109, 159, 234
    aggression, 104
    life stories, 235, 243
    masculinity, 111
    sexuality, 55, 65
    work, 174
parents *see also* fathers; mothers
pastoral care, 23–5, 91, 107, 111
patriarchy, 6, 8, 14, 18–19
    language, 166
    warriors, 250, 252–4, 260
Patten, John, 51
pecking order, 7, 233
Pecora, Norma, 148
peer-group pressure, 9, 121,
        233–4
    blow-out, 157, 158, 159
    ideal bodies, 192–3
    life stories, 236–8
    risk, 219
    sanctuaries, 207–8
    schools, 33–4
    sexuality, 54, 55–6
performance, 45–7, 56, 222
personal challenge, 213–14
personal and social education (PSE), 21,
        26, 28–9, 218
Phillips, Angela, 9
physical education (PE), 12, 20–1
    authority, 32
    harassment, 91
    mixed games, 210–11
    National Curriculum, 212
    personal challenge, 214
pleasure
    fathers, 285
    sexual, 40–1, 44, 46–7, 49, 51
Plow Hatch Hall School, 5
policy statements, anti-bullying, 109
Pollock, S., 277
pornography, 5, 47–8, 54, 95, 101, 255,
        279
Postman, Neil, 139

power, 19–20, 28–32, 48–9,
        112
    bullying, 108, 134–5
    fathers, 276
    harassment, 89, 92
    imbalances, 217
    language, 166–7
    media, 149–50
    military, 255
    oppression, 97
    sport, 208
    staffrooms, 170
    staring, 95
primary schools, 91, 248
privilege, 12, 48, 51–2, 112
probation services, 16–17
product-orientated activities, 27
propaganda, 139–41
prostitution, 96
psychodramatic methods, 121–9
public schools, 206–7, 211

questionnaires
    bullying, 114–16
    harassment, 102–3
    sexuality, 77–85
    violence, 262

racism, 12, 30, 108, 110
    media, 149
    playing war, 258
    sport, 207
rape, 5, 50, 94, 280
    harassment, 96, 101
    marital, 95
Rashleigh, Andy, 274–5
reading schemes, 4, 34
real men
    advertising, 143, 149
    bullying, 107, 121
    concept of, 2
    fathers, 284, 285
    harassment, 89–92
    lads, 97–100, 219, 232–49
    sexuality, 49–52
    sport, 109, 205
Reay, Diane, 9
recession, 141
Redhill Comprehensive School,
        213
registers, 4
relationships, 221–2
relaxation techniques, 58–9, 222
respect, 223–5, 233, 283

responsibility, 3, 5, 109, 221
  bullying, 107
  caring, 218, 226
  childcare, 266–7
  decision-making, 65
  emotions, 51–2
  fathers, 274
  home life, 27
  life stories, 243
  mothers, 277
  sexuality, 49, 50, 222
ridicule, 22–3, 34
rights, 48, 86–92, 95
Riley, D., 112
risk, 3, 49–52, 72–6, 218–19, 238
Robinson, M., 280
role-playing, 44, 131–2, 260
Ross, Carole, 6, 90
Rossi, Alice, 277
routines, 1–2, 105
Rykneld Support Service, 118

safe sex, 3, 49–52, 72–6, 222
sanctuaries, male, 207–8
Sarah, E., 3
schools, 1–17, 108–13, 255–60
  conflict resolution, 265–8
  ethos, 110
  harassment, 89
Schools Council for Sex Differentiation, 4
science, 12, 25, 26–7, 33
secondary schools, 18–39
secrecy, 110
Sedwall, Christina, 155
Seidler, Vic, 106
self-esteem, 111, 207, 214, 244
  bullying, 112
  girls, 26
self-images, bodies, 189–90
senior management teams (SMT), 18, 29
sensitivity, 21, 41, 44
sessions
  bullying, 121–9
  caring, 223–5
  fathers, 281–3
  harassment, 92–6
  ideal bodies, 195–9
  introduction, 15–16
  language, 173–5
  manly characteristics, 156–9
  playing war, 261–4
  real lads, 236–8
  respect, 223–5
  sexuality, 52–5

Sex Discrimination Act, 4
sex education, 5, 50–1, 62, 232, 247–9
sex role theory, 6–7
sexual harassment *see* harassment
sexual responsibility, 3, 5
sexuality, 40–85, 245, 279
  life stories, 235
  responsibility, 222
  sex education, 247–9
sexually transmitted diseases, 3, 49–52
shame, 40–1, 206
shaving, 192
Sheffield Men against Sexual Harassment
  (SMASH), 5, 97
significant men, 283–4
sin bins, 86, 169, 236
single-parent families, 42, 166
Skills for Living course, 5
social costs, 280
social studies, 267
socialization, 6, 14
sons, 274–91
space, 48, 86, 89, 96, 170
Spender, Dale, 3, 26, 89, 167
sport, 12, 32, 91, 275, 285–6
  ideal bodies, 190
  life stories, 243
  making of men, 204–15
  sexuality, 43
staff handbooks, 29
staffrooms, 8, 16, 30, 87, 104
  competition, 31
  language, 169–72
Stanley, L., 89
Stanworth, M., 3, 26
staring, 94–5, 101
stereotypes, 9, 34, 50, 62–3
  advertising, 142–5
  bullying, 121
  challenging, 175–7
  dance, 212, 213
  homosexuality, 275–6
  internalization, 6–7
  manly characteristics, 157
  media, 160–2
Stoke Newington School, 110
Stouffer, 253
Strate, Lance, 142, 144
Strathclyde University, 13
streaming, 10
subject choices, 4, 32, 34
suicide, 216, 223, 252
supervision, 113
support staff, 28

surveys
  bullying, 114–21
  ideal male bodies, 194
survival skills, 221, 222–3, 226
Sutton, J., 277

teachers, 1–2, 15, 27–8, 104–7, 111
  bullying, 112–13, 116, 128–9
  competition, 108
  harassment, 87–9
  inservice training, 10, 16, 30, 37–8
  language, 171, 176
  life stories, 236
  PE, 212
  real lads, 233
teaching methods, 13–14, 27–9, 34–5
technology, 12, 25–7, 29, 34–5
television *see also* media, 139, 209
'telling school' concept, 110
text books, 4, 34
textile technology, 35
theory
  ideal bodies, 189–94
  introduction, 1–2, 15
  media education, 139–56
  playing war, 250–61
  real lads, 232–5
  secondary schools, 18–19
  sexuality, 40–52
  violence, 104–13
Thomas, Clarence, 88
timetabling, 21

touching-up *see also* harassment, 12, 94, 101
toys, 91, 240–1, 256–8, 260, 267, 286
Trade Union Congress (TUC), 88
traditional models, 3–4, 33, 141
  awareness, 142–8
  fathers, 276
  masculinity, 216–20
  media, 152–6
  social costs, 280
training in masculinity, 2
truancy, 3, 32

underachievement, 3
unemployment, 141, 147, 149, 166
uniforms, 25, 251, 263
United States of America, 255
unwanted attentions, 86–92

video games, 139, 193
violence, 104–38, 226, 276

Walkerdine, Valerie, 26, 106
war, playing, 250–73
weapons, 53, 166–88, 255, 257
well-being, 216–31
Wernick, Andrew, 148
whole-school policy, 114–21
Whyld, Janie, 214
Winnicott, D., 260
Wise, S., 89
Working with Boys Initiative, 5
workplaces, 88